FROM THE EARTH TO THE TABLE

John Ash's
Wine Country Cuisine

FROM THE EARTH TO THE TABLE

John Ash

with Sid Goldstein

A DUTTON BOOK

DUTTON
Published by the Penguin Group
Penguin Books USA Inc., 375 Hudson Street, New York, New York 10014, U.S.A.
Penguin Books Ltd, 27 Wrights Lane, London W8 5TZ, England
Penguin Books Australia Ltd, Ringwood, Victoria, Australia
Penguin Books Canada Ltd, 10 Alcorn Avenue, Toronto, Ontario, Canada M4V 3B2
Penguin Books (N.Z.) Ltd, 182–190 Wairau Road, Auckland 10, New Zealand

Penguin Books Ltd, Registered Offices: Harmondsworth, Middlesex, England

First published by Dutton, an imprint of Dutton Signet,
a division of Penguin Books USA Inc.
Distributed in Canada by McClelland & Stewart Inc.

First Printing, October, 1995
10   9   8   7   6   5   4   3   2   1

From the Earth to the Table is a registered trademark of FETZER VINEYARDS.
All photographs courtesy of FETZER VINEYARDS.

 REGISTERED TRADEMARK—MARCA REGISTRADA

LIBRARY OF CONGRESS CATALOGING-IN-PUBLICATION DATA
Ash, John.
From the earth to the table : John Ash's wine country cuisine /
John Ash with Sid Goldstein.
p.   cm.
Includes bibliography references.
ISBN 0-525-94000-6
1. Cookery, American—California style.   2. Cookery—California, Northern.
3. Wine lists.   I. Goldstein, Sid.   II. Title.
TX715.2.C34A83   1995
641.59794—dc20   95-22041
CIP

Printed in the United States of America
Set in Palatino
Designed by Eve L. Kirch

This book is printed on acid-free paper.

Acknowledgments

I've been lucky to have been surrounded by a number of inspired cooks in my life. The whole crew over the years at Valley Oaks is in many ways as responsible for this book as I. Cal Uchida and Jim Rhodes lead the pack along with a whole colorful band who have spent time with us there including Jane Selover, Petra Arguelles, Jacquie Lee, Mark Gordon, Jim Stuart, Jim "Elvis" Mitchell, Eliza Miller, Karen Hadley, and many others. Special note must be given to Michael Maltas and Jeff Dawson, the garden directors at Valley Oaks, who taught me so much about the importance of the earth connection to great food. This book would not ever have gotten done without Marj Caulfield, the best assistant and most patient friend I've ever had. Also, thanks are due to Amy Mintzer, editor extraordinare, who helped so much in forming and shaping the book.

Finally, to all those growers, farmers, foragers, fishermen, winemakers, and other producers in the wine country of California who have given me and my cook compatriots so much to work with, I offer my heartfelt thanks. They are the real inspiration and reason for great food. I feel blessed to be part of this time and place.

J.A.

To Suzanne and Zack, the best mother-son team on the planet, for patience, love, and great testing palates; to Mom, for letting me drink cheap kosher wine at the family table at an early age, thereby setting a standard that's been hard to replicate; to Dorothy Woll, for manuscript assistance; to Jeff Dawson, for the world's most beautiful garden; to Carole DeSanti, for her patience and unwavering support of the project; and to all my friends at Fetzer Vineyards, who really care about making a difference in the world: "Live right. Eat right. Pick the right grapes."

S.G.

Contents

Introduction

The food production chain is really very simple. We plant it; we grow it; we gather it; we cook it and then we eat it. When this process occurs with a certain immediacy and a minimum of interference, and if it is nurtured by people who are truly passionate about what they are doing, the results can be glorious.

This book is largely about that process from my perspective at the Fetzer Food and Wine Center at Valley Oaks in Mendocino County, California, where I am involved not only in cooking but also in developing and utilizing what I believe is one of the world's most spectacular culinary gardens. Valley Oaks, a completely organic experiment, has well over one thousand varieties of fruits, vegetables, and herbs, and I have the good fortune to be able to cook from this garden every day. This particular vantage point greatly affects my understanding of cooking and the current state of our relationship to it.

The thrust of this book is to capture the spirit of Valley Oaks and to share the results of this ambitious culinary experiment in which I am involved. You do not need to have a thousand varieties of fruits, vegetables, and herbs growing in your backyard to cook and enjoy the recipes in this book. You do not need to have a garden at all. But by sharing what I have at Valley Oaks, I hope to encourage you to reconceive your mental shopping list—to think about what's grown locally, what's in season, to buy organically produced foods whenever possible. The wholesomeness of our food supply is at stake, as is the exquisite flavor of "real" foods—something our ancestors took for granted that has been largely denied to us.

Changes in American Cooking

Americans are undergoing a profound change in how they think about and prepare what they eat. I have been especially fortunate to be at the center of this revolution, in California's wine country, where everyone involved brings a heightened appreciation to the art of eating—whether they are in the fields and vineyards, which provide the finest raw materials available, in the kitchens and wineries, where these ingredients are transformed with consummate skill and loving care, or at the table, where we enjoy the fruits of our labors.

This book represents my evolution as a cook. It began with my grandmother Maud, with whom I spent a lot of my childhood, and in tribute several of her recipes are in this book. Being poor on an isolated mountain ranch in Colorado, she had to use *everything*, and she taught me how to as well. This meant I got an early crash course in such archaic practices as boiling the hooves of calves in order to extract the gelatin. I also learned to appreciate and love the process of cooking. It still seems pretty magical to me that yeast and flour come together to make bread.

Like so many of my contemporaries, I learned to cook formally by studying French cooking both in America and abroad. In the late 1960s and 1970s there was no question that, if you wanted to study the highest order of Western cooking, you went to France to learn your skills and discipline. At that time, if you hadn't "been to France" you were out of the culinary loop. With the exception of a few outposts of indigenous regional cuisine, such as Cajun–Creole or American Indian–Mexican, which managed to hold their own, most of American haute cuisine came to us from French or European discipline and technique. Wine country cuisine represents an evolution from those roots, but it has clearly begun to take on an identity of its own.

What Is "Wine Country" Cuisine?

The very existence of a wine country cuisine is a direct response to the great wines that are being produced here in California. In the "early days" of wine in California (which really was only the 1960s), winemakers tried to duplicate the great wines of Europe, especially those of France. Big, blockbuster Cabernets and Chardonnays were so intense that they overpowered almost any food they accompanied. We cooks tried our best to create dishes that would match these wines. Because of our training, we tended to create variations on French and to some extent Italian dishes. It was a gestation period for both winemakers and cooks.

Then, a curious and wonderful thing happened. For winemakers, it was the blind tastings in France in 1976 in which a California Cabernet and Chardonnay beat the best of their French counterparts. For cooks, it was that we began to travel to other parts of the world (especially Latin America and Asia) and bring back flavors, ingredients, and techniques that were altogether foreign to the French tradition. We also opened our eyes to the new ingredients beginning to appear in our markets courtesy of the new waves of immigrants, many of whom came from Latin America and Asia. In that sense, we began to create our own little culinary global village in California and finally had enough confidence to explore and define territory that was uniquely our own.

In the 1980s and 1990s California wines changed dramatically. And this time it was in response to the food. Big Cabernets and Chardonnays became subtler, more approachable. "Lesser" varieties that better complement the strong flavors of "ethnic" foods (such as Sauvignon Blanc, Gewürztraminer, and Pinot Noir with spicy Asian dishes) became more important. California chefs and winemakers began working together to create harmony and synergy at the table rather than fight for attention.

During this time, we (both winemakers and cooks) began exploring the unique and rich agricultural microclimates available in the California wine country to grow a broad spectrum of grapes and foods. In Sonoma County, my original base of operations, we saw the reestablishment of small family farms devoted to growing all kinds of spectacular new produce and raising animals such as game birds and organic Sonoma lamb that fired the cook's imagination. In a real sense, we were learning the very thing that had made French and European food and wine so great—the importance of the land and its connection to the cook.

My passion became to explore with farmers and ranchers all that could be produced locally. This approach was consistent with my lifelong passion for the farming stage of cooking and for simple preparations. In 1980, when I started my restaurant, John Ash & Company, in Santa Rosa in Sonoma County, I enlisted every grower I could find to supply us with ingredients. (Here I must recognize and offer my gratitude to Alice Waters and her pioneering efforts at Chez Panisse. She encouraged us all to be proactive in finding wholesome and unusual ingredients.) At first, my colleagues and I would sift through seed catalogs each winter and select different varieties just to see if they would grow. Sometimes it worked—sometimes not. But it instilled in me a credo that I believe in even more strongly today: Farming is the first step in cooking. A great cook is only as great as his or her ingredients.

In my view, great meals result from spending *more* time finding great ingredients than in the kitchen preparing them. On its own, a great recipe does not create a unique taste experience. The raw ingredients are the stars of the show.

The role of the cook, then, is like that of a stage director in a play: to coax and encourage the best out of his or her stars—in this case, the vine-ripened tomato, the fresh-from-the-water snapper, the dead-ripe berry, the bundle of fresh, bright basil. Winemakers have a saying that applies equally to food: "The secret of making great wine is to grow great grapes and then not screw them up."

Preservation of the Land

California has a kind of split personality when it comes to taking care of the land. On the one hand, it is home to some of the country's most innovative approaches to organic agriculture, natural farming without the use of the "cide" sisters (herbicides, fungicides, insecticides), combined with techniques that recycle and replenish the soil. On the other hand, California has come to depend on some of the country's most abusive agricultural practices, which involve a vicious circle of ever-increasing amounts of the "cide" sisters and other chemical additives. In this scenario, there is never a chance for the land to recover and renew.

In extending my thoughts about the importance of great ingredients to great cooking, I would add also that great ingredients come from great land. I strongly believe that the preservation of the planet is directly tied to the food supply. The choices that each of us makes every day about what we eat is like a vote for the planet. These choices affect the diversity and quality of the food as well as how it is grown or raised, and distributed.

My decision to join Fetzer Vineyards was greatly motivated by the Fetzer family's commitment to organic viticulture and agriculture. They evidenced this commitment by creating a magnificent food and wine education center, Valley Oaks, anchored by one of the world's great organic gardens—truly a cook's dream. Fetzer has been a leader in the organic movement, which, ironically, is not only contributing to the health of the planet but also improving the quality of grapes and wine, since chemicals have been totally eliminated in all of their farming practices.

The Importance of "Ethical Food"

In addition to being concerned about the use of chemicals in agriculture, like many of you I worry about the existence of what I call "ethical food." The biological revolution of the twentieth century has opened the door to such developments as "genetic engineering" of our foods. I find this troubling, because it diverts attention and effort from the preservation of the vast and diverse gene pool that nature has already provided us with and that we are allowing to become extinct.

In commercial animal husbandry, as another example, we've all become increasingly aware of the use of growth hormones, massive doses of antibiotics, and other means to raise animals in ways that are occasionally inhumane, that homogenize the flavor, and that have health consequences only beginning to be understood. Happily, consumer demand can have a positive effect on how meat is produced. I remember a time in my restaurant when we didn't serve beef because we couldn't find a supplier who raised and processed it "naturally." We finally found one and have used him ever since.

This concern about wholesomeness was an important reason Sid Goldstein and I wrote a book called *American Game Cooking*. One of the basic tenets of the book was that farm-raised game was one of the few remaining meat sources that was not manipulated genetically or chemically and therefore was still a wholesome food.

How food is grown, harvested/slaughtered, fumigated/packaged, stored and handled should be of concern to us all, as cooks and eaters as well as residents of the planet. One sensible response is to eat seasonally and locally. We don't really need tasteless tomatoes for salad in December, which come from halfway around the world. Cabbage, fennel, and citrus can make an equally interesting salad, more in harmony with the season, the ecology, and our appetite.

Another way to cast your "vote" for ethical forms of agriculture is to patronize local farmers' markets that showcase locally farm-raised seasonal foods. If your city or township doesn't have one, it should. You can help nurture this important movement along by working with the local Chamber of Commerce or your state's Department of Agriculture or agricultural extension.

The Importance of Health

Perhaps the most important new influence that is changing how I cook is the concern about good health and longevity. My increased understanding of what good nutrition means has forever changed the way I cook. My training in French cooking taught me to "enrich" a sauce or dish by adding a bit more cream or butter or egg yolks or, better yet, all of them! As I explore now, I discover that food can be "enriched" in myriad ways—and that food that starts with great ingredients doesn't need to be "enriched" after all.

We know now that controlling our fat intake is probably the most important dietary contribution we can make to our health. Following the controversial USDA "Eating Pyramid" (controversial because pressure from the meat and dairy industries affected the final recommendations) and its refined version provided by the Harvard University School of Public Health has become a personal goal and is reflected in the vast majority of the recipes in this book. At the same time I've tried to maintain some balance: Food is about pleasure, too, which is my way of saying that I've included a few truly decadent dishes, and I hope you enjoy them. I remember a time when Julia Child was doing a demonstration at our Food and Wine Center for an overflow crowd of admirers and press. She stopped in the middle of her demo and shook her finger at the assembled press and noted that they were making us a nation of "food hysterics." She exclaimed, "God gave us butter and cream to enjoy." The key, she explained, was to understand your individual metabolism and enjoy everything in moderation.

The Use of Raw Eggs in Cooking

Traditionally raw or uncooked eggs were used to make emulsified sauces such as mayonnaise and aïoli. In recent years, however, there has been some concern about eating raw-egg dishes because of possible salmonella contamination. While it is extremely rare for salmonella poisoning to be fatal, the very young, old, or health-compromised should be careful. Interestingly, it is estimated that only 10 percent of the 2 million cases or so of salmonella poisoning reported each year are caused by raw eggs. Undercooked meat or poultry are much more likely to be the culprits. If you are concerned, however, please be sure to use "coddled" eggs (eggs that have been heated to at least 145 degrees) or use flash pasteurized raw eggs wherever uncooked eggs are called for.

The New "Mother Sauces"

One of the best examples I can think of that illustrates new American and especially wine country cuisine is what I call the development of the new "mother sauces." Any of you who have spent time cooking traditional French food will no doubt recall the so-called mother sauces (see Julia Child's *Mastering the Art of French Cooking*, Volume I, page 54, for a complete description). These included brown sauces derived from brown stocks, white sauces, and hot and cold emulsion sauces such as hollandaise or mayonnaise derived from egg yolk–fat combinations, etc. In much of my cooking today, the original "mothers," which were often high in butter, cream, or other saturated fats, have been replaced by new lighter mothers, such as vinaigrettes, salsas, pestos, chutneys, natural stock reductions, and juices. These new "mothers" come to us from many cuisines, and their appearance recognizes a new understanding of how to add flavor and zing to the ever-increasing variety of new foods that are becoming available to us with less fat but—most important—more flavor.

Food as Art

Before I became a chef, my training was in art, specifically painting. Looking back on it now, the connection between painting and cooking was pretty direct. I discovered that everything I ever wanted to do on canvas I could also do with food.

Mechanically and intellectually, pushing paint around on a canvas was similar in process to manipulating food on a plate, plus I had the advantage of feeding the body as well as the soul. The enjoyment of food, I believe, is as much visual as it is oral, and, like many of my contemporaries, I care very much about how food is presented. Many of my recipes have several components, because I love the way certain foods look together as well as how they taste together. That's also why I include suggested garnishes with most of the recipes. It's true I can do things in my restaurant kitchen that I wouldn't expend the energy on in my home kitchen, but even at home I take care with the look of the dish, the look of the plate, because I take pleasure in the activity. Food gives us the opportunity every day to create a "masterpiece." And even if each plate doesn't turn out to be a masterpiece, then at least we can enjoy the process of creating it. Cooking can and should remind us of our connection to our bodies, our fellow human beings, and our planet.

You will find in these recipes some things familiar and traditional, some things very new, but all of them are wrapped around a consciousness of this special place where foods and wines are grown together and made in proximity.

What I hope to share with you is my experience, passion, and love for creating wholesome, delicious recipes. In the process, I hope I'll strike a few chords and inspire you to explore your own concept of the natural food chain—from the earth to the table.

As my friend and mentor, the late M. F. K. Fisher, said: ". . . We must eat. If, in the face of that dread fact, we can find other nourishment, and tolerance and compassion for it, we'll be no less full of human dignity. There is a communication of more than our bodies when bread is broken and wine drunk."

John Ash, Mendocino County, 1995

SALADS

Salads and Wine

Traditionally, we have been told *not* to serve wine with salads. Vinegary, acidic dressings and raw greens and vegetables don't usually flatter wine, so why bother? This seems to have been the conventional wisdom.

It may be true that most wines don't do much for iceberg lettuce doused with oil and vinegar (or vice versa), but today's salads are different. Salads are made with a range of greens—romaine and arugula, mâche, frisée, spinach—that are fuller flavored; salads can include grilled vegetables, nuts, meats and fish, cheeses. They're often the main event and they can be perfect partners to a full range of wines, from a crisp Sauvignon Blanc to earthy reds.

There are two keys to good salad-wine matches:

1. Make sure there isn't too much acid or vinegar in the dressing; this can kill the fruit in wine. Cut down the amount of vinegar or don't use it at all. For an acid component that's more complementary to wine, you can use citrus juice, a mellow vinegar such as balsamic or rice, or even wine itself.
2. Look to "bridge" ingredients to connect the salad and wine: That is, include ingredients in the salad whose flavors are a natural complement to the wine. An aged Parmesan cheese is a nice bridge to a buttery, oaky Chardonnay; grilled portabello mushrooms are an earthy bridge to mellow reds like Merlot; fresh pear or melon is a natural with Riesling or Gewürztraminer.

In the same way that salads are different creatures from what they used to be, so are wines. A fine old Cabernet from Bordeaux is not a great wine for most salads, but a fresh young California Pinot Noir could be sublime.

Asparagus Salad with Pickled Ginger Vinaigrette

Asparagus celebrates the coming of spring, so it occupies a special place in my culinary cravings. As soon as the markets start carrying fresh asparagus, I gravitate to this savory Asian-style preparation. Charcoal grilling really changes the nature of asparagus: The dark, smoky flavors it brings out make the vinaigrette a perfect foil, so do try this when you can grill the asparagus. You may never steam, blanch, or boil it again!

Serves 2 to 3

1	teaspoon chopped shallots	2	teaspoons rice wine vinegar
2	tablespoons chopped pickled ginger (available in Asian markets)	4	tablespoons dark sesame oil Kosher salt and freshly ground black pepper
¼	teaspoon wasabi powder	1½	pounds fresh asparagus

Prepare a charcoal fire. In a small bowl, combine the shallots, pickled ginger, wasabi powder, rice wine vinegar, and sesame oil. Whisk thoroughly to blend. Season to taste with salt and pepper.

Brush the asparagus with some of the vinaigrette. Grill the asparagus over hot coals until bright green and tender.

Serve the asparagus drizzled with the remaining vinaigrette.

 Recommended wine: A herbal-tinged Sauvignon/Fumé Blanc will contrast with the spicy rush of ginger in this dressing.

Grilled Kale Salad

This salad was suggested by Jeff Dawson, one of the garden directors at Valley Oaks. Its very simple approach can be used for any variety of kale or other savory winter green. Grilling gives the greens a special smoky flavor, which is heightened by the sherry vinegar. You may not find Lacinato kale in your supermarket, but it is a great variety to track down and grow in your garden.

Serves 4

1½ pounds Lacinato, Verdura, or other kale, washed, stems removed

⅓ cup extra-virgin olive oil

Kosher salt and freshly ground black pepper

3 tablespoons sherry vinegar (or to taste)

Prepare a charcoal fire. Brush the kale leaves very lightly with some of the olive oil. Season with salt and pepper.

Grill the kale leaves over hot coals until they soften and the edges are lightly browned. In a bowl, toss the kale with the remaining olive oil and the sherry vinegar. Season to taste with salt and pepper.

 Recommended wine: Kale has a very rich, "meaty" flavor, so this salad goes well with lighter reds, such as Pinot Noir or Chianti-style wines.

SALT

Salt has many faces and, believe it or not, many flavors. Most salt sold in markets today is rock salt, which is mined from salt deposits left behind from ancient, extinct seas. You can also buy sea salt, which comes from existing seas and is simply sea water that has been evaporated by the sun. One of the most interesting tastings I've ever gone to was a tasting of sea salts from around the world. There was a substantial difference in flavor depending on location. Some were very "minerally" while others were almost sweet—so even something as simple as salt can add subtle flavor differences to a recipe.

Most tasters (including me) prefer sea salt to ordinary table, or mined, salt. It simply seems to have a more complex flavor. Some cooks also believe that sea salt is nutritionally superior to rock salt, but unfortunately there is no truth to this. Any extra minerals that may be in sea salt are in such small amounts that they wouldn't make any dietary difference.

In this book I often call for the use of kosher salt. Kosher salt has large, flaky crystals and dissolves much more slowly than ordinary salt—qualities that are helpful in drawing the blood out of meats before cooking, which is a requirement of Jewish dietary law. I like its large crystals as a garnishing salt when you want to see and taste the pure salt flavor.

Other salt mixtures: Dry herb and salt mixtures have become available in most markets. They are easy to put together on your own and have the advantage of adding interesting flavors while cutting down on the amount of sodium in your diet, if that is of concern to you.

Two other salt mixtures that I keep on hand for everyday use are:

- *Sesame salt* (Gomasio), from Japanese cooking, is a blend of 6 or more parts toasted, ground sesame seeds to 1 part sea salt. It adds a nutty, earthy note when sprinkled on foods.
- *Sour salt*, used in Indian cooking, is a blend of 6 or more parts sea salt with 1 part citric acid crystals. It adds a tart-salt flavor that I love with fresh tomatoes and on grilled fish.

Cucumber-Yogurt Salad with Toybox Tomatoes

This refreshing salad shines during the summer, when tomatoes are at their peak. Toybox tomatoes are baby red and yellow tomatoes that may be found in specialty produce markets. (Regular cherry tomatoes will certainly do in their place.) This salad is great for making ahead, since the flavors develop best after about 2 hours in the refrigerator. The combination of cucumbers and yogurt is derived from Indian cuisine, where the raita is used as a condiment to calm the palate alongside hot curries.

Serves 6 to 8

2 large English cucumbers	½ teaspoon seeded and minced
Kosher salt	serrano chile
1 cup minced red onions	(or to taste)
1 teaspoon minced garlic	1¼ cups plain yogurt

1 tablespoon chopped fresh basil
   (or 1 teaspoon dried)
1 tablespoon chopped fresh mint
   (or 1 teaspoon dried)
½ teaspoon toasted and crushed
   cumin seed (page 36)
¼ teaspoon freshly ground black
   pepper
2 teaspoons sugar (or to taste)

3 tablespoons seasoned rice wine
   vinegar
¼ cup toasted pine nuts or
   blanched, toasted, and
   slivered almonds
1 pint toybox tomatoes or 2 cups
   cherry tomatoes, quartered
   Garnish: Mint sprigs

With a vegetable peeler, remove the skin from the cucumbers in alternating strips. Cut the cucumbers in half lengthwise and scrape out any seeds with a teaspoon. Slice into ¼-inch slices. Place in a colander in the sink. Lightly sprinkle the cucumber slices with salt, toss, and set aside to drain for at least 1 hour.

In a large bowl, combine the onions, garlic, chile, yogurt, herbs, cumin, pepper, and sugar. Using paper towels, blot the cucumber slices dry. Toss the cucumbers with the rice wine vinegar and add them to the onion-yogurt mixture. Cover and refrigerate at least 2 hours before serving.

At serving time, stir in the pine nuts or almonds and the tomatoes. Serve on chilled plates, garnished with mint sprigs.

 Recommended wine: An herbal-tinged Fumé/Sauvignon Blanc offers a pleasing crispness and tartness that go well with the mint and basil flavors in this salad.

 Black Bean Gazpacho Salad

This is a variation on a traditional gazpacho, with the addition of black beans. It makes a terrific summer lunch salad or first course since it's extremely refreshing, even though it's hearty. While the length of the ingredients list may seem a little daunting and some time is involved in chopping the vegetables, the salad comes together very easily. It's great for a crowd and stores well in the refrigerator for up 3 days.

Serves 10 to 12

2   cups cooked black beans (or
    canned beans, drained and
    rinsed)
2   cups thinly sliced small red
    onions
1   tablespoon minced garlic
2   cups peeled, seeded, and
    diagonally cut cucumbers
2   cups seeded and diced tomatoes
1½ cups diced red bell peppers
1½ cups diced yellow bell peppers
1½ cups diced green bell peppers
2   teaspoons seeded and finely
    minced serrano chiles
½   cup husked and julienned
    tomatillos

1   cup fresh raw corn kernels
    (about 2 large ears)
½   cup chopped fresh cilantro
⅓   cup fresh lime juice
2   teaspoons raspberry vinegar
1   tablespoon Tabasco (or to taste)
¼   cup olive oil
1   cup fresh or canned tomato juice
2   tablespoons chopped fresh
    oregano (or 2 teaspoons
    dried)
Kosher salt and freshly ground
    black pepper
Garnish: Cilantro sprigs

Combine all of the ingredients. Chill at least 2 hours to allow the flavors to blend. Season to taste with additional salt and pepper, and add more Tabasco as desired. Serve chilled, garnished with cilantro sprigs.

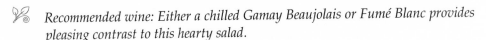 *Recommended wine: Either a chilled Gamay Beaujolais or Fumé Blanc provides pleasing contrast to this hearty salad.*

 # Summer Squash Salad with Feta

Anyone who has ever grown zucchini or yellow summer squash knows that you have to be creative to find ways to use all that even a small garden will produce. This Provençal-inspired dish is an excellent accompaniment to grilled seafood or may be served as a first-course salad.

Serves 6 to 8 as a first course or side dish

¾   pound zucchini, diced
½   pound yellow summer squash,
    diced
½   cup drained and chopped oil-
    packed sun-dried tomatoes

½   cup pitted and sliced Kalamata
    or Niçoise olives
1   red bell pepper, chopped
1½ tablespoons chopped shallots
6   tablespoons olive oil

3   tablespoons raspberry vinegar
1   tablespoon honey
1   tablespoon chopped fresh basil
1   tablespoon chopped fresh mint

3   ounces crumbled feta cheese
    Kosher salt and freshly ground
       black pepper

In a large bowl, combine all the ingredients. Refrigerate until ready to serve.

 Recommended wine: A citrusy Fumé/Sauvignon Blanc is the perfect selection for this garden-fresh salad.

 # Fire and Ice Melon with Figs

This is a perfect dish for a warm summer day. The fiery heat of the serrano chiles makes a startling and delightful contrast to the cool, refreshing melon. This counterpoint of hot and cool is carried through by the mint and lime juice. A confetti of edible flower petals is a dazzling garnish for this as well as many other dishes in this book. (For more information on using edible flowers, see page 397.)
Serves 8 as a first course

SYRUP:

⅓   cup sugar
¼   cup water
2   teaspoons seeded and minced
       serrano chiles
¼   cup fresh lime juice
1   tablespoon minced fresh mint
2   teaspoons minced red bell pepper
2   teaspoons minced green bell
       pepper

2   teaspoons minced yellow bell
       pepper

2   large honeydew, cantaloupe,
       crane, or other ripe melons
8   large fresh, ripe figs, sliced
    Garnish: Edible flower petals, if
       available

In a small saucepan, combine the sugar and water. Boil until the sugar is dissolved. Remove from the heat and cool. Add the chiles, lime juice, mint, and peppers. The syrup can be stored refrigerated for up to 1 week.
    Cut the melons in half and scoop out the seeds. Remove the rind. Then cut into an assortment of pleasing shapes.
    To serve, arrange the melon and figs on well-chilled plates. Spoon the syrup over the fruit and garnish with flower petals if desired.

Recommended wine: A slightly sweet, spicy Gewürztraminer is the perfect match for this lively dish, particularly if it is served on a warm summer day.

CHILE HEAT

The Scoville Scale for measuring the heat level of chiles was developed back at the turn of the century by W. L. Scoville. His method involved extracting the heat-producing chemical compounds known as capsaicin,* which he then diluted to a point where they were barely detectable to the taste. For example, if a gram of chile extract had to be diluted in 40,000 ml of water and alcohol to be barely perceptible then that chile was rated at 40,000 Scoville heat units. Although this is not a precise test, since each of us has some differences in sensitivity to chiles, it does give a good estimate of the relative heats of different chiles.

Here are some Scoville heat ratings for various popular chiles:

Bell peppers: 0
Anaheims: 800–1200
Poblanos: 800–1200
Jalapeños: 8000–10,000

Serranos: 10,000–18,000
Japanese: 25,000–40,000
Thai types: 40,000–60,000
Pure capsaicin: 1,000,000

*Capsaicin is thought to be the most potent of the heat-producing chemicals in chiles.

Watermelon and Red Onion Salad

Ideal for summer lunches when melons are at their peak of ripeness, this refreshing salad is an appetite stimulator as well as a radiant color complement to any outdoor buffet. Blueberries or fresh figs make a wonderful addition to this salad.

Serves 6

1   tablespoon chopped shallots
⅓   cup raspberry vinegar
⅓   cup fresh or frozen raspberries,
        puréed and strained

2   teaspoons honey (or to taste)
⅓   cup olive oil
        Kosher salt and freshly ground
        black pepper

2 medium red onions, thinly
   sliced
2 bunches watercress, stems
   removed

8 cups watermelon cut into 1-inch
   cubes (use both red and yellow
   watermelon, if available)
Garnish: Julienned mint leaves

In a medium bowl, whisk together the shallots, vinegar, raspberry purée, honey, and oil. Season to taste with salt and pepper. Separate the onions into rings. Pour the vinaigrette over the onions and marinate in the refrigerator for at least 15 minutes.

To serve, arrange a bed of watercress on each chilled plate. Top with the cubed watermelon and drape the onion rings on top. Drizzle with the vinaigrette and garnish with the mint leaves if desired.

 Recommended wine: A fruity, slightly sweet Gewürztraminer or Johannisberg Riesling accentuates the sweet melon and raspberry tastes in this salad.

WATERMELON

Watermelons are traditionally known for their dark-green exterior and ruby-red flesh, but there are an extraordinary variety of melons available. There are many delicious yellow-fleshed varieties, and the combination of red and yellow melon on a plate is particularly beautiful. In the Valley Oaks garden we're growing an heirloom variety called "Moon and Stars," which displays a radiant large yellow oval splash (resembling the moon) and tiny yellow dots in constellations (the stars) on its green skin. Under the right conditions—a good, warm summer and sandy soil—melons can be grown easily by the home gardener, and many unusual, flavorful melon varieties are available through seed companies. (A source list is on page 410.)

Whole watermelons should always be stored at room temperature after being purchased, while cut melons keep better in the refrigerator.

Watermelon seeds are edible, by the way. The Chinese roast and salt them to eat as a snack. I've also had them when they've been soaked in soy sauce, lightly dusted with hot pepper, and then roasted at 350 degrees just until crunchy.

Fennel, Pear, and Persimmon Salad with Fig Vinaigrette

This is a wonderful salad for the fall and winter months, as it takes advantage of seasonal produce. For a more substantial course, drape some paper-thin slices of prosciutto or coppa salami around the plate. There are two different varieties of persimmons on the market. I've specified Fuyu persimmons in this recipe because they are fully ripe and really at their peak while they are still firm—thus sliceable. The variety called Hachiya is not ripe until very soft and sweet and it's usually used mashed or puréed in baking.

Serves 6

3 cups mixed savory greens, such as arugula, watercress, tat tsoi, endive, or radicchio	1 medium fennel bulb, thinly sliced vertically
2 firm Fuyu persimmons, thinly sliced	½ cup lightly toasted pecan halves
2 ripe pears, sliced in wedges	Fig Vinaigrette (recipe follows)

To serve, divide the greens among 6 well-chilled plates. Arrange the persimmons, pears, and fennel bulb on and around the greens. Sprinkle with the pecan halves. Drizzle some of the Fig Vinaigrette over all.

Fig Vinaigrette

Makes approximately 1¼ cups

⅔ cup chopped dried figs	1½ tablespoons minced shallots
½ cup water	¼ cup sherry vinegar
½ cup dry white wine	⅓ cup olive oil
½ cup apple juice or cider	Kosher salt and freshly ground black pepper
2 teaspoons minced fresh thyme	
2 teaspoons toasted black mustard seed (optional; page 36)	

In a saucepan, combine ⅓ cup of the figs with the water. Bring to a boil. Reduce the heat and simmer, covered, until the figs are soft, about 5 minutes. Cool.

Pour the fig mixture into a blender or food processor and purée. Transfer to a medium bowl. Whisk in the wine, apple juice, thyme, mustard seed, shallots, vinegar, and olive oil. Season to taste with salt and pepper. Stir in the remaining figs.

Recommended wine: The dressing is fairly sweet, so a fruity Riesling or Chenin Blanc would work well. I've also had a Pinot Gris that I liked with this salad.

Orange, Olive, and Fennel Salad with Cranberry Vinaigrette

This is another lovely salad for the winter months, when it is difficult to find good tomatoes and greens. Sometimes I like to use Baked Olives (page 278) in place of the brine-cured olives in the recipe. Dried cranberries are becoming more widely available and can be found in natural food and gourmet stores, as well as anywhere dried fruits are sold in bulk. Dried cherries are also great in this vinaigrette. If you are concerned about fat in your diet, the vinaigrette is also delicious made without oil beyond that used to sauté the shallots.

Serves 6

3 large navel oranges, peeled and sliced ¼ inch thick
1 large fennel bulb, thinly sliced vertically, fronds reserved for garnish
1 small red onion, thinly sliced

⅔ cup mixed brine-cured black olives, such as Niçoise, Kalamata, and Picholine
Cranberry Vinaigrette (recipe follows)
Garnish: Fennel fronds

Arrange oranges, fennel, and onion attractively on a platter. Scatter the olives around and drizzle with the Cranberry Vinaigrette. Garnish with fennel fronds.

Cranberry Vinaigrette

Makes approximately 1¼ cups

3 cups unsweetened cranberry juice
½ cup dry red wine
¼ cup dried cranberries
2 tablespoons olive oil
2 tablespoons finely minced shallots
2 tablespoons fresh orange juice

1 tablespoon red wine vinegar (or to taste)
2 teaspoons chopped fresh dill or feathery fronds from fennel
Honey to taste
Kosher salt and freshly ground black pepper

In a saucepan, combine the cranberry juice, wine, and dried cranberries and bring to a boil. Boil over high heat until the liquid is reduced to approximately 1 cup (6 to 8 minutes).

Meanwhile, in a small sauté pan, heat 1 tablespoon of the olive oil and sauté the shallots until soft but not brown. Remove to a medium bowl and set aside.

In a blender or food processor, purée the reduced cranberry–cranberry juice mixture. Add the purée to the softened shallots. Whisk in the rest of the ingredients, including the remaining olive oil, seasoning to taste with salt and pepper.

Store covered in the refrigerator for up to 1 week.

 Recommended wine: The sweet-tart flavor of the vinaigrette goes well with a wine that has some sweetness and a lot of fruit. I'd serve this salad with either a chilled Gamay, Gewürztraminer, or White Zinfandel.

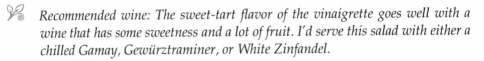

EATING SEASONALLY

I can't emphasize enough the value of eating seasonally. By that I mean eating ingredients that are properly available to us during specific seasons. I've never understood why restaurants or markets insist on serving items like tomatoes in winter salads (or why we continue to expect them) when we all know that winter tomatoes are generally pretty awful. Instead, why not serve a winter salad that takes advantage of ingredients that are at their peak in winter? (Of course, making that kind of determination has been vastly complicated by jet shipping. Oranges are at their peak in winter, so I think of the recipe here as a winter salad, but they have to be flown long distances to reach markets anywhere outside of Florida or California—no matter what the season.)

Part of the joy of eating is the anticipation of seasonal foods. For me, the first asparagus of spring or the first raspberries in the summer are a cause for celebration. Eating with the seasons helps ground us and reminds us of our connections to the earth. Thoreau said: "Live in each season as it passes; breathe the air, drink the drink, taste the fruit, and resign yourself to the influence of each."

Oranges, Watercress, and Endive with an Oriental Orange Vinaigrette

This simple, pretty salad is notable for its combination of sweet and slightly bitter tastes, which are complemented by the sweet, spicy dressing. A variation on the preceding recipe, it also takes advantage of winter and spring ingredients that often appear together in the market at the border of the seasons. The recipe for the vinaigrette makes more than you'll need.

Serves 8

2 large Belgian endive, separated into leaves
2 cups cored, finely slivered radicchio
4 large navel oranges, peeled and thickly sliced

2 bunches watercress, stems removed
1 medium red onion, thinly sliced
   Oriental Orange Vinaigrette (recipe follows)

To serve, arrange the endive in a circle. Place a mound of the radicchio on the endive with the oranges, watercress, and onion on top. Drizzle the vinaigrette generously over the top.

Oriental Orange Vinaigrette

Makes approximately 2 cups

6 ounces unsweetened frozen orange juice concentrate
⅓ cup low-sodium soy sauce
⅓ cup rice wine vinegar
1 tablespoon peeled and minced fresh ginger

1½ teaspoons dark sesame oil
½ cup chopped scallions, white and pale-green parts
¼ cup chopped fresh parsley
1 cup olive or peanut oil

In a food processor or blender, combine all ingredients except the oil. Process until smooth. Transfer to a bowl. Stir in the oil, being careful not to emulsify; otherwise the dressing will get too thick. Store any unused dressing, covered and refrigerated, for up to 2 weeks.

 Recommended wine: A fruity, citrusy Johannisberg Riesling mirrors the flavors in this salad.

PARSLEYS

There are two kinds of parsley which are now generally available in the market: curly and flat leaf. They can be used interchangably, but many cooks (me included) prefer the more pronounced herbal flavor of flat leaf for most dishes. Although we typically think of parsley as a garnish, it makes a wonderful side dish vegetable when it's cooked briefly in a little stock and then puréed.

The vinaigrette used in the recipe on page 15, as well as most of the fruity vinaigrettes in this book, also makes a wonderful marinade for grilled or roasted chicken, fish, and shellfish. Try this Oriental Orange Vinaigrette next time you're cooking chicken breasts or shrimp.

Goat Cheese, Figs, and Savory Greens with Sherry-Shallot Vinaigrette

This is one of those very simple recipes that epitomizes summer—sweet figs, rich, aged goat cheese, and uncomplicated vinaigrette. I particularly like a goat cheese with a little age on it in this salad—it's deep in flavor and has a firm texture. I especially like Laura Chenel's Crottin or Taupinière (page 402). Try adding slices of ripe pear or apple for an interesting variation.

Serves 4

4   ounces aged goat cheese
4   cups loosely packed mixed
     savory greens, such as
     arugula, mizuna, mustard,
     watercress, etc.
8   small ripe figs, sliced in half and
     fanned

Sherry-Shallot Vinaigrette
   (recipe follows)
Garnish: Mixture of edible flower
   petals, such as calendula,
   bachelor's button, or chive

Slice the cheese into small wedges and set aside. Arrange the greens and figs on chilled plates and dress with Sherry-Shallot Vinaigrette. Arrange the goat cheese on top and sprinkle with a confetti of edible flower petals.

Sherry-Shallot Vinaigrette

1½ tablespoons fino or amontillado sherry	1 tablespoon finely minced shallots
1½ tablespoons balsamic vinegar	¼ cup olive oil
1 teaspoon roasted garlic (page 247)	Salt and freshly ground black pepper

Whisk all the ingredients together until just combined.

 Recommended wine: A soft Riesling or Chenin Blanc with just a touch of residual sugar would go well with the figs and nutty, aged goat cheese. If using a fresh goat cheese, with its tarter flavor, a barrel-aged Sauvignon Blanc would work best.

Minted Romaine Salad with Blue Cheese and Pecans

This is a simple salad with really punchy flavors to it. It would be a perfect accompaniment to simply grilled chicken or pork.
Serves 4

2 large heads of romaine Blue Cheese and Mint Vinaigrette (recipe follows)	Garnish: Mint sprigs, cherry tomato halves, toasted whole pecans, and additional crumbled blue cheese, if desired

Discard the outer leaves of the romaine to reveal the light-green core and heart. Wash the cores and hearts in cold water and shake dry. Cut crosswise into thick sections. Refrigerate until ready to use.

To serve, toss the romaine with the vinaigrette. Garnish with mint sprigs, cherry tomatoes, pecans, and blue cheese.

Blue Cheese and Mint Vinaigrette

Makes approximately 1 cup

¼ cup white wine vinegar
1 tablespoon minced shallots
2 tablespoons Dijon-style mustard
2 teaspoons minced fresh mint
1½ tablespoons toasted and chopped
     pecans
¼ cup walnut oil

3 tablespoons olive oil
¼ cup apple juice
1 ounce crumbled blue cheese,
     such as Maytag or Dietrich's
     (pages 407, 406)
Kosher salt and freshly ground
     black pepper

In a medium bowl, combine the vinegar, shallots, mustard, mint, and pecans. Whisk in the oils and apple juice to form a smooth mixture. Stir in the blue cheese. Season to taste with salt and pepper. (Taste carefully, since the blue cheese can be very salty.) Store, covered and refrigerated, for up to 5 days.

    Recommended wine: The mint, mustard, and cheese make for a complex flavor combination, which goes best with a crisp, clean, straightforward wine, such as a Fumé/Sauvignon Blanc.

 # Grilled Portabello Mushrooms on Savory Greens with Parmesan Chips

I've specified portabello mushrooms because they are widely available during most of the year, but during the late fall, after the rains have come, my favorite mushroom to use for this recipe is fresh boletus. They are found wild up and down the northern California coast. Fresh oyster mushrooms would be delicious too. To make this a main course, add some roasted beets and carrots and grilled red onions.

Serves 6

2 teaspoons balsamic vinegar
2 teaspoons roasted garlic (page 247)
1 teaspoon chopped fresh
     rosemary
2 teaspoons chopped fresh sage
¼ cup olive oil
1½ pounds stemmed and trimmed
     portabello mushrooms

Kosher salt and freshly ground
     black pepper
4 cups mixed young, tender, savory
     greens, such as mizuna, arugula,
     watercress, or red mustard
Mustard Seed Vinaigrette (recipe
     follows)
Parmesan Chips (recipe follows)

Prepare a charcoal fire or preheat a stovetop grill. In a medium bowl, whisk together the vinegar, roasted garlic, rosemary, sage, and oil. Brush the mushrooms liberally with the mixture. Season with salt and pepper.

Grill the mushrooms over hot coals or moderate heat, until just softened, turning once or twice.

To serve, arrange the greens on individual plates. Lightly drizzle with the vinaigrette. Slice the mushrooms thickly and arrange on the greens. Surround with the Parmesan Chips and serve immediately.

Mustard Seed Vinaigrette

Makes about ⅓ cup

1 tablespoon Dijon-style mustard
2 teaspoons toasted mustard seed
    (page 36)
2 tablespoons seasoned rice wine
    vinegar

2 tablespoon fresh orange juice
2 teaspoons chopped fresh dill
¼ cup olive oil
    Kosher salt and freshly ground
       black pepper

In a small bowl, whisk all the ingredients until combined. Prepare the vinaigrette at least 30 minutes before serving to allow the flavors to marry.

Parmesan Chips

Makes 12 chips

Vegetable spray
1 cup freshly and finely grated Parmesan or aged Asiago cheese

Preheat the oven to 350 degrees. Line a baking sheet with parchment or waxed paper. Lightly spray the paper with vegetable spray. Sprinkle the cheese into thin 3-inch rounds, 4 inches apart. Bake until the cheese melts and the chips begin to brown, 5 to 10 minutes. Using a metal spatula, carefully remove each chip and place on a rack or drape over a dowel or rolling pin to form curls. Cool. The Parmesan Chips should be used within a few hours.

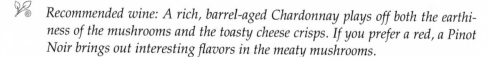 *Recommended wine: A rich, barrel-aged Chardonnay plays off both the earthiness of the mushrooms and the toasty cheese crisps. If you prefer a red, a Pinot Noir brings out interesting flavors in the meaty mushrooms.*

Warm Radicchio Salad with Lemon-Garlic Cream

The perfect round shape of radicchio makes it ideal for many uses where other lettuces and greens won't do. In this variation, quartered heads are deep-fried and served with a luscious, garlicky lemon cream. The joy of this dish is biting into the radicchio and tasting the various levels of warmth and crispness inside—a textural treat! If you're really going all out, deep-fry some capers according to the directions and use them for garnish.

Serves 4

4   small heads radicchio
2   large eggs
⅓   cup all-purpose flour
¾   cup fresh breadcrumbs
½   cup freshly grated dry Jack or
       Parmesan cheese
1   teaspoon kosher salt
½   teaspoon ground white pepper

Olive oil for frying
2   cups baby greens, such as arugula,
       frisée, and mâche
Lemon-Garlic Cream (recipe
       follows)
Garnish: Chopped chives and
       fried capers (page 21)

Cut the radicchio in quarters through the core.

In a small bowl, beat the eggs with 1 tablespoon water. Spread the flour on a plate. On a second plate, combine the breadcrumbs, cheese, and salt and pepper. Dredge the radicchio in the flour, shaking off the excess. Coat thoroughly in the egg mixture and then lightly and evenly pat with the breadcrumb mixture, shaking off any excess. Chill, uncovered, for at least 30 minutes to make the coating adhere.

In a sauté pan, pour olive oil to a depth of ¼ inch and heat. Add the radicchio and evenly brown over moderate heat. Transfer to paper towels to drain.

To serve, arrange the baby greens on individual plates and place sautéed radicchio on each plate. Drizzle with the Lemon-Garlic Cream and scatter the chives and fried capers over the top. Serve immediately while the radicchio is still warm.

Lemon-Garlic Cream

1   large egg
1   tablespoon roasted garlic
       (page 247)
2   tablespoons fresh lemon juice

½–¾   cup olive oil
1   tablespoon drained capers
       Kosher salt and freshly ground
       black pepper

In a blender or food processor, combine the egg, garlic, and lemon juice. Blend. With the motor running, slowly add the olive oil to form an emulsion. Do not overbeat. The sauce should be thick but not stiff (still pourable). Transfer to a bowl or storage container. Stir in the capers and season to taste with salt and pepper. Store, covered and refrigerated, for up to 3 days.

 Recommended wine: A Fumé/Sauvignon Blanc provides a nice foil for the lemony dressing and the bittersweet radicchio.

FRIED CAPERS

Something magical happens to capers when you quickly deep-fry them. They lose a lot of their vinegar sharpness and become crisp and crunchy—a terrific garnish.

Drain the capers and place them on a paper towel to absorb as much moisture as possible. In a small, deep-sided saucepan, heat ¼ inch of olive oil until it shimmers (350 degrees on a frying or candy thermometer). Add the capers to the hot oil and fry for 2 to 3 minutes until they begin to crisp. Drain carefully and place on paper towels to absorb excess oil. The capers can be made 3 to 4 hours ahead; keep them uncovered at room temperature.

 Warm Red Cabbage Salad with Pancetta and California Goat Cheese

I love this salad when the weather is cool. When you cook red cabbage with vinegar it turns a beautiful fluorescent red. Select a young goat cheese that is creamy in texture. I really like the fresh Chabis from Redwood Hill Farms or Bodega Goat Cheese (pages 402, 401).

Serves 6

⅓ pound good-quality pancetta,
     chopped
1   teaspoon roasted garlic (page 247)
½ cup olive oil
1   tablespoon honey
¼ cup red wine vinegar
     Kosher salt and freshly ground
     black pepper

1½ pounds cored and finely
      shredded red cabbage
3   cups mixed baby greens, such as
      arugula, frisée, mizuna, and
      mâche
6   ounces fresh California goat
      cheese, thinly sliced
      Garnish: Watercress sprigs

In a large sauté pan over moderate heat, cook the pancetta until it just begins to color, approximately 7 to 8 minutes. Remove to paper towels and set aside. Discard the fat.

In a small bowl, combine the garlic, olive oil, honey, vinegar, salt, and pepper.

Return the sauté pan to high heat and heat the olive oil mixture. Add the cabbage and sauté for 1 to 2 minutes, stirring constantly. Cabbage should still be crisp. Add the pancetta to the cabbage.

To serve, arrange the greens on individual plates. Divide the cabbage among the plates. Arrange the slices of goat cheese around the cabbage and drizzle the greens with any remaining cooking juices from the cabbage pan. Garnish with watercress sprigs.

Recommended wine: The sweet-tart flavors of the warm salad are complemented by a lightly chilled Gamay.

Warm Vegetable Salad with Chanterelle and Portabello Mushrooms

I love mushrooms and use them as often as I can. Here in the wine country we have access to many varieties of wild mushrooms, which appear after the first rains in the fall. In this recipe, I've used wild chanterelles and cultivated portabellos for a double mushroom flavor. (For convenience, I've suggested cooking the portabellos under the broiler or on the stove, but if you can cook them on an outdoor grill, by all means do it.)

Serves 4 to 6

4   tablespoons olive oil
1   cup peeled and finely julienned
      parsnips or turnips

⅔ cup finely julienned carrots
⅔ cup finely julienned red bell pepper
⅔ cup finely julienned fennel bulb

1 tablespoon minced shallots
½ pound cleaned chanterelles,
   sliced ¼ inch thick
2–3 large portabello mushrooms,
   stemmed
   Kosher salt and freshly ground
   black pepper

2 cups savory greens, such as
   arugula, red mustard,
   watercress, and radicchio
   Honey-Lemon Vinaigrette
   (recipe follows)
   Garnish: Watercress or chervil
   sprigs

In a sauté pan, heat 1 tablespoon of the olive oil. Add the vegetables and sauté until tender but still crisp, approximately 2 minutes. Set aside and keep warm.

In the same sauté pan, heat 2 tablespoons of the olive oil. Add the shallots and chanterelles and sauté until lightly browned. Remove and combine with the julienned vegetables.

Preheat the broiler or stovetop grill. Brush the cleaned portabellos with the remaining 1 tablespoon olive oil. Season with salt and pepper. Broil or grill the portabellos until softened. Keep warm.

To serve, toss the vegetables with half of the Honey-Lemon Vinaigrette. Divide the greens among the plates. Place the vegetables on top. Thickly slice the portabellos and arrange on the salads. Drizzle with some of the remaining vinaigrette and garnish with watercress or chervil, if desired.

Honey-Lemon Vinaigrette

Makes approximately 1 cup

2 tablespoons finely minced
   shallots
⅓ cup olive oil
½ cup fresh lemon juice

3 tablespoons honey (or to taste)
   Salt and freshly ground black
   pepper

Sauté the shallots in the olive oil until soft but not brown. Set aside in a mixing bowl to cool. Whisk in the lemon juice, honey, and salt and pepper to taste. Store refrigerated up to 2 weeks.

Recommended wine: A toasty, barrel-aged Chardonnay mirrors the earthy flavors of the mushrooms.

CHANTERELLE MUSHROOMS

Chanterelles, also known as girolle or pfifferling, are a true wild mushroom that no one has yet figured out how to cultivate. In the United States, most are gathered in the Pacific Northwest everywhere from Northern California to British Columbia. They have a wonderful nutty flavor. Although you can buy them dried or canned, they are best fresh. Like most mushrooms, it is best to clean them with a soft brush. Don't immerse them in water unless they are so full of sand and pine needles that you absolutely have to. And don't wrap chanterelles (or any other mushroom) in plastic to store them; they are best stored refrigerated in a basket covered with a very lightly moistened cloth.

Pecan-Polenta Salad with Grilled Scallions and Crème Fraîche

This robust salad can serve as the centerpiece for the meal. Everything can be made ahead of time and the polenta sautéed just before serving. This is another dish that pairs hot ingredients (the polenta) with cold (crisp greens) for an intriguing contrast. The oven-dried tomatoes called for as a garnish are made by slicing the tomatoes ¼ inch thick. These are gently patted with paper towels to dry them as much as possible. They are then placed in a single layer on a baking sheet lined with parchment paper and put in a 200-degree oven and allowed to dry out. The drying process takes 6 to 8 hours or overnight. You can certainly use a good, oil-packed sun-dried tomato in place of the oven-dried. Drain well before adding.

Serves 6

POLENTA:

3 tablespoons unsalted butter	Salt and freshly ground black pepper
¾ cup minced yellow onions	
3 cups rich chicken stock	¾ cup minced pecans
1 cup polenta	⅓ cup fresh breadcrumbs
¼ cup freshly grated Asiago cheese	2 tablespoons flour
2 tablespoons minced chives	2 large eggs, beaten with 1 tablespoon water

SALAD:

12 large scallions, split lengthwise
    Olive oil
    Kosher salt and freshly ground
      black pepper
3   cups savory greens, such as
      arugula and frisée

½ cup crème fraîche (page 314)
   Garnish: Balsamic vinegar, extra-
     virgin olive oil, and oven-dried
     or sun-dried tomatoes

To make the polenta: In a small saucepan, melt the butter and sauté the onions over moderate heat until they are soft and sweet. Add the stock, increase the heat, and bring to a boil. Slowly sprinkle in the polenta, stirring constantly. Reduce the heat and cook for 10 to 12 minutes, stirring often. The polenta will be thick and soft and will pull away from the sides of the pot when it's done. Stir in the cheese and chives. Season to taste with salt and pepper. Transfer the polenta to an oiled 10-inch pie plate or pan and spread it evenly. Refrigerate for 1 hour. Cut the chilled polenta into even diamond or wedge shapes.

In a small bowl, combine the pecans and breadcrumbs. Lightly dust each polenta piece with flour, dip it into the beaten egg mixture, and then into the pecan mixture, patting to coat evenly. Set on a rack and refrigerate until serving time.

To make the salad: Lightly brush the scallions with olive oil. Season with salt and pepper. Grill or broil until they just begin to soften. Set aside.

To serve, arrange the greens on chilled plates. In a sauté pan, heat 2 tablespoons olive oil. Add the polenta and sauté until golden-brown. Place on top of the greens. Arrange the scallions around. Top with a good tablespoon of crème fraîche. Arrange the oven-dried tomatoes around the plate and drizzle with the balsamic vinegar and extra-virgin olive oil. Finish with a grinding or two of black pepper and a sprinkling of salt.

 Recommended wine: A barrel-aged Chardonnay nicely complements the nutty polenta and the crème fraîche.

ENSURING A CRISP CRUST

You'll note that this recipe suggests refrigerating the coated polenta pieces briefly before they are sautéed. This is an important step when using the flour-egg-crumb technique. It is also important to make sure that the oil is the right temperature: The ideal is 350 to 360 degrees—the point at which the oil "shimmers." Placing chilled food in hot oil is key to ensuring a crisp crust around an inside that isn't soggy or greasy.

 Hangtown Fry Salad

"Hangtown" is Placerville in the California gold country. The nickname comes from its gold rush days, when justice was often handed down quickly at the end of a rope. A Hangtown fry combined fresh oysters, eggs, and bacon—rare ingredients in a gold rush town. It was reputedly the dish most often ordered by those who had either struck it rich or were about to have their last meal. I've translated the traditional fry into a salad that delights not only with the mix of flavors, but also with its mix of temperatures and textures. The greens can be chilled and ready to go at any time. The crêpes, which go into the salad at room temperature, can be made as much as a day or two ahead—just wrap them up well and refrigerate. You can also make the crêpes while the oysters are "bathing" in the milk—a step that makes them less fishy. The chilled greens, egg crêpes, warm pancetta, and hot oysters are brought together with a drizzle of Walnut Oil Vinaigrette—a new "mother sauce" unknown in gold rush days.

Serves 6

24 small shucked oysters	2 tablespoons chopped fresh parsley
1 cup milk	12 thinly sliced rounds of pancetta
1 cup Panko or other dry	5 cups loosely packed mixed baby
breadcrumbs	greens, such as arugula,
¼ cup yellow cornmeal	mizuna, and mustard
1 teaspoon kosher salt	Herbed Egg Crêpes, sliced
½ teaspoon pure California or New	(recipe follows)
Mexico chile powder	Walnut Oil Vinaigrette (page 30)

In a bowl, combine the oysters and the milk. Let stand up to 1 hour at room temperature or up to 3 hours refrigerated. In a separate bowl, combine the breadcrumbs, cornmeal, salt, chile powder, and parsley. Drain the oysters. Roll each oyster in the crumb mixture until well coated. Separate them on a sheet of wax paper and refrigerate, to set the coating, while you sauté the pancetta.

In a nonstick sauté pan, cook the slices of pancetta until firm and lightly browned but not crisp. Remove the pancetta, leaving the drippings in the pan, and keep warm. In the same pan, quickly sauté the oysters until they are lightly brown and their edges begin to curl, about 2 minutes.

To serve, mound the greens on plates. Arrange the strips of Herbed Egg Crêpes on the greens. Place the oysters on top, along with 2 slices of the pancetta, and drizzle with some of the Walnut Oil Vinaigrette.

Herbed Egg Crêpes

3 large eggs
1 tablespoon unsalted butter
2 tablespoons minced shallots
2 tablespoons minced fresh basil

2 tablespoons minced red bell pepper
Salt and freshly ground black pepper

In a small bowl, beat the eggs with 2 tablespoons water. In an 8-inch nonstick sauté pan, melt the butter. Add the shallots and sauté until soft but not brown. Put them in the bowl with the egg mixture and stir in the basil and red pepper. Season with salt and pepper.

Wipe the sauté pan and reheat over moderate heat. Ladle in a thin layer of the egg mixture. Cook until just set, about 1 minute. With a spatula, turn the crêpe over and cook 30 seconds more. Remove. Repeat with the rest of the egg mixture. (You should end up with 3 or 4 crêpes.) Carefully cut the crêpes into fine, long strips. (If you make the crêpes ahead of time, wrap them well after they've cooled and refrigerate them. Slice them and let them return to room temperature when you are ready to serve the salads.)

 Recommended wine: Classically, oysters and a crisp Sauvignon Blanc are a great match. This recipe, however, adds some rich, round flavors that link it wonderfully to a barrel-fermented and aged Chardonnay that has some lemony notes in the flavor.

PANKO

Panko is a type of breadcrumb used in Japan. It is becoming widely available in the U.S., especially in areas with a Japanese population. I think it is the best dry breadcrumb to use, both in mixtures as well as for coating foods for frying or sautéing. When Panko is made, the crumb is expanded in a way that makes it very light and crisp, so it doesn't "sog out" like ordinary breadcrumbs. Furthermore, the crumbs are larger than ordinary commercially available bread-crumbs; this helps keep the foods lighter and more delicate. Panko has become one of my pantry staples.

 Lobster and Grilled Portabello Mushroom Salad

The rich taste of lobster combined with the earthy, meaty texture of portabello mushrooms is terrific. I've used stock for some of the oil in the Walnut Oil Vinai-grette as a way of reducing the total fat content. (In fact, if you wish to reduce fat in your diet, a reduced stock can substitute for all the oil in vinaigrettes.) Due to the price of lobsters, this recipe would have to fall into the special occasion cate-gory, but, hey, why not?

Serves 4

2	1½-pound live Maine lobsters	2	cups young savory greens, such as
2	large stemmed portabello		arugula, watercress, mustard,
	mushrooms		and frisée
2	tablespoons olive oil		**Walnut Oil Vinaigrette (page 30)**
	Kosher salt and freshly ground		**Garnish: Fresh salmon roe**
	black pepper		

In a large stockpot of lightly salted boiling water, plunge the lobsters, head first. Cook for 10 to 12 minutes. Remove them from the pot and wait until they are cool enough to handle. Remove the tail and claw meat intact. Set aside.

Prepare a charcoal fire. With the blunt side of a paring knife, scrape the black gills from the underside of the portabellos. Lightly brush the mushrooms with the olive oil. Season with salt and pepper. Quickly grill on both sides until just soft-ened. Or broil them. Remove and set aside.

To serve, arrange the greens on plates. Slice the lobster tail into medallions and fan over the greens. Slice the portabellos into ¼-inch thick slices and arrange around the lobster meat.

Drizzle with a little of the Walnut Oil Vinaigrette and garnish with the lobster claw meat (one per plate) and a scattering of salmon roe if desired.

🌿   *Recommended wine: A rich, barrel-aged Chardonnay adds an intensity of flavor and a matching richness to this delicious lobster salad.*

Tempura Soft-Shell Crab Salad

This is a delightful salad, with lots of crunch from both the raw vegetables and the crisply fried crab. Soft-shell crabs are available fresh from late spring to midsummer. Since they also freeze very well, they are available frozen year round; ask your fishmonger if they can be ordered for you. I like to garnish this salad with edible flower petals when they're available.

Serves 6

6 cleaned soft-shell crabs	2 cups mixed savory baby greens, such as mizuna, watercress, red mustard, and arugula
1 large egg yolk	
1 cup ice water	
1 cup flour (or ½ cup *each* wheat and rice flour)	2 cups *each* finely julienned carrots, beets, and parsnips (see note)
Flour for coating crab	Walnut Oil Vinaigrette (page 30)
Vegetable oil for deep-frying	Garnish: Salmon roe and edible flower petals (page 397)

Rinse the soft-shell crabs and pat them dry. Set aside. Make the tempura batter: In a medium bowl, beat the egg yolk and water together until just mixed. Dump the flour in all at once and whisk with a few strokes until the ingredients are loosely combined. Batter will be a little lumpy. Use immediately.

Lightly dust each crab with some flour. In a large saucepan or deep-fryer, pour the oil to a depth of 2 inches and heat to 350 degrees. (It should be shimmering. If it's simmering or smoking, it's too hot.) Dip the floured crabs in the tempura batter. Quickly but carefully place the crabs in the hot oil for 3 to 4 minutes or until they are golden brown and crisp. Fry one or several depending on your pan, but do not crowd. Transfer to paper towels to drain. Keep warm.

To serve, arrange the greens on individual plates. Place a crab on each plate along with the julienned vegetables. Drizzle with the vinaigrette and garnish with the salmon roe and a sprinkling of edible flower petals if desired. Serve immediately.

Note: To julienne vegetables I like to use either a mandoline or a Japanese "turner-slicer"; my favorite is manufactured by Benriner of Japan. It's a great tool that makes long, thin "spaghetti" out of any root vegetable with very little effort.

Recommended wine: Crisp-textured vegetables and crab should be mirrored in the wine. A clean, crisp Chardonnay, a dry Chenin Blanc, or a crisp sparkling wine would all work well. Although most people don't know it, dry sparkling wines and deep-fried foods are really terrific together.

WALNUT OIL

Walnut oil, as well as its cousin hazelnut oil, is a robust flavoring agent for vinaigrettes and marinades. The truth about these rich, flavorful oils is that they must be refrigerated after opening and they can't be kept too long, as they will go rancid after more than a couple of months. I particularly like the French Vivier brand, but there are many good ones. They are somewhat expensive, but worth it for a special treat, like this salad.

WALNUT OIL VINAIGRETTE

This rich-tasting dressing, which has a lower fat content than that of a traditional vinaigrette because stock replaces some of the oil, is a perfect complement to the three warm shellfish-based salads in this chapter: the Hangtown Fry Salad, which uses oysters, the Lobster and Grilled Portabello Mushroom Salad, and the Tempura Soft-Shell Crab Salad. Once you've tasted how it works with these dishes, you'll think of many other uses for it. Shellfish stock is available frozen in better gourmet shops, and a recipe to make your own (which you can freeze) is on page 53, but in the absence of either, you can certainly use chicken stock, which everyone who cooks should have on hand. A recipe is on pages 52–53, but a good-quality canned broth, defatted, is an acceptable substitute.

Makes ¾ cup

¼ **cup walnut oil**
½ **teaspoon minced garlic**
¼ **cup rich chicken or shellfish stock**
1 **teaspoon white-wine Worcestershire**
1½ **tablespoons Dijon-style mustard**

1 **teaspoon sherry vinegar**
2 **teaspoons chopped fresh parsley**
2 **teaspoons chopped fresh chives**
2 **teaspoons chopped fresh dill Kosher salt and freshly ground black pepper**

In a blender or food processor, combine the walnut oil, garlic, stock, Worcestershire, mustard, and vinegar. Blend until fully combined and creamy. Transfer to a bowl. Whisk in the herbs and add salt and pepper to taste. Store the vinaigrette, covered and refrigerated, for up to 3 days. Bring to room temperature before using.

 ## Fresh Corn, Orzo, and Smoked Chicken Salad with Pine Nuts

This makes an excellent lunch salad or light supper for summer, and it can be made ahead of time and chilled. Smoked or corned chicken is now available at many supermarket deli counters as well as gourmet stores. (Actually, any smoked meat or fish would be tasty in this salad.) If the corn isn't perfectly young, sweet, and tender, I suggest blanching it for a few seconds and cooling it before using. Orzo is a type of very small pasta that is shaped like rice.

Serves 6 to 8

2 teaspoons red chile flakes	⅓ cup minced fresh basil
½ cup seasoned rice wine vinegar	½ cup minced scallions, white and
2 tablespoons light corn syrup	pale-green parts
2 bay leaves	½ cup julienned and blanched red
3 tablespoons fresh lime juice	bell pepper
¼ pound dry orzo pasta	Kosher salt and freshly ground
2 tablespoons olive oil	black pepper
¾ pound julienned smoked or	½ cup toasted pine nuts
corned chicken (page 187)	Garnish: Basil sprigs and lime
2½ cups fresh raw white or yellow	wedges
corn kernels	

To make the dressing, combine the chile flakes, vinegar, corn syrup, bay leaves, and lime juice in a small saucepan. Simmer for 5 minutes. Remove from the heat and cool. Remove and discard the bay leaves.

In a pot of lightly salted, boiling water, cook the orzo until al dente, approximately 3 to 4 minutes. Drain and run cold water over the orzo to stop the cooking. Drain, scoop into a large bowl, and toss with the olive oil.

Then add the dressing and lightly toss to combine. Add the smoked chicken, corn, basil, scallions, and red pepper. Lightly toss to combine. Season with salt and pepper to taste. Chill for 2 hours.

Serve the salad sprinkled with pine nuts and garnished with basil sprigs and lime wedges.

 Recommended wine: I love matching corn with a Chardonnay that has not been overoaked. The fresh, fruity flavors of the wine mirror those of the sweet corn.

PINE NUTS

It goes by many names: pignolia, piñon, Indian nut, pinocchio, as well as pine nut. The seeds of all pine trees are probably edible, but the best culinary pine nuts come from the European stone pine and the piñon tree of the American Southwest. Pine nuts have a very long culinary history. They were found among the foods in the ruins of Pompeii, and they are mentioned in the works of Virgil, Theocritus, and Ovid, who referred to them as one of the great aphrodisiacs of his time. Their rich flavor is at its best after they've been lightly toasted. Shelled pine nuts, because of their high oil content, can become rancid fairly quickly. Buy them at a store that has a rapid turnover and be sure to store them tightly sealed in a cool, dark place. I keep pine nuts refrigerated or frozen.

 Fusilli Salad with Asparagus and Smoked Mozzarella

This is a pasta salad that I particularly like in the spring, when asparagus comes into season. Toward summer, substitute young "haricot vert" green beans for the asparagus. Alternately, you can either roast or grill the asparagus instead of blanching it. Grilling the asparagus emphasizes the sweetness of the vegetable.

Serves 4 to 6

1 **pound slender asparagus, diagonally cut into 3-inch pieces**	2 **tablespoons slivered garlic**
	½ **cup dry white wine**
½ **pound fusilli or other shaped dry pasta**	1 **large roasted red bell pepper, cut into ½-inch pieces**
⅓ **cup extra-virgin olive oil**	1 **large roasted yellow bell pepper, cut into ½-inch pieces**

1   cup seeded and slivered plum
      tomatoes
¼   cup coarsely chopped fresh
      basil
2   teaspoons chopped fresh mint
      Sweet Rice Wine Vinaigrette
      (recipe follows)

      Kosher salt and freshly ground
        black pepper
½   pound smoked mozzarella cheese,
        sliced into thin rounds
¼   pound paper-thin slices of
        prosciutto or hot coppa salami
      Garnish: Fresh basil sprigs

In a large pot of lightly salted boiling water, blanch the asparagus until crisp-tender, about 2 to 3 minutes. Using a skimmer, remove the asparagus from the pot and immediately run cold water over it to stop the cooking. Drain and set aside.

Return the asparagus water to the boil. Add the pasta to the pot and cook until just al dente. Drain the pasta and immediately run cold water over it to stop the cooking. Drain, transfer to a large bowl, and toss with 2 tablespoons of the olive oil.

In a small sauté pan, heat the remaining olive oil and sauté the garlic over low heat until soft but not brown. Add the wine and increase the heat to moderate. Cook 3 to 4 minutes or until most of the wine has evaporated.

Combine the pasta with the asparagus, roasted peppers, tomatoes, basil, and mint. Add the garlic and wine mixture. Toss to combine. Add enough of the Sweet Rice Wine Vinaigrette to coat the ingredients thoroughly. Season with salt and pepper to taste.

Serve the pasta surrounded by the mozzarella and prosciutto. Garnish with the basil sprigs.

Sweet Rice Wine Vinaigrette

¼   cup rice wine vinegar
1   tablespoon fresh lemon juice
1   teaspoon Dijon-style mustard
1   teaspoon minced garlic

½   teaspoon kosher salt
2   teaspoons light-brown sugar
½   cup extra-virgin olive oil
      Freshly ground black pepper

In a medium bowl, whisk all the ingredients together.

Recommended wine: The smoky mozzarella beautifully plays off a fruity Chardonnay or White Zinfandel.

DILL

This herb has a long history of culinary, medicinal, and celebratory uses. The feathery leaves of the plant are used both fresh and dried in salads and often with fish. The seeds, which have a stronger flavor, are more often found in longer-cooking recipes and pickling mixes. Herbalists use both dill leaves and seeds in infusions to dispel flatulence, increase mother's milk, relieve colic in babies, and soothe upset stomachs. Dill was also used as a charm against witches— you could combat an evil spell by carrying a bag of dried dill over your heart.

Rotelle Salad with Smoked Trout and Fresh Dill

This is a lovely salad for the summertime, when good tomatoes and fresh dill are available. Any smoked fish could be substituted for the trout.

Serves 4 to 6

¼ pound rotelle or other corkscrew-shaped dry pasta	2 tablespoons drained and rinsed capers
2 tablespoons olive oil	1 cup thinly sliced small red onions
½ cup buttermilk	12 ounces skinned and boned smoked trout, cut into ½-inch cubes
½ cup mayonnaise, preferably homemade (page 35)	
3 tablespoons prepared horseradish	Salt and freshly ground black pepper
¼ cup chopped fresh dill (or 2 tablespoons dried)	Lemon juice
1½ cups seeded and diced ripe plum tomatoes	Garnish: Arugula and/or frisée leaves

In a large pot of lightly salted boiling water, cook the rotelle until just al dente. Drain and immediately run cold water over it to stop the cooking. Drain again, transfer to a bowl, and toss with the oil. Set aside.

In a large bowl, combine the buttermilk, mayonnaise, horseradish, and dill.

Stir until smooth. Add the pasta, tomatoes, capers, and red onions and toss gently to combine. Carefully fold in the trout. Season to taste with salt and pepper and drops of lemon juice.

Serve the rotelle salad on a bed of arugula and/or frisée.

 Recommended wine: An herbal-tinged Fumé/Sauvignon Blanc captures and complements the fresh dill and smoky flavors of the trout.

HOMEMADE MAYONNAISE

Homemade mayonnaise is so simple I don't know why anyone buys the commercial stuff. It can be made in a couple of minutes in the food processor or blender and flavored in an infinite variety of ways to enhance the dish you're serving it with. I've listed some of my favorite variations below.

Makes approximately 1½ cups

2 whole eggs	2–4 teaspoons fresh lemon juice
½–1 teaspoon salt	1 cup olive or other vegetable oil
1–2 teaspoons Dijon-style mustard	Freshly ground pepper to taste, preferably white pepper

Place eggs, ½ teaspoon salt, 1 teaspoon mustard, and 2 teaspoons fresh lemon juice in a blender or food processor. Combine ingredients with 2 or 3 short bursts.

With the motor running, slowly add the oil in a steady stream to form a thick emulsion. Taste and season with pepper and additional salt, mustard, and lemon juice as desired. If the mayonnaise is too thick, mix in a little water, stock, or buttermilk. Store covered in the refrigerator up to 1 week.

Mayonnaise variations

Add ingredients to the eggs before adding oil.

CAPER-TARRAGON:	1 tablespoon drained capers 2 teaspoons chopped fresh tarragon
CURRY-APPLE:	2–4 teaspoons toasted curry powder ¼ cup peeled, chopped tart apple Honey to taste
MUSTARD:	1–3 additional tablespoons Dijon-style mustard ½ teaspoon grated lemon zest

RED PEPPER:	¼–⅓ cup chopped roasted and peeled red pepper (page 246)
	Drops of Tabasco to taste
BASIL:	⅓–½ cup roughly chopped fresh basil

TOASTING SPICES

If your spices have spent some time on the shelf, I recommend toasting them lightly before using. You can do this by placing them dry in a sauté pan over moderate heat or in a 375-degree oven. It only takes a couple of minutes. Surface oils in spices tend to oxidize and go rancid, and toasting drives off these tired flavors, yielding fresh ones.

 White Bean Salad with Grilled Tomatoes

For those looking to add more healthy legumes to their diet, this Mediterranean-influenced salad is a flavorful way to do it. Accompany this with the Baked Olives on page 278, a loaf of crusty French bread, and a glass of red wine and you've got a perfect summer supper.
Serves 6

6   halved and seeded large plum tomatoes
3   tablespoons extra-virgin olive oil
    Kosher salt and freshly ground black pepper
2   teaspoons mashed anchovy fillets or paste (or to taste)
1   tablespoon roasted garlic (page 247)

2   cups (¾ cup dried) cooked white beans (or canned beans, drained and rinsed)
1   cup chopped red onions
2   tablespoons drained and minced capers
1   tablespoon minced fresh mint
3   cups young arugula leaves
    Garnish: Mint sprigs

Prepare a charcoal fire. In a bowl, lightly toss the tomatoes with 1 tablespoon of the olive oil. Season with salt and pepper. Grill the tomatoes over hot coals until lightly colored but still firm. Or broil them. Set aside.

In a large bowl, combine the remaining 2 tablespoons olive oil, the anchovy fillets, and the roasted garlic. Add the cooked white beans, red onions, capers, mint, and plenty of freshly ground black pepper. Toss to combine.

Serve the bean salad on the arugula leaves, surrounded by the grilled tomatoes. Garnish with mint sprigs.

 Recommended wine: A smooth, barrel-aged Merlot is well suited to this hearty salad; however, a clean, crisp Fumé/Sauvignon Blanc offers a refreshing contrast if you're in the mood for a white.

Orecchiette Salad with Goat Cheese, Olives, and Basil

One of the things I like most about pasta salads is that you can create a great-tasting dish in about 20 minutes with a few key complementary ingredients. This salad is perfect for a light luncheon but is also wonderful as part of a larger buffet.
Serves 4 to 6

½ **pound orecchiette or other small shaped dry pasta**
⅓ **cup extra-virgin olive oil**
2 **tablespoons thinly slivered garlic**
¼ **teaspoon red chile flakes**
⅓ **cup finely diced red bell pepper**
½ **cup slivered Niçoise or Kalamata olives**

⅓ **cup dry white wine**
½ **pound mild California goat feta, crumbled**
⅓ **cup loosely packed basil leaves, chopped**
Freshly ground black pepper
Garnish: Lightly toasted pine nuts and basil sprigs

In a large pot of lightly salted boiling water, cook the pasta until just al dente. Immediately run cold water over it to stop cooking. Drain and toss with 2 tablespoons of the olive oil to prevent sticking. Set aside in a bowl.

In a medium sauté pan, heat the remaining olive oil. Add the garlic and sauté over low heat until soft but not brown. Add the chile flakes, red pepper, olives, and wine. Simmer for 4 to 5 minutes or until most of the wine has evaporated. Remove from the heat and toss with the orecchiette. Add the goat feta and basil and toss gently. Season with pepper.

Serve garnished with pine nuts and basil sprigs.

> *Recommended wine: I've always loved the combination of feta and Fumé/ Sauvignon Blanc. This salad gives me the perfect excuse.*

Lemony Potato Salad with Olives, Corn, and Cashews

This is a summertime barbecue favorite and a sure-fire, crowd-pleasing twist on the classic. The Lemon Vinaigrette is lighter and fresher tasting than a traditional mayonnaise dressing—and vinaigrette is a safer keeper in warm weather.
Serves 12

4 pounds small red potatoes, unpeeled	½ cup lightly toasted and chopped unsalted cashews
1¾ cups fresh raw corn kernels (about 3 large ears)	½ cup chopped fresh parsley Lemon Vinaigrette (recipe follows)
½ cup chopped Kalamata olives	

To a large pot of lightly salted, boiling water, add the potatoes. Return to a boil. Reduce heat to a simmer and cook the potatoes for 12 to 15 minutes, or until just fork-tender. Do not overcook; the potatoes should remain firm. Drain the potatoes and spread them on a baking sheet in a single layer to cool completely. When cool, cut the potatoes into quarters. (If the corn is not perfectly young and tender, then quickly blanch the kernels in boiling water.)

In a bowl, combine the quartered potatoes, corn kernels, olives, cashews, and parsley, reserving some of the parsley for garnish. Add the Lemon Vinaigrette and gently toss with the potatoes. (The salad can be prepared up to 1 day in advance. Store covered in the refrigerator. Bring to room temperature before serving.) Serve garnished with the remaining parsley.

Lemon Vinaigrette

1 tablespoon minced lemon zest	2 tablespoons Dijon-style mustard
3 tablespoons fresh lemon juice	2 teaspoons minced fresh tarragon (or 1 teaspoon dried)

½ cup chopped scallions, both white
   and pale-green parts
⅓ cup extra-virgin olive oil

⅛ teaspoon red chile flakes
   (or to taste)
   Kosher salt

In a bowl, combine the lemon zest, lemon juice, mustard, tarragon, and scallions. Whisk in the olive oil. Add the chile flakes and salt to taste. Whisk again just before serving.

 Recommended wine: A lighter-style Chardonnay, preferably with little or no oak aging, is ideal for this delicious salad.

ZESTING CITRUS

A lemon zester is an invaluable kitchen tool. In place of a good zester, you can use a vegetable peeler to pull long, thin slices of zest off a lemon. Always avoid the bitter white pith beneath the zest when zesting any citrus.

 # *Tomatoes Stuffed with Couscous and Feta*

This makes a great first course or summer lunch dish, particularly at the height of the tomato season, when you're looking for some different ways to utilize them.

Serves 6

2 cups dry quick-cooking couscous
1¾ cups rich chicken or vegetable
   stock
½ cup olive oil
⅔ cup dry white wine
½ teaspoon saffron threads
2 tablespoons white wine vinegar
3 tablespoons chopped fresh basil
2 tablespoons chopped fresh mint

   Fresh lemon juice
   Kosher salt and freshly ground
      black pepper
⅓ cup toasted pine nuts
½ cup crumbled feta cheese
6 ripe medium tomatoes
3 cups mixed baby greens, such as
   arugula, mâche, frisée, and
   spinach

Place the couscous in large bowl. In a saucepan, heat the stock and 1 table-spoon of the olive oil. Bring to a boil and pour over the couscous; the stock should just moisten the couscous. Stir and let stand for 5 minutes. Gently fluff with a fork.

In a small saucepan, combine the wine and saffron. Simmer over moderate heat for 3 minutes. Remove from the heat and cool.

In a medium bowl, combine the wine mixture, vinegar, basil, and mint. Whisk in the remaining oil and correct the seasoning with lemon juice, salt, and pepper. Reserving ⅓ cup of the dressing, pour the remainder over the couscous. Stir in the toasted pine nuts and feta. Set aside.

Slice off the tops of the tomatoes. Carefully scoop out and discard the seeds and pulp. Season the insides of the tomatoes with salt and pepper. Fill with the couscous mixture.

Serve the tomatoes on a bed of the baby greens and drizzle with the reserved dressing.

Recommended wine: A fruity, herbal-tinged Fumé/Sauvignon Blanc plays counterpoint to the salty feta.

 # Tomatoes Stuffed with Souffléed Goat Cheese and Savory Greens

The combination of warm elements with cool salad greens is very typical of wine country cooking. The trick of this recipe is that the baking "dish" for the soufflé is entirely edible.

Serves 6

6 ripe medium tomatoes	2 eggs, separated
Salt	3 tablespoons minced fresh chives
4 teaspoons unsalted butter	2 teaspoons minced fresh savory or
1½ tablespoons minced shallots	tarragon
2 teaspoons minced garlic	Freshly ground white pepper
1½ tablespoons all-purpose flour	3 cups mixed savory baby greens,
⅓ cup half-and-half	such as arugula, frisée,
1 tablespoon dry sherry	watercress, and mizuna
½ cup fresh, soft cream cheese- or	Lemon-Garlic Vinaigrette (recipe
log-style goat cheese	follows)

Slice the tops off the tomatoes and scoop out the seeds and pulp. Sprinkle the insides with salt and invert the tomatoes on paper towels to drain.

In a small saucepan, melt the butter. Add the shallots and garlic and sauté until soft but not brown. Add the flour and continue cooking for 2 to 3 minutes, stirring continuously. Whisk in the half-and-half and the sherry, cooking for 3 minutes longer and continuously whisking until the mixture is smooth. Transfer the mixture to a bowl and let cool slightly. Whisk in the goat cheese, egg yolks, chives, savory, salt, and pepper.

In a separate bowl, beat the egg whites until they hold stiff peaks. Stir ¼ of the whites into the cheese mixture to lighten it. Carefully fold in the remaining whites.

Preheat the oven to 400 degrees. Spoon the soufflé mixture into the tomato shells, mounding it slightly. Place the tomatoes, with their sides touching, in a lightly oiled baking dish. Bake for 20 to 25 minutes or until the tops are lightly puffed and browned.

Serve the hot tomatoes immediately on a bed of the mixed greens on chilled plates. Drizzle with about ¼ cup of the vinaigrette and finish with a sprinkling or two of white pepper. If you have some basil oil on hand (page 68), a few drops on each tomato would be delicious.

Lemon-Garlic Vinaigrette

Makes ¾ cup

3 tablespoons white wine vinegar	½ teaspoon kosher salt
1 tablespoon fresh lemon juice	1 tablespoon light-brown sugar or
2 teaspoons Dijon-style mustard	honey
½ teaspoon roasted garlic (page 247)	½ cup extra-virgin olive oil

In a bowl, whisk together all the ingredients. Store any unused vinaigrette (you won't need more than ¼ cup for the tomatoes) tightly covered in the refrigerator for up to 5 days.

Recommended wine: Goat cheese and Sauvignon Blanc are a great combination. A dry, crisp sparkling wine would also work well.

Roasted Potato, Beet, and Onion Salad

This is more an approach than a hard and fast recipe. I love the color/flavor/texture mix of potatoes, beets, and onions, but eggplant, asparagus, or carrots could be added or substituted. If you don't have access to baby vegetables, quarter and roast large ones, adjusting the cooking time accordingly. Any varieties of whole herb leaves, mixed together, make a sprightly addition, but if fresh herbs aren't available, you could always serve the dressed vegetables on a bed of young savory greens such as arugula, mustard, and frisée.

Serves 6

12 fingerling or creamer potatoes	½ pound peeled cipolline or pearl onions
12 garlic cloves	
4 tablespoons olive oil	¾ pound scrubbed and stemmed baby red, chioggia, or golden beets
Sprigs of fresh rosemary or thyme	
Kosher salt and freshly ground black pepper	1 cup loosely packed mixed fresh herb leaves

VINAIGRETTE:

1½ tablespoons balsamic vinegar	Kosher salt and freshly ground black pepper
3 tablespoons olive oil	
2 teaspoons chopped fresh parsley or chives	Garnish: Edible flower petals, if available (page 397)

Preheat the oven to 375 degrees. Prepare the vegetables in separate roasting pans. Halve or quarter the potatoes lengthwise. In a bowl, toss the potatoes and garlic cloves with 2 tablespoons of the olive oil and the rosemary or thyme and season liberally with salt and pepper. Arrange the potatoes and garlic in a single layer in a roasting pan. Toss the onions with 1 tablespoon of olive oil and season with salt and pepper in a pan; do the same for the beets. Cover all three pans tightly with foil and roast the vegetables for 35 to 40 minutes (or until tender), uncovering the potatoes and garlic after 20 minutes to allow them to brown and crisp slightly. Reserve any juices from the beets and onions for the vinaigrette. While the beets are still warm, gently rub their skins off using paper towels.

To make the vinaigrette: In a small bowl, combine the beet and onion juices, the balsamic vinegar, the olive oil, and the parsley or chives. Whisk and add salt and pepper to taste.

Serve the roasted vegetables surrounding a mound of the herb "salad" and drizzle with the vinaigrette. Serve warm or at room temperature.

 Recommended wine: A crisp Fumé/Sauvignon Blanc goes with the green-herb components of the dish and a lighter-style red such as Pinot Noir goes with the roasted vegetables. Maybe half a glass of both?

COOKING BEETS

As you may have surmised from glancing at the recipes in this book, I love beets. I don't think we pay enough attention to most root vegetables, but I really love beets. Too often, old recipes called for boiling beets to death in water (one old cookbook I have specifies 8 hours!). No wonder we grew up disliking beets—the flavor and texture were cooked out of them.

Beets have the highest sugar content of any vegetable, and the absolute best (and I think only) way to cook them is to bake or roast them. Alexandre Dumas, in his *Grand Dictionaire de Cuisine* (published after his death, 1870), gives this advice: "The best way to cook beets is in the oven. First they should be washed in ordinary brandy. Then they are placed on grills in the brick oven. Which is heated as for large loaves of bread. They are left in the oven until it cools, and the following morning cooked again the same way and at the same temperature. The beet is not really cooked until its skin is carbonized."

In one small French village that I spent time in years ago, the locals brought their large beets and onions to the *boulangerie* after the afternoon's bread had come out. The baker would then put these vegetables in the still-hot brick oven and roast them overnight for pickup the next morning. In parts of Italy, roasted beets and onions have for centuries been sold together by street vendors.

Roasting caramelizes the sugar in beets and concentrates the flavor. Try it once and you'll never boil a beet again. You'll also find yourself (as I do) looking for ways to utilize this great food.

Prawn and Cabbage Salad with Red Pepper–Orange Vinaigrette

This salad was created by Eliza Miller, a talented young student from the C.I.A. (not *that* C.I.A. but the Culinary Institute of America) who studied with us at Valley Oaks. This is a wonderful main-dish salad for any time of the year. You will find many uses for the unusual vinaigrette besides as an accompaniment for the delicious marinated and grilled prawns. (I think it's best to make this vinaigrette ahead, if possible, to give the flavors time to develop.) If you have the time or the inclination, add some roasted vegetables (I like beets, celery root, and carrots), which is all you need to make a great meal.

Make the Red Pepper–Orange Vinaigrette first.

Serves 6

MARINADE:

- ¼ cup chopped fresh parsley
- ½ cup loosely packed basil leaves, finely chopped
- 2 tablespoons minced scallions
- 1 tablespoon minced garlic
- 1 teaspoon minced fresh oregano
- 2 teaspoons kosher salt
- ½ teaspoon freshly ground black pepper
- ¼ teaspoon red chile flakes
- ⅓ cup dry white wine
- ¾ cup olive oil

- 1 pound large prawns, slit down the back for deveining, shells left on
- 1 tablespoon olive oil
- ½ medium head green cabbage, thinly shredded
- ¼ teaspoon celery seed
  Kosher salt and freshly ground black pepper
  Red Pepper–Orange Vinaigrette (recipe follows)

To make the prawns: In a medium bowl, whisk together all the marinade ingredients. Rub the marinade into the prawns. Marinate, covered and refrigerated, for at least 30 minutes.

To make the cabbage: In a sauté pan, heat the tablespoon of olive oil and sauté the cabbage and celery seed until the cabbage is softened. Season to taste with salt and pepper and set aside.

Prepare a charcoal fire or preheat the broiler. Grill the prawns, with the shells left on, over hot coals or under the broiler until just done. They should just turn pink. The meat will be opaque. Please don't overcook the prawns or you will lose their lovely sweet flavor and texture. Remove the shells, leaving the tail segment and its shell intact.

To serve, place a small mound of cabbage in the center of each plate. Arrange prawns upright against the cabbage and drizzle with a little of the Red Pepper–Orange Vinaigrette.

Red Pepper–Orange Vinaigrette

¼ teaspoon crushed coriander seed
4 teaspoons chopped fresh sage
2 teaspoons fresh thyme leaves
2 roasted and diced medium red bell peppers (page 246)
1½ teaspoons minced shallots
6 tablespoons balsamic vinegar

2 teaspoons minced orange zest
2 tablespoons frozen orange juice concentrate
Kosher salt and freshly ground black pepper
6 tablespoons extra-virgin olive oil

In a bowl, whisk together all ingredients except the olive oil. Slowly whisk in the olive oil. Cover and refrigerate for at least 1 hour to allow the flavors to marry. Season to taste with salt and pepper. Bring to room temperature before serving. (The vinaigrette can be stored, tightly covered, in the refrigerator for up to 3 days.)

 Recommended wine: A rich, oaky Chardonnay or a Pinot Noir made in a fruity style would work well with this dish.

 ## Pork Tenderloin Salad with Roasted Beet Vinaigrette

This main-course salad has been a personal favorite for a long time. I love the quality of roasted beets, as the natural sugars of the beets intensify during the roasting process. This salad is vividly red and green, a stunning visual statement. (I usually garnish this dish with grilled or roasted red onion. You can roast the onions alongside the beets for the vinaigrette, if you like.) The marinade is useful for a wide range of meat and poultry, but for the flavor to really develop here, the pork needs to be marinated for 4 to 6 hours, so plan ahead.

Serves 6 to 8

ORANGE-MOLASSES MARINADE:

1   tablespoon olive oil
1½ cups chopped red onions
1½ tablespoons chopped garlic
1   teaspoon cracked black pepper
½   cup balsamic vinegar
1¼ cups fresh orange juice
⅓   cup dark molasses
1   tablespoon toasted and crushed
     coriander seed (page 36)

1   tablespoon grated orange zest

2   ¾-pound trimmed pork tenderloins
2   tablespoons olive oil
1   pound mixed baby greens, such
     as arugula, mizuna, and red
     mustard
    Roasted Beet Vinaigrette (recipe
     follows)

To make the marinade: In a small saucepan, heat the olive oil. Add the onions and garlic. Sauté until lightly browned. Add the pepper, vinegar, orange juice, molasses, coriander seed, and orange zest. Bring to a boil. Reduce the heat and simmer for 5 minutes. Remove from the heat and cool before using.

In a baking dish, combine the pork tenderloins and the marinade, turning to coat. Marinate, refrigerated, for 4 to 6 hours, turning occasionally.

Remove the tenderloins from the marinade and pat dry. In a large sauté pan, heat the 2 tablespoons olive oil over high heat. Quickly sear the pork on all sides. Lower the heat and continue to cook on the stove, approximately 6 to 8 minutes. Do not overcook. Pork should remain slightly pink and juicy.

To serve, divide the greens among individual plates and drizzle with a little of the Roasted Beet Vinaigrette. Slice the tenderloins on the bias and arrange on top. Serve while the pork is still warm.

Roasted Beet Vinaigrette

Makes approximately 2½ cups

2   pounds large red beets
¼   cup olive oil
    Kosher salt and freshly ground
     black pepper
1¼ cups rich chicken stock, fat
     removed

⅓   cup balsamic vinegar
1   tablespoon sherry vinegar
1   tablespoon honey (or to taste)
1   teaspoon toasted and crushed
     anise seed (page 36)

Preheat the oven to 375 degrees. Wash, dry, and lightly oil the beets with 1 tablespoon of the olive oil. Place in a roasting pan and season with salt and pepper. Roast until cooked through and skins begin to shrivel, approximately 45 minutes depending on the size of the beets.

While still warm, remove the beet skins by rubbing with a paper towel. Cut into ¼-inch dice.

In a blender or food processor, purée the chicken stock and 1 cup of the beets. Transfer the purée to a bowl. Whisk in the vinegars, honey, anise seed, and remaining olive oil. Season to taste with salt and pepper. Stir in the remaining diced beets.

Store, covered and refrigerated, up to 5 days.

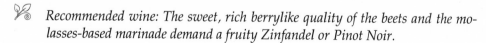 *Recommended wine: The sweet, rich berrylike quality of the beets and the molasses-based marinade demand a fruity Zinfandel or Pinot Noir.*

PATRICIA BRABANT

Orange, Watercress, and Endive Salad

Watermelon and Red Onion Salad

Beggars Purses with Savory Greens and Warm Lemon Sauce

ED AIONA

Oyster–Spinach Chowder

ED AIONA

Chilled Fresh Tomato Soup with Summer Relish

Prawns Wrapped in Zucchini with a Red Pepper Aïoli

Creamy Garlic Polenta with Wild Mushrooms

Grilled Vegetables shown with Roast Chicken and Shrimp

SOUPS

Stocks

Soups

Soup and Wine

As with salads, we've been told that wine isn't traditionally served with soup, but I've included wine recommendations for each of the soups in this chapter because for me soup often *is* the meal and I think wine is a perfect beverage to serve with it. The choice of wine should reflect complementing flavors in the soup. As you'll note, many of the soups contain wine as an ingredient, which is a good tip-off that wine can work very well as an accompaniment.

Besides looking for linking flavors, I think it's important to select a wine that has a similar body or mouth feel to the soup: For example, a creamy pumpkin or butternut squash soup really works best with a rich-bodied, creamy-tasting barrel-aged Chardonnay and probably doesn't work well with a light-bodied, tart Sauvignon Blanc. Keep in mind that soups—even broth-based soups—are full-bodied taste experiences because of the way soup coats the mouth; choose a wine with a similar mouth-feel.

Two notes on soup making: Soups come in two basic styles—"chunky," where the solid ingredients retain their distinctiveness, and "smooth," where the ingredients are cooked together and then puréed. For soups that are to be puréed, it's a good idea to let the soup base cool slightly or even completely before transferring it to the blender or food processor, because an accident involving a high-powered motor and boiling hot liquid is not pleasant. In fact, most soups benefit from being cooled completely, even refrigerated overnight, before the heating and serving: The flavors have a chance to develop and the soup is much easier to degrease—this is especially necessary for soups made with meat.

Stocks

Good homemade stocks are really very easy to make and are the basis for good soups and sauces. I look on stock making as a "rainy day" project—something to do when I'm going to be around the house for a few hours. Stocks don't take much attention—just an occasional check to make sure they aren't boiling hard (which causes them to get cloudy) and are developing the flavors you want.

Although I've included recipes for several stocks, I believe that you really only need to know how to make two stocks: chicken, to cover all your meat/fish needs, and a good vegetable stock. In addition to the stocks included here, note that there are several other stocks attached to specific recipes (e.g., a chile stock with the Vegetarian Red Chile with Pepitas on page 273) which can be used in a number of ways.

About the stock recipes:

1. All of the recipes yield about 1 gallon of stock. If storage space is a problem in your refrigerator or freezer, then reduce the strained stocks uncovered over high heat by up to half. Not only will they require less space but their flavors will be more concentrated and intense.
2. If you anticipate that you are going to reduce the stocks either for storage or to make a sauce, then don't add any salt, pepper, or strong spice or herb. In the reduction those flavors will become too dominant. Wait until the dish is nearing completion to do the final seasoning and flavoring.
3. Fresh juices can substitute wholly or in part for stocks in many recipes. Once you start with juices you'll come up with your own favorite combinations.
4. For simple stocks, remember to save the cooking liquid from potatoes and beans. They both can provide a base for the addition of fresh herbs, chile peppers, or what have you for soups and sauces.

Chicken Stock
(Western version)

5–6 pounds meaty chicken parts, such as wings, backs, necks, or a large stewing hen, quartered	1 cup chopped mushrooms (optional)
2 tablespoons vegetable oil	2 cups dry white wine
2 cups chopped onions	2 large bay leaves
1 cup chopped carrots	1 teaspoon dried thyme
1 cup chopped celery	2 whole cloves
4 large garlic cloves, unpeeled	½ teaspoon whole black peppercorns
	Water

Rinse the chicken and set aside. Add oil and vegetables to a stockpot and cook over moderately high heat until the vegetables are lightly browned. Add the chicken, wine, herbs, cloves, peppercorns, and enough water to cover the chicken by at least 3 inches. Bring to a boil. Reduce the heat and simmer slowly partially covered for 1½ to 2 hours, carefully skimming off any scum or froth that rises to the surface. Remove from the heat, cool slightly, and strain carefully. Chill the stock and remove the fat layer. Store covered in the refrigerator up to 5 days or frozen up to 2 months.

Chicken Stock
(Asian version)

6 **pounds meaty chicken parts, including feet if available**	3 **half-dollar-size slices fresh ginger**
6 **whole scallions, smashed**	**Water**

Rinse the chicken and add to a stockpot along with the scallions and ginger. Add enough water to cover the chicken by at least 3 inches and bring to a boil. Reduce the heat and simmer slowly, carefully skimming off any scum, partially covered for 2 to 2½ hours. Remove from the heat, cool slightly, and strain carefully. Chill the stock and remove the fat layer. Store covered in the refrigerator up to 5 days or frozen up to 2 months.

Easy Shellfish Stock

One tip that I always give in my cooking classes is to **never** throw away shrimp shells. There is as much or more flavor in the shell as there is in the meat of the shrimp. If you are peeling raw shrimp for a recipe, **always** save the shells and store them in a plastic bag in your freezer. Then, when you need to make a good fish/shellfish stock, all you have to do is to take your basic chicken stock (either version), add as many shrimp shells as you can along with a good splash or two of dry white wine, and simmer for 5 minutes. Strain, and you have a delicious stock for your favorite fish soup or sauce.

A final admonition—**never, never** use bottled clam juice (even though a recipe may suggest it). It has a very salty, metallic taste and I think it's thoroughly disagreeable. If you don't have shrimp shells to make this simple stock, then you are better off just using your homemade chicken stock.

Traditional Fish Stock

Choose mild white fish for this stock. Oily, heavier-flavored fishes such as salmon or tuna are too strongly flavored for a basic stock.

6–7 pounds fresh fish bones, trimmings, and/or heads	2 large bay leaves
2 tablespoons olive oil	1 teaspoon whole coriander seed (optional)
4 cups chopped onions	2 teaspoons chopped fresh lemon zest
2 cups chopped carrots	5 quarts water
2 garlic cloves, smashed	
2 cups dry white wine	
1 cup roughly chopped parsley stems and leaves	

Rinse the fish well and remove gills if using heads. Set aside. Add the olive oil and vegetables to a stockpot and cook over moderate heat until the vegetables are just beginning to color. Add fish, wine, herbs, coriander seed, lemon zest, and water and bring to a boil. Reduce the heat and simmer partially covered for 30 to 45 minutes. Carefully skim any scum or froth that rises to the surface. Remove from the heat, cool slightly, and strain. Chill the stock and remove any fat. Store covered in the refrigerator for 3 days or frozen for up to 2 months.

Lamb or Other Meat Stock

The procedure is the same for most brown meat stocks, such as beef, venison, pork, etc. To make sure the stock has enough flavor, be sure to add some meat trimmings along with the bones.

6–8 pounds cracked lamb shanks and meat trimmings without fat	2 ribs celery, chopped
2 medium onions, quartered	1 head garlic, cloves separated but unpeeled
2 large carrots, chopped	2 cups hearty red wine
	2 bay leaves

1	bunch fresh parsley, coarsely chopped	¼	cup tomato paste or chopped
2	teaspoons dried thyme		dried tomatoes
1	teaspoon whole black peppercorns		Water

Preheat the oven to 450 degrees. Place the bones, trimmings, and vegetables in a roasting pan and roast for 45 to 50 minutes or until the bones are nicely browned. Turn bones and vegetables occasionally.

Transfer the bones and vegetables to a large stockpot, leaving fat behind. Pour off the fat from the roasting pan and place the pan over moderate heat. Pour in the wine, scraping up any of the browned bits on the bottom. Add to the stockpot, along with the bay leaves, parsley, thyme, peppercorns, and tomato paste. Add enough cold water to cover the bones by at least 2 inches and slowly bring to a boil. Reduce the heat and simmer partially covered for 4 to 6 hours. Check occasionally to make sure the bones are covered with liquid. Be sure to skim any froth or scum that rises to the surface. Strain the stock carefully, chill, and remove the fat from the surface. Store refrigerated up to 1 week or frozen up to 3 months.

 Rich Vegetable Stock

8	cups sliced onions	½	ounce dried porcini or dried
4	cups diced carrots		wild mushrooms
2	cups sliced celery, including tops	5	cups chopped canned or fresh
4	cups sliced leeks, both white and		tomatoes
	tender green parts	2	teaspoons whole black
3	cups sliced parsnips or celery root		peppercorns
	(optional)	6	bay leaves
¼	cup chopped garlic	1	tablespoon dried thyme
¼	cup olive or other light vegetable oil	2	teaspoons fennel seed
6	quarts water	2	cups roughly chopped parsley
2	cups dry white wine		leaves and stems

In a large pot put the onions, carrots, celery, leeks, parsnips, garlic, and olive oil and very lightly brown over moderate heat. Add the remaining ingredients, bring to a boil, then reduce the heat and simmer partially covered for 2 to 2½ hours. Remove from the heat, cool slightly, and strain carefully, pressing on solids to extract all the juices. Chill the stock and remove any fat. Store covered in the refrigerator up to 7 days or frozen up to 3 months.

Corn Stock

When corn is plentiful, I love to make this stock. Use as much corn as will fit in your stockpot. You can also add fresh or dried chiles and/or toasted cumin or coriander seeds (page 36) for variation.

16 large ears fresh corn, shucked	2 tablespoons chopped garlic
2 tablespoons olive oil	2 cups dry white wine
6 cups chopped onions	2 bay leaves
4 cups chopped carrots	½ teaspoon whole peppercorns
2 cups chopped celery	Water

Remove the kernels from the cobs and reserve both. Put the olive oil in a stockpot along with the onions, carrots, celery, and garlic and cook over moderate heat until the vegetables are just beginning to brown. Break the corn cobs into 2 or 3 pieces each and add to the pot along with the wine, bay leaves, peppercorns, and enough water to cover all by at least 3 inches. Bring to a boil, then reduce the heat and simmer for 1½ hours. Strain the stock, pressing on the vegetables and cobs to extract all liquid, return to the stockpot, and add the reserved corn kernels. Simmer for an additional 25 to 30 minutes. Strain, cool, and store covered in the refrigerator for up to 5 days or 3 months in the freezer.

Note: To add body and texture to the stock, purée the strained corn kernels and add back to the stock. Roasting the corn before making the stock adds an additional interesting flavor dimension too.

Tomato Stock

7–8 pounds ripe tomatoes, stems removed	2 cups chopped mushrooms
Olive oil	2 tablespoons slivered garlic
4 cups chopped red onions	1 cup chopped carrots
	3 cups dry white wine

3	large bay leaves	2	teaspoons whole black peppercorns
2	teaspoons chopped fresh thyme	½	teaspoon fennel seed
¼	cup fresh (page 255) or canned tomato paste (or chopped dried tomatoes)	¼	teaspoon saffron threads (optional)
		6	quarts water

Place the tomatoes in a single layer in a lightly oiled baking pan. Place in a preheated 400-degree oven for 40 to 50 minutes and roast until the tomatoes are lightly browned. Set them aside.

Put a tablespoon or two of olive oil in a stockpot along with the vegetables and sauté over moderate heat until just beginning to color. Add the wine, herbs, tomato paste, peppercorns, fennel seed, saffron, roasted tomatoes, and water and bring to a boil. Reduce the heat and simmer partially covered for 30 minutes. Remove from the heat, cool slightly, and strain, pressing on the solids. Chill the stock and remove any fat. Store covered in the refrigerator up to 7 days or frozen up to 3 months.

Mushroom Stock

This is a great stock to make when your market is offering half-price, "over the hill" mushrooms—those that have opened up completely and are getting soft (but not moldy). Buy a lot of them and store them in the freezer if you don't have time to make the stock right away. Add to this any mushroom stems and pieces or leftover wild mushrooms you might have. The secret here is to sauté the mushrooms in small batches so they have a chance to brown, which intensifies their flavor dramatically.

¼	pound or more unsalted butter	3	large bay leaves
5–6	pounds chopped fresh mushrooms	2	teaspoons chopped fresh rosemary
6	cups chopped onions	2	teaspoons whole black peppercorns
¼	cup chopped garlic		
1	ounce dried porcini or dried wild mushrooms, soaked, strained, and chopped	3	cups canned diced tomatoes in juice
3	cups chopped carrots	3	cups dry white wine
		6	quarts water

In a stockpot melt the butter and sauté the mushrooms in small batches until they are well browned and almost "crisp." Set aside. Add a bit more butter to the stockpot and sauté the onions, garlic, dried mushrooms, and carrots until lightly browned. Add the herbs, peppercorns, tomatoes, wine, and water and bring to a boil. Reduce the heat and simmer partially covered for 1 hour. Strain, pushing down on the solids, and chill. Remove fat if desired. Store covered in the refrigerator up to 1 week or frozen up to 3 months.

 # Leek and Potato Stock with Fresh Herbs

This is another basic vegetable stock using leeks and potatoes and whatever fresh herbs you may have a lot of to add a spike of flavor. Here I've suggested using tarragon, but you could use leafy herbs like basil, chervil, or cilantro or woody-stemmed herbs like thyme or rosemary. Use less (start with one third as much) of the woody herbs because they tend to be stronger and sometimes more bitter in flavor.

3 tablespoons olive oil	1 small head garlic, cloves smashed but unpeeled
12 cups chopped leeks, both white and tender green parts	2 cups roughly chopped fresh parsley, including stems
4 cups chopped red or white waxy potatoes, unpeeled	4 large bay leaves
4 cups chopped carrots	2 cups roughly chopped fresh tarragon, including stems
3 cups chopped mushrooms, including stems	1 teaspoon whole black peppercorns
2 cups chopped celery, including leaves	3 cups dry white wine
	Water

Heat the olive oil in a stockpot, add the leeks, and cook over moderate heat until soft but not brown. Add the remaining vegetables, herbs, and peppercorns and continue cooking for 5 to 6 minutes. Add the wine and enough water to cover the vegetables by about 4 inches. Bring to a boil, then reduce the heat and simmer partially covered for 1 hour. Strain carefully and store refrigerated up to 7 days or frozen up to 3 months.

JUICES

An alternative or interesting addition to stocks are fresh vegetable and fruit juices. Juicers vary, but I like the kind that capture all the pulp and provide a clear, sparkling juice. If your juice is cloudy, slowly heat it in a saucepan just to simmer. Skim away the froth that rises and then strain the liquid through cheesecloth or a coffee filter. There are no hard and fast rules to substituting juices for some or all of stocks. Here are some ideas to encourage you:

- Use a combination of chicken stock and fresh fennel juice to poach chicken breasts for salad.
- Use fresh carrot or sweet red pepper juice as a beautiful garnish to ladle around a risotto.
- Intensify the flavors of corn and mushroom stocks by adding juices of each at the end, and roast the corn or mushrooms first to add even more flavor.
- Use fresh juices as a basis for vinaigrettes or marinades.
- Reduce juices until they become syrupy to drizzle over grilled or roasted meats, cooked vegetables, or fresh fruits.

Yields, of course, vary depending on the fruit, herb, or vegetable used and the type of juicer, but I usually figure on approximately 1 cup of juice for each pound of product.

Soups

Butternut Squash Soup

I'm a big fan of simple, soul-satisfying, seasonal soups, and this one has always been one of my favorites. If I want to make this a main-course soup, I add some sautéed shiitake mushrooms just before serving. If you can find fresh wild mushrooms such as chanterelles or morels, so much the better.

Serves 8

3	tablespoons unsalted butter	1	tablespoon honey
3	cups chopped yellow onions	1	cup heavy cream, light cream, or milk
3	cups baked butternut squash (see box below)	3	tablespoons dry sherry
6	cups rich chicken or vegetable stock		Kosher salt and freshly ground white pepper
1½	tablespoons high-quality curry powder, lightly toasted (page 36)		Garnish: Toasted pepitas (pumpkin seeds) or slivered almonds
¼	teaspoon freshly grated nutmeg		

In a large sauté pan, melt the butter and sauté the onions until very soft but not brown. In a food processor, in batches if necessary, purée the onions and baked squash. Transfer to a large saucepan and add the stock, curry powder, nutmeg, and honey. Whisk to combine and bring to a simmer. Simmer for 10 to 15 minutes, stirring occasionally. Stir in the cream and sherry and correct the seasoning with salt and pepper. Serve in warm bowls garnished with pepitas or almonds.

 Recommended wine: The lightly spiced curry flavor in the squash calls for a barrel-aged Chardonnay with its natural hint of spice and its creamy flavor and texture.

BUTTERNUT SQUASH

An oval-shaped squash with a dark orange skin, butternut is extremely flavorful and offers a dense, sweet flesh. Butternut squash is extremely high in fiber and vitamin A. To cook, cut the squash in half, remove seeds, and bake in a 375-degree oven for 40 to 45 minutes. Clean and toast the seeds for a garnish or a snack. Scoop out the flesh after baking.

Butternut is now widely grown and distributed. It has opened the door for several new hard winter squashes that work equally well in this soup, including buttercup and kabocha, a sweet Japanese variety.

Beet Soup with Mint

This is a very simple but rich soup with a beautiful color; it is equally good hot or cold. It is one I like to serve in little demitasse cups to begin a meal. Be careful when adding the honey so that the soup doesn't get too sweet; roasted beets are very sweet on their own.

Serves 8 to 10

2 pounds scrubbed beets	1 tablespoon honey (or to taste)
2 tablespoons olive oil	½ teaspoon toasted and crushed
Kosher salt and freshly ground	caraway seed (page 36)
black pepper	¼ teaspoon ground cloves
4–5 cups rich chicken stock or	2 tablespoons chopped fresh mint
mushroom stock (page 57)	Garnish: Plain yogurt and fresh
1 tablespoon fresh lemon juice	mint sprigs

Preheat the oven to 350 degrees. In a roasting pan, lightly coat the beets with the olive oil and season with salt and pepper. Roast for 30 to 40 minutes or until the flesh is soft and skins are loose. While the beets are still warm, peel off the skins by rubbing gently with a paper towel.

In a blender or food processor, purée the beets with 4 cups stock, the lemon juice, honey, caraway seed, cloves, and mint. (It will be necessary to do this in batches.) Strain the purée and season to taste with salt and pepper. Add additional stock if a thinner consistency is desired.

Serve hot or cold. Garnish each serving with a dollop of plain yogurt and a sprig of fresh mint.

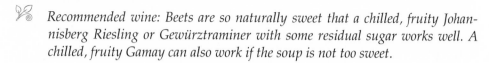

Recommended wine: Beets are so naturally sweet that a chilled, fruity Johannisberg Riesling or Gewürztraminer with some residual sugar works well. A chilled, fruity Gamay can also work if the soup is not too sweet.

"Five Lilies" Chowder

The "Five Lilies" here refer to the onions, shallots, leeks, garlic, and chives—all members of the lily, or allium, family. In addition to being very tasty, this soup is low in fat. The trick to this dish is not to overcook the vegetables added at serving time; they should have some crunch left. To turn this into a main-course soup, add some cooked wild rice, sautéed mushrooms, and/or any other favorite vegetable.

Serves 8

3 tablespoons olive oil	2 teaspoons minced fresh oregano
4 cups diced yellow onions	(or 1 teaspoon dried)
¼ cup sliced shallots	½ cup minced celery
1 tablespoon chopped garlic	1 cup sliced leeks, both white and
1 cup dry white wine	tender green parts
1 bay leaf	2 tablespoons dry sherry
6 cups mushroom stock (page 57)	2 tablespoons minced chives
or rich chicken stock, fat	Garnish: Gremolata
removed	(1 tablespoon minced garlic,
Kosher salt and freshly ground	2 tablespoons minced parsley,
black pepper	and 2 tablespoons minced
2 teaspoons minced fresh thyme (or	lemon zest, combined in a
1 teaspoon dried)	bowl)

In a medium saucepan, heat the olive oil. Add the onions, shallots, and garlic and sauté until they just begin to color. Transfer half the onion mixture to a blender or food processor. Purée and return to the pan. Add the wine, bay leaf, and stock and simmer for 10 minutes. Season with salt and pepper. (The soup base may be prepared in advance to this point and stored refrigerated for up to 3 days or frozen indefinitely and reheated before finishing.)

Just before serving, add the thyme, oregano, celery, leeks, and sherry to the hot soup base. Bring to a simmer and simmer for 2 minutes. Do not overcook; the vegetables should retain their crunchy texture. Remove the bay leaf, stir in the chives, and garnish with a sprinkling of the gremolata.

Recommended wine: Fumé/Sauvignon Blanc is one of my favorite wines with many different vegetable dishes, but its herbal, flinty flavors particularly complement this one.

Lentil "Cappuccino"

This is a whimsical approach to soup in a coffee cup. Because the color of the soup is similar to coffee, I played with the idea of adding a dollop of steamed milk or whipped cream to make it look like cappuccino. If you wanted to be really decadent, a shaving or two of fresh truffle to mimic chocolate could complete the presentation.

Serves 8 to 10

½ ounce dried porcini mushrooms	1 tablespoon chopped fresh oregano (or 1 teaspoon dried)
2 tablespoons olive oil	
½ cup chopped celery	1 teaspoon toasted and crushed cumin seed (page 36)
1 cup chopped carrots	
1 cup chopped onions	1¼ cups green or brown lentils
½ cup chopped leeks, white part only	Kosher salt and freshly ground black pepper
1 tablespoon chopped garlic	Garnish: Steamed milk (if you have an espresso machine) or unsweetened, lightly whipped cream, chopped chives, and sprigs of fresh herbs
6 cups rich lamb stock (page 54) or mushroom stock (page 57)	
1 cup dry white wine	
1 large bay leaf	

Place the dried mushrooms in a small bowl and add warm tap water to cover. Weight the mushrooms with a small plate to completely submerge them. Let stand 1 hour to rehydrate. Drain, rinse, and coarsely chop. Set aside.

In a large saucepan, heat the olive oil. Add the celery, carrots, onions, leeks, garlic, and porcini over moderate heat and sauté until the vegetables are soft and lightly colored. Add the stock, wine, bay leaf, oregano, cumin, and lentils. Simmer for 40 to 45 minutes or until the lentils are very soft. Remove the bay leaf and season to taste with salt and pepper. Transfer to a blender or food processor. Purée, in batches if necessary, and strain through a medium sieve. Adjust the consistency, if desired, by adding more stock.

Serve in warm 6-ounce coffee cups with a saucer. Garnish with steamed milk, chopped chives, and an herb sprig "stirrer."

 Recommended wine: This is a rich, earthy dish and could go with a "soft" red wine such as Pinot Noir or Merlot.

Spicy Black Bean Chowder with Pineapple-Banana Salsa

This hearty black bean chowder draws heavily from Latin American cuisines, such as Brazilian and Cuban. The hot-sweet spice flavors are typical of those cuisines. The salsa is also delicious on grilled fish and chicken. (And if you're grilling fish or chicken, grill the pineapple and red onions for the salsa, too.)

Serves 10

2 tablespoons olive oil	1 tablespoon fennel seed
4 cups chopped onions	1½ tablespoons fresh oregano
¼ cup chopped garlic	(or 2 teaspoons dried)
1 cup diced celery	½ teaspoon ground cloves
2 pounds smoked ham hocks	1½ teaspoons ground cinnamon
1¾ cups black beans, soaked	Kosher salt and freshly ground
overnight and drained	black pepper
6 cups rich chicken stock	3 cups seeded and diced fresh or
2 cups fresh orange juice	drained canned tomatoes
3 tablespoons pure California or	½ cup chopped fresh cilantro
New Mexico chile powder	Pineapple-Banana Salsa
1 tablespoon seeded and minced	(recipe follows)
serrano chiles	Garnish: Cilantro sprigs
2 bay leaves	
1 tablespoon thyme leaves	
(or 1½ teaspoons dried)	

In a stockpot, heat the olive oil. Add the onions, garlic, and celery and sauté until they just begin to color. Add the ham hocks, beans, stock, orange juice, chile powder, chiles, bay leaves, thyme, fennel seed, oregano, cloves, and cinnamon. Bring to a simmer. Simmer, partially covered, until the beans are tender, approximately 1 hour. (At this point, the soup can be refrigerated overnight, if desired, to develop the flavors and to congeal the fat so that it is easily removed.)

Skim any fat from the soup. Remove the bay leaves and ham hocks, discard any skin or fat, shred the meat and return it to the soup. Heat the soup through and season to taste with salt and pepper. Just before serving, stir in the tomatoes and cilantro. Top each serving with a spoonful of the Pineapple-Banana Salsa and garnish with a cilantro sprig.

Pineapple-Banana Salsa

Makes approximately 1½ cups

½	cup diced fresh pineapple	2	teaspoons seeded and minced
⅓	cup diced firm, ripe banana		serrano chiles
¼	cup minced red onion	2	tablespoons chopped fresh cilantro
¼	cup diced fresh orange segments	1	tablespoon fresh lime juice

In a bowl, gently combine all the ingredients. Refrigerate at least 30 minutes to allow the flavors to blend.

 Recommended wine: You can either mirror the hearty flavors with a Zinfandel or contrast them with a White Zinfandel or Fumé/Sauvignon Blanc.

 ## Wine Country Borscht

This is a rich stew that is a meal in a bowl, particularly when accompanied by crusty French bread. In this recipe we've made the presentation a little more elegant by straining out the cooking vegetables and adding separately cooked potatoes and cabbage at the end to give more color and texture. You could, however, leave the cooking vegetables in the stew if you prefer a more rustic borscht. I recommend making the soup a day ahead and refrigerating it overnight: This makes it easier to degrease and you can then prepare the beets, potatoes, and cabbage just before you reheat the soup.

Serves 8

3	tablespoons olive oil	2	teaspoons thyme leaves
3	pounds cubed lean stewing beef,		(or 1 teaspoon dried)
	such as brisket or tri-tip	2	tablespoons balsamic vinegar
1½	cups diced carrots		Kosher salt and freshly ground
1½	cups sliced onions		black pepper
2	tablespoons chopped garlic	¼	cup finely chopped fresh parsley
½	cup diced celery	1½	cups diced red potatoes
5	cups peeled and diced raw beets	2½	cups finely shredded green cabbage
2	cups seeded and diced tomatoes	1	teaspoon caraway seed
8	cups rich beef stock	1½	pounds roasted and peeled beets
3	cups dry red wine		(page 46), cut into ¼-inch dice
1½	teaspoons fennel seed		Garnish: Sour cream

In a stockpot, heat 2 tablespoons of the olive oil. Add the beef in batches and quickly brown on all sides. Remove the meat and reserve. Add the carrots, onions, garlic, and celery. Sauté until the vegetables are lightly colored. Return the beef to the pot and add the raw beets, tomatoes, stock, wine, fennel seed, and thyme. Bring to a boil. Reduce the heat and simmer partially covered for 1½ to 2 hours or until the beef is very tender. Occasionally skim off the fat as the borscht simmers.

Strain the soup carefully, pressing down gently on the meat and vegetables to extract as much liquid as possible. Set aside the beef cubes and discard the remaining vegetables, if desired. Return the beef and strained liquid to the stockpot. (The soup can be made ahead to this point and refrigerated overnight.) Add the balsamic vinegar and salt and pepper to taste. Stir in the parsley and keep warm.

In a separate saucepan, in lightly salted boiling water, blanch the potatoes until just tender, about 5 minutes. Drain and keep warm. In a medium sauté pan, heat the remaining 1 tablespoon olive oil. Add the cabbage and caraway seed. Sauté until crisp-tender, about 2 minutes.

To serve, ladle the borscht into warm soup bowls. Add the roasted beets, potatoes, and sautéed cabbage. Garnish with a dollop of sour cream.

Recommended wine: The natural sweetness of the beets suggests a fruity red wine, such as Pinot Noir, Zinfandel, or Gamay Beaujolais, to heighten the impact.

Fresh Pea Soup with Tarragon

With fresh peas from the garden, this soup makes a lovely, light springtime alternative to the traditional split pea soup of winter. The addition of romaine lettuce further enhances the brilliant color and springtime freshness of the peas. Plan to serve this shortly after it is made in order to enjoy the bright color and the flavor of the soup.

Serves 6

2 tablespoons unsalted butter	¼ cup chopped carrot
1 cup chopped onions	3½ cups rich vegetable or chicken
1 cup chopped leeks, both white	stock
and tender green parts	½ cup dry white wine
½ cup chopped celery	4 cups shelled fresh peas

1   cup loosely packed tarragon
    leaves
3   cups loosely packed and finely
    sliced romaine or other green
    lettuce

Kosher salt and freshly ground black
    pepper
Garnish: Fresh tarragon leaves and
    fennel oil (page 68)

In a medium saucepan, melt the butter. Add the onions, leeks, celery, and carrot and sauté until soft but not browned. Add the stock and wine. Bring to a boil. Reduce the heat and simmer for 10 minutes. Add the peas and tarragon. Simmer for 5 minutes longer or until the peas are soft. Add the lettuce and simmer for 2 minutes or until the lettuce is just wilted and tender. Transfer to a blender or food processor, in batches if necessary, and purée the soup. Strain and return the soup to the saucepan. Bring back to a simmer and season to taste with salt and pepper.

Serve garnished with fresh tarragon leaves and a drizzle of fennel oil.

 Recommended wine: The fresh licorice flavor from the tarragon is a great link to a richer-style Sauvignon Blanc—that is, one that has seen some barrel-aging.

INFUSED OILS

Once you start playing with these, I think you'll become as hooked on them as I am. For me, they are part of the basic pantry and add not only color, but often intense and unusual flavor to a wide variety of foods. They are easy to make and I always have a few around stored in the refrigerator in handy squirt bottles so that I can squirt a rainbow of color and flavor on almost anything.

I've divided the infused oils into ingredient categories. As you'll note, however, the approach is basically the same. I encourage you to come up with your own combinations—even mix categories if you want. A couple of other comments:

- There is nothing sacred about the quantities you use, adjust according to your taste.
- For the oil I usually use a good olive or canola oil. Both of these are neutral in flavor and a good carrier for the infusion. I don't generally use extra-virgin olive oil unless that is a flavor component I want in the final infusion.

- I suggest storing your infused oils in the refrigerator because I think it keeps them fresher tasting. Most oils tend to solidify when cold. If this happens, simply place in a pan of warm water or in the microwave for a few seconds before using.

Fresh leafy herb oils (basil, mint, chive, cilantro, parsley, shiso, etc.)

2 cups lightly packed herbs, large stems removed	1–2 cups olive oil Salt and pepper to taste

Blanch the herbs in lightly salted, boiling water until they turn a bright green (about 5 seconds). Drain and plunge immediately into ice water to stop the cooking and set the color. This blanching step inactivates the enzymes that cause the herbs to turn brown and develop an oxidized flavor.

Pat the herbs dry and add to a blender or food processor along with enough oil to cover. Blend briefly to make a thick paste. Pour into a clean tall jar and cover with up to 2 inches of oil. Stir well or shake and store covered in the refrigerator for at least 1 day or up to 3 to 4 days depending on color and flavor desired. Strain the oil carefully through a fine filter or cheesecloth. The oil should be a very bright green and very fragrant. Season with salt and pepper if desired and store covered in the refrigerator for up to 3 weeks.

Note: I've had oils last for more than 8 weeks before they begin to fade or develop off flavors.

Spice oils (chile, curry, saffron, mustard, ginger, fennel, cumin, cinnamon, juniper berry, etc.)

Lightly toast whole or ground spices in a dry pan over moderate heat for a minute or two. This "refreshes" their flavor, helping to drive off any rancid oils or flavors. If you are using whole spices, grind them after toasting and add enough water to make a smooth paste. Place the paste in a clean jar and cover with a couple of inches of oil. Stir or shake and allow the oil to infuse for at least 2 days. When the desired taste/color is achieved, carefully strain and store covered in the refrigerator for up to 6 weeks.

Fresh vegetable and fruit oils (carrot, beet, roasted garlic, red or yellow pepper, tomato, orange, lemon, cranberry, mango, etc.)

With a mechanical juicer, juice the fruit or vegetable. You should start with at least 3 cups. Place the juice in a saucepan and reduce it over moderately high heat until it begins to become syrupy in texture (¾ cup).

Strain this and add to the oil in whatever concentration desired. I suggest you try equal amounts of reduced syrup and oil. Store covered in the refrigerator for up to 6 weeks.

Dried fruit and vegetable oils (apricot, sun-dried tomato, dried mushroom, etc.)

For most dried fruits, simply chop to use. For dried tomatoes (not packed in oil) rehydrate briefly in warm water, drain, and chop. For mushrooms such as porcini or morel, briefly rehydrate in warm water and rinse thoroughly to remove any sand or grit.

In a blender or food processor add enough oil to cover and blend to form a thick paste. Place in a clean jar and cover with at least 2 inches of oil and stir or shake to combine. Allow to sit for at least 2 days. Strain carefully and store covered in the refrigerator for up to 8 weeks.

Mussel, Leek, and White Bean Chowder

This is reminiscent of the soupy stews found in Italy. Any cooked white beans can be used. The flavor of the soup will be greatly influenced by the stock you use. Try the Corn Stock (page 56) or the Tomato Stock (page 56).

Serves 6

3 tablespoons olive oil
2 cups thinly sliced leeks, white part only
2 tablespoons finely slivered garlic
3 pounds scrubbed fresh mussels, beards removed
1 cup dry white wine
4 cups rich fish, chicken, or vegetable stock
1 cup cooked cannellini or baby lima beans

1 cup seeded and diced ripe tomatoes
2 teaspoons minced fresh parsley
2 teaspoons minced fresh basil
  Kosher salt and freshly ground black pepper
  Drops of fresh lemon juice
1 bunch trimmed young spinach
  Garnish: Red Pepper Aïoli (page 164)

In a large saucepan, heat the olive oil and sauté the leeks and garlic until soft but not brown. Add the mussels, wine, and stock. Simmer, covered, until the mussels open, approximately 3 minutes. Discard any unopened mussels. Remove from the heat. Strain, reserving both the stock and the solids. Return the stock to the pan and reduce by one quarter over high heat to intensify the flavors.

Meanwhile, remove the mussels from their shells and discard the shells. Return the mussels and leek mixture to the reduced stock. Add the beans, tomatoes, parsley, and basil. Heat to warm through. Season to taste with salt and pepper and drops of lemon juice.

To serve, place 3 or 4 spinach leaves in warm soup bowls. Ladle the hot soup over the spinach. Garnish with a dollop of Red Pepper Aïoli if desired.

 Recommended wine: This hearty soup engages a full-bodied Chardonnay beautifully.

MUSSELS

Mussels found in the market today all come from farm-raised sources and are much more uniform, meatier, and cleaner than those gathered in the wild. Also, because the farms are regularly inspected you don't have to worry about "red tides" and other contamination. Mussels are raised on both the east and west coasts of America and are readily available. One of the simplest and best fish stocks you can make involves simply poaching mussels in white wine and then straining the liquid through cheesecloth to remove any debris that remains from the mussels.

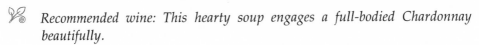

My Grandmother's White Bean Soup

My friends tease me about how often I say "my grandmother's this or that," but the truth is that my grandmother was the one who instilled in me a real passion for cooking. Living in the mountains of Colorado, she knew how to whip up a hearty bean soup to combat the bone-chilling weather. Here's to you, Grandma.

Serves 10 to 12

2 cups dried Great Northern or navy beans
2 tablespoons olive oil
2 cups thinly sliced onions
2 tablespoons chopped garlic
1 cup diced carrots
1 cup diced celery
2 quarts rich chicken stock or vegetable stock
2 cups dry white wine
1 pound meaty smoked ham hocks
1 teaspoon dried oregano

1 teaspoon dried thyme
1 teaspoon fennel seed
2 bay leaves
½ teaspoon red chile flakes
1 cup seeded and diced fresh tomatoes or 1 cup drained and chopped canned tomatoes
3 tablespoons chopped fresh parsley
1 cup finely shredded green cabbage
Garnish: Freshly grated Parmesan cheese

Sort through the beans to remove any stones or dirt. Rinse thoroughly and soak overnight in enough water to cover the beans by at least 2 inches.

In a stockpot, heat the olive oil. Add the onions, garlic, carrots, and celery and sauté until they just begin to color. Add the stock, wine, ham hocks, herbs, and chile flakes. Bring to a simmer and cook, partially covered, for 30 to 40 minutes or until the beans are tender. Add the tomatoes and parsley. Remove from the heat. (At this point, the soup can be refrigerated overnight, if desired, to develop the flavors and to congeal the fat so that it is easily removed.)

Skim any fat from the soup. Remove the bay leaves and the ham hocks, discard any skin or fat, shred the meat, and return it to the soup. Heat to a simmer. Just before serving, stir in the cabbage.

Serve the soup and pass the Parmesan cheese.

 Recommended wine: I like the rustic quality of Zinfandel with this extremely hearty soup.

Oyster-Spinach Chowder

Over the past few years, I've gravitated away from cream-based soups due to dietary concerns. Every once in a while, however, I can't resist the way cream enhances the texture and flavor of a soup.

Serves 8

2   tablespoons unsalted butter
3   cups thinly sliced onions
2   cups thinly sliced leeks, both white and tender green parts
3   garlic cloves, thinly sliced
6   cups rich shellfish stock
2   teaspoons fresh thyme leaves (lemon thyme preferred)
    Kosher salt and freshly ground black pepper

2   cups washed and thinly sliced new potatoes
2   cups heavy cream
⅓   cup dry sherry
1   pound small fresh oysters, shucked and drained
1   pound young spinach leaves, washed and trimmed
    Garnish: Small garlic croutons and chopped chives

In a medium saucepan, melt the butter and sauté the onions, leeks, and garlic until soft but not brown. Add the stock and thyme. Simmer for 5 minutes. Season to taste with salt and pepper. (The soup base may be prepared in advance to this point. Store, covered, in the refrigerator for up to 3 days; reheat before continuing.)

Add the potatoes and simmer for 5 minutes or until the potatoes are almost done. Just before serving, add the cream, sherry, oysters, and spinach leaves in order so that the oysters are not overcooked. Barely bring to a simmer and cook for approximately 2 minutes.

Serve garnished with garlic croutons and chives.

Recommended wine: A citrus-tinged Chardonnay is just the right counterpoint to this lush soup.

NO-CREAM "CREAM"

Although my approach in this book and in my kitchen is to reduce the use of cream and other high-fat products, I do use some cream if it adds a desirable richness to the final dish. You can always cut down on the amount of cream and substitute stock, low-fat milk, or rice milk, found in natural food stores, in most recipes—certainly in these soups. A great alternative that allows you to use *no* cream at all but still have most of the richness and mouth-feel that cream provides is the very low-fat no-cream "cream" that follows. Use it in place of cream in soups or sauces.

Makes approximately 2½ cups

2   teaspoons olive oil
½   cup chopped yellow onions
⅓   cup rice (preferably medium- or
      short-grain, which is
      starchier)

2   cups defatted rich chicken or
      vegetable stock
1   cup dry white wine
      Salt and freshly ground white
      pepper

In a saucepan, heat the olive oil, add the onions, and sauté over moderate heat until soft but not colored. Add the rice and sauté 2 minutes longer, stirring regularly. Add ⅔ cup of the stock and the wine, cover, and simmer until the liquid is mostly absorbed (about 25 minutes). Cool slightly, transfer the mixture to a blender or food processor, and purée. With the motor running, add more stock (up to 1½ cups) until you reach the desired consistency. Season to taste with salt and pepper. Make a double batch and freeze it in 1-cup portions; it keeps indefinitely.

Roasted Red Pepper Soup with Poached Eggs

This is a peasant-style Italian soup that could be a meal in itself. For a multi-course meal, serve it in small cups or bowls with a poached quail egg, if you can find them. The recipe calls for puréeing the soup, but you could certainly serve it as a chunky soup if you prefer.

Serves 8

3 tablespoons olive oil, plus additional for brushing the bread	3 tablespoons Arborio or other short-grain rice
4 cups minced onions	4 large roasted red bell peppers, cut into thick strips (page 246)
1 cup minced carrots	Kosher salt and freshly ground black pepper
1 cup thinly sliced fennel bulb	
5 cups rich chicken or vegetable stock	Drops of balsamic vinegar
1 cup dry white wine	8 slices Italian bread
⅛ teaspoon red chile flakes	2 garlic cloves, halved
1 teaspoon fennel seed	8 eggs
1 tablespoon chopped fresh rosemary (or 1 teaspoon dried)	White vinegar for poaching
2 tablespoons chopped fresh basil (or 1 tablespoon dried)	Garnish: Freshly grated Parmesan cheese

In a stockpot, heat the olive oil. Add the onions, carrots, and fennel and sauté until soft but not brown. Add the stock, wine, red chile flakes, herbs, rice, and roasted peppers. Bring to a boil. Reduce the heat and simmer partially covered for 20 minutes or until the rice is tender.

Transfer to a blender or food processor and purée, in batches if necessary. Return to the stockpot. Correct the seasoning with salt, pepper, and drops of balsamic vinegar. The soup may be prepared to this point in advance; store covered in the refrigerator for up to 3 days.

Lightly brush the slices of bread with olive oil and rub with the cut side of the garlic. Toast or grill the bread and set aside.

At serving time, in a large sauté pan, add water to a depth of 3 inches. Add 2 tablespoons white vinegar and heat the water to just below the simmer. Crack each egg into a ladle and then place gently in the water. Poach the eggs for 3 minutes.

To serve, place a slice of the grilled bread in the bottom of a warm soup bowl. Place an egg on the bread and ladle the hot soup over. Top with Parmesan.

Recommended wine: With the sweet roasted red peppers in this soup, I love a soft red wine such as Pinot Noir or Gamay.

WHEN IS A PEPPER A CHILE?

Recipes can sometimes be confusing in their use of the terms "peppers" and "chiles." In England peppers are known either as "chiles" or "capsicums" and hot ones are called "hot chiles." In Latin America, hot peppers are called "chiles" while mild peppers are called "peppers." In the United States, the word "peppers" usually refers to the mild bell peppers (pimientos are included in the pepper category as one of the varieties) and "chiles" refer to those peppers that are hot. Furthermore, the original Nahautl word was *chilli*, the Spanish *chile*, and in English you can find *chili* or *chilli*. I've used the Spanish spelling, which is slowly taking over in the U.S.

 Tomato-Curry Soup with Riso

This is a simple recipe, easily put together at the last moment. I like to use white onions rather than yellow because they provide a different texture and flavor. Commercial curry powders vary greatly in strength; make sure to taste the soup carefully, adjusting the amount of curry you use. (To make your own curry powder, see page 87.) The riso suggested here is a rice-shaped pasta; orzo or any other grain-shaped soup pasta can be used.

Serves 8 to 10

1 tablespoon olive oil
½ pound white onions, diced
1 tablespoon chopped garlic
2 teaspoons high-quality curry
    powder
1 16-ounce can diced tomatoes in
    juice (Muir Glen brand preferred)
4 cups rich chicken or vegetable
    stock

1 cup dry white wine
½ teaspoon minced fresh ginger
¼ teaspoon fennel seed
⅛ teaspoon red chile flakes
    Kosher salt and freshly ground
      black pepper
¼ cup dry riso pasta
    Garnish: Parsley pesto (page 99)

In a large saucepan, heat the oil. Add the onions, garlic, and curry powder and sauté over moderate heat until the onions just begin to brown. Add the tomatoes, stock, wine, ginger, fennel seed, and red chile flakes. Simmer for 10 minutes. Season to taste with salt and pepper. Just before serving, add the riso pasta and simmer for 5 minutes or until the pasta is al dente.

Serve garnished with a dollop of parsley pesto, if desired.

 Recommended wine: The soup is richly flavored and fairly acidic, so it demands a wine with similar acidity. A crisp, clean, non-oaked Chardonnay would work here, as would a crisp brut sparkling wine. Alternately, a slightly sweet, lower-alcohol Gewürztraminer would be an interesting contrast to the spicy heat from the chile and curry.

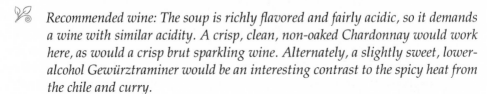

CANNED TOMATOES

Diced tomatoes in juice are generally in supermarkets, but if you can't find them, use whole peeled tomatoes and chop them up and add them along with their juice. Among the many brands of canned tomatoes, I prefer Muir Glen tomatoes, which I think are the best-tasting canned tomato product on the market (and they're organic!). Address: Muir Glen, P.O. Box 1498, Sacramento, CA 95812.

 ## *Chilled Corn, Jicama, and Buttermilk Soup with Shrimp*

The potato-and-curry base of this soup can be made ahead in a larger quantity and frozen for use at any time. Any combination of raw vegetables can be used in place of or in addition to the corn and jicama—such as cucumbers, red onions, and sweet peas.

Serves 6 to 8

3 tablespoons olive oil
½ cup peeled and diced new
    potatoes
1½ cups chopped onions

2 teaspoons minced garlic
2 teaspoons minced fresh ginger
1 teaspoon high-quality curry
    powder (page 87)

½   teaspoon seeded and minced
      serrano chile
½   cup dry white wine
2   cups rich chicken or shellfish
      stock
½   cup minced red bell pepper
⅔   cup heavy cream or light cream
3   cups buttermilk
2   tablespoons lime juice

1½   cups fresh raw corn kernels
        (about 2 ears)
⅓   cup chopped fresh cilantro
⅔   cup peeled and minced jicama
½   pound bay shrimp
      Kosher salt and freshly ground
        black pepper
      Tabasco or other hot pepper sauce
      Garnish: Chopped fresh chives

In a large saucepan, heat 2 tablespoons of the olive oil. Add the potatoes, onions, garlic, ginger, curry powder, and chile and sauté over moderate heat until soft but not brown. Add the wine and stock and bring to a boil. Reduce the heat and simmer until the vegetables are very tender, approximately 8 to 10 minutes. Remove from the heat and cool. Transfer to a blender or food processor and purée the cooled soup base, in batches if necessary. Chill for at least 4 hours or overnight.

In a small sauté pan, heat the remaining 1 tablespoon olive oil. Add the red bell pepper and sauté until softened. Set aside.

Combine the chilled soup base, cream, buttermilk, lime juice, corn, cilantro, jicama, shrimp, and sautéed pepper. Season to taste with salt and pepper and drops of Tabasco.

Serve cold, garnished with chopped chives.

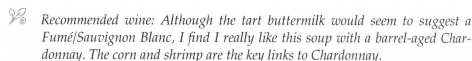

Recommended wine: Although the tart buttermilk would seem to suggest a Fumé/Sauvignon Blanc, I find I really like this soup with a barrel-aged Chardonnay. The corn and shrimp are the key links to Chardonnay.

JICAMA

A native of Central and South America, jicama is now grown widely throughout the Pacific Rim. It is a fleshy, crisp, sweet root that ranges in size from less than a pound to 5 pounds or more. I think it is best eaten raw, although some Chinese dishes call for it to be steamed or stir-fried. It does need to be peeled. It makes a great addition to a salad and has an excellent affinity for tart-sweet vinaigrettes. Jicama is the best alternative for fresh water chestnuts in Chinese cuisine, as it has a similar sweet, crunchy flavor and texture. It is generally available year-round, especially in Latin American and Chinese markets.

Chilled Fresh Tomato Soup with Summer Relish

Unfortunately, hothouse tomatoes don't work in this recipe. Wait until tomatoes are in season and select the most flavorful vine-ripened ones you can find. Usually when I present this, I drizzle some basil or chive oil (page 68) on top of the soup, which adds an interesting color contrast as well as a flavor note.

Serves 6

4 pounds coarsely chopped ripe
    tomatoes
¼ cup balsamic vinegar
    Kosher salt and freshly ground
      white pepper

Summer Relish (recipe follows)
Garnish: Fresh mint or basil
    sprigs

Using a food mill, purée the tomatoes—a food mill is preferred because a blender or food processor tends to incorporate too much air. Discard the skins and seeds. Add the vinegar and season the purée with salt and pepper. Cover and refrigerate until very cold.

Serve in chilled soup bowls with 1 or 2 tablespoons of the Summer Relish on top and garnish with the herb sprigs.

Summer Relish

¼ cup plain yogurt
1 tablespoon minced fresh basil
2 teaspoons minced fresh mint
¼ cup diced red onion
2 tablespoons diced red bell pepper

2 tablespoons seeded and diced
    lemon or English cucumber
¼ cup diced firm ripe avocado
    Salt and freshly ground black
      pepper

In a bowl, combine the relish ingredients. Season to taste with salt and pepper.

Recommended wine: A Fumé/Sauvignon Blanc really expresses the flavors and aromas of a summer vegetable garden. Mint and basil are a perfect match for the fresh "green" herbal flavors of Sauvignon Blanc.

Chilled Tomatillo-Tequila Soup

Here's another marvelous cold summer soup. Light, clean, and refreshing, it's the perfect starter course for a rich, Mexican-style meal.

Serves 8

2 tablespoons olive oil	4 cups rich chicken stock
1½ cups chopped yellow onions	¼ cup tequila
1 tablespoon seeded and diced jalapeño chile	1 tablespoon fresh lime juice
	Kosher salt
2 pounds husked and quartered tomatillos	Tabasco or other hot pepper sauce
2 tablespoons minced garlic	¼ cup chopped fresh cilantro
½ teaspoon ground cumin	1 tablespoon sugar
1½ teaspoons dried oregano (Mexican preferred)	1 cup low-fat plain yogurt

In a large saucepan, heat the olive oil and sauté the onions until soft and lightly browned. Add the jalapeño, tomatillos, garlic, cumin, and oregano. Sauté 5 minutes more. Add the stock, bring to a boil, then lower the heat and simmer for 10 minutes.

Transfer to a blender or food processor and purée, in batches if necessary. Refrigerate until well chilled.

At serving time, stir in the tequila, lime juice, salt and Tabasco to taste, cilantro, sugar, and yogurt.

 Recommended wine: A fresh, fruity, lower-alcohol wine, such as a Riesling or Chenin Blanc, is a nice contrast to the tartness of the tomatillos and the lime.

Corn, Coconut, and Fennel Chowder

Reminiscent of the flavors of Southeast Asia, this is a rich, luscious soup that can be served hot or cold. I often add some freshly sautéed rock shrimp to make this soup a main course.

Serves 12

4   cups rich chicken stock
4   cups fresh raw corn kernels, cut
      from the cob, with cobs reserved
3   tablespoons olive oil
4   cups thinly sliced yellow onions
2   cups sliced leeks, both white and
      tender green parts
3   tablespoons chopped garlic
1   teaspoon fennel seed
½   teaspoon red chile flakes
1   teaspoon seeded and slivered
      serrano chile

1   tablespoon cornstarch
6   cups unsweetened coconut milk
1   tablespoon finely slivered lime or
      lemon zest
2   cups thinly sliced fennel bulb
      Kosher salt and freshly ground
        white pepper
¼   cup roughly chopped cilantro
      leaves
    Garnish: Fresh cilantro or mint
      leaves and finely slivered red
      bell peppers

In a saucepan, combine the chicken stock and the corn cobs and bring to a simmer. Simmer, covered, for 10 to 15 minutes. Meanwhile, in a stockpot, heat the olive oil. Add the onions, leeks, garlic, fennel seed, chile flakes, and serrano and sauté until the vegetables are just beginning to soften, approximately 3 minutes. Strain the stock, discarding the cobs, and add to the sautéed vegetables. Return to a simmer, stirring occasionally.

In a small bowl, dissolve the cornstarch in the coconut milk. Stir into the soup along with the citrus zest. Simmer for 5 minutes. Add the corn kernels and fennel and simmer until they are just heated through. (The corn and fennel should retain some crunch.) Season with salt and pepper.

Just before serving, stir in the chopped cilantro. Garnish with whole cilantro or mint leaves and the slivered bell peppers.

 Recommended wine: The sweet, spicy flavors in the soup would nicely match a fruity Chenin Blanc or Sémillon.

COCONUT MILK

Coconut milk is not the liquid inside fresh coconuts; it is, rather, the meat of the coconut that has been puréed and blended with hot water or milk. The interest in Thai and Southeast Asian cooking in recent years has made prepared coconut milk easy to obtain. Canned or frozen coconut milk is certainly acceptable and is widely available in Asian markets as well as large supermarkets. Several brands are available, but my favorite (introduced to me by Longtiene de Montinero, chef–owner of Elephant Walk in Boston) is the Mae Ploy brand. It has a fresh, naturally sweet flavor without the starchiness of many other brands. Sweetened coconut milk is also available in the market; it's used for desserts and drinks. Make sure not to use sweetened coconut milk where unsweetened is called for. Fat-reduced coconut milks are also fairly available now.

Crab and Corn Chowder with Ginger

In this soup I use our California Dungeness crab, which is very rich and sweet, but any fresh or frozen crab could be used. Crab and corn are an unbeatable combination, particularly when accented by fresh ginger. This recipe calls for ¾ cup heavy cream, but it's also delicious without any cream (or milk) at all.
Serves 8

4 cups rich chicken or shellfish stock	1 teaspoon lightly toasted coriander seed (page 36)
3 cups fresh, raw corn kernels, cobs reserved	2 cups peeled and diced waxy potatoes
2 tablespoons olive oil	1 cup fruity white wine, such as Riesling
1 tablespoon chopped fresh ginger	¾ cup heavy or light cream
1½ cups diced onions	10 ounces cooked crabmeat
½ cup minced fennel bulb or celery	⅓ cup chopped fresh cilantro
¼ cup minced red bell pepper	Kosher salt and freshly ground black pepper
¼ teaspoon chopped chipotle chiles in adobo sauce (available where Mexican food products are sold)	Garnish: Crab Tomalley Toasts (recipe follows)

In a saucepan, combine the stock and the corn cobs and simmer, covered, for 10 to 15 minutes. Remove the cobs and discard. Set aside the stock.

In a stockpot, heat the olive oil and sauté the ginger just to soften it. Add the onions, fennel or celery, red bell pepper, and chipotle. Sauté over medium heat for 2 minutes. Add the coriander seed, potatoes, wine, and stock. Bring to a boil, then reduce the heat and simmer until the potatoes are almost done, about 8 minutes. In a blender, combine 1 cup of the corn with 1 cup of the hot soup stock and blend. Return to the stockpot and add the remaining corn kernels, cream, and crabmeat. Warm just until heated through.

Just before serving, stir in the cilantro and season to taste with salt and pepper. Serve with Crab Tomalley Toasts on the side.

TOMALLEY

If you are lucky enough to get fresh cooked crab, be sure to take it home whole and clean it yourself so that you can retrieve the tomalley (the liver). The tomalley, a greenish or yellowish matter, is found inside the shell or carapace; scoop it out, strain it, and use it to make the Tomalley Toasts or simply stir it into the chowder to enhance the crab flavor. Recently there has been some concern about using the tomalley from crab and lobsters because of pollution. If you're unsure of the waters from which the crab comes, then don't make the toasts.

Crab Tomalley Toasts

16 2 inch-wide slices French bread,
      sliced ½ inch thick
 5 tablespoons unsalted butter
 2 tablespoons chopped
      shallots

¼ cup cooked crab tomalley
 2 teaspoons minced fresh parsley
      or sorrel
      Freshly ground white pepper

Toast bread slices until crisp and golden brown.

In a small sauté pan, melt 2 teaspoons of the butter. Add the shallots and sauté until soft but not brown. Remove from the heat and cool. In a small bowl, combine the shallots, remaining butter, tomalley, and parsley. Stir until well combined and add pepper to taste. Spread on the toasts.

 Recommended wine: The rich flavors of corn, crab, and ginger all would be a great match for a rich barrel-fermented and/or aged Chardonnay. If you find one, a Viognier from one of the new American producers would also be delicious.

Chipotle in adobo

Chipotle in adobo—cooked chipotle chiles in adobo sauce—is a canned product that is always available in Hispanic markets and often available in the Mexican food section of large supermarkets. Both the chiles and the sauce are wonderfully tasty; I use them a lot and once you try them, you will too. Chipotle in adobo is, however, very hot, and you'll generally want to use it in small amounts (like the ¼ teaspoon called for in the crab and corn chowder). After you open the can, you can either freeze the contents or transfer to a little glass jar and refrigerate. It keeps indefinitely.

 Lavender-Blueberry Soup

The floral quality of the lavender adds an interesting flavor to the blueberries. Add the honey a bit at a time to make sure the soup doesn't end up being too sweet—it's not supposed to be a dessert soup! It can be served hot or cold, and it couldn't be easier to make.

Serves 8 to 10

2 quarts fresh or frozen blueberries	Juice and grated zest of 1 large lemon
1 cup dry red wine	1 4-inch cinnamon stick
1½ cups water	½ teaspoon freshly ground black pepper
¾ cup honey (or to taste)	
¼ cup frozen orange juice concentrate	½ teaspoon ground cloves
1½ tablespoons dried lavender flowers	Garnish: Crème fraîche, whole blueberries, and fresh mint sprigs

In a large saucepan, combine all the ingredients. Bring to a boil. Reduce the heat and simmer for 8 minutes. Remove the cinnamon stick.

The soup may be served hot or cold. Garnish with a dollop of crème fraîche, a sprinkling of fresh blueberries, and a mint sprig.

Recommended wine: A fruity, slightly sweet Gewürztraminer amplifies the fruity-floral notes in the soup.

LAVENDER

Lavender flowers are wonderfully fragrant and add a lot of character to savory dishes. They are inexpensive and can be purchased in most health food stores. (Be sure that the lavender you're using is intended for cooking. Do not use lavender that has been sprayed or designed for use in sachets.) Store lavender in a sealed plastic container in your pantry. Lavender flowers make a particularly good dry marinade, or "rub," for poultry or fish (like the Seared Ahi Tuna with a Lavender-Pepper Crust, page 160). Culinary lavender (both flowers and leaves) is used to flavor vinegars, oils, and jellies, and when infused into a sugar syrup it makes an interesting ice or sorbet. It is also a key ingredient in that famous French mixture "herbes de Provence."

Historically, lavender was known as the herb of love. It worked both ways, however: On the one hand, it was considered an aphrodisiac; on the other, a sprinkle of lavender water on the head purportedly kept the wearer chaste.

 Mendocino Gazpacho

Gazpacho is a Spanish chilled soup that perfectly echoes the essence of summer. This version resounds with garden-fresh flavors. Vine-ripened tomatoes add immeasurably to the quality of the gazpacho. Make it several hours in advance, so it has time to really chill before being served.

Serves 8 to 10

1 tablespoon roasted garlic (page 247)	⅓ cup extra-virgin olive oil
1 cup cubed French bread, crusts removed	1½ teaspoons lightly toasted and crushed cumin seed (page 36)
¼ cup red wine vinegar	2–3 cups fresh tomato juice or V-8

2–3	cups fish stock	¼	cup minced fresh cilantro
3	pounds ripe tomatoes, seeded and finely diced	¾	pound cooked whole bay shrimp
⅔	cup minced red onion		Fresh lemon juice or balsamic vinegar
1	cup minced cucumber		
½	cup minced red bell pepper	¼–1	teaspoon chipotle in adobo (optional)
½	cup minced celery		
1	teaspoon seeded and minced serrano chiles		Kosher salt and freshly ground black pepper
2	tablespoons minced fresh basil (or 1 tablespoon dried)		Garnish: Diced avocado, thinly sliced lemon, and cilantro sprigs
1	tablespoon minced fresh mint (or ½ tablespoon dried)		

In a food processor, combine the garlic, cubed bread, vinegar, olive oil, and cumin seed. Process until smooth. Transfer to a large bowl. Add 2 cups of the tomato juice, 2 cups of the stock, tomatoes, red onion, cucumbers, bell pepper, celery, serranos, basil, mint, cilantro, and shrimp and stir to combine. Correct the seasoning with lemon juice, chipotle, and salt and pepper. Add more juice and stock if a thinner consistency is desired. Chill, covered, for 2 to 3 hours.

Serve in chilled soup bowls and garnish with the avocado, lemon slices, and cilantro sprigs.

 Recommended wine: A Fumé/Sauvignon Blanc would beautifully complement the fresh herbs and fish in the soup.

 # Curried Apple and Mussel Chowder

This Indian-inspired soup is really fast to make. We used to gather wild mussels off the California coast in the fall and winter. Unfortunately, concerns about pollution from land-based run-off have kept us from continuing the harvest. Farm-raised mussels are an excellent alternative and are generally available year round. They are constantly monitored and much more consistent in quality than their wild cousins.

Serves 6

2	tablespoons olive oil	6	cups rich shellfish stock or chicken stock
3	cups peeled and diced tart green apples, such as Pippin or Granny Smith	1	teaspoon toasted and crushed coriander seed (page 36)
2½	cups chopped red onions	1	teaspoon toasted and crushed fennel seed (page 36)
2	cups bias-cut leeks, both the white and tender green parts	1	cup thinly sliced fennel bulb
2–3	tablespoons high-quality curry powder, or homemade (page 87)	2	pounds scrubbed mussels, beards removed
			Big pinch cayenne pepper (optional)
1	cup dry white wine		Garnish: Fennel fronds

In a medium sauté pan, heat 1 tablespoon of the olive oil and sauté the apples over moderately high heat until lightly browned. Set aside.

In a stockpot, heat the remaining 1 tablespoon olive oil. Add the onions, leeks, and curry powder and sauté until the onions and leeks just begin to soften but not brown. Add the wine, stock, coriander seed, and fennel seed and simmer for 5 minutes. Add the sliced fennel and mussels. Simmer, covered, until the mussels open, about 3 minutes. Add the sautéed apples and cayenne, if using, and heat through. Remove and discard any mussels that did not open. Reserve 18 mussels in their shells for garnish.

To serve, remove the remaining mussels from their shells and divide among 6 warm soup bowls. Ladle in the hot chowder. Garnish with the reserved mussels in their shells and the fennel fronds.

Recommended wine: This is a terrific match with Gewürztraminer, since the sweet spice and fruit in the chowder mirror the same flavors in the wine.

CURRY POWDER

The world of curry is as diverse as the cultures that use it and as personal as the people making them. Curries range from mild, as in the curries of Indonesia, to fiery hot Thai and India curries. Basic curry called for in this book and in most recipes refers to a mild to medium-hot Indian-style curry powder. You should definitely make your own! Curry powders should begin with toasted whole spices, which are then ground finely and stored in airtight containers. Toasting brings out the rich flavor of the spice. Once ground, the spices begin to lose their subtle flavors and aroma quickly, so you should plan to use up whatever you've made within 3 months. Most commercial curries are simply mixtures of un-toasted spices and who knows how long ago they were ground.

Here is a basic curry mixture that you can make at home. Health food stores are usually a good source for whole spices at a reasonable price, but be sure to investigate any Asian or Caribbean markets in your area.

1   ounce *each* seeds of coriander, cumin, fenugreek, poppy, and cardamon
¼   ounce mustard seed
½   ounce dried chiles (or to taste; see note)

1   cinnamon stick, broken in small pieces
½   ounce ground ginger
1   ounce ground turmeric

Preheat the oven to 375 degrees. Place the seeds, chiles, and cinnamon stick is a baking pan and toast for 3 to 4 minutes or until the spices are fragrant. Cool; then in a spice grinder or with a mortar and pestle grind to a powder. Transfer to a small bowl. Stir in the ginger and turmeric. Store in an airtight container in the refrigerator or freezer for up to 3 months.

Note: The heat of the chiles will determine the heat of the curry. Use ancho, pasilla, or chile negro for a milder curry and red chile flakes from any of the hot chiles, such as chipotle, for a fiery version.

Apple-Herb Vichyssoise

One of the first "serious" cookbooks I remember buying was the book Albert Stockli wrote after he had retired from "21" in New York City—*Splendid Fare*. He was a real fan of vichyssoise with fruit in it—so this recipe is in remembrance of him.

Serves 6 to 8

1 tablespoon olive oil	¼ cup apple brandy, such as Calvados, or 2 tablespoons dry sherry
1½ cups chopped leeks, white part only	1½ cups light cream (or half-and-half)
½ cup chopped onion	2 tablespoons *each* minced fresh chervil and chives
¼ cup chopped celery	1 tablespoon minced fresh tarragon
1 pound tart-sweet apples, peeled and chopped, such as McIntosh or Gravenstein	1 teaspoon minced fresh mint
	Sea salt and freshly ground white pepper
½ pound boiling potatoes, peeled and chopped	Garnish: Finely diced apples, chervil sprigs, and chive flowers and a drizzle of chive oil (page 68), if desired
3 cups rich vegetable stock or rich chicken stock, fat removed	
½ cup dry white wine	

In a large stockpot, heat the olive oil. Add the leeks, onion, celery, and half of the apples; sauté until soft but not brown. Add the potatoes, stock, and wine. Simmer, partially covered, until the vegetables are very soft. Remove from heat. Add the Calvados and the remaining apples. Transfer to a blender or food processor and purée, in batches if necessary, until very smooth. Strain. Add the half-and-half and the herbs. Refrigerate until well chilled or up to 2 days. Season to taste with salt and pepper.

Serve in chilled soup bowls, garnished with apples, chervil sprigs, chive flowers, and optional chive oil.

Recommended wine: A clean, young Chardonnay with a minimum of oak aging accentuates the crisp apple and herb flavors in the soup.

CHERVIL

One of the subtlest of the herb family, chervil is worth seeking out or even growing in a pot. It's a "warm" herb, in the sense that its parsley-anise flavor and fragrance tend to warm, or blend and fill in the background when used with other herbs.

The flavor and fragrance of chervil resemble myrrh, one of the gifts brought by the Wise Men to the baby Jesus. Because of this it became a tradition in Christian Europe to serve chervil soup on Holy Thursday.

Blue Cheese and Apple Soup

Apples and cheese are great together, so why not in soup? This rich combination is best served in small bowls, but it works equally well either hot or cold. For an interesting alternative garnish, add some chopped freshly roasted chestnuts if serving warm or peeled and diced tart apple if serving cold.

Serves 6 to 8

2	tablespoons unsalted butter or vegetable oil	½	pound sweet Gorgonzola, Cambozola, Maytag blue, or other blue cheese
⅓	cup finely minced shallots or scallions	1¼	cups light cream
3	cups peeled and diced tart-sweet apples such as McIntosh or Gravenstein		Kosher salt and freshly ground black pepper
⅓	cup dry white wine		Drops of fresh lemon juice
2–3	cups rich vegetable stock or chicken stock		Garnish: Minced fresh chives

In a medium saucepan, melt the butter and sauté the shallots until soft but not brown. Add the apples and cook until they just begin to soften. Add the wine and 2 cups of the stock and bring to a boil. Reduce the heat to a simmer. Crumble and add the cheese and stir until the cheese melts. Add the cream and season with salt, pepper, and lemon juice. Transfer to a blender or food processor and purée, in batches if necessary, adding more stock if desired for a thinner consistency. At this point the soup can be either chilled (for up to 2 days) to serve cold or heated to serve hot. Do not allow the soup to boil, or it will tend to curdle.

Serve hot or cold, garnished with the minced chives.

Recommended wine: A big, luscious barrel-fermented and aged Chardonnay is a great choice here to go with the apple and rich cheese flavors. These flavors echo the toasty, creamy nuances in the wine.

 # Maui Onion and Ginger Soup

This soup was inspired by Roger Dikon, the affable chef at the Maui Prince Hotel in Kihei. The soup has gone through some changes in the Valley Oaks kitchen but it still reminds me of Maui. It works equally well hot or cold.

Serves 6

2	tablespoons unsalted butter	1	13-ounce can unsweetened coconut milk
2	pounds sweet onions, such as Maui, Walla Walla, or Vidalia, sliced	1	cup half-and-half
½	cup chopped fresh ginger	½	teaspoon grated lime zest
1	teaspoon seeded and minced jalapeño chile	1	tablespoon fresh lime juice (or to taste)
1	teaspoon high-quality curry powder (page 87)		Kosher salt and freshly ground white pepper
1½	cups dry white wine		Garnish: Chopped fresh basil leaves (lemon basil, if available)
4	cups rich vegetable or chicken stock		

In a large saucepan, melt the butter. Add the onions, ginger, jalapeño, and curry powder and sauté 8 to 10 minutes or until the onions are translucent. Add the wine, stock, and coconut milk. Bring to a boil. Reduce the heat and simmer for 15 minutes or until the onions are very tender. Remove from heat. Transfer to a blender or food processor and purée, in batches if necessary. Return the soup to the saucepan. Add the half-and-half, lime zest, and lime juice. Season to taste with salt and pepper.

Serve with chopped basil sprinkled on top.

Recommended wine: A floral Gewürztraminer mirrors the spicy, ginger notes in the soup and flatters the natural sweetness of the onions.

 ## Poblano and Smoked Chicken Chowder with Hominy

This hearty, unusual soup could be the centerpiece of a meal. The smoky flavor of the poblano chile is even better if you char-roast it before adding it in. If poblanos are not available, Anaheim chiles can substitute nicely. If neither are available, regular green bell peppers, which have been char-roasted and peeled, will work, but you'll need to add a little chile powder to approximate the zing of the poblanos.

Serves 6 to 8

2 tablespoons olive oil	1½ cups seeded and diced tomatoes (drained if using canned)
1 pound yellow onions, halved and sliced lengthwise	6 cups rich chicken stock
3 medium poblano chiles, seeded and sliced into thin strips	2 cups fruity white wine, such as Gewürztraminer or Riesling
1 tablespoon finely slivered garlic	½ pound smoked chicken, julienned
2 cups husked and quartered tomatillos	¾ cup canned, drained white hominy
½ teaspoon fennel seed	Kosher salt and freshly ground black pepper
½ teaspoon cumin seed	Garnish: Chopped fresh cilantro, diced avocado, and fresh lime juice
2 teaspoons dried oregano (Mexican preferred)	
¼ teaspoon ground cinnamon	

In a saucepan, heat the olive oil. Add the onions, poblanos, and garlic. Sauté until soft but not brown, about 5 minutes. Add the tomatillos, fennel seed, cumin seed, oregano, cinnamon, tomatoes, stock, and wine. Simmer gently for 15 minutes. Add the smoked chicken and hominy. Simmer to heat through. Season to taste with salt and pepper.

Garnish with chopped cilantro, diced avocado, and lime juice just before serving.

 Recommended wine: The tart flavors of the tomatillos and fruity stock are augmented by a similarly fruity Johannisberg Riesling or Gewürztraminer.

Pumpkin Soup with Wild Mushrooms

This seasonal soup, perfect for the Thanksgiving or harvest table, shows off flavors that are unusually complex and earthy.

Serves 6 to 8

1 ounce dried porcini mushrooms, rinsed	⅛ teaspoon ground cloves
	1 teaspoon lemon juice
1 tablespoon olive oil or unsalted butter	4 cups rich chicken or mushroom stock (page 57)
2 cups sliced yellow onions	¾ cup milk
1 cup sliced leeks, white part only	½ cup heavy cream
1 tablespoon minced garlic	Kosher salt and freshly ground white pepper
2 pounds fresh pumpkin, to measure 5 cups peeled and diced	3 tablespoons dry sherry
1 tablespoon wild honey	Garnish: Lightly sautéed fresh wild mushrooms and minced fresh chives
2 teaspoons minced fresh sage (or 1 teaspoon dried)	

Place the porcini in a small bowl and cover with 1 cup warm tap water. Weight the mushrooms with a small plate to submerge them completely. Let stand for 1 hour. Remove the mushrooms from the soaking liquid. Strain the liquid through a double thickness of rinsed cheesecloth or through a paper coffee filter and reserve. Rinse and chop the mushrooms.

In a medium saucepan, heat the olive oil. Add the onions, leeks, and garlic and sauté until soft and lightly brown. Add the chopped porcini and sauté 2 to 3 minutes longer. Add the pumpkin, honey, sage, cloves, lemon juice, stock, and the porcini-soaking liquid. Simmer for 25 minutes or until the pumpkin is soft.

Transfer to a food processor and purée, in batches if necessary. Return the purée to the saucepan. Add the milk and cream and season with salt and pepper. Bring just to a simmer. Add the sherry just before serving.

Serve garnished with sautéed fresh wild mushrooms and a sprinkling of chives, if desired.

Note: The soup may be served as more of a chowder by not puréeing it. For a lighter version, the cream and milk may be omitted and an equivalent amount of stock added in their place.

Recommended wine: The creamy texture of this soup plays nicely off the buttery texture of many Chardonnays.

Roasted Eggplant Soup with Sweet Peppers

This is one of my oldest and most favorite soups. It originated as a clear tomato broth with slices of roasted eggplant and vegetables in it; the soup was transformed accidentally when I appeared as a guest chef in a restaurant in Chicago, and the kitchen staff decided it was easier to prepare this way. I found I liked it better their way too. The soup is particularly wonderful in the summer, when the bounty of peppers, eggplant, onions, and tomatoes bursts forth in our gardens.
Serves 8

1 **large eggplant, sliced into ¼-inch-thick rounds**	**Kosher salt and freshly ground black pepper**
2 **tablespoons chopped garlic**	½ **cup seeded and thinly slivered ripe tomatoes**
½ **cup loosely packed basil leaves**	
¼ **cup chopped scallions**	6 **cups tomato stock (page 56) or chicken stock**
⅛ **teaspoon red chile flakes**	
½ **cup olive oil**	**Garnish: Fresh basil leaves and freshly shaved Asiago or Parmesan cheese**
1½ **cups thinly sliced red bell peppers**	
1½ **cups thinly sliced red onions**	

Preheat the oven to 375 degrees. Oil a baking sheet and arrange the eggplant in a single layer. In a food processor, combine the garlic, basil, scallions, chile flakes, and 6 tablespoons of the olive oil. Process briefly to make a smooth mixture. Spread evenly over the eggplant slices and bake for 12 to 15 minutes or until the eggplant is soft and lightly browned. Remove, roughly chop, and set aside.

In a small sauté pan, heat the remaining olive oil and sauté the peppers and onions until softened. Season with salt and pepper. Transfer to a food processor. Add the tomatoes and reserved eggplant and process thoroughly. Add the stock, in batches if necessary, and continue to process until thoroughly puréed. The soup can be prepared up to this point and stored, refrigerated, for up to 2 days. Heat, season to taste with salt and pepper, and serve garnished with basil leaves and the shaved cheese.

 Recommended wine: Fumé/Sauvignon Blanc complements this hearty, intensely flavorful soup.

Pastas, Pizzas, Risottos, and Gnocchis

Penne with Grilled Asparagus and Tomatoes

This is a simple and very flavorful pasta with some zing. It's the grilling of the vegetables that makes it special. If asparagus is not available, try using thin sliced fennel bulb or even black kale.

Serves 6

½ cup extra-virgin olive oil
1 pound young, tender asparagus
3 pounds plum tomatoes, insides scooped out and discarded
Kosher salt and freshly ground black pepper
4 tablespoons roasted garlic (page 247)
8 anchovy fillets, rinsed and finely chopped

½ cup chopped fresh basil
3 tablespoons chopped fresh parsley
1 tablespoon chopped fresh mint
½ teaspoon red chile flakes (or to taste)
1 pound penne or other shaped dry pasta
Garnish: Freshly grated Parmesan cheese, fried capers (page 21), if desired

Prepare a charcoal fire. Using 2 tablespoons of the olive oil, lightly oil the asparagus and tomatoes and season with salt and pepper. Grill over hot coals until just tender but well marked. Cut the asparagus at an angle into 2-inch lengths and set aside. Coarsely chop the tomatoes and toss with the roasted garlic, anchovies, herbs, chile flakes, and the remaining olive oil.

Cook the pasta in boiling salted water until just al dente. While the pasta is cooking, heat the tomato mixture in a large sauté pan. When the pasta is done, drain and add to the pan along with asparagus. Toss to combine. Season to taste with salt and pepper. Serve immediately, garnished with Parmesan and fried capers, if desired.

 Recommended wine: Try a crisp, clean Sauvignon Blanc with herbal notes; it is a great match to this dish. A crisp Italian or Spanish white would also be fun.

Purslane and Penne

Foraging for wild foods has always had a personal attraction for me. It started years ago when I read Euell Gibbons' classic *Stalking the Wild Asparagus* and Billy Joe Tatum's *Wild Foods Cookbook and Field Guide*. Purslane is basically a weed *(Portulaca oleracea)* that grows in many parts of the country. It has the texture of a succulent and a tart, citric flavor. My grandmother and I used to gather it often and cook it with lamb's-quarter, another wild green. It is best when young, before it gets woody, from late spring to early summer. It is one of those humble peasant ingredients that is beginning to appear in upscale markets and restaurants. Purslane is worth buying or foraging for when you see it. In Italy, purslane leaves are often sprinkled on tomato salads.

Serves 4

¼   pound lean, smoky bacon, cut crosswise into short, ¼-inch-wide strips

¾   pound young purslane, washed and woody stems removed

½   pound penne or other tubular-shaped dry pasta

⅓   cup extra-virgin olive oil

2–3   tablespoons red wine vinegar

½   teaspoon sugar

2   cups seeded and diced ripe plum tomatoes

½   cup finely diced feta
      Kosher salt and freshly ground black pepper

In a sauté pan, cook the bacon until crisp. Using a slotted spoon, remove the bacon to paper towels and set aside. Discard all but 2 tablespoons of the bacon fat.

Cook the penne in lightly salted boiling water until just al dente. Drain and toss with 1 tablespoon of the olive oil. Keep warm.

In a large skillet or wok over moderately high heat, sauté the purslane quickly in the reserved bacon fat until just tender but not limp, approximately 2 to 3 minutes. Add 2 tablespoons of the vinegar and the sugar and cook for 30 seconds more.

Add the cooked pasta, remaining olive oil, tomatoes, feta, and bacon, and toss just to combine. Season to taste with salt and pepper and additional drops of vinegar, if desired.

Serve immediately.

Recommended wine: A crisp Sauvignon Blanc or dry Chenin Blanc are good choices.

Rigatoni with Roasted Cauliflower and Parsley Pesto

I think of this as a fall or winter dish, but it could just as easily be served as part of a summer buffet. Roasting cauliflower, like the root vegetables discussed in other recipes, brings out deeper, sweeter flavors. I greatly prefer roasted cauliflower to steamed or boiled. Slivered sun-dried tomatoes are a nice addition to this recipe.

Serves 6

2 pounds cauliflower, trimmed and separated into large florets
1 cup extra-virgin olive oil
   Kosher salt and freshly ground black pepper
2 cups firmly packed parsley leaves
¼ cup lightly packed mint leaves
1 teaspoon grated lemon zest
½ cup blanched slivered almonds, lightly toasted

2 teaspoons minced garlic
1 pound rigatoni or other shaped dry pasta
¾ cup slivered Niçoise, Kalamata, or other oil-cured black olives
1 cup cooked cannellini, borlotti, or other bean (optional)
   Garnish: Thinly shaved Asiago or Parmesan cheese and mint sprigs

Preheat the oven to 425 degrees. Liberally brush the cauliflower florets with ¼ cup of the olive oil and season with salt and pepper. Place in a single layer on a baking sheet and roast for 15 to 20 minutes or until the cauliflower is lightly browned and tender. Slice the florets into ½-inch-thick pieces.

While the cauliflower is roasting, combine the parsley, mint, lemon zest, almonds, garlic, and the remaining ¾ cup olive oil in a blender or food processor, and blend until smooth. Season to taste with salt and pepper. Thin if desired with a little stock or water.

Cook the rigatoni in lightly salted boiling water until just al dente. Drain. Toss the hot pasta with the parsley pesto, cauliflower, olives, and beans, if using. Serve warm or at room temperature. Garnish with the shaved cheese and mint sprigs.

Recommended wine: The rich green pesto is great with Sauvignon Blanc.

Farfalle with Feta, Olives, and Golden Raisins

The interplay of salty olives and feta with sweet golden raisins makes for an intriguing palate teaser. For me, this combination evokes memories of a long-ago summer spent in Greece.

Serves 4 to 6

3   tablespoons olive oil
1   cup thinly sliced small red onions
1   cup slivered red or yellow bell pepper
2   teaspoons minced garlic
1   28-ounce can diced Italian tomatoes with juice
⅔   cup sliced Niçoise or Kalamata olives
½   cup golden raisins
½   cup dry white wine
2   tablespoons drained capers

3   tablespoons minced fresh basil (or 2 teaspoons dried)
1   teaspoon seeded and minced serrano chile (or ¼ teaspoon red chile flakes)
    Kosher salt and freshly ground black pepper
½   pound farfalle or other shaped dry pasta
¼   cup minced fresh parsley
½   cup crumbled feta cheese

Heat 2 tablespoons of the olive oil in a large sauté pan. Add the onions, bell pepper, and garlic and sauté until the vegetables are soft but not brown, about 10 minutes. Add the tomatoes, olives, raisins, wine, capers, basil, and serrano. Simmer, uncovered, for 10 to 12 minutes, or until slightly thickened. Season to taste with salt and pepper. Keep warm.

Bring a large pot of lightly salted water to a boil. Add the pasta and cook until just al dente. Drain and toss with the remaining 1 tablespoon olive oil and parsley. Top with the sauce and feta and serve immediately.

Recommended wine: The infinitely versatile fruitiness and acidity of Fumé/ Sauvignon Blanc provide the necessary counterpoint for this pasta.

Fusilli with Collards, Bacon, and Garlic

Except for the olives, this pasta is reminiscent of a Southern "mess of greens." It's a delicious, simple wintertime dish.

Serves 4 to 6

1½ pounds collard greens, Swiss chard, or kale, coarsely chopped, woody stems discarded	½ cup pitted and sliced Niçoise, Kalamata, or other oil-cured black olives
⅓ pound good smoked bacon, roughly chopped	½ cup rich chicken or vegetable stock
3 tablespoons extra-virgin olive oil	1 pound fusilli or other corkscrew-shaped pasta
1½ cups thinly sliced red onions	2 tablespoons balsamic vinegar (or to taste)
½ teaspoon seeded and minced serrano chile	Kosher salt and freshly ground black pepper
4 tablespoons roasted garlic	Garnish: Freshly grated or shaved Parmesan

Blanch the greens in lightly salted boiling water for 2 minutes to soften. Drain and rinse in cold water to stop the cooking, drain again, and set aside.

Cook the bacon in a skillet over moderate heat until browned. Using a slotted spoon, remove the bacon to paper towels and pour off all but 1 tablespoon of the fat. To the pan, add the olive oil, onions, and serrano and sauté until just softened but not brown. Add the garlic, olives, blanched greens, and stock and cook over moderate heat 6 to 8 minutes, or until the greens are tender. Keep warm.

Cook the fusilli in lightly salted boiling water until just done. Toss with the greens mixture and bacon. Season to taste with the vinegar, salt, and pepper. Garnish with Parmesan. Serve immediately.

 Recommended wine: The slight bitterness of the greens and saltiness of the bacon are counterpointed by a crisp Fumé/Sauvignon Blanc. A soft red with subtle herbal notes, such as a Merlot or Pinot Noir, also works.

Conchiglie with Sweet and Sour Lamb

Conchiglie are one of the seemingly endless number of pasta shapes; they look like little conch shells. You, of course, can use any shape of dry pasta you please or try this with the fresh Gremolata Pasta on page 107. The sauce in this dish is magnificent, and I would suggest making a double batch so you can freeze one for later use. Like most stewed meat sauces, this one tastes even better a day or two after being made.

Serves 6

4 tablespoons olive oil	½ cup red wine vinegar
3 pounds boneless lamb neck or shoulder, well trimmed and cut in 1-inch cubes	⅓ cup golden raisins
	1 tablespoon light-brown sugar
	2 cups rich lamb or chicken stock
Kosher salt and freshly ground black pepper	½ cup dry white wine
2½ cups sliced onions	1 tablespoon chopped fresh rosemary (or ½ teaspoon dried)
1 tablespoon slivered garlic	1 teaspoon cinnamon
½ cup finely diced carrots	1 pound conchiglie or other shaped dry pasta
½ cup finely diced fresh fennel bulb or celery	⅓ cup minced fresh parsley
2 cups seeded and diced tomatoes	Garnish: Toasted pine nuts

Heat 3 tablespoons of the olive oil in a heavy-bottomed pot and brown the lamb quickly and evenly, seasoning lightly with salt and pepper. Do this in batches if necessary. Remove the meat and set aside. Add the onions, garlic, carrots, and fennel to the pot and sauté over moderate heat until just beginning to color. Return the meat to the pot and add the tomatoes, vinegar, raisins, sugar, stock, wine, rosemary, and cinnamon. Simmer for 1½ to 2 hours or until the meat is very tender. Skim off fat occasionally. Season with salt and pepper and keep warm.

At serving time, cook the pasta in lightly salted boiling water until just al dente. Drain, toss with the remaining 1 tablespoon olive oil and the parsley. Ladle the lamb sauce over the pasta and garnish with toasted pine nuts.

Recommended wine: Try a low-tannin red wine such as a Pinot Noir or Merlot with this dish. A light, fruity white wine such as a Chenin Blanc with just a touch of residual sugar (1 percent or so) also works, because it mirrors the slight sweetness and sweet-spice aromas in the dish.

Orecchiette with Red Wine–Braised Chicken

This is a rich, peasant-style chicken stew that can be served with pasta (as it is here) or with rice or roasted potatoes. Use whatever fresh herbs you like; for example, rosemary and savory could substitute for the thyme, sage, and basil.
Serves 6

6 large chicken thighs, skinned and boned
   Kosher salt and freshly ground black pepper
2 tablespoons olive or canola oil
½ pound fresh shiitake mushrooms, stemmed and thickly sliced
1 cup sliced yellow onions
3 tablespoons slivered garlic
½ cup diced carrots
½ cup thinly sliced celery
2 cups hearty red wine
2 cups seeded and diced ripe tomatoes

1 teaspoon *each* chopped fresh thyme and sage
4 cups chicken stock
   Balsamic vinegar (optional)
⅓ cup finely chopped fresh parsley
½ pound orecchiette or other shaped dry pasta
¼ cup chopped fresh basil
¼ cup drained and finely chopped sun-dried tomatoes in oil
   Garnish: Fresh basil sprigs and freshly shaved Asiago or Parmesan cheese

Season the chicken liberally with salt and pepper. In a large, heavy-bottomed saucepan, heat the oil and quickly brown the chicken over high heat. Remove and set aside. Add the mushrooms, onions, garlic, carrots, and celery, and sauté until very lightly browned.

Return the chicken to the pan and add the wine, tomatoes, thyme, sage, and stock and bring to a simmer. Cover and simmer until the chicken is tender, 25 to 30 minutes. Remove the chicken and cut the meat into bite-sized pieces and set aside. Strain the braising liquid, reserving the vegetables, and return the liquid to the pot. Bring it to a boil and cook over high heat for 8 to 10 minutes to reduce and thicken it lightly and concentrate the flavors. Taste and adjust the seasoning with salt, pepper, and drops of balsamic vinegar, if using. Add the reserved chicken and vegetables and heat through. Stir in the parsley. Keep warm.

Cook the orecchiette in lightly salted boiling water until just al dente. Drain and toss with the chopped basil and sun-dried tomatoes. Moisten with a little of the liquid from the chicken mixture. Serve the pasta in the center of large shallow bowls, surrounded by the braised chicken sauce. Garnish with fresh basil sprigs and shaved cheese. Serve immediately.

Recommended wine: This simple, hearty dish would be great with the black-pepper and spice flavors of Zinfandel.

 # Rotelle with Chicken Livers and Basil

This dish originated when a local chicken farmer stopped by the restaurant and gave me a big tub of fresh chicken livers. This is the kind of dish my grandmother on the ranch would have made had she known about balsamic vinegar.

Serves 4

½	pound chicken livers, cut into large dice	¼	pound good-quality (no-water-added) ham, finely slivered
5	tablespoons olive oil	1	tablespoon drained capers (optional)
½	pound rotelle or other shaped dry pasta	⅓	cup chopped fresh basil
2	cups thinly sliced red onions		Kosher salt and freshly ground black pepper
1	cup thinly sliced red bell pepper		Drops of balsamic vinegar
1	tablespoon slivered garlic	½	cup freshly grated Parmesan cheese
⅓	cup dry white wine		
1	cup rich chicken stock		

In a sauté pan over high heat, sauté the chicken livers in 2 tablespoons of the olive oil until browned but still pink and juicy inside. Set aside and keep warm.

Cook the rotelle in lightly salted boiling water until just al dente. Drain and toss with 1 tablespoon of the oil.

Wipe the sauté pan, add the remaining 2 tablespoons of the olive oil, and sauté the onions, bell pepper, and garlic over moderate heat until they just begin to soften and lightly color. Add the wine and stock and cook until the liquid is reduced slightly. Stir in the ham, capers, and cooked chicken livers. Turn off the heat.

Toss the pasta with the chicken liver sauce and chopped basil. Season with salt, pepper, and drops of balsamic vinegar. Top with the cheese and serve immediately.

Recommended wine: This rich concoction needs a peppery red wine such as Zinfandel.

Fiochetti with Leeks and Smoked Salmon

This dish is reminiscent of one prepared for me during a trip to Norway several years ago. In addition to the ingredients below, the chef added some sautéed chanterelles and garnished it with a few tart huckleberries.

Serves 4

2   cups sliced leeks, white part only
4   tablespoons unsalted butter
1   cup chicken, shellfish, or rich
    vegetable stock
2   tablespoons Dijon-style mustard
1¼ cups heavy cream
1   tablespoon grated lemon zest
    Kosher salt and freshly ground
    black pepper to taste

3   tablespoons chopped fresh dill
½   pound fiochetti or other dry
    bowtie pasta
⅓   pound smoked salmon, cut into
    wide strips
⅓   pound diced smoked mozzarella
    Garnish: Dill sprigs and fried
    capers (page 21), if desired

In a large skillet, slowly sauté the leeks in the butter until translucent but not brown, approximately 10 minutes. Set aside. In a saucepan, combine the stock, mustard, cream, and lemon zest and reduce over moderate heat to a light sauce consistency, approximately 8 to 10 minutes. Season with salt and pepper and stir in the fresh dill.

Meanwhile, cook the pasta in lightly salted boiling water until just al dente. Drain the pasta and toss with the sauce, leeks, salmon, and mozzarella. Serve immediately, garnished with dill sprigs and fried capers, if desired.

 Recommended wine: A complex, barrel-aged Sauvignon Blanc will provide smoky flavors and enough body to balance this dish, while the leeks and dill will accent the classic fresh herbal notes in the wine.

MAKING FRESH PASTA

Traditional Italian pasta is a combination of flour and eggs and nothing else. Marcella Hazan, in her excellent book *Marcella's Italian Kitchen*, makes the point succinctly: "Olive oil, salt, colorings, seasonings have no gastronomic reason for being in pasta. Some, such as olive oil, which makes the pasta slicker, are wholly undesirable and a detriment to good pasta."

Fresh flour is, of course, the most important ingredient in making good pasta. Depending on the region, Italians make pasta out of both soft "all-purpose" flour and hard wheat (durum) flour, also known as semolina. The durum has a higher gluten content, which is desirable when making pasta with a machine. Different flours produce different flavors and textures in the pasta, so you might try both types and decide which you like better.

Being a little less of a purist than Marcella, I love experimenting with fresh herbs and other seasonings in pasta to add some highlights. I do agree, however, that it is easy to get carried away. In a restaurant recently, I saw a fresh pasta described as "squid ink pasta made with lemon grass, coriander, and hot chile"— and that didn't include the sauce! More is not always better.

Basic Pasta

Yields approximately 1 pound of pasta, serving 4

**2 cups unbleached all-purpose flour
    or durum semolina flour**
	**3 large eggs
	    Drops of water as needed**

Food processor method: Place the flour in the bowl of the food processor. With the motor running, add the eggs, one at a time. Continue processing for 10 seconds after the last egg has been added. Add drops of water if the dough seems too dry. Turn out onto a lightly floured work surface and knead for 6 to 8 minutes or until the dough is smooth and satiny and springs back when pressed with a finger.

Hand-mix method: Place the flour in a mound on a clean work surface. Form a well in the center and break the eggs into the well. Mix the eggs with a fork. Pulling from the sides of the well, gradually incorporate the flour into the eggs. Continue to mix until the dough forms a ball, adding drops of water as necessary. Begin kneading the dough, pushing the dough with the heel of your hand. Knead until soft and satiny. Most important, the dough should spring back when poked with your finger. This will take 10 to 15 minutes of continuous kneading.

Divide the dough into 4 pieces, wrap in plastic wrap, and refrigerate for at least 45 minutes. The dough may also be frozen at this point; thaw in the refrigerator before proceeding.

Roll out by hand or with a hand-cranked pasta machine, according to the manufacturer's directions.

Spinach-Basil Pasta

3 cups lightly packed spinach leaves	2 cups unbleached all-purpose flour
1 cup lightly packed basil leaves	2 large eggs

In a saucepan of lightly salted boiling water, blanch the spinach and basil 5 seconds. Remove and immediately plunge into ice water to set the color. Drain, pat dry, and then squeeze in a towel to remove any excess liquid. Chop very fine and add as the eggs are incorporated into the flour. Proceed as directed above.

Carrot-Sage Pasta

¼ cup fresh carrot purée or juice	2 cups unbleached all-purpose flour
2 teaspoons minced fresh sage	2 large eggs

Add the carrot purée or juice and minced sage to the eggs as they are incorporated into the flour. Proceed as directed above.

Gremolata Pasta

2 teaspoons finely grated lemon zest	2 cups unbleached all-purpose flour
1 tablespoon finely minced garlic	
1 tablespoon finely minced fresh parsley	2 large eggs

Add the zest, garlic, and parsley to the eggs as they are incorporated into the flour. Proceed as directed above.

Saffron–White Wine Pasta

¼ cup dry white wine	2¼ cups unbleached all-purpose flour
¼ cup water	
1 teaspoon crumbled saffron threads	2 large eggs

In a small saucepan, combine the wine, water, and saffron. Bring to a boil. Remove from the heat and let cool. Add the mixture to the eggs as they are incorporated into the flour mixture. Proceed as directed above.

Fettuccine with Fresh and Sun-Dried Tomatoes

This is the simplest of summer pastas and is meant to be served at room temperature. It is best if you can use several varieties of ripe tomatoes. I am blessed to be able to work from the Valley Oaks garden, where we have over a hundred varieties of tomatoes. Many of these tomatoes are scarce heirloom varieties for which garden director Jeff Dawson is the "keeper of the seed." You can cook the pasta and make the rest of the dish ahead of time, if you like, but wait until the last minute to toss the pasta with the tomato mixture.

Serves 4

1 pound fresh Gremolata Pasta, cut into fettuccine (page 107)	1 teaspoon grated lemon zest
½ cup extra-virgin olive oil	1 tablespoon balsamic vinegar (or to taste)
¼ cup slivered shallots or red onion	Kosher salt and freshly ground black pepper
1 tablespoon roasted garlic (page 247)	½ cup freshly grated Parmesan, Asiago, or pecorino
2½ cups seeded and diced fresh tomatoes, several varieties if possible	Garnish: A drizzle of basil oil (page 68) and basil sprig
½ cup slivered fresh basil	
⅓ cup slivered oil-packed sun-dried tomatoes	

Cook the pasta in lightly salted boiling water until just al dente, about 3 to 4 minutes if fresh. Drain and immediately run cold water over to stop the cooking. Drain again and toss with 2 tablespoons of the olive oil to prevent the pasta from sticking.

Warm the remaining olive oil in a pan, add the shallots and garlic, and sauté for 3 minutes. Remove from heat and cool. Combine the oil, shallots, and garlic with the remaining ingredients, except the cheese. Season with salt and pepper and toss with the pasta. Serve in bowls, sprinkled with freshly grated cheese, a drizzle of basil oil around, and a basil sprig.

Recommended wine: A lighter-style Cabernet or Merlot would add a rich note to this dish.

SUN-DRIED TOMATOES

Sun-dried tomatoes are an Old World delicacy that have found their definitive place in wine country cuisine due to their sweet, tangy taste and their ability to enliven many dishes.

When the tomato was introduced in Europe during the fifteenth and sixteenth centuries, its sour taste perplexed Europeans. As tomatoes became more and more accepted, new uses were created. Like most fruit crops, tomatoes tend to ripen within a brief period and provide more bounty than can be used at once. Accordingly, the sun-dried tomato was developed as a means of preservation. High in the sun-drenched hills of Liguria in Italy, surplus Roma tomatoes (selected for their meatiness and low moisture) were sprinkled with salt and placed on shaded cane beds to dry naturally. They were then marinated in extravirgin olive oil and herbs. Ligurian sun-dried tomatoes continue to this day to be among the best produced.

The oven is the easiest way to make your own dried tomatoes unless you have flow-through wire trays and constant daytime temperatures of 80 degrees. Stem the tomatoes and cut them in half lengthwise. Using your fingers, squeeze out the seeds and juice. Spread the halves on a cake rack, cut side up, and sprinkle with kosher salt. Place in a 200-degree oven for about 8 hours or overnight. They should be pliable and leathery, not crisp.

Store dried tomatoes, wrapped in plastic wrap, in your refrigerator or place in a jar and cover with good olive oil and a few sprigs of your favorite herbs.

 Curried Sweet Potato Ravioli

The sweet potato filling used here has a myriad of other uses: by itself as a garnish for roasted meats, as a filling in deep-fried wontons, or as a soup base, thinned with stock and cream to make a lovely soup. I particularly like it in these ravioli, which are served here in a simple stock; they could also be tossed with fresh herb butter and a little grated Parmesan or pecorino.

Makes 24 to 30 ravioli, serving 4 to 6

2 pounds sweet potatoes
⅓ cup minced shallots
2 teaspoons high-quality curry
     powder (page 87)
3 tablespoons unsalted butter
½ cup dry white wine
½ cup heavy cream
1 tablespoon *each* chopped fresh
     parsley and chives

1 teaspoon minced fresh mint
     Kosher salt and fresh ground
       black pepper
1 pound fresh pasta sheets
     (page 106)
2 cups hot rich chicken stock
     (page 52)

Roast the whole sweet potatoes in a 375-degree oven until soft, about 1 hour. Cool and remove the skins. With a potato masher or food mill (don't use a food processor) mash the potatoes and set aside. You should have about 2 cups.

In a saucepan, sauté the shallots and curry powder in the butter until the shallots are soft but not brown and the curry is fragrant. Add the wine, bring to a boil, and reduce the liquid by half. Add the mashed sweet potato and cream. Stir to combine thoroughly and heat the mixture through. Remove from the heat and stir in the parsley, chives, and mint; season to taste with salt and pepper. Cool.

Cut the pasta sheets into strips about 4 inches wide. Place a row of rounded tablespoonfuls of potato mixture along the bottom half of the long pasta strip at 1-inch intervals. Fold the top half of the strip over to enclose the filling. Cut the ravioli with a knife, or a fluted cutter if you have one. Seal the dough around the filling by pressing gently with your finger to expel any air. If the dough is very fresh, it should stick to itself easily. If the dough has dried out at all, paint a little water around the filling and then seal. (Ravioli can be made ahead and stored, frozen, for up to 2 months. Defrost in the refrigerator before proceeding.)

To serve: Place the ravioli in lightly salted boiling water and simmer until they begin to float, approximately 3 to 4 minutes. Remove the ravioli carefully with a slotted spoon and divide among warm soup bowls. Ladle in enough hot stock just to moisten the ravioli and serve immediately.

Recommended wine: The heat from the curry is softened and rounded with a fruity white wine such as Riesling or Chenin Blanc.

Eggplant–Goat Cheese Ravioli

Grilled eggplant and goat cheese are one of my favorite flavor combinations. Use any fresh goat cheese you can find, but be on the lookout for those wonderful cheeses from Laura Chenel, Bodega Goat Cheese, or Redwood Hill Farms (pages 401–402). I've suggested two different sauces. Go all out and serve the ravioli with both.

Makes 30 ravioli, serving 6

1   **3-pound globe eggplant, cut into ¾-inch-thick rounds**
4   **tablespoons olive oil**
    Salt and freshly ground black pepper
1   **cup chopped shallots or scallions**
2   **tablespoons chopped garlic**
1   **cup fresh goat cheese, crumbled**
1   **cup freshly grated Parmesan cheese**
½   **cup finely chopped toasted walnuts**

3   **tablespoons finely chopped fresh basil**
1   **teaspoon freshly ground black pepper**
2   **tablespoons finely chopped fresh sage**
1   **pound fresh pasta, rolled into thin sheets (page 106)**
    Creamy Tomato Sauce (page 116) or Warm Basil Cream (page 147)
    Garnish: Shaved Parmesan and fresh basil leaves cut in fine chiffonade

Paint the eggplant rounds on both sides with 2 tablespoons of the olive oil. Lightly season with salt and pepper and grill or broil until lightly browned and softened. Finely chop and set aside in a bowl.

Sauté the shallots and garlic in the remaining 2 tablespoons olive oil until soft but not brown. Remove from heat and toss the shallot mixture with the eggplant, goat cheese, Parmesan, walnuts, basil, 1 teaspoon black pepper, and the sage. Season to taste with salt.

Cut the pasta sheets into strips about 4 inches wide. Place a row of rounded tablespoonfuls of the eggplant-cheese mixture along the bottom half of each pasta strip at 1-inch intervals. Fold the top half of the strip over to enclose the filling. Cut the ravioli apart using a knife, or a fluted cutter if you have one. Seal the ravioli around the filling by pressing gently with your finger to expel any air. Make sure the dough is well sealed. If the dough is very fresh, it should stick to itself easily. If the dough has dried out at all, paint a little water around the filling and then seal. (Ravioli can be made ahead and stored, frozen, for up to 2 months. Defrost in the refrigerator before proceeding.)

To serve: Place the ravioli in lightly salted boiling water and simmer until the ravioli begin to float, approximately 3 to 4 minutes. Drain and serve with melted butter or with either (or both!) of the suggested sauces. To do this, drizzle both sauces decoratively around the ravioli. Garnish with shaved Parmesan and basil chiffonade and serve immediately.

 Recommended wine: A light red wine, such as a Gamay or Chianti, works well with this dish; for contrast try a fresh, clean Fumé/Sauvignon Blanc with little or no oak. In fact, try a glass of both.

 ## Lobster and Fennel Lasagne with Shiitake Cream Sauce

This dish takes a bit of labor but is well worth the effort. It's beautiful to look at, and the marriage of lobster and fennel is one made in heaven!
Serves 4

2 2½-pound live lobsters	½ cup minced Niçoise olives
5 tablespoons olive oil	1 teaspoon roasted garlic
3 cups finely sliced fennel bulb (tops reserved for garnish)	½ pound fresh pasta (page 106), rolled into sheets with a hand-crank pasta machine and cut into 16 3-inch squares
Salt and freshly ground black pepper	
½ cup minced red onions	Shiitake Cream Sauce (recipe follows)
3 cups seeded and chopped ripe tomatoes	Garnish: Fresh fennel sprigs and chopped chives
2 teaspoons fresh tarragon (or 1 teaspoon dried)	
1 cup finely diced shiitake mushroom caps (stems reserved for sauce)	

Steam or boil the lobsters until done, approximately 12 to 15 minutes. Be sure not to overcook. When the lobsters are cool enough to handle, remove the meat from the tail and claws and slice thinly. Set aside.

Heat 2 tablespoons of the oil in a skillet and sauté the fennel over moderate heat until tender, approximately 2 to 3 minutes. Season to taste with salt and pepper, remove with a slotted spoon, and set aside.

Add 1 tablespoon of the oil to the pan with the onions and sauté until soft but not brown. Add the tomatoes and tarragon and cook until the liquid is mostly evaporated. Season lightly with salt and pepper, remove, and set aside.

Add 1 tablespoon of the oil to the pan and sauté the shiitakes until tender. Combine with the olives and roasted garlic and set aside.

Cook the pasta squares in a pot of lightly salted boiling water until just al dente, about 2 to 3 minutes. Drain and rinse under cold water to stop the cooking and coat with the remaining 1 tablespoon olive oil.

To assemble: Preheat the oven to 350 degrees. Arrange a square of pasta in the center of each of 4 ovenproof plates. Divide the fennel evenly on top of the squares along with half of the slices of the lobster. Top with another pasta square and spread with some of the tomato mixture. Top with the remaining slices of the lobster. Add the third pasta square and spread with some of the shiitake-olive mixture. Top with the fourth pasta square. Cover with foil and heat for 8 to 10 minutes or until just heated through. Spoon the Shiitake Cream Sauce over the little lasagnes and garnish with fennel sprigs and chopped chives.

Shiitake Cream Sauce

3 tablespoons unsalted butter	1 cup rich fish stock
¼ cup minced shallots or scallions	½ cup heavy cream
¼ cup chopped mushroom stems (from shiitakes above)	Kosher salt and freshly ground black pepper
1 cup dry white wine	

Melt 1 tablespoon of the butter in a saucepan and sauté the shallots and mushrooms over medium heat until lightly colored. Add the wine and stock and reduce by half. Add the cream and simmer until reduced to the consistency of a light sauce. Whisk in the remaining 2 tablespoons butter, season to taste with salt and pepper, and strain. The sauce can be made ahead and kept warm (110 degrees) off the heat for up to 2 hours. (A thermos is best.)

Recommended wine: A rich, barrel-aged Chardonnay is the perfect companion for this wonderful, decadent dish.

Tonnarelli with Dungeness Crab Sauce

This very rich dish comes from the wrong end of the nutrition pyramid, but it's a worthwhile treat when fresh Dungeness crab is available. To lighten (or at least brighten) it up, I often add some crisply cooked sugar snap or snow peas. Tonnarelli refers to a flat, irregularly cut (but essentially square) pasta. You can use any pasta shape you like.

Serves 4

1	pound fresh pasta (page 106), rolled into sheets		Kosher salt, cayenne pepper, and dry sherry
4	tablespoons olive oil	2	tablespoons chilled unsalted butter, cut in small dice
¼	cup minced shallots or scallions	1	pound fresh Dungeness crabmeat (or thawed if frozen), coarsely shredded
2	teaspoons minced garlic		
¾	cup dry white wine	3	tablespoons chopped chives
1½	cups rich shellfish stock	1	teaspoon grated lemon zest
1	cup heavy cream	½	cup seeded and slivered firm ripe tomato
1	tablespoon tomato paste		
¼	pound shiitake mushrooms, cut into ¼-inch dice		

Cut the pasta sheets into 1-inch squares. Loosely cover with waxed paper and set aside.

In a large saucepan, heat 2 tablespoons of the olive oil and sauté the shallots and garlic over moderate heat until soft but not brown. Add the wine and stock and bring to a boil, reducing the liquid by half. Add the cream and tomato paste and return to a boil. Lower heat and simmer, uncovered, for 5 minutes to reduce to a light sauce consistency.

In a separate sauté pan over high heat, sauté the mushrooms in the remaining 2 tablespoons olive oil until browned; remove from the heat and set aside.

Season the sauce to taste with salt, cayenne pepper, and drops of sherry. Whisk in the cold butter to form a smooth sauce. Add the crabmeat, chives, lemon zest, and sautéed mushrooms. Keep warm.

To serve: Cook the pasta in lightly salted boiling water until just al dente, 3 to 4 minutes if fresh. Drain and gently toss with the crab sauce and tomato. Spoon into warm bowls and serve immediately.

Recommended wine: A barrel-aged Chardonnay is a great complement to this luscious dish. Be sure the wine has some forward acidity and citrus notes to help cut through the richness of the sauce.

Shrimp and Fresh Herb Spaetzle with Creamy Tomato Sauce

Spaetzle is a staple in German-Austrian cooking. Because of its national origins we don't think of it as a pasta, but it certainly is a member of the pasta family. Spaetzle is traditionally made with only flour or with a flour and potato mixture; it is poached and then sautéed. Jim Rhodes, one of the talented chefs at Valley Oaks, and I created this dish to use an excess of shrimp we had one day. We've also made it with a combination of shrimp, scallops, and smoked salmon. Okay, it's not a low-fat dish, but the delicious spaetzle could also be served in a fish or shellfish stock as a lighter alternative.

Serves 4 to 6

½   **pound peeled and deveined shrimp**
¾   **cup heavy cream**
1   **cup flour**
2   **egg yolks**
2   **tablespoons mixed chopped herbs such as parsley, basil, and chives Kosher salt and freshly ground black pepper**

3   **tablespoons clarified unsalted butter or canola oil**
    Creamy Tomato Sauce (recipe follows)
    Garnish: Basil-mint oil (page 68), seeded, diced tomatoes, chopped fresh parsley

Purée the raw shrimp in a food processor. Add the cream and purée until smooth. In a bowl, combine the purée with the flour, egg yolks, herbs, salt, and pepper to make a smooth batter. (The batter should be the consistency of a very stiff pancake batter. Add a bit of water, if necessary, to achieve this consistency.)

Over a pot of lightly salted boiling water, force the batter through the holes of a colander and into the water. Cook for 2 to 3 minutes or until the spaetzle floats to the surface. Drain and cool immediately under cold running water. Drain again. (The spaetzle can be made ahead to this point. Toss with a few drops of olive oil and store, covered and refrigerated, for up to 24 hours.)

When ready to finish the dish, sauté the spaetzle in clarified butter until lightly browned and crispy. Drain on paper towels and keep warm.

To serve: Spoon Creamy Tomato Sauce onto plates and distribute the spaetzle on top. Drizzle basil-mint oil, if desired, around the perimeter of the plate and sprinkle the diced tomatoes and chopped parsley on top. Serve immediately.

Creamy Tomato Sauce

Makes about 3 cups

2	tablespoons olive oil	1	teaspoon minced fresh
1½	cups minced red onions		rosemary
½	cup dry white wine	½	cup heavy cream
1¼	cups rich shellfish stock		Kosher salt and freshly ground
1	28-ounce can Italian plum		black pepper
	tomatoes, drained and sliced		

Combine the olive oil and onions in a saucepan and sauté until just beginning to color. Add the wine, stock, tomatoes, and rosemary, and cook over moderately high heat for 5 to 6 minutes to reduce slightly. Strain the sauce. Return to the pan, add the cream, and reduce to a light sauce consistency. Season to taste with salt and pepper. Can be made up to 2 hours ahead of time. Cover and keep warm. (A thermos is best.)

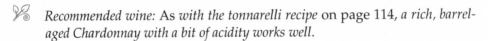

Recommended wine: As *with the tonnarelli recipe* on page 114, *a rich, barrel-aged Chardonnay with a bit of acidity works well.*

Ricotta-Herb Gnocchi with Two Sauces

I love gnocchi because they are easy to prepare and can be made well ahead of time and then frozen. This dish uses two sauces: a rich wild mushroom cream and a refreshing spinach–arugula pesto for balance. Try these gnocchi with any of the other savory pasta sauces—they'll be delicious too!

Serves 4 to 6

1	pound fresh whole-milk ricotta,	4	tablespoons mixed finely minced
	drained (page 333)		fresh herbs, such as tarragon,
⅓	cup unbleached flour		chives, chervil
½	teaspoon freshly ground white	½	teaspoon ground fennel seed
	pepper	½	teaspoon salt

Large pinch freshly grated
  nutmeg
2 tablespoons kosher salt
  Wild Mushroom Cream (recipe
  follows)

Spinach-Arugula Pesto (recipe
  follows)
Garnish: Chive flowers and fresh
  herb sprigs

In a food processor, combine the ricotta, flour, white pepper, herbs, fennel seed, salt, and nutmeg. Process until combined. Or you can knead by hand 4 to 5 minutes, or until very smooth. The dough should be somewhat sticky. (If it is too sticky, add a little bit of flour, but be careful about adding too much or the gnocchi may become heavy.)

Divide the dough into egg-size portions and roll into logs about ½ inch thick. With a sharp knife, cut the logs into ¾-inch pieces. (If you'd like, you can roll the pieces up the back of a fork to create the traditional ridged surface.) Place the gnocchi on floured waxed paper on a baking sheet. Refrigerate, uncovered, for at least 30 minutes. (The gnocchi may also be frozen at this point; freeze in a single layer on the baking sheet until hard and then store in tightly closed plastic bags.)

Bring 4 quarts water to a gentle boil, adding 2 tablespoons kosher salt. Carefully place all the gnocchi in the water, in batches if necessary, and simmer until they rise to the surface, about 2 to 3 minutes. Cook 30 seconds longer and then remove with a slotted spoon and drain. If desired, the gnocchi may be made up to 2 hours in advance to this point; rinse them in cold water and toss gently with a little olive oil to prevent sticking. Reheat with a little olive oil in a sauté pan or a hot oven, until hot throughout.

To serve: Gently combine the gnocchi with the Wild Mushroom Cream and place on warm plates. Drizzle Spinach-Arugula Pesto over the top. Garnish with chive flowers and herb sprigs.

Wild Mushroom Cream

Makes about 2 cups

½ ounce dried morels or porcini
    mushrooms
1 cup minced fresh shiitake or other
    wild mushrooms
2 tablespoons olive oil
3 tablespoons minced shallots

½ cup dry white wine
1½ cups heavy cream
1 tablespoon minced fresh parsley
1 tablespoon Dijon-style mustard
  Salt and freshly ground black
    pepper

Soak morels or porcini in 1 cup warm water until softened, swishing around occasionally to dislodge any sand. Remove the mushrooms, carefully strain the soaking liquid through a paper coffee filter or a cheesecloth-lined sieve to remove any sand, and reserve the liquid. Slice the mushrooms thinly and set aside with the fresh wild mushrooms.

In a saucepan, heat the olive oil and sauté the shallots until very lightly colored. Add all the mushrooms and sauté 3 minutes longer. Add the wine and reserved soaking liquid and reduce the liquid over moderately high heat for 5 minutes. Add the cream and reduce to a light sauce consistency. Stir in the parsley, mustard, and salt and pepper to taste and keep warm.

Spinach-Arugula Pesto

Makes about 2 cups

2 tablespoons toasted, skinned, and chopped hazelnuts	3 tablespoons freshly grated Parmesan cheese
1½ cups packed spinach leaves	½ cup olive oil
1½ cups packed arugula leaves (or extra 1½ cups spinach)	Chicken or vegetable stock
	Salt and freshly ground black pepper

In a food processor or blender, process until smooth all of the ingredients except the stock and salt and pepper. Add stock to reach the desired consistency. Season to taste.

 Recommended wine: The earthy notes of Pinot Noir are magical with the flavors of the Wild Mushroom Cream. A barrel-aged Chardonnay works well as a white wine alternative.

DRAINING RICOTTA

Draining ricotta rids the cheese of excess water, undesirable in a recipe like this.

To drain ricotta, simply scoop it into a superfine-mesh sieve or into a colander or sieve lined with a double thickness of well-rinsed cheesecloth. Suspend the sieve over a bowl and refrigerate at least 6 hours or overnight, stirring at least 2 or 3 times.

Gratin of Prosciutto and Chard Gnocchi with Tomato-Eggplant Sauce

This is a great make-ahead dish: You can prepare the gnocchi and sauce the day before serving, then finish at the last moment under the broiler.

Serves 6

2 pounds Swiss chard, center stems removed	½ teaspoon freshly grated nutmeg
	Kosher salt and freshly ground
2 tablespoons olive oil	black pepper
2 tablespoons chopped fresh basil (or 1 teaspoon dried)	3 tablespoons melted unsalted butter
2 cups whole-milk ricotta	¼ cup fresh breadcrumbs
1¼ cups freshly grated Parmesan, Asiago, or pecorino cheese	2 teaspoons grated lemon zest
	Tomato-Eggplant Sauce (recipe follows)
⅔ cup chopped prosciutto	Garnish: Fresh basil sprigs and
2 egg yolks, lightly beaten	basil-mint oil (page 68), if
6 tablespoons flour	desired

Chop the chard roughly and sauté in the olive oil over moderate heat for 3 to 4 minutes, or until completely wilted. (You should have approximately 2 cups.)

In a bowl, combine the chard, basil, ricotta, ¾ cup of the Parmesan, and the prosciutto. Add the egg yolks, 4 tablespoons of the flour, the nutmeg, and salt and pepper to taste. Mix with a fork until well combined. (The mixture will be very soft and sticky.)

Flour your hands generously with the remaining flour and form the mixture into small logs, approximately 1½ inches long and ½ inch wide. Place on a floured baking sheet and refrigerate, uncovered, for at least 30 minutes. (The gnocchi may also be frozen at this point; freeze in a single layer on the baking sheet until hard and then store in tightly closed plastic bags.)

Working in batches, if necessary, carefully place the gnocchi into lightly salted simmering water. Gently cook the gnocchi for 2 to 3 minutes or until they rise to the surface. With a slotted spoon, transfer them to a lightly buttered oven-proof gratin dish large enough to hold the gnocchi in one layer. Paint with the remaining melted butter. Mix the remaining ¾ cup Parmesan with the breadcrumbs and lemon zest and sprinkle evenly over the buttered gnocchi.

To serve: Place the gnocchi under a preheated broiler, about 3 inches from the heat, and lightly brown. Spoon the Tomato-Eggplant Sauce onto warm plates and place the hot gnocchi on top. Serve immediately, garnished with fresh basil sprigs and a drizzle of basil-mint oil decoratively around.

Tomato-Eggplant Sauce

1¼ pounds eggplant, trimmed
2   tablespoons olive oil plus more
        for brushing the eggplant
    Kosher salt and freshly ground
        black pepper
1½ cups minced onions
1   tablespoon minced garlic
½   cup finely diced cremini or
        shiitake mushrooms

½   cup dry white wine
1   35-ounce can plum tomatoes
1   cup rich chicken stock or
        mushroom stock (page 57)
2   teaspoons dried oregano
1   teaspoon fennel seed
¼   teaspoon red chile flakes
    Balsamic vinegar

Preheat the oven to 400 degrees. Slice the eggplant lengthwise into ½-inch thick slices, paint lightly with olive oil, and season both sides with salt and pepper. Place in a single layer on a baking sheet and roast for 10 to 12 minutes or until soft and lightly browned. Set aside.

In a saucepan, heat 2 tablespoons olive oil and sauté the onions, garlic, and mushrooms until they just begin to color. Add the wine, tomatoes, stock, oregano, fennel seed, and chile flakes and simmer for 15 minutes, stirring occasionally to break up the tomatoes. Dice the roasted eggplant, leaving the skin on, and add to the sauce. Season to taste with salt and pepper and drops of balsamic vinegar. You can also purée the mixture at this point to make a smooth sauce, if you prefer. The sauce can be stored, covered in the refrigerator, for 1 day.

 Recommended wine: This dish calls out for an Italian red wine. A Bandolino will have both the subtle herbal notes and smoky flavors to accent this complex dish.

Pizza

Good pizza, like good pasta, depends on a good dough. I have included two variations on pizza dough, and I like both for the different qualities of the crusts they make. Basic Pizza Dough results in a plain, thin, crisp crust, making it a good foil for more elaborate toppings. The Pizza Dough with Sun-Dried Tomatoes and Herbs creates a crust that is a bit thicker and, because it includes lots of flavorful ingredients, is best suited to simple toppings such as a scattering of freshly grilled vegetables or garden-ripe tomatoes with a drizzle of fresh pesto. Both pizza doughs can be made ahead of time and stored, wrapped in plastic, for a day or two in the refrigerator or up to a month in the freezer. If frozen, defrost overnight in the refrigerator before using. Following the dough recipes, I've included a few of my favorite pizza toppings.

At its simplest (which is often when it's best), a pizza needs only a topping of a simple tomato sauce, a few roasted or grilled vegetables, and just a little cheese to make it fantastic. Included below is a recipe for a simple pizza sauce, which of course can also be used with pasta or as a topping for grilled meats or fish. I also love a fresh pizza dough spread with a generous layer of one of the several pestos in this book and topped with a scattering of good olives. This can be done quickly, especially if you've made the pizza dough ahead of time and have it available from the freezer.

 Basic Pizza Dough

Makes 1 14-inch or 2 8- to 10-inch pizzas

¼   cup warm water (110 degrees)
2   teaspoons active dry yeast
2   tablespoons olive oil
¼   cup coarse rye or whole-wheat flour
1¾ cups all-purpose flour, plus additional as needed

1   teaspoon salt
½   cup warm water
    Coarse cornmeal for sprinkling on pan

In a small bowl, sprinkle the yeast over ¼ cup of the warm water and let sit 8 to 10 minutes or until foamy. In a food processor with the plastic or metal blade, an electric mixer fitted with the dough hook, or by hand, combine the yeast mixture, 1 tablespoon olive oil, rye flour, 1¾ cups of the all-purpose flour, salt, and remaining ½ cup water. Mix until the dough forms a ball. If the dough is very sticky, add a little extra flour. Continue to knead for about 1 minute in the food processor, about 3 minutes in the electric mixer, or about 4 to 5 minutes by hand, until the dough is smooth and satiny.

Smear a large bowl with the remaining tablespoon of olive oil. Place the dough in the bowl and turn it to coat with oil. Cover with plastic wrap and let the dough rise in a warm place until it has doubled, 1 to 2 hours. Lightly flour a board and roll the dough out into a 14-inch circle. Sprinkle cornmeal on a pizza pan or cookie sheet and place the dough on it. Cover with a towel and allow to rest for 30 minutes.

Top the pizza and bake in a preheated 475-degree oven on the top rack for 10 to 12 minutes or until the dough is nicely browned and the topping is hot.

 ## *Pizza Dough with Sun-Dried Tomatoes and Herbs*

Makes 1 14-inch or 2 8- to 10-inch pizzas

1 cup lukewarm water
2 teaspoons active dry yeast
1 teaspoon sugar
2 tablespoons chopped fresh mixed herbs, such as basil, thyme, oregano, parsley, and chives, or just one of your favorites
2 tablespoons minced sun-dried tomatoes

¼ cup plus 1 tablespoon extra-virgin olive oil
2 teaspoons kosher salt
3 cups all-purpose flour plus additional flour for kneading
   Coarse cornmeal for sprinkling on pan

Pour the warm water into a bowl, sprinkle the yeast into the water, then sprinkle the sugar onto the yeast. Stir and let this mixture sit for 8 to 10 minutes or until foamy.

Pour the yeast mixture into a food processor fitted with the plastic blade. Add the herbs, tomatoes, ¼ cup of the olive oil, salt, and 3 cups flour. Process in short bursts until the mixture forms a ball. Or mix the ingredients by hand.

Remove the dough from the food processor and knead on a lightly floured surface until smooth and elastic. The time will vary depending on the method used to make the dough. (Hand-mixed dough may need more kneading.) If the dough is very sticky, use a little extra flour.

Smear a large bowl with the remaining 1 tablespoon olive oil. Place the dough in the bowl and roll it around to coat with oil. Cover with plastic wrap and let the dough rise in a warm place until it has doubled, 1 to 2 hours. Lightly flour a board and roll the dough out into a 14-inch circle. Sprinkle cornmeal on a pizza pan or cookie sheet and place the dough on it. Cover with a towel and allow to rest for 30 minutes. Scatter desired topping over pizza. Bake in a preheated 475-degree oven on the top rack for about 20 minutes or until the crust is golden brown and well puffed.

Simple Pizza Sauce

Makes about 4 cups

4 cups canned plum tomatoes in
    heavy purée
2 tablespoons extra-virgin olive oil
2 tablespoons thinly slivered garlic
¼ teaspoon red chile flakes (or to taste)

¼ cup loosely packed fresh basil
    leaves, coarsely chopped
Salt and freshly ground black
    pepper

In a food processor, pulse the tomatoes briefly 2 or 3 times to coarsely chop. Or do it by hand. Set aside.

Heat the olive oil in a skillet and sauté the garlic and chile flakes over moderate heat until the garlic is softened but not brown. Add the tomatoes and basil, bring to a simmer, and cook for 3 to 5 minutes or until lightly thickened. Correct seasoning with salt and pepper. Store covered in the refrigerator for up to 7 days or frozen indefinitely.

Blue Cheese and Caramelized Onions with Sage

Enough topping for 1 16-inch pizza or 2 10-inch pizzas

1 recipe Pizza Dough with Sun-
    Dried Tomatoes and Herbs
    (page 122)
3 tablespoons olive oil
1½ pounds thinly sliced yellow
    onions

Kosher salt and freshly ground
    black pepper
¾ pound Bavarian Blue, sweet
    Gorgonzola, or other creamy
    blue cheese, crumbled
⅓ cup fresh sage leaves

Prepare the pizza dough. Preheat the oven to 475 degrees.

To a deep, heavy-bottomed pan, add olive oil and onions and slowly sauté until onions are golden brown, stirring regularly to prevent burning. This may take 20 minutes or more to completely brown the onions. Season with salt and pepper.

Scatter the onions evenly over the top of the prepared dough. Scatter the blue cheese and sage leaves on top. Bake the pizza, preferably on the top rack, for about 20 minutes or until the dough is puffed, golden, and cooked through.

 Recommended wine: A Petite Sirah or Zinfandel with bright, jammy, berry notes would be heaven with this decadent pizza.

Potato, Red Onion, Arugula, and Brie

Enough topping for 1 16-inch or 2 10-inch pizzas

1 recipe Basic Pizza Dough (page 121)	¾ pound red potatoes, scrubbed
1 cup sliced red onions	¼ cup grated Parmesan
Kosher salt and freshly ground black pepper	6 ounces Brie, thinly sliced
	1 cup loosely packed arugula leaves
1 tablespoon olive oil	⅔ cup finely diced red bell peppers

Prepare the pizza dough. Preheat the oven to 475 degrees.

Season the onion slices lightly with salt and pepper and sauté in the olive oil until crisp-tender. Set aside.

Thinly slice the potatoes and blanch in lightly salted boiling water until just tender, about 5 minutes. Cool in ice water to stop the cooking, drain, and pat dry.

Sprinkle the dough with the Parmesan. Layer the potatoes evenly on top, followed by the slices of Brie and the onions. Season with salt and pepper.

Bake the pizza for 10 to 12 minutes on the top rack. Scatter the arugula and red peppers on top and slice and serve immediately.

 Recommended wine: Brie is great with lush red wines such as Pinot Noir or Merlot.

Spicy Pork with Basil-Mint Pesto

This spicy pizza can be made with a variety of meats: I've done it with pork, lamb, and turkey. It is also delicious with chopped prawns or rock shrimp, which I suggest adding halfway through baking so they won't overcook. The Basil-Mint Pesto makes more than you'll want for one pizza; freeze the leftover sauce for another use.

Enough for 1 16-inch or 2 10-inch pizzas

1   recipe Basic Pizza Dough (page 121)

BASIL-MINT PESTO:

½   cup loosely packed mint leaves
¾   cup tightly packed basil leaves
3   tablespoons lightly toasted pine
     nuts
1   tablespoon roasted garlic
     (page 247)
½   cup olive oil
     Kosher salt and freshly ground
     black pepper

½   pound lean, freshly ground pork
¼   cup finely chopped red onion

1   teaspoon minced garlic
¼   teaspoon cayenne (or to taste)
½   teaspoon ground cumin
1   cup coarsely grated mozzarella
     cheese
⅓   cup slivered Kalamata, Niçoise,
     or other oil-cured black
     olives
⅓   cup crumbled feta cheese
     Garnish: ½ cup coarsely chopped
     fresh basil or mint

Prepare the pizza dough. Preheat the oven to 475 degrees.

In a blender or food processor, combine the mint, basil, pine nuts, and roasted garlic. With the machine running, slowly add the olive oil to make a smooth paste. Season to taste with salt and pepper. Reserve.

In a bowl, combine the pork with the onions, garlic, cayenne, and cumin. Spread the mozzarella evenly over the prepared dough. Crumbling the meat mixture, spread it evenly over the cheese. Top with some of the pesto and the olives. Bake the pizza on the top rack until the crust is brown and the cheese is melted, about 10 to 15 minutes. Just before removing the pizza from the oven, sprinkle with the feta. Serve immediately, garnished with the herbs.

 Recommended wine: A crisp, refreshing Fumé/Sauvignon Blanc is perfect with the lively flavors of mint and feta cheese in this pizza.

 # Double Olive and Peppers with Prosciutto

This is a perfect Sunday night pizza: full of flavor, great for the family, easy to prepare. It also makes for delicious appetizers, sliced in smaller pieces.

Enough for 1 16-inch pizza or 2 10-inch pizzas

1 recipe Basic Pizza Dough (page 121)	½ cup chopped oil-cured black olives
½ cup tomato sauce	¼ pound prosciutto, julienned
2 tablespoons tomato paste	½ cup freshly grated Parmesan cheese
½ pound mushrooms, thinly sliced	
1 red bell pepper, julienned	¼ cup chiffonade of fresh basil
½ cup sliced green olives	¼ teaspoon red chile flakes

Prepare the pizza dough. Preheat the oven to 475 degrees. Combine the tomato sauce and tomato paste and spread evenly over the dough. Distribute the mushrooms, pepper, olives, and prosciutto all over the top of the dough. Sprinkle the Parmesan, basil, and chile flakes evenly over the top. Bake for 10 to 20 minutes, depending on thickness of the crust.

 Recommended wine: Soft Italian red wines such as Chianti or Valpolicella are always great companions to pizza.

Risottos

If I had to choose only one food to live on, it would be rice. Although rice is an important agricultural crop in California, Americans are way behind the rest of the world in consumption. Happily, the popularity of rice has increased dramatically in recent years, due in great part to dishes like risotto. Following are four of my favorite risottos.

Anyone who can cook can make risotto. Marie Simmons in her insightful book *Rice the Amazing Grain* succinctly describes the process: "To make risotto the rice is first sautéed in fat and then simmering broth is added slowly while the mixture is stirred. The rice expands as it absorbs the broth, and the friction of the stirring softens the outside of the grain, forming a creamy almost sauce-like consistency. The center of the rice remains firm to the bite or al dente." That's all it takes. You can experiment with different broths and additions (vegetables, cheeses, bits of meat), but don't improvise with the process.

The key to good risotto is the right variety of rice. Classically, Italian Arborio or Vialone Nano are used, but you can make a wonderful risotto with California medium-grain rice. The primary differences between Italian and California rice are in the sturdiness of the grain and the price, since the Italian is much more expensive. California medium-grain rice is softer and not as sturdy as Italian Arborio. If you decide to use it, stir only occasionally and add the liquid in no more than three "doses," rather than a half cup at a time. If you stir California rice too much it becomes soft and mushy and loses the classic risotto bite.

Since making risotto typically takes 20 to 25 minutes of steady stirring, home cooks sometimes consider it impractical both for entertaining and for family dinners. A trick used in restaurants is to prepare the risotto in two stages: Cook it to the point where half of the liquid has been added; then spread the rice out as thinly as possible on a baking sheet to cool. It can keep this way for several hours at room temperature or covered and refrigerated for up to a day. To complete the risotto, return the rice to the pan and continue adding the remaining liquid in appropriate increments.

 Asparagus, Roasted Garlic, and Lemon Risotto

Risottos are quickly becoming a signature dish of the wine country, but with distinctly Italian roots. They are infinitely versatile, and I particularly like the addition of seasonal vegetables. Here, the asparagus must be very young and tender since it's added at the last minute and barely cooked.

Serves 6

4 tablespoons unsalted butter	**¼ cup freshly grated Parmesan or Asiago cheese**
¼ cup sliced shallots	
1½ cups Arborio rice	**2 teaspoons grated lemon zest**
¾ cup sliced shiitake mushrooms	**¾ cup diagonally sliced young asparagus, in ½-inch pieces**
1½ tablespoons roasted garlic (page 247)	**¼ cup minced fresh chives**
½ cup dry white wine	**Kosher salt and freshly ground black pepper**
5–6 cups rich vegetable or chicken stock, heated	**Garnish: Chopped fresh chives and shaved Parmesan cheese**

Melt 3 tablespoons of the butter in a medium saucepan and sauté the shallots over moderate heat until soft but not brown. Add the rice and shiitakes and sauté evenly until the rice is translucent, about 3 minutes.

Add the garlic, wine, and ½ cup of the hot stock and cook, stirring constantly, until the liquid is absorbed. Continue adding small amounts of stock and cooking in this manner until the rice is creamy but the center is firm, about 15 minutes.

When the risotto is done, stir in the remaining 1 tablespoon of butter, the cheese, lemon zest, asparagus, and chives, and season with salt and pepper. Serve in warm bowls garnished with chopped chives and shaved Parmesan.

Recommended wines: Asparagus has a reputation for not matching well with wine. The other elements in this dish, however, temper its tendency to make wine taste sweet. A crisp, clean Chardonnay without too much oak or a barrel-aged Fumé/Sauvignon Blanc could both work here.

Carrot Risotto

Carrots add a sweetness and beautiful orange color to this risotto. The addition of the lemon juice helps balance that sweetness. I have included an alternative version for the fun of it that uses fresh fennel and carrot juices in place of the vegetable stock.

Serves 6

3 tablespoons unsalted butter	1 tablespoon minced fresh marjoram
½ cup minced shallots	
1½ cups Arborio rice	½ cup freshly grated Parmesan cheese
½ cup dry white wine	
1½ cups grated carrots	2 tablespoons lemon juice (or to taste)
5–6 cups vegetable stock, heated	
2 tablespoons minced fresh parsley	Garnish: Sautéed wild mushrooms, such as Oyster Cinnamon Cap, or whatever is seasonally available in your market
2 tablespoons minced fresh tarragon	

Melt the butter in a medium saucepan and sauté the shallots over moderate heat until soft but not brown. Add the rice and sauté evenly until rice is translucent, about 3 minutes. Add the wine and stir over medium heat until it is absorbed. Stir in the grated carrots and begin adding the hot stock by ½-cup increments, stirring constantly. When each addition is absorbed, add the next ½ cup, until the stock is mostly (or all) incorporated and the risotto is creamy but not overcooked. Stir in the herbs and the Parmesan. Add the lemon juice to taste. Serve garnished with wild mushrooms, if desired.

For a richer wintertime version (and another use for your juicer): Substitute for 3½ cups of the vegetable broth (follow instructions for whatever juices you may have):

1¾ cups fresh carrot juice	1½ cups grated carrots, reserved till end of recipe
1¾ cups fresh fennel juice	

Combine the vegetable juices with 1½ to 2½ cups stock and heat to simmer. Proceed as above. Add the grated carrots at the end along with the herbs and Parmesan.

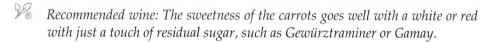   *Recommended wine: The sweetness of the carrots goes well with a white or red with just a touch of residual sugar, such as Gewürztraminer or Gamay.*

 # Sun-Dried Tomato and Olive Risotto

Jim Rhodes and I developed this risotto especially to go with young Cabernets and prove the point that a vegetable-based dish could match up with a lusty red wine.
Serves 6

5 tablespoons extra-virgin olive oil	¼ cup chopped Niçoise or other oil-cured black olives
1 cup finely minced yellow onion	
1 tablespoon minced garlic	1 tablespoon drained small capers
1½ cups Arborio rice	⅓ cup loosely packed mint leaves, chopped
1 cup dry white wine	
5–6 cups rich chicken or vegetable stock, heated	2 tablespoons chopped fresh parsley
¾ cup peeled, seeded, and diced plum tomatoes	1 cup freshly grated Parmesan cheese
⅓ cup slivered oil-packed sun-dried tomatoes, drained	Garnish: Mint sprigs

In a large saucepan over medium heat, heat the olive oil and sauté the onions and garlic until soft but not brown. Add the rice and sauté until it is translucent, about 3 minutes.

Add the wine and cook, stirring constantly, until the liquid is absorbed. Add the hot stock in ½-cup increments, stirring until the liquid is almost absorbed. After the last increment of stock has been absorbed and the risotto is creamy but not overcooked, add the fresh tomatoes, sun-dried tomatoes, olives, and capers. Finish by adding the mint, parsley, and Parmesan. Spoon into warm bowls and garnish with mint sprigs.

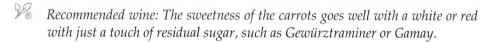   *Recommended wine: Cabernet, of course, is the choice to go with this dish. The mint in the dish is an important link to Cabernet, which often has a minty characteristic of its own.*

New World Risotto

"New World" in the title refers to the ingredients below that were indigenous to the Americas. Margaret Visser, in her book *Much Depends on Dinner*, notes how over and over again early explorers were amazed at the ingenuity and efficiency of Native American farmers. The Iroquois and other Eastern tribes would prepare the soil in mounds and plant corn. A few days later, in the same place, they would plant beans and squash. When the seedlings emerged from the mound of soil, the corn grew straight and strong, the beans climbed the corn, and the squash trailed down the side of the mound and covered the flat land between the mounds, keeping it shaded and moist. This recipe honors the kinship of these three ingredients and includes others from the New World larder.

Serves 6

4 tablespoons olive oil	½ cup husked and diced tomatillos
1 cup finely diced onions	¼ cup *each* diced red and yellow peppers
¼ cup slivered garlic	
1½ cups Arborio rice	½ cup green beans sliced into tiny rounds
2 teaspoons toasted cumin seed (page 36)	½ cup diced yellow summer squash
¼ teaspoon red chile flakes	½ cup freshly grated dry Jack or Parmesan cheese
½ cup dry white wine	
5–6 cups hot corn stock (page 56) or vegetable stock	¼ cup chopped fresh cilantro Kosher salt and freshly ground black pepper
2 cups fresh raw corn kernels, cut from the cob (about 3 large ears)	

In a deep saucepan over moderate heat, heat the olive oil and sauté the onions and garlic until soft but not brown. Add the rice and sauté, stirring, until the rice is translucent, about 3 minutes. Add the cumin seed and chile flakes.

Add the wine and cook, stirring constantly, until completely absorbed. Add the hot stock in ½-cup increments, stirring constantly until the liquid is almost absorbed. When the risotto is almost complete, add the corn, tomatillos, peppers, beans, and squash. Continue stirring and add the last of the stock, cooking until the vegetables are tender and the risotto is creamy but not overcooked. Stir in the cheese and cilantro and season to taste with salt and pepper. Spoon into warm bowls. I like to surround the risotto with a small ladleful of any leftover corn stock.

Recommended wine: A barrel-aged Chardonnay with good fruit is a great match for this dish, especially if you use the corn broth.

FISH AND SHELLFISH

Calamari Bruschetta with Tomatoes, Goat Cheese, and Mint   *133*

Scallop Seviche with Cilantro, Lime, and Serrano Chiles   *135*

Crab Wontons with Orange-Chipotle Sauce   *136*

Oysters on the Half Shell with Pickled Ginger Salsa   *137*

Barbecued Oysters with a Zesty Barbecue Sauce   *139*

Mussels Baked with Serrano Chiles and Fresh Mozzarella   *140*

Smoked Salmon Cheesecake with a Walnut Crust   *142*

Salmon Grilled in a Japanese Style   *143*

Grilled Salmon with Black Bean Salsa and Chipotle-Tangerine Vinaigrette   *144*

Grilled Salmon with Roasted White Corn Salsa and Warm Basil Cream   *146*

Salmon in a Fennel Crust with a Roasted Red Pepper–Blood Orange Vinaigrette   *148*

Salmon Cakes   *150*

Salmon Cured with Tequila and Herbs   *151*

Pacific Rock Cod Stewed with Oranges, Tomatoes, and Olives   *152*

Halibut Baked with Tomatoes, Capers, and Herbs with a Feta-Crumb Crust   *153*

Sturgeon with Pancetta, Capers, Parsley, and Lemon   *154*

Swordfish "Sandwiches" with Raisins, Herbs,
and Capers in a Fresh Tomato Broth   *155*

Fish Tacos with Citrus Salsa and Cabbage Slaw   *157*

Grilled Ahi Tuna with Japanese Noodles, Ginger-Soy Sauce,
and Wasabi Mousse   *159*

Seared Ahi Tuna with a Lavender-Pepper Crust   *160*

Ahi Tuna–Eggplant "Tarts"   *162*

Prawns Wrapped in Zucchini with a Red Pepper Aïoli   *163*

Marinated and Grilled Prawns with a Melon-Pineapple Salsa   *164*

Rock Shrimp Cakes with Salsa Cruda   *166*

Rock Shrimp Tamales with Four-Pepper Cream   *168*

Dungeness Crab in Wine and Vermouth   *171*

Shellfish in a Saffron-Scented Stock   *172*

Grilled Scallops with Fennel and a Lemon-Tarragon Vinaigrette   *173*

Seared Dayboat Scallops with Sautéed Apples and Vanilla-Scented Sauce   *175*

Fish and Wine

There is a wonderful affinity between wine and fish and shellfish. The delicate flavors of fish usually call for subtle white wines, but earthy ingredients—wild mushrooms, tomatoes, bay leaves, olives—and cooking techniques such as grilling can make fish and shellfish perfect with a red wine, too. Rich shellfish stews are another example of red wine–friendly fish dishes. In fact, most fish preparations that are "in the Mediterrean style" or influenced by Mediterranean cooking have an affinity for lighter style red wines. (A good discussion on this subject is Josh Wesson and David Rosengarten's book *Red Wine with Fish.*) I've been asked a few times what my "last meal" would be if I had a choice. There's no question—a piece of grilled wild king salmon and a glass of good California Pinot Noir.

A note on the recipes in this section (and throughout the book): You'll notice that many of the recipes contain marinades plus a sauce or two. Please don't be deterred by the length of some of the recipes. I've given you the elements that I like to assemble for the final dish, but the results will be (nearly!) as good if you choose to prepare only one or two of the elements. For example, the Grilled Salmon with Roasted White Corn Salsa and Warm Basil Cream is terrific unmarinated and accompanied with either the salsa or the basil cream.

 ## Calamari Bruschetta with Tomatoes, Goat Cheese, and Mint

Calamari, or squid, were historically a major fish resource for California, especially around the Monterey Bay. Overfishing, climate changes, and other factors have significantly reduced the squid population off the California coast.

In cooking calamari there is no in between. Either you cook them very briefly or simmer them for a long time. Anything in between results in a tough, chewy, and thoroughly uninteresting (not to say inedible) product. This recipe uses the fast-cook method. The recipe can also be done under a hot broiler if you don't want to fire up the grill, but the smoky flavor the grill adds is a real plus. This is also a wonderful mixture to use, without the toasts, on hot or cold pasta dishes.

Makes 12 to 16 individual toasts

⅓ cup plus up to 2 tablespoons extra-virgin olive oil

3 tablespoons fresh lemon juice

3 tablespoons chopped fresh basil
Sea salt and freshly ground black pepper

1½ pounds cleaned small calamari, bodies separated from tentacles

1 pound firm ripe plum tomatoes, halved and seeded

1 medium red onion, sliced into ¼-inch-thick rounds

1 tablespoon roasted garlic (page 247)

3 tablespoons coarsely chopped fresh mint

2 tablespoon chopped fresh chives
Red wine vinegar

½ pound aged goat cheese, such as Laura Chenel's Cabecou or Tomme, crumbled (page 402)

1 crusty Italian or French baguette, cut into ½-inch-thick slices
Garnish: Small mint leaves and fried capers (page 21)

In a large bowl, combine ⅓ cup of the olive oil, the lemon juice, basil, 1 teaspoon sea salt, and a grinding or two of black pepper and whisk together. Add the squid bodies and tentacles and marinate for 1 hour at room temperature.

Prepare a charcoal fire or preheat the broiler. Remove the squid from the marinade and reserve the marinade. Over hot coals or under the broiler, grill bodies and tentacles until they just begin to firm and turn opaque, only a few minutes. Be careful not to overcook or the calamari will be tough. Slice bodies into bite-size rings and tentacles into bite-size portions. Set aside. (Do not refrigerate.)

Add the tomatoes halves and onion rounds to the reserved marinade, stir to coat, then drain and grill briefly. Coarsely chop them and then put them in a large bowl with the calamari, garlic, mint, chives, and red wine vinegar, olive oil, salt, and pepper to taste. Gently stir in the goat cheese. Lightly paint the bread with the remaining olive oil and grill over hot coals until lightly toasted with grill marks. Place a heaping tablespoon or two of the calamari mixture on toast and garnish with a mint leaf and fried capers.

 Recommended wine: The classic combination of goat cheese and Sauvignon Blanc is further enhanced by the fresh mint and seafood in this dish.

Scallop Seviche with Cilantro, Lime, and Serrano Chiles

This is a very simple dish to put together and can be used in a number of different ways. I like the seviche rolled up in *crisp* romaine or iceberg lettuce leaves and eaten out of hand, like a kind of Latin American spring roll. The seviche is also delicious served on crisp corn or flour tortilla wedges with a spoonful of Salsa Cruda (page 167) on top.

Serves 4 as an appetizer

½ pound bay scallops or sea scallops, sliced ¼ inch thick

3 tablespoons minced shallots or scallions

½ teaspoon seeded and minced serrano and jalapeño chiles (or to taste)

1 tablespoon chopped fresh cilantro

1 teaspoon kosher salt (or to taste)

4 tablespoons fresh lime juice

½ teaspoon sugar

1 tablespoon olive oil

In a medium bowl, combine all the ingredients, cover, and place in the refrigerator. Let the seviche "cook" 4 hours or to taste.

  Recommended wine: The tartness of seviche requires the balancing acidity of a crisp Fumé/Sauvignon Blanc or sparkling wine.

"COOKING" FISH WITH ACIDITY

Seviche is the best-known dish that "cooks" fish through the use of acidity, without heat. A number of different acidic elements will work, but lime juice and vinegar are the two most popular. In this dish, the scallops are marinated for 4 hours, which causes a change in the actual protein structure of the shellfish, simulating the effect of cooking with heat. After more than 7 or 8 hours, the fish "overcooks" and becomes rubbery.

Crab Wontons with Orange-Chipotle Sauce

China and Mexico meet in California in this delicious, unusual dish. The wontons and sauce can be made ahead of time and frozen if desired. To freeze the wontons, place uncovered in a single layer on a baking sheet lined with waxed paper and freeze until hard. Wontons can then be carefully placed in freezer bags. Thaw in the refrigerator before frying.

Makes 40 wontons, serving 8 to 10

½ cup golden raisins	2 tablespoons minced fresh oregano
1 cup dry white wine	
3 cups fresh or frozen Dungeness crabmeat, picked over to remove any pieces of shell	1 teaspoon minced lime zest
	2 tablespoons soy sauce
	1 teaspoon kosher salt (or to taste)
3 cups fresh raw corn kernels (about 4 to 5 large ears)	½ teaspoon freshly ground black pepper
2 cups minced red bell peppers	80 wonton wrappers
1 tablespoon olive oil	Cornstarch or rice flour
¼ cup minced fresh cilantro	Peanut, corn, or canola oil for deep-frying
2 teaspoons toasted and crushed cumin seed (page 36)	Orange-Chipotle Sauce (recipe follows)
1 tablespoon finely minced fresh ginger	Garnish: Cilantro sprigs

In a small bowl, combine the raisins and the wine. Let stand at room temperature for 4 hours or overnight to plump. Drain.

In a large bowl, combine the plumped raisins with the crab, corn, red bell peppers, olive oil, cilantro, cumin, ginger, oregano, lime zest, soy sauce, salt, and pepper. Place 1 tablespoon crab filling in the middle of each of 40 wonton wrappers. Lightly brush the edge of each wrapper with water and place a second wrapper on top, pressing the edges together to seal completely. Dust a sheet of waxed paper with cornstarch, placing the wontons on top.

In a large saucepan, heat about 3 inches of oil to 350 degrees on a candy or deep-fry thermometer. Place the wontons in the hot oil in batches and deep-fry for 3 to 4 minutes or until golden brown and puffed. Remove carefully and drain on paper towels. Serve immediately, drizzled with Orange-Chipotle Sauce and garnished with cilantro sprigs.

Orange-Chipotle Sauce

Makes about ½ cup

2–3 roasted red bell peppers
    (page 246)
  1 cup fresh orange juice
  1 teaspoon minced orange zest
  ½ teaspoon minced lime zest
  1 tablespoon fresh lime juice
  ½ teaspoon sherry vinegar
  ½ teaspoon honey
  ¾ teaspoon minced fresh oregano

  ½ teaspoon toasted and crushed
    cumin seed (page 36)
  ½ teaspoon chile powder, ancho
    preferred
  2 teaspoons minced canned chipotle
    in adobo (or to taste)
    Kosher salt
  ¼ cup olive oil

In a blender or food processor, combine the roasted peppers and ¼ cup of the orange juice. Purée, adding additional juice as necessary to make a puree. Set aside. In a saucepan over moderate heat reduce the remaining orange juice by half. Cool.

In the blender combine the reduced orange juice, the roasted pepper purée, the orange zest, lime zest, lime juice, vinegar, honey, oregano, cumin, chile powder, and chipotle. Blend well. With the motor running, slowly add the oil to form a smooth sauce. The sauce may be made up to 1 week in advance and stored covered and refrigerated.

 Recommended wine: Gewürztraminer is a showstopper with this eclectic dish. The orange-blossom and spice flavors in the wine are accentuated by the Orange-Chipotle Sauce, and the wine's fruitiness helps mellow the heat in the sauce.

 # Oysters on the Half Shell with Pickled Ginger Salsa

Absolutely fresh oysters on the half shell are one of God's best gifts to us. In California we get oysters from several "farms" ranging from Tomales Bay, north of San Francisco, all the way up to British Columbia. A single variety, Miyagi from Japan, makes up most of what is cultivated in this region. It is an amazingly adaptable creature and will take on varying characteristics depending on where and how it is grown. (It also takes on the name of the area it's farmed in.)

Serves 4 to 6

**24 fresh oysters, such as Hog Island, Preston Point, Fanny Bay,
or any good half-shell oysters**

Pickled Ginger Salsa

Makes about 1 cup

¼ cup peeled and diced jicama
½ cup peeled, seeded, and diced
    cucumber
¼ cup finely diced red onion
3 tablespoons chopped pickled
    ginger
1 tablespoon seasoned rice wine
    vinegar

1 teaspoon fresh lemon juice
1 tablespoon coarsely chopped
    fresh cilantro
1 teaspoon toasted sesame seeds
    (page 36)
¼ teaspoon sugar (or to taste)
    Kosher salt and freshly ground
    black pepper

In a medium mixing bowl, combine all the ingredients. Cover and refrigerate. This salsa is best used the day it is made, as it tends to lose its crisp character over time.

To serve: Shuck each oyster by carefully inserting the point of an oyster knife between the shells and twisting; don't lose the juices. Free the oyster from the bottom shell by gently sliding a knife underneath it. Top with a teaspoon of the Pickled Ginger Salsa. Serve immediately.

 Recommended wine: A crisp, lean California sparkling wine or dry Gewürztraminer would be a great match.

FOOD AND LOVE

The two have always been connected—an intimate dance of the senses. I know in my own experience that the most memorable (and sensuous) times of my life have all been around food.

For all of recorded history, claims have been made that certain foods increase sexual potency and desire. The Chinese tout shark fin and bird's nest (real ones) soups. The French made Champagne and wine essential to the process (which I definitely approve of). The Scottish swear by haggis, a mixture of minced sheep innards mixed with oatmeal and spices and then stuffed into a sheep's stomach and boiled for 4 hours. (The Scots obviously have a different sense of sensuality!) Other cultures include cocoa and chocolate (forbidden by the Aztecs to their women), pine nuts (according to Ovid), hippopotamus snout and hyena eyes (from Pliny), and, of course, oysters. Caviar, snails, and the eggs, glands, and sexual organs of all kinds of birds, animals, and fish have been credited with special powers. Even prunes were so highly regarded as an aphrodisiac in Elizabethan times that they were served free in brothels.

Foods from the garden that have been endowed with special sexual potential at one time or another include apples, figs, bananas, cucumbers, leeks, peppers, tomatoes, and potatoes. (The obvious connection is that many of them resemble human genitalia!) The noted anthropologist Peter Farb observed that the association between food and sex has probably existed since humans started walking upright. Eating brings people into close proximity in a situation that does not call for defensive tactics; the table, after all, is less fraught than the bed. Eating can bind a couple more effectively than sex simply because people have dinner more often and more predictably than they have sex. M. F. K. Fisher notes in her wonderful little book *An Alphabet for Gourmets* that gastronomy has always been connected with its sister art of love. [Passion and sex is the] "come-and-go, the preening and the prancing, the final triumph or defeat, of two people who know enough, subconsciously or not, to woo with food as well as flattery."

There are physiological reasons for us to connect the two desires: For one, the same very sensitive structures, called "Krause's end bulbs," are found in both the taste buds of the mouth and in the sensitive parts of our sexual organs. (This could explain why sexual desire and delicious food aromas both cause our mouths to water.) But, for me, the connection is both subtler and more all-encompassing than physiology can explain. It is the total sensuality of cooking and eating—the way I experience food as something to be touched and smelled, my love of its look and sound and savor—that makes it a sensual experience as well.

Barbecued Oysters with a Zesty Barbecue Sauce

During the spring and fall, I love to go to Tomales Bay, where oysters of all sizes are grown. We take the largest oysters (which are up to 5 inches long and just too fleshy to eat raw), put them on the grill until they just pop open, and then slather them with a warm, zesty barbecue sauce. As they say, "It doesn't get any better than this!" The recipe makes more than enough sauce for 6 dozen large oysters; try any leftover sauce with grilled chicken or ribs.

Serves 12 to 18

BARBECUE SAUCE:

2 cups finely minced onions	3 bay leaves
1 tablespoon minced garlic	4 cups catsup
3 tablespoons olive oil	1 cup dark molasses
1 tablespoon ground cumin	1 teaspoon Tabasco or other hot sauce
1 tablespoon ground ginger	
1 tablespoon salt	¼ cup dark-brown sugar
1 teaspoon freshly ground black pepper	¼ cup hoisin sauce
	¼ pound unsalted butter
1 cup apple cider vinegar	
1 cup fresh orange juice	72 large oysters, in their shells

In a large saucepan over medium heat, sauté the onions and garlic in the olive oil until soft but not brown. Stir in the cumin, ginger, salt, and pepper. Add the vinegar, orange juice, bay leaves, catsup, molasses, Tabasco, brown sugar, hoisin sauce, and butter. Bring to a simmer, cover, and cook 1 hour, or until thick. Remove bay leaves amd keep sauce warm.

Place the oysters in their shells on a hot grill. As soon as they pop open, spoon the warm barbecue sauce over them, and serve immediately. Some will open rather quickly, in a couple of minutes. Discard those that do not open.

 Recommended wine: A chilled Gamay, a crisp sparkling wine, or a locally brewed beer would go beautifully with this.

 # Mussels Baked with Serrano Chiles and Fresh Mozzarella

I really love mussels. In addition to their great taste, they are also relatively inexpensive. As with clams and oysters, the shells should be tightly closed when you purchase mussels, since this indicates they are still alive and fresh. Use the mussels as close to the time of purchase as possible.

Serves 6 as an appetizer

2 cups dry white wine	¼ cup finely minced scallions
36 large mussels, well scrubbed	2 teaspoons seeded and finely minced serrano chiles
½ pound bacon in slices	
2 tablespoons finely minced garlic	

2 tablespoons extra-virgin olive oil,
     plus additional for
     breadcrumbs
6 tablespoons finely minced fresh
     parsley

6 tablespoons dry white
     breadcrumbs
6 ounces fresh mozzarella cheese
1 large bunch spinach, well washed
     and stems removed

In a large pot, bring the wine and 2 cups water to a boil over high heat. Place the mussels in the poaching liquid and cover. Shaking the pan occasionally, cook the mussels until the shells just begin to open, approximately 3 minutes. Discard any unopened mussels. Using a slotted spoon, remove the mussels and set aside. Strain the poaching liquid through a cheesecloth-lined sieve to remove any sediment and pieces of shell; reserve the liquid. Remove and discard the top shell from the mussels, along with the "beard," if any. Replace any mussels that have been dislodged during cooking in their shells.

In a sauté pan, cook the bacon until crisp. Drain the slices on paper towels and chop finely.

In a separate pan over medium heat, briefly sauté the garlic, scallions, and chiles in the olive oil until soft but not brown, approximately 2 to 3 minutes. Combine the bacon, garlic mixture, and parsley in a bowl and set aside. Place the breadcrumbs in a small bowl and add a few drops of olive oil to very lightly coat them.

Place the prepared mussels in a shallow casserole or other ovenproof pan. Divide the bacon mixture evenly on top of the mussels and moisten with a few drops of the reserved poaching liquid. Thinly slice the mozzarella and cover each mussel. Sprinkle the oiled breadcrumbs on top. (If not serving immediately, cover and refrigerate before proceeding.)

Preheat the broiler. Pour ¼ cup of the reserved poaching liquid into a large sauté pan. Heat until boiling. Add the clean spinach and blanch briefly until just wilted. Using a slotted spoon, remove and keep warm.

Place the mussels under the broiler until the cheese just melts, approximately 4 minutes. Divide the wilted spinach into small beds on each plate; arrange 6 mussels on top. Serve immediately.

Recommended wine: A Fumé/Sauvignon Blanc is a good counterpoint to the briny, spicy mussels.

SERRANO CHILES

The serrano is a small, medium-hot green chile, having a little more fire than a jalapeño. Serranos are becoming more and more available in grocery stores. As with all chiles, be sure to wash your hands thoroughly with soap and water after removing the seeds and inner ridges, where the heat from the active ingredient capsaicin is located. For a more detailed discussion of chile heat, see page 10.

Smoked Salmon Cheesecake with a Walnut Crust

This makes a very elegant first course or lunch dish, and it is simple to make. I'd serve a small slice of this savory cheesecake with a salad of baby greens drizzled with a little vinaigrette. To test that the cheesecake has set, a toothpick in the center should come out clean.

Serves 12

CRUST:

2 cups Panko or other dry breadcrumbs	¼ cup grated Gruyère or Asiago cheese
¾ cup toasted and finely chopped walnuts	2 teaspoons chopped fresh dill (or 1 teaspoon dried)
½ cup melted unsalted butter	

Combine all the ingredients in a food processor. Process to mix. Press the crumb mixture into the bottom and up sides of a buttered 10-inch springform pan. (The crust will not come all the way up the sides of the pan.) Chill.

FILLING:

3 tablespoons unsalted butter	½ teaspoon salt
1 medium yellow onion, minced	¼ teaspoon freshly ground white pepper
1¾ pounds cream cheese at room temperature	4 eggs, separated
⅓ cup half-and-half	½ pound high-quality smoked salmon, finely chopped
⅔ cup grated Gruyère or Asiago cheese	

Preheat the oven to 350 degrees. In a small sauté pan, melt the butter and sauté the onion until soft but not brown. Set aside. In a mixer or by hand, blend the cream cheese, half-and-half, sautéed onion, Gruyère, and salt and pepper until smooth. Beat in the egg yolks one at a time. In a separate bowl, beat the egg whites to stiff peaks, but not dry. Mix in the salmon. Carefully fold the beaten whites into the cream cheese mixture. (It should have the consistency of a thick batter. If it's too stiff, add a little milk or cream.) Pour into the prepared pan. Bake for 1 hour and 10 minutes or until set. Remove from the oven and allow to cool in the pan. To serve, remove the ring from the springform pan and cut the cheesecake into slices with a warm knife. Serve at room temperature.

 Recommended wine: This cheesecake is particularly nice with a fruity Gewürztraminer or Johannisberg Riesling

 ## *Salmon Grilled in a Japanese Style*

This simple salmon preparation works equally well on fresh halibut or sea bass. The dish can be served either hot or at room temperature, either as an entrée or as a salad, sliced or flaked on a bed of mixed greens. (How's that for flexibility?) If you use salmon, try marinating and grilling the skin until it's crisp, to use as a garnish; instructions are on page 144.

Serves 4

¼ **cup soy sauce**	2 **tablespoons sugar**
¼ **cup sake or dry white wine**	2 **tablespoons chopped fresh ginger**
¼ **cup mirin (Japanese sweetened rice wine)**	1 **small lemon, thinly sliced**
	4 **5-ounce salmon fillets**

To make the marinade: In a small saucepan, combine the soy sauce, sake, mirin, sugar, and ginger. Bring to a boil. Remove from the heat and allow the marinade to cool to room temperature. Once cooled, pour the marinade over the fish (a glass dish is best) and scatter the lemon slices over the fish. Marinate refrigerated for at least 4 hours or overnight, turning the fish occasionally.

Grill or broil the salmon on both sides until just done, approximately 4 to 5 minutes per side.

 Recommended wine: Though simple, this is a richly flavored dish, so soft reds like Pinot Noir or Merlot are a good match.

Grilled Salmon with Black Bean Salsa and Chipotle-Tangerine Vinaigrette

I have left the skin on the salmon in this recipe to add an interesting flavor and to help keep the salmon moist. (Of course, it is essential to scale the fish if leaving the skin on.) Cooked quickly over high heat, the skin takes on the character of "cracklins," which is delicious. Even if I cook salmon without the skin, I'll often grill or roast the scaled skin separately until crisp, then slice or chop it to use as a garnish. Don't be daunted by the salsa and the vinaigrette. Each can be assembled in 5 to 10 minutes; the vinaigrette keeps beautifully for up to 2 weeks and the salsa keeps for up to 3 days.

Serves 6

6   5-ounce salmon fillets, cut ¾ inch
      thick, skin on and scales
      removed
Salt and freshly ground black
      pepper
Olive oil

Black Bean Salsa (recipe follows)
Chipotle-Tangerine Vinaigrette
      (recipe follows)
Garnish: Cilantro sprigs, grilled
      salmon skin (if desired)

Prepare a charcoal fire or preheat a broiler or stovetop grill. Remove any bones from the salmon: Pin bones in the center can be most easily removed using a needle-nosed pliers. Season with salt and pepper and lightly rub with olive oil. Quickly grill the salmon until it is just done, approximately 3 to 4 minutes per side (making sure the skin is crisp). Serve each salmon steak on ½ cup salsa and drizzle the vinaigrette over, reserving any extra for another use. Garnish with cilantro sprigs and grilled salmon skin, if desired. Serve warm or at room temperature.

Black Bean Salsa

Makes about 3 cups

1½   cups cooked black beans, or
        canned beans, drained and
        rinsed
¼   cup minced red bell pepper
¼   cup minced green bell pepper
¼   cup minced yellow bell pepper

½   cup minced red onion
2   teaspoons seeded and minced
        jalapeño or serrano chile
1½   teaspoons chopped fresh cilantro
½   cup seeded and diced plum
        tomatoes

1   teaspoon chopped garlic
½   teaspoon ground cinnamon
2   tablespoons fresh lime juice
1½ tablespoons raspberry vinegar

3   tablespoons olive oil
    Kosher salt and freshly ground
        black pepper to taste

Combine all the ingredients and refrigerate at least 2 hours before using. Before serving, season to taste with salt and pepper.

Chipotle-Tangerine Vinaigrette

Makes approximately 2 cups

1¼ cups fresh tangerine or orange
        juice
1   teaspoon minced chipotle in
        adobo
⅓   cup olive oil
2   teaspoons grated tangerine or
        orange zest
1   teaspoon grated lime zest
1   tablespoon fresh lime juice
1   teaspoon sherry vinegar
2   teaspoons honey (or to
        taste)

½   teaspoon tamarind concentrate
        (optional), available in Asian
        markets
1½ teaspoons chopped fresh
        oregano (or ½ teaspoon dried)
2   tablespoons chopped fresh
        cilantro
1   teaspoon toasted and ground
        cumin seed (page 36)
1   teaspoon ancho chile powder
        (optional)
    Kosher salt

In a small saucepan, over moderate heat, reduce the tangerine juice by half. Cool. In the jar of a blender, combine the reduced juice with the remaining ingredients, seasoning to taste with salt. Blend on high speed for a minute or so until the vinaigrette is smooth.

Store the vinaigrette, covered, in the refrigerator up to 2 weeks.

 Recommended wine: The Chipotle-Tangerine Vinaigrette is spicy and mildly sweet, so an off-dry Gewürztraminer would be a great match for the citrus flavors as well as the sweetness. A Gamay Beaujolais would also be an intriguing match, especially accenting the smoky chipotle flavors.

CHIPOTLE CHILES

Chipotle chiles are jalapeños that have been dried and smoked. Using them, you get the double hit of hot spice and smoke. They can be purchased in their dry form or canned as "chipotle in adobo," in which they are stewed with tomato, garlic, vinegar, and other spices. Chipotles in adobo are readily available in Mexican markets and generally available in the Mexican food aisle of the supermarket. Chipotles are pretty powerful, so if you have a low threshold for heat, add a little less than the recipe calls for. You can always add more. If you're like me, however, you'll soon be using them in everything.

Grilled Salmon with Roasted White Corn Salsa and Warm Basil Cream

This dish epitomizes summertime cooking in the wine country. Our California wild-caught king salmon is one of the great fish of the world. The Roasted White Corn Salsa can be made a day ahead, but the Warm Basil Cream does not keep well: Make it while the salmon is marinating.

Serves 6

⅓ **cup olive oil**
2   **teaspoons grated lemon zest**
2   **tablespoons chopped fresh mint**
½   **teaspoon kosher salt**
¼   **teaspoon freshly ground black pepper**

6   **6-ounce salmon fillets or steaks, cut ½ inch thick**
    Warm Basil Cream (recipe follows)
    Roasted White Corn Salsa (recipe follows)
    Garnish: Cilantro or mint sprigs

In a mixing bowl, whisk together the olive oil, lemon zest, mint, salt, and pepper. Rub the salmon with the marinade and marinate for 1 hour. Make the Warm Basil Cream. Have the salsa ready.

Prepare a charcoal fire or preheat the broiler or stovetop grill. Grill the salmon over hot coals until done, about 4 to 5 minutes on each side. To serve, spoon a few tablespoons of Warm Basil Cream on each plate. Place a salmon fillet on top, followed by a heaping tablespoon or two of the Roasted White Corn Salsa. Garnish with the herb sprigs. Serve immediately.

Warm Basil Cream

1 tablespoon olive oil	4 cups lightly packed basil leaves
¼ cup chopped shallots or scallions	1 tablespoon *each* chopped fresh parsley and mint
2 tablespoons chopped garlic	Kosher salt and freshly ground black pepper
½ cup dry white wine	Fresh lemon juice
2 cups rich shellfish or chicken stock	½ cup peeled, seeded, and diced plum tomatoes
1 teaspoon fennel seed	
1 cup heavy cream	

In a saucepan, heat the olive oil and sauté the shallots and garlic until soft and brown. Add the wine, stock, and fennel seed; bring to a boil, then lower the heat and reduce by half. Add the cream and reduce to a light sauce consistency. Strain into a blender or food processor.

Blanch the basil leaves quickly in lightly salted boiling water. Drain and run cold water over them immediately to stop the cooking and set the color. Pat dry.

Add the blanched basil leaves and the chopped parsley and mint to the cream mixture in the blender and process until smooth. Return the contents to a saucepan and season with salt, pepper, and drops of lemon juice. At serving time, stir in the tomatoes and serve immediately.

Roasted White Corn Salsa

2 cups fresh raw white corn kernels (about 3 to 4 large ears)	1 teaspoon seeded and minced serrano chile
¼ cup olive oil	2 tablespoons seasoned rice wine vinegar
Kosher salt and freshly ground black pepper	1 tablespoon sherry vinegar
⅓ cup finely diced red bell pepper	1 teaspoon fresh lemon juice (or to taste)
⅓ cup finely diced red onion	
⅓ cup chopped fresh cilantro or basil (or a combination)	1 teaspoon honey (or to taste)

Preheat the oven to 425 degrees. Toss the corn kernels with the olive oil and lightly season with salt and pepper. Spread out the kernels in a single layer on a baking sheet and roast until very lightly browned, about 15 minutes. Set aside.

In a separate bowl, combine the remaining ingredients. Stir in the roasted corn. Season with additional salt and pepper, lemon juice, and honey, if necessary (depending on the sweetness of the corn). Cover and store refrigerated for up to 5 days.

Recommended wine: Chardonnay seems to have a special affinity for sweet corn, so in concert with the salmon's richness and the creamy texture of the sauce, a well-balanced Chardonnay would be delicious.

Farmed versus Wild Fish

As more of the world's waters are overfished or become polluted we see the growth of farm-raised fish. For example, most of the salmon offered in our markets comes from farm-raised sources. Is one "better" than the other?

Almost all cooks I know who have had experience with both would without question pick a wild salmon over a farm-raised one. The texture and flavor are better and the wild salmon is also less fatty than its farm-raised cousin.

Unfortunately, as wild supplies dwindle we'll have to depend on farmed fish more. The real advantage to farmed fish is that by farming we ensure a commercial supply. We're also seeing that many fish farmers can generate more protein per "acre" and at a lower cost than farmers of land animals such as cows, pigs, or poultry can.

 # Salmon in a Fennel Crust with a Roasted Red Pepper–Blood Orange Vinaigrette

The flavors of fennel seed, roasted peppers, and blood oranges somehow express the cooking of the wine country. If blood oranges are not available, regular oranges or grapefruit may be substituted.

Serves 4

1½ tablespoons crushed fennel seed
½ teaspoon crushed white
      peppercorns
1 teaspoon kosher salt
4 6-ounce salmon fillets or steaks,
      cut ¾ inch thick

2 tablespoons olive oil
3 cups mixed baby greens
      Red Pepper–Blood Orange
         Vinaigrette (recipe follows)

Combine the crushed fennel seed, peppercorns, and salt. Rub the salmon with 2 teaspoons of the oil and lightly coat both sides of the salmon with the spice mixture. In a large sauté pan over medium-high heat, add the remaining oil and heat until just smoking. Add the salmon and sear for 4 to 5 minutes. Turn and sear on the other side for 2 to 3 minutes or until cooked through. Do not overcook the salmon.

Serve the salmon on a bed of the baby greens and drizzle with the vinaigrette.

Red Pepper–Blood Orange Vinaigrette

2 large roasted and chopped red
   bell peppers (page 246)
1 shallot, minced
⅔ cup blood-orange juice
1 teaspoon crushed fennel seed
2 teaspoons minced fresh thyme (or
   1 teaspoon dried)

1 tablespoon sherry vinegar
¾ cup extra-virgin olive oil
2 tablespoons hazelnut oil
   Kosher salt and freshly ground
      white pepper

In a mixing bowl, whisk together the roasted peppers, shallot, orange juice, fennel seed, thyme, and sherry vinegar. Slowly add the olive and hazelnut oils, whisking to emulsify. Season to taste with salt and white pepper.

 Recommended wine: This is a very full-flavored recipe, with lots of depth to it. It requires a complex, rich white wine, such as a Chardonnay or red wine with lots of flavor but not a lot of tannins, like Pinot Noir or Merlot.

BLOOD ORANGES

Until recent years, blood oranges were grown almost exclusively around the Mediterranean; now they are grown fairly extensively in California. Their name is derived from the color of their flesh, which can range from rosy to very deep burgundy in color. Blood oranges have a unique tart-sweet flavor and are definitely worth seeking out.

Salmon Cakes

Since we use a lot of salmon in the wine country, there always seem to be a few small pieces left over. I developed this recipe to take advantage of those tidbits. I often serve these cakes on a bed of savory salad greens and garnish them with a dollop of aïoli or one of the mayonnaises on page 35. You'll note that I call for the salmon to be both diced and finely chopped. This gives some texture to the finished cake.

Serves 8 as an appetizer

THE SALMON MIXTURE:

4 ounces fresh salmon, cut into
   ¼-inch dice
2 ounces very finely chopped fresh
   salmon
2 ounces fresh, uncooked shrimp,
   cut into ¼-inch dice
1 egg white, beaten
1 tablespoon finely diced celery
2 tablespoons finely diced red or
   yellow pepper (or a combination)
1 tablespoon chopped scallions
2 teaspoons grated lemon zest
¼ teaspoon seeded and minced
   jalapeño chile (or to taste)

¼ teaspoon chopped garlic
1 teaspoon mayonnaise
½ teaspoon finely chopped rosemary
   (or ¼ teaspoon dried)
1 teaspoon rinsed and drained
   capers
   Kosher salt and freshly ground
   black pepper

¼ cup plus 2 tablespoons Panko or
   other dry breadcrumbs for
   dredging
   Vegetable oil for sautéing

In a medium bowl, combine all the ingredients for the salmon mixture. Divide the mixture and pat to form into 8 cakes no thicker than 1 inch. (The salmon cakes may be prepared in advance to this point. Store loosely covered in the refrigerator for up to 4 hours.)

Dredge the salmon cakes in breadcrumbs that you've seasoned with salt and pepper. In a large sauté pan pour in oil to a depth of ⅛ inch. Heat the oil and sauté the cakes until golden brown, about 3 minutes per side.

Recommended wine: These meaty, succulent salmon cakes would be wonderful with a soft red wine like Merlot or Pinot Noir or a buttery, oaky Chardonnay.

Salmon Cured with Tequila and Herbs

This preparation, essentially a New World gravlax, is delicious. I like to layer the thinly sliced salmon on warm Grilled Flat Bread (page 352) with a scattering of sweet red onions, fresh salmon roe, and a dollop of sour cream or crème fraîche. This salmon is also wonderful to use in old-fashioned English-style tea sandwiches made with white or whole-grain bread, fresh herb butter, and thinly sliced cucumbers.

Serves 12

1 3- to 4-pound salmon fillet, all bones removed, skin left intact	2 teaspoons freshly ground black pepper
¼ cup kosher salt	⅔ cup mixed fresh herbs, such as basil, tarragon, parsley, chives, mint, chervil, and cilantro
3 tablespoons sugar	
1 tablespoon grated lemon zest	⅓ cup high-quality tequila

Place a layer of cheesecloth in a pan just large enough to hold the salmon. Lay the salmon on the cheesecloth, skin side down.

In a mixing bowl, combine the salt, sugar, lemon zest, and pepper. Sprinkle evenly over the salmon. Roughly chop the herbs and scatter over the fish. Place a second piece of cheesecloth over the salmon, gently tucking under the edges. Sprinkle with the tequila. Turn the salmon skin side up. Cover the pan tightly with plastic wrap and allow the salmon to cure in the refrigerator for 3 days, turning occasionally.

To serve, gently wipe off the marinade. Slice the salmon very thinly, leaving the skin behind.

Note: To give the salmon a firmer texture, place a smaller pan or tray, weighted with bricks or canned goods, on top of the wrapped salmon.

Recommended wine: I'd choose either a crisp California sparkling wine or a fairly grassy/herbal Sauvignon Blanc to go with this recipe.

Pacific Rock Cod Stewed with Oranges, Tomatoes, and Olives

This whole dish can be prepared and cooked in less than 25 minutes and can be made with any mild white fish, such as sole, halibut, or even scallops. I'd serve it with steamed rice finished with a good amount of chopped fresh cilantro.

In California, rock cod (a rockfish, not cod) is also known as "red snapper," another misnomer, since it bears no relationship to the true red snapper from the Gulf of Mexico. I think it originally was named this as a marketing ploy—"Pacific red snapper" sounds a lot more enticing and expensive then "red rock cod." If you can get it, my very favorite fish for both this recipe and overall is ling cod, an ugly but delicious member of the greenling family.

Serves 4

2 tablespoons olive oil	¼ teaspoon ground black pepper
1½ cups thinly sliced red onions	2 tablespoons slivered Kalamata or
1 tablespoon slivered fresh garlic	Niçoise olives
¾ cup canned diced tomatoes in juice	2 medium oranges, peeled and cut into segments
¾ cup dry white wine	1 pound rock cod fillets
½ teaspoon salt	

In a large sauté pan, heat the olive oil over medium heat and sauté the onions and garlic, stirring occasionally, until the onions are just beginning to brown (about 3 minutes).

Add the tomatoes, wine, salt, and pepper and simmer for 2 minutes. Stir in the olives and oranges and simmer 1 minute longer.

Lay the fillets over the mixture in a single layer, cover the pan, and simmer on moderate heat until the fish is just cooked through, about 3 to 4 minutes.

Serve immediately, spooning some of the onion mixture on top of the fish.

 Recommended wine: This is a wonderful dish to have with a crisp Chardonnay that has a bit of oak aging. A dry Chenin Blanc or sparkling wine would also be very good.

Halibut Baked with Tomatoes, Capers, and Herbs with a Feta-Crumb Crust

This great casserole dish can be prepared ahead of time, refrigerated, and then baked just before serving. It's also wonderful served at room temperature as part of a summer buffet. You can use other fish or shellfish, such as sea bass or scallops, in place of the halibut if you wish.

Serves 6

6   tablespoons olive oil
3   cups thinly sliced white onions
2   tablespoons thinly slivered garlic
1   cup thinly sliced fennel bulb
4   rinsed and finely minced anchovies
2   tablespoons chopped fresh parsley
3   pounds ripe plum tomatoes, peeled, seeded, and diced, or 3 cups diced and drained canned Italian tomatoes

Salt and freshly ground black pepper
2½   pounds fresh halibut, cut into 1-inch pieces
¼   cup chopped fresh basil
3   tablespoons rinsed and drained small capers
¼   cup dry red wine
⅓   cup freshly grated Parmesan cheese

TOPPING:

½   cup crumbled feta cheese
3   tablespoons finely chopped pine nuts
½   cup Panko or other dry bread-crumbs

1   tablespoon minced fresh thyme (lemon thyme, if available)

Preheat the oven to 350 degrees. In a sauté pan, heat 3 tablespoons of the olive oil and sauté the onions, garlic, and fennel bulb until softened but not brown. Add the anchovies and parsley and cook 2 minutes more. Remove from the heat.

Lightly oil a 3-quart baking dish with 2 tablespoons of the olive oil and spread half the onion mixture in the bottom of the dish. Scatter half the tomatoes on top and season with salt and several grindings of black pepper. Arrange the fish evenly on top of the tomatoes and scatter the basil and capers on top. Season well with salt and pepper. Drizzle with the red wine. Layer with the remaining onion mixture followed by the remaining tomatoes. Sprinkle the Parmesan cheese on top.

To make the topping: Finely crumble the feta cheese and drain on paper towels. Combine the feta, pine nuts, breadcrumbs, thyme, and the remaining 1 tablespoon olive oil together to form a loose topping. Scatter evenly over the top of the halibut casserole. (The casserole can be refrigerated, covered, at this point for up to 6 hours.)

Bake for 30 to 35 minutes (40 to 45 if it has been refrigerated) or until the fish is done and the topping is a light golden brown.

Recommended wine: A crisp, clean Chardonnay or Sauvignon Blanc with a lot of oak would go nicely with this dish. Light-style reds such as Gamay also are a good choice.

Sturgeon with Pancetta, Capers, Parsley, and Lemon

Sturgeon is a fish with excellent flavor. It is a great sport fish in California, although it is becoming scarce and is now being farm-raised in several locations, including the upper Sacramento river. If you can't find sturgeon, any firm-fleshed fish, such as halibut, sea bass, mahi mahi, or swordfish, will do.

Serves 6

12 very thinly sliced rounds of pancetta	1 tablespoon minced garlic
6 5-ounce sturgeon fillets	½ cup dry white wine
Kosher salt and freshly ground black pepper	1 cup rich fish or shellfish stock
2 tablespoons plus 1 teaspoon flour	1½ tablespoons fresh lemon juice (or to taste)
2 tablespoons olive oil	⅔ cup seeded and diced tomatoes
2 tablespoons unsalted butter	2 tablespoons minced fresh parsley
3 tablespoons minced shallots	3 tablespoons drained capers

Preheat the oven to 375 degrees. Lay the slices of pancetta on a baking sheet and place in the oven for 4 to 5 minutes to firm. Do not brown. When cool, finely chop 6 of the rounds; reserve the remaining 6 rounds.

Lightly season and flour the sturgeon. In a heavy-bottomed pan, heat the olive oil and sauté both sides of the fish until golden brown and cooked through, about 6 minutes. Remove and keep warm.

Add 1 teaspoon flour and the butter to the pan and cook and stir for 2 minutes to make a light roux. Add the shallots and garlic and cook until softened, approximately 2 minutes. Add the wine, stock, lemon juice, and tomatoes and, over high heat, reduce to a light sauce consistency.

Add the parsley, capers, and chopped pancetta and season with salt and pepper. Return the fish to the pan to heat through. (Note: Sturgeon must be cooked all the way through or it will be tough).

Serve the fish on warm plates topped with some of the sauce and a round of pancetta.

 Recommended wine: The smoky, salty flavors of the pancetta and capers require a crisp, citrus-tinged Fumé/Sauvignon Blanc for contrast.

CAPERS

A staple of Mediterranean cooking since their introduction by the Greeks in 600 B.C., capers have a prominent place in wine country cuisine. Basically the dried and pickled flower buds of the sun-loving caper plant (a relative of the rose), capers provide a piquant lift to almost any dish.

 Swordfish "Sandwiches" with Raisins, Herbs, and Capers in a Fresh Tomato Broth

Cal Uchida, the managing chef at Fetzer's Food and Wine Center at Valley Oaks, and I made this dish one year at the Telluride Wine Festival and people loved it. You may substitute any meaty, firm-fleshed fish or even skinless, boned chicken breast for the swordfish.

Serves 4

⅓ cup olive oil
1 cup finely minced red onions
3 tablespoons minced garlic
3 tablespoons Panko or other dry
     breadcrumbs
2 tablespoons capers, rinsed,
     drained, and chopped
3 tablespoons golden raisins,
     plumped in ½ cup warm water
     for 15 minutes, drained, and
     chopped
2 tablespoons chopped fresh
     parsley
2 teaspoons chopped fresh mint
1 tablespoon chopped fresh
     basil

⅓ cup freshly grated Parmesan
     cheese
   Kosher salt and freshly ground
     black pepper
8 pieces fresh swordfish, cut
     ¼ inch thick, trimmed into
     approximately 3- by 5-inch
     slices
2 tablespoons balsamic vinegar
   Fresh Tomato Broth (recipe
     follows)
   Garnish: Small dice of red,
     yellow, and green bell peppers,
     freshly grated Parmesan
     cheese, and drops of basil oil
     (optional; page 68)

Prepare a charcoal fire or preheat a broiler or stovetop grill. In a medium sauté pan, heat 3 tablespoons of the olive oil and sauté the onions and garlic until soft but not brown. Transfer the mixture to a bowl and stir in the breadcrumbs, capers, raisins, parsley, mint, and basil. Stir in the Parmesan and season to taste with salt and pepper.

Place 4 slices of swordfish on a baking sheet. Place one quarter of the bread-crumb mixture on each of the swordfish slices. Top with the remaining slices of swordfish to make "sandwiches."

Whisk the remaining olive oil with the balsamic vinegar and brush the bundles generously with the mixture. Season with salt and pepper.

Grill the swordfish bundles over moderately hot coals, approximately 3 minutes on each side, or broil until just cooked through. Be careful not to overcook. To serve, place the bundles in warm soup bowls and ladle the Fresh Tomato Broth around. Garnish with the diced peppers, freshly grated Parmesan cheese, and a drizzle of bright-green basil oil, if desired. Serve immediately.

Fresh Tomato Broth

1¼ cups strained fresh ripe tomato
      juice (page 59)
⅔ cup rich shellfish or chicken
      stock
¼ cup dry white wine
½ cup loosely packed basil leaves

   Drops of fresh lemon juice
   Kosher salt and freshly ground
     white pepper
1 tablespoon chilled unsalted
     butter, cut into bits
     (optional)

Bring the tomato juice, stock, wine, and basil to a boil. Lower the heat and simmer for 5 minutes to reduce slightly and concentrate the flavors. Strain and discard the basil. Season to taste with lemon juice, salt, and pepper. Whisk in the butter, if desired.

 Recommended wine: A Chardonnay with bright tropical fruit flavors will stand up to the raisins and capers in the relish.

 ## Fish Tacos with Citrus Salsa and Cabbage Slaw

Fish tacos have become all the rage in recent years, especially in southern California. This is a fairly simple recipe in which all of the components can be made ahead of time and the fish grilled at the last moment. I developed this recipe with Jim Stuart, a talented young chef who studied with me at Valley Oaks. He and I both agree that the very freshest tortillas make all the difference. If you want to make your own, a recipe is on page 362.

Serves 4

⅓ cup olive oil
1 tablespoon ancho or New Mexico
     chile powder
1 tablespoon fresh lime juice
     Kosher salt and freshly ground
       black pepper
4 4-ounce fillets of halibut, sea bass,
     or cod

4 lightly grilled 10-inch flour or
     corn tortillas
   Cabbage Slaw (recipe
     follows)
   Citrus Salsa (recipe follows)
   Cilantro Aïoli (recipe follows)

Prepare a charcoal fire or preheat a stovetop grill. In a small bowl, combine the olive oil, chile powder, lime juice, salt, and pepper. Brush liberally on the fillets. Grill the fish until it is just done. To serve, place a warm grilled tortilla on each plate. Top with one quarter of the Cabbage Slaw, a portion of the grilled fish, a heaping tablespoon or two of the Citrus Salsa, and a spoonful of the Cilantro Aïoli. Fold or roll and eat.

Cabbage Slaw

2   cups finely shredded green
      cabbage
½   cup thinly sliced red bell pepper
⅓   cup thinly sliced red onion
¼   cup finely sliced basil leaves

1   tablespoon seasoned rice wine
      vinegar
2   tablespoons corn or other light oil
      Kosher salt and freshly ground
      black pepper

Combine all the ingredients but the salt and pepper in a bowl. Gently toss and then season to taste with the salt and pepper. This may be prepared a day in advance and kept covered and refrigerated.

Citrus Salsa

2   oranges, peeled and segmented
      and membrane removed
1   blood orange, peeled and
      segmented (or 1 additional
      regular orange) and membrane
      removed
1   lemon, peeled and segmented and
      membrane removed
1   lime, peeled and segmented and
      membrane removed

1   teaspoon chopped fresh cilantro
1   teaspoon seeded and minced
      serrano chile
2   teaspoons seasoned rice wine
      vinegar
1   tablespoon olive oil
      Kosher salt and freshly ground
      pepper

Cilantro Aïoli

1   teaspoon drained capers
⅓   cup chopped fresh cilantro
2   teaspoons minced garlic
4   tablespoons minced scallions,
      green part only
1   teaspoon seeded and minced
      serrano chile

1   egg
½–¾ cup olive oil
      Kosher salt and freshly ground
      black pepper

In a blender or a food processor, combine all the ingredients except the oil and salt and pepper. Process to combine. With the motor running, slowly drizzle in the oil until the aïoli is emulsified. Scoop the aïoli into a bowl and season with salt and pepper. This may be prepared a day in advance and kept tightly covered and refrigerated.

Combine the citrus segments in a bowl. Add all the other ingredients and gently toss to combine. Season with salt and pepper.

Recommended wine: A light, fruity well-chilled white wine, such as a Chenin Blanc, Riesling, or Sémillon, would hit the mark with this dish.

Grilled Ahi Tuna with Japanese Noodles, Ginger-Soy Sauce, and Wasabi Mousse

Ahi is yellowfin tuna, which is the tuna most often used in Japanese restaurants for sushi and sashimi. Its beautiful deep, dark red, firm-fleshed meat truly is the beef of the sea. "Ahi" is the term used in Hawaii to describe this variety of tuna, and I think it sounds more appealing than yellowfin. I originally prepared this dish for an article on low-fat cooking in *Bon Appétit* magazine. The recipe was coupled with the "Five Lilies" Chowder (page 62) and fresh fruits to provide a menu in which only 14 percent of the calories came from fat. (That version, however, didn't include the Wasabi Mousse.) Low fat isn't the only reason to try this: I think it's very tasty and it's simple! The Wasabi Mousse and Chive Mixture may be made up to 2 hours in advance.

Serves 4

4 center-cut ahi tuna steaks, cut 1 inch thick	½ cup rice wine vinegar
2 tablespoons olive oil	⅓ cup reduced-salt soy sauce
Kosher salt and freshly ground black pepper	½ cup chicken stock, all fat removed
1½ tablespoons minced garlic	2 teaspoons sugar
2 tablespoons minced fresh ginger	1 pound soba or somen noodles
½ teaspoon seeded and minced serrano chile (or ¼ teaspoon red chile flakes)	½ cup diagonally sliced scallions, white and pale-green parts
½ teaspoon minced lemon zest	Wasabi Mousse (recipe follows)
	Chive Mixture (recipe follows)

Prepare a charcoal fire or preheat a stovetop grill.

Rub the tuna steaks with 1 teaspoon of the olive oil and lightly season with salt and pepper. Set aside. Add the remaining oil to a small saucepan and sauté the garlic and ginger over medium heat until they just begin to color. Add the chile, lemon zest, vinegar, soy sauce, stock, and sugar and bring to a boil. Reduce slightly. Remove from the heat and set aside. Keep warm.

Cook the noodles in lightly salted boiling water until just al dente, according to package directions. Drain and toss with half of the ginger-soy sauce mixture, and the scallions.

Grill the tuna on both sides over medium coals until just done, approximately 2 to 3 minutes per side (the center should remain very pink). Remove and keep warm.

Serve the tuna steaks on a bed of the noodles and drizzle with the remaining ginger-soy sauce. Place a dollop of the Wasabi Mousse on the ahi and sprinkle with the Chive Mixture. Serve immediately.

Wasabi Mousse

1½ teaspoons wasabi powder	Salt to taste
½ cup heavy cream	Lemon juice to taste

In a medium bowl, whisk the wasabi powder into the heavy cream. Lightly season with salt and drops of lemon juice. Whisk until the mixture is stiff.

Chive Mixture

2 tablespoons minced fresh chives	2 teaspoons minced fresh mint
2 teaspoons minced lemon zest	½ teaspoon seeded and minced serrano chile (optional)

In a small bowl mix together the chives, lemon zest, mint, and serrano.

Recommended wine: A fruity red wine with low tannins, such as Gamay Beaujolais, or a great rosé would be an ideal accompaniment to this Oriental-influenced dish.

Seared Ahi Tuna with a Lavender-Pepper Crust

This makes an elegant first course. The crust is especially intriguing because of the use of lavender, a highly aromatic flower usually used in soaps and cosmetics. Used in moderation, lavender is also an interesting culinary herb.

Serves 8

1½ pounds center-cut ahi tuna
 1 teaspoon kosher salt
 2 teaspoons black peppercorns
 1 teaspoon white peppercorns
 2 teaspoons fennel seed
1½ teaspoons dried lavender flowers

3 tablespoons olive oil
4 cups savory greens and herbs,
      such as mâche, arugula, chervil
   Mustard Seed Dressing (recipe
      follows)

Trim and cut the tuna into a block, approximately 2 inches across (depending on the size of the original piece). Crush the salt, peppercorns, fennel seed, and lavender with a mortar and pestle or a rolling pin. Lightly oil the tuna pieces with 2 teaspoons of the olive oil and coat evenly with the lavender-pepper mixture, patting off the excess. Heat the remaining olive oil in a large skillet over high heat, and when it just begins to smoke, quickly sear the tuna on all sides. Don't overcook; the tuna should be very rare inside. This will not take any more time than just to brown the outside of the fish. Immediately refrigerate the tuna for 1 hour (but no more than 3).

To serve, arrange the greens on chilled plates. Drizzle with Mustard Seed Dressing. Thinly slice the tuna and arrange on top of the dressed greens.

Mustard Seed Dressing

4 tablespoons whole-grain mustard
2 tablespoons olive oil
2 teaspoons toasted mustard seed
      (page 36)
2 tablespoons seasoned rice
      vinegar

3 tablespoons vegetable stock or
      water
1 teaspoon honey (or to taste)
   Kosher salt and freshly ground
      black pepper

Whisk all the ingredients together and season to taste.

 Recommended wine: Fumé/Sauvignon Blanc offers some balancing acidity to the peppery, mustardy flavors in the dish. A young, vibrantly fruity Pinot Noir works beautifully as a red wine accompaniment.

Ahi Tuna–Eggplant "Tarts"

The "tart" shell in this recipe is simply a round of roasted eggplant, which serves as the base for the chopped vegetables and seared tuna—a sort of "Mediterranean meets Japan" idea that I really like. The tart is served at room temperature. For a dramatic presentation, I like to drizzle reduced balsamic vinegar and basil oil around the plate. I just reduce inexpensive balsamic over medium heat until it is a sauce consistency and coats the back of a spoon.

Serves 4

¾ pound center-cut ahi tuna, cut into a rectangular block

1 large eggplant
  Olive oil
  Kosher salt and freshly ground black pepper

¾ cup finely minced red onions

2 large plum tomatoes, seeded and diced

1 tablespoon *each* minced fresh basil and parsley

1½ tablespoons drained and chopped capers

1 small red bell pepper, roasted, skinned, seeded, and coarsely chopped (page 246)

1 teaspoon fresh lemon juice
  Lemon Zest Mixture (recipe follows)
  Garnish: Reduced balsamic vinegar, basil oil, and Frizzled Onions (page 228)

In a sauté pan or on a stovetop grill, sear the tuna quickly over very high heat only until lightly browned. Chill the seared tuna for at least 30 minutes. Remove from the refrigerator and slice thinly.

Preheat the oven to 400 degrees. Slice the eggplant into ½-inch-thick rounds. Brush the slices lightly with olive oil and season both sides with salt and pepper. Place on a baking sheet in a single layer and bake for 6 to 8 minutes or until lightly browned and cooked through. The slices should still hold their shape.

While the eggplant is baking, sauté the onions in 1 tablespoon olive oil until they just begin to soften. Season lightly with salt and pepper and set aside.

Select the 4 largest rounds of eggplant to form the base of the tarts and set aside. Coarsely chop the remaining eggplant and add to the onion mixture along with the basil, parsley, capers, and roasted pepper. Mix thoroughly. Season lightly with salt and pepper.

To assemble the tarts, on each plate place one of the reserved eggplant rounds, then one quarter of the chopped eggplant, then one quarter of the tuna slices on top. Drizzle with lemon juice and sprinkle with the Lemon Zest Mixture.

Add salt and pepper to taste. Garnish the plate with the reduced balsamic vinegar and the basil oil, if desired, and place a nest of Frizzled Onions on top.

Lemon Zest Mixture

½ teaspoon minced garlic
1 teaspoon minced fresh basil or mint

1 teaspoon minced lemon zest

Combine all the ingredients.

🍃 *Recommended wine: A barrel-aged Fumé/Sauvignon Blanc or a peppery Zinfandel would work well with this full-flavored dish.*

 ## Prawns Wrapped in Zucchini with a Red Pepper Aïoli

This idea evolved from the Italian tradition of wrapping prawns or scallops in prosciutto before grilling. It is also a way to use up the abundance of zucchini that always seems to hit us in midsummer. When they're available, I love to take small or baby artichokes and grill or deep-fry them as an addition to this dish.

Serves 8 as an appetizer or 4 as a main course

16   medium prawns

MARINADE:

3 tablespoons olive oil
¼ cup dry white wine
1 teaspoon minced lemon zest
1½ teaspoons minced fresh oregano
     (or ½ teaspoon dried)
1½ teaspoons minced fresh thyme
     (or ¾ teaspoon dried)
1 teaspoon minced garlic
1 tablespoon minced fresh parsley
½ teaspoon red chile flakes
½ teaspoon kosher salt

2 large zucchini, sliced very
     thinly lengthwise to yield
     16 slices
16   large basil leaves
16   bamboo skewers or rosemary
     branches, leaves removed
     Red Pepper Aïoli (recipe
     follows)
     Garnish: Basil sprigs and lemon
     wedges

Shell and devein the prawns, leaving the tail segment and its shell intact. In a mixing bowl, whisk the marinade ingredients together and toss with the prawns. Marinate for 1 hour. Meanwhile, blanch the zucchini slices in lightly salted boiling water for 5 seconds. Remove and immediately plunge into cold water to stop the cooking. Drain, pat dry, and set aside.

Place a basil leaf on top of each prawn. Curl a zucchini slice around the prawn, enclosing the basil leaf. Thread a bamboo skewer or rosemary branch through the prawn and zucchini slice to hold in place. Grill or broil the prawns approximately 3 minutes, turning once, until just done. Be careful not to overcook. Serve immediately, garnished with a dollop of Red Pepper Aïoli, basil sprigs, and lemon wedges.

Red Pepper Aïoli

Makes approximately 2 cups

2 egg yolks	⅔–1 cup olive oil
1 tablespoon or more chopped garlic	Fresh lemon juice
2 cups roasted and chopped red bell	Salt and freshly ground black
peppers (page 246)	pepper
2 tablespoons Dijon-style mustard	Drops of Tabasco

In a food blender or food processor, combine the egg yolks, garlic, red peppers, and mustard. With motor running, slowly add the olive oil to form an emulsion. The mixture should be thick but not stiff. Season with lemon juice, salt, pepper, and Tabasco to taste. Cover and store refrigerated for up to 1 week.

Recommended wine: The piquant flavors of this dish are nicely balanced by a Fumé/Sauvignon Blanc or a lighter red such as a Gamay or Chianti-style wine.

Marinated and Grilled Prawns with a Melon-Pineapple Salsa

In this dish, the prawns can be served warm, right off the grill, or at room temperature as part of a summer buffet. You can either peel the prawns, as suggested, or grill them with the shell on, which makes them harder to handle at the table but adds a lot of flavor. To grill with the shell on, simply take a pair of scissors and snip the shell along the back so that you can remove the sand vein.

Serves 4, as an appetizer or lunch

1   pound large prawns
⅓   cup olive oil
1   teaspoon finely minced garlic
1   tablespoon finely minced
    scallions
½   teaspoon finely chopped fresh
    oregano (or ¼ teaspoon dried)

½   teaspoon kosher salt
¼   teaspoon red chile flakes
2   tablespoons dry white wine
    Melon-Pineapple Salsa (recipe
    follows)
    Garnish: Cilantro sprigs and
    avocado slices, if desired

Peel and devein the prawns, leaving the tail segment and its shell intact. Whisk the remaining ingredients together and marinate the prawns for up to 2 hours in the refrigerator. (The prawns will toughen if they marinate too long; be careful not to overmarinate.) Skewer, if desired, to facilitate grilling.

Grill or broil the prawns quickly, approximately 1 to 2 minutes per side, until they begin to turn pink. Be careful not to overcook—prawns should remain slightly transparent in the middle. Divide the salsa among the plates and place the prawns on top. Garnish with cilantro sprigs and avocado slices.

Melon-Pineapple Salsa

1½ cups diced cantaloupe,
    honeydew, or other melon
½   cup diced fresh pineapple
    (see note)
1   teaspoon seeded and minced
    serrano chile
¼   cup finely diced red onion
2   tablespoons olive oil

½   teaspoon finely minced garlic
1   tablespoon raspberry vinegar
1   tablespoon fresh lemon or lime
    juice
½   teaspoon honey
    Kosher salt and freshly ground
    white pepper
2   tablespoons minced fresh cilantro

Gently combine the melon, pineapple, serrano, and onion in a bowl. In a separate bowl, whisk together the olive oil, garlic, vinegar, lemon juice, and honey. Season to taste with salt and pepper. Just before serving, combine the oil mixture with the fruit and gently toss with the cilantro.

Recommended wine: The Melon-Pineapple Salsa is particularly embellished by the tropical fruit flavors of Gewürztraminer, Riesling, or Chenin Blanc.

Note: For additional flavor, lightly oil and grill slices of pineapple, about 2 minutes on each side, before cutting them up.

Rock Shrimp Cakes with Salsa Cruda

Rock shrimp are so named because they have a rock-hard shell, which is generally removed mechanically during commercial processing; this causes the shrimp to have a "broken" appearance. The flavor of rock shrimp, however, is phenomenal. When cooked, they have all the richness and texture of lobster meat at a much lower price. While rock shrimp are widely available, you can substitute regular shrimp if necessary. Be sure not to overcook either kind of shrimp.

Serves 4

1 pound rock shrimp	10 drops Tabasco or other hot sauce (or to taste)
¼ cup dry white wine	Kosher salt and freshly ground black pepper
1 large egg, beaten lightly	
½ cup Panko or other dry homemade breadcrumbs	Clarified unsalted butter or vegetable oil for sautéing
5 tablespoons mayonnaise	2 cups spicy greens, such as red mustard, arugula, mizuna
½ teaspoon dry mustard	
2 tablespoons minced fresh parsley	Salsa Cruda (recipe follows)
2 tablespoons scallions, white parts only	Garnish: Cilantro sprigs, Frizzled Onions (page 228)
2 teaspoons white-wine Worcestershire	

In a large sauté pan over medium-high heat, combine the shrimp and wine and cook for 1 minute. The shrimp will still be translucent and not quite done. Drain the shrimp, reserving any liquid. Cool and chop coarsely. Return the shrimp liquid to the pan and, over medium heat, reduce until almost a syrup. In a bowl, combine the egg, breadcrumbs, mayonnaise, mustard, parsley, scallions, Worcestershire, and Tabasco. Fold in the sautéed rock shrimp and the reduced liquid. Season with salt and pepper to taste. Form into 8 cakes. Refrigerate if not cooking and serving immediately.

In a large sauté pan, heat the butter or vegetable oil and sauté the cakes until lightly brown on both sides. Remove and drain on paper towels. Serve the shrimp cakes on a bed of the greens, topped with salsa. Garnish with cilantro and Frizzled Onions, if desired.

Salsa Cruda

Makes approximately 1 cup

¾ pound ripe tomatoes, seeded and
   diced
⅓ cup diced red onion
1 teaspoon seeded and minced
   serrano chile

2 tablespoons chopped fresh cilantro
   Drops of lime or lemon juice
   Pinch of sugar
   Kosher salt and freshly ground
   black pepper

In a medium bowl, combine all the ingredients and allow the flavors to blend for at least 1 hour before using. Store covered in the refrigerator for up to 2 days.

 Recommended wine: Fumé/Sauvignon Blanc brings out the flavors of the succulent shrimp cakes and emphasizes the fresh piquant salsa.

When I make Rock Shrimp Cakes with Salsa Cruda I often use one more sauce, which I place in a squeeze bottle and squirt decoratively around the edge of the plate. You certainly don't have to add it, but I wanted to share the recipe with you because it's one of my favorite sauces with fish, poultry, and roasted vegetables. It's very easy to make and I'll bet you'll adopt it as one of your "all-purpose" sauces too!

ROASTED TOMATILLO AND AVOCADO SAUCE

Makes about 1 cup

¾ pound tomatillos, husked
1 large onion, peeled and quartered
1 medium serrano or jalapeño
   chile, stemmed
6 cloves garlic, peeled
3 tablespoons olive oil
½ teaspoon *each* whole
   coriander and cumin seed

   Salt and freshly ground black
   pepper
1 large avocado (10–12 ounces),
   chopped
¼ cup chopped fresh cilantro
½ cup or so chicken or vegetable
   stock

Preheat the oven to 375 degrees. Toss the tomatillos, onion, chile, and garlic cloves with the olive oil and place in an ovenproof baking dish. Sprinkle coriander and cumin seeds on top along with a light seasoning of salt and pepper. Toss again.

Roast uncovered for approximately 40 minutes, or until the tomatillos and onion are lightly browned and soft. Cool slightly and transfer to a food processor or blender, being sure to include all juices and browned bits from the dish.

Add the avocado and cilantro and process briefly. With the motor running, add enough stock to make a nice smooth sauce. Season to taste with salt and pepper. Serve warm or at room temperature. The sauce can be made up to 1 day in advance but is best served soon after it is made. Store refrigerated.

 Rock Shrimp Tamales with Four-Pepper Cream

I am fascinated by wrapped foods in general and tamales in particular. At one point I even wanted to write a global tamale book, describing different types of doughs and fillings. My better judgment prevailed, but this zesty contribution was one of the results. For other tamale inspirations, see Sticky Rice "Tamales" with Star Anise Beef (page 210) and Mediterranean Polenta Tamales (page 257).

Serves 4

8   large dried corn husks, available in Latin American markets, soaked in
    warm water for 30–40 minutes to soften

MASA DOUGH:

¼   cup unsalted butter, softened
2   cups masa harina
1   teaspoon baking powder
1   teaspoon salt

1   tablespoon minced chipotle in
    adobo
¼   cup canola oil
1   cup hot chicken or shellfish stock

In the bowl of an electric mixer fitted with the paddle attachment, or by hand with a wooden spoon, beat the butter until light and fluffy. Add the masa harina, baking powder, salt, and chipotle. Mix until well blended. With the motor running, slowly add the canola oil and the hot stock. Continue mixing until you hear a slapping sound, approximately 2 minutes. The dough will be soft. Set aside. You can do this all by hand with a wooden spatula, but it will take some energy!

FILLING:

2	slices bacon, finely diced
2	tablespoons minced red bell pepper
2	tablespoons minced green bell pepper
2	tablespoons minced yellow bell pepper
2	tablespoons minced red onion
1	teaspoon minced garlic
½	cup chicken or shellfish stock

8–10	ounces coarsely chopped rock shrimp or bay shrimp
½	teaspoon adobo sauce from canned chipotles above
1	tablespoon chopped fresh cilantro
	Four-Pepper Cream (recipe follows)
	Garnish: Cilantro sprigs and diced bell peppers

In a large sauté pan over medium heat, sauté the bacon until translucent. Add the peppers, onion, and garlic and sauté slowly until tender, approximately 3 minutes. Add the stock, shrimp, and adobo sauce. Cook, stirring, until the shrimp are barely cooked through, approximately 1 minute. Remove from the heat, strain, set the solids aside, and return the liquid to pan. Over high heat, reduce the liquid until syrupy and add to the shrimp mixture. Add the cilantro and stir to combine.

To assemble, remove the husks from the water, drain, and pat dry. Spread out the corn husks on a dry work surface. Pinch off an egg-size piece of the masa mixture. Pat it into the corn husk, flattening the dough to approximately 4 inches square and ¼ inch thick, leaving a border of husk at least ½ inch wide around the perimeter of the dough. Spread a tablespoon of the filling lengthwise in the center of the dough. Fold the husk together until the edges overlap and the masa and its filling are completely enclosed by the husk. Gently flatten the top and bottom of the husk and fold the ends up to enclose. Repeat with the other 7 husks. Place folded side down in a steamer over boiling water and steam, covered, for 45 minutes.

To serve, open the husks to reveal the tamales and place on a warm plate. Spoon the Four-Pepper Cream over the tamales and garnish with cilantro sprigs and diced peppers. Serve immediately.

Four-Pepper Cream

Makes 2 to 3 cups

1 tablespoon olive oil	2 tablespoons finely diced yellow
¼ cup minced shallots	bell pepper
2 teaspoons seeded and chopped	2 tablespoons finely diced green
serrano chiles	bell pepper
1 cup dry white wine	Kosher salt and freshly ground
2½ cups rich shrimp or chicken stock	white pepper
¾ cup heavy cream	Drops of fresh lemon or lime
2 tablespoons finely diced red bell	juice
pepper	

In a medium sauté pan, heat the olive oil and sauté the shallots and serranos until soft but not brown. Add the wine and stock and bring to a boil. Continue to boil until the mixture is reduced by half. Add the cream and continue to boil until the mixture is reduced to a light sauce consistency. Stir in the diced bell peppers and season to taste with salt, pepper, and drops of lemon juice. Serve warm. (Four-Pepper Cream can be made up to a day ahead, stored in the refrigerator, and reheated gently in a water bath.)

 Recommended wine: With dishes that have a lot of flavor and spice, I like softer, fruity wines, like Gewürztraminer or Johannisberg Riesling.

MASA HARINA, MASA, CORNMEAL, AND POLENTA

It's easy to see why these terms are confused, but they shouldn't be used interchangeably. They are really different things!

Masa harina is corn that has been dried, treated with limewater, and then ground to make a flour. Masa harina is widely available in supermarkets today. It is sold under many brand names, but it is always labeled "masa harina." Masa harina is the dried raw material for making "masa," which refers to the prepared dough used to make corn tortillas and tamales.

Ordinary ground cornmeal of the kind used in this country, primarily for making corn bread, dusting bread and pizza pans, and coating foods for frying, does not go through the limewater processing and lacks the flavor and texture necessary to make good tortillas or tamales.

Polenta, the Italian dish of cooked cornmeal served either as mush or cooled and sliced, is made from either very finely ground or coarsely ground cornmeal. Ground cornmeal labeled "polenta" is available at gourmet food stores and markets that carry Italian products. That is what I'm referring to in the recipes that call for "polenta" as an ingredient. If you can't find this product, you can certainly substitute regular [coarse yellow] cornmeal.

 Dungeness Crab in Wine and Vermouth

This simple dish celebrates one of the real treasures of California and the Northwest—Dungeness crab! Unfortunately, Dungeness crab is not generally available outside that area. You can substitute the eastern blue crab or the Alaskan king crab. Fresh mussels, clams, and shrimp can also be used. Serve with a big stack of napkins and lots of crusty French bread.

Serves 2 as a main course or 4 as an appetizer

3–4 **pounds cooked and cleaned Dungeness crab in the shell**	1½ **tablespoons soy sauce**
¼ **pound unsalted butter**	1 **tablespoon fresh lemon juice**
⅔ **cup dry vermouth**	2 **teaspoons sugar**
½ **cup dry white wine**	1 **teaspoon cornstarch, dissolved in 1 teaspoon cold water**
1½ **cups clear fish stock (page 54)**	3 **tablespoons minced fresh parsley**
2 **tablespoons minced garlic**	**Freshly ground black pepper**
2 **teaspoons minced fresh ginger**	

Crack and separate the crab into sections. Set aside.

In a saucepan, combine the butter, vermouth, wine, stock, garlic, ginger, soy sauce, lemon juice, sugar, and dissolved cornstarch. Bring to a simmer and cook, covered, for 10 minutes. Add the crab, parsley, and pepper to taste and warm through.

Ladle into large bowls. Serve immediately.

 Recommended wine: I've had this dish with both a good, full-bodied Chardonnay and with a good amber ale; I like them both.

Shellfish in a Saffron-Scented Stock

This is an elegant presentation for shellfish that looks even better if you have deep, wide-rimmed white bowls to frame the fish in its jewel-like stock. For the full visual effect, make the stock as clear as possible. I've done this dish with other seafood, including grilled salmon and sea bass. In other words, use whatever selection of fish and shellfish you want as long as they are absolutely fresh!

Serves 6

12   large prawns, shelled and
    deveined

12   large sea scallops, rinsed

MARINADE:

⅓   cup finely chopped parsley
¼   cup chopped fresh basil
1   tablespoon minced shallots or
    scallions
2   teaspoons minced garlic
1   tablespoon minced fresh sage
    (or ½ teaspoon dried)
½   teaspoon minced fresh oregano (or
    ¼ teaspoon dried)

¾   teaspoon kosher salt
½   teaspoon freshly ground black
    pepper
½   teaspoon red chile flakes
2   teaspoons grated orange zest
⅓   cup dry white wine
⅓   cup extra-virgin olive oil

STOCK:

6   cups rich, clear shellfish stock
    (page 53)
1   cup dry white wine
½   teaspoon saffron threads
2   bay leaves

¼   cup julienned leeks, white part only

¼   cup julienned carrots
24   mussels
    Garnish: Watercress sprigs,
    chopped fresh chives,
    finely sliced strips of nori
    (Japanese dried seaweed), if
    desired

Prepare a charcoal fire or preheat a stovetop grill. In a medium bowl, combine all the marinade ingredients. Add the cleaned prawns and scallops and marinate, refrigerated, for approximately 30 minutes. Remove from the marinade and grill quickly over hot coals until done, 1 to 2 minutes. Be careful not to overcook. The shellfish should be slightly translucent in the middle. Set aside.

In a large saucepan, bring the stock, wine, saffron, and bay leaves to a boil. Reduce the heat and allow to simmer for 5 minutes to develop the saffron aroma and color. Strain carefully. In another large pot, quickly blanch the julienned leeks and carrots in lightly salted, boiling water (just 5 seconds) and remove. Pour off most of the water, return to a boil, and steam the mussels until just open. (Discard any that don't open.)

To serve, divide the prawns, scallops, mussels, and blanched leeks and carrots among 6 warm soup bowls. Ladle steaming stock over the seafood. Garnish with the watercress, chives, and nori, if using.

 Recommended wine: This is a rich dish and requires a rich wine. An elegant, barrel-aged Chardonnay, Viognier, or Pinot Blanc would be great!

SAFFRON

Saffron, the world's most expensive and exotic spice, is the stigma of a small purple crocus called *Crocus sativus;* it can be harvested only by hand. It is estimated that it takes over a quarter million crocus flowers to yield one pound of saffron. Luckily, very little saffron is needed to flavor a dish. It yields an intense color and flavor like nothing else in the world. Most saffron comes from Spain, where it is used to flavor many dishes, the most famous of which is paella.

 Grilled Scallops with Fennel and a Lemon-Tarragon Vinaigrette

Cal Uchida developed this dish to accompany Fetzer's Sauvignon Blanc. It is also a simple dish to make, and lends itself to all kinds of garnishes. I've used pea tendrils, bronze fennel sprigs, nasturtium flowers and leaves, along with any available roasted baby vegetables, to create a beautiful presentation. Even without these garnishes, it's a magnificent dish.

Serves 4 as an appetizer

1 large fennel bulb, trimmed of
     fronds
   Olive oil
   Kosher salt and freshly ground
     black pepper
12 fresh jumbo sea scallops

1 roasted red pepper, peeled and
     cut into triangles (page 246)
   Lemon-Tarragon Vinaigrette
     (recipe follows)
   Garnish: Tarragon sprigs

Prepare a charcoal fire or preheat a stovetop grill. Slice the fennel bulb vertically into ¼-inch-thick "fans." Lightly toss the slices in olive oil, season with salt
and pepper, and grill over medium coals until attractively marked on both sides
and tender, about 10 minutes. Set aside. Lightly toss the scallops in olive oil and
season with salt and pepper. Grill until done, approximately 2 to 3 minutes per
side. Be careful not to overcook—the centers should still be slightly translucent.
To serve, divide the fennel slices and pepper triangles among the plates, place
3 scallops on top for each plate, and drizzle a tablespoon or two of vinaigrette
over the scallops. Garnish with tarragon and serve immediately.

Lemon-Tarragon Vinaigrette

Makes almost 2 cups

½ cup fresh lemon juice
1 teaspoon grated lemon zest
2 tablespoons white wine vinegar
1 tablespoon minced shallots
2 tablespoons minced fresh
     tarragon

2 teaspoons honey (or to taste)
½ cup olive oil or ½ cup defatted
     chicken stock
   Kosher salt and freshly ground
     white pepper

In either the bowl of a food processor or a mixing bowl, combine the lemon
juice, lemon zest, vinegar, shallots, tarragon, and honey. Slowly incorporate the
olive oil or stock, either by whisking by hand or pulsing 2 to 3 times in a food
processor. The vinaigrette should not be emulsified but remain very light in body.
Season to taste with salt and pepper. Store covered in the refrigerator for up to
3 days.

*Recommended wine: A Fumé/Sauvignon Blanc captures the fresh lemony fla-
vors in the vinaigrette. Tarragon is also a great link to Sauvignon Blanc.*

Seared Dayboat Scallops with Sautéed Apples and Vanilla-Scented Sauce

The high quality of the scallops called for here is crucial to this dish. "Dayboat" refers to scallops that have not been packed in brine or treated with chemical whiteners, which are often used with commercial scallops. Natural, unadulterated scallops are available—you just have to demand them! If dayboats are not available, the recipe will certainly work with the freshest scallops you can find. I often garnish this dish with a sprinkling of fresh lemon thyme leaves and a tablespoon or two of fresh salmon caviar, if it's available.

Serves 4

1   **pound very fresh jumbo scallops**
    Sea salt and freshly ground white pepper
½   **cup chopped mushrooms**
⅓   **cup diced shallots or scallions, white part only**
4   **tablespoons clarified unsalted butter or olive oil**
2   **cups peeled cored and julienned tart green apples (Pippin or Granny Smith)**

1½   **cups dry white wine**
2½   **cups rich shellfish stock**
1   **3-inch vanilla bean**
1   **cup heavy cream**
1   **teaspoon Dijon-style mustard (or to taste)**
    Garnish: Oven-dried apple slices, if desired (page 176)

Gently remove any side muscle from the scallops. Rinse and pat dry. Lightly season the scallops with salt and pepper. Set aside.

In a saucepan over medium heat, sauté the mushrooms and shallots in 2 table-spoons of the clarified butter until they just begin to color. Add 1 cup of the apples, the white wine, stock, and vanilla bean and reduce by half over moderately high heat, approximately 10 minutes. Add the cream and mustard and reduce to a light sauce consistency. Strain the sauce carefully. Season to taste with salt and pepper and keep warm.

In a large sauté pan over high heat, add the remaining 2 tablespoons butter and sear the scallops for approximately 1 minute on each side. Be careful not to over-cook; scallops should remain slightly translucent in the center. Remove the scallops and keep warm. Add the remaining 1 cup apples and sauté until crisp-tender.

To serve, arrange the scallops and apples on warm plates. Spoon the warm sauce over and garnish with dried apple slices, if desired.

Recommended wine: This is a classic dish to highlight the apple-vanilla flavors and creamy texture of a barrel-aged Chardonnay.

OVEN-DRIED APPLE SLICES

Preheat the oven to 250 degrees. Peel and slice the apples into very thin rounds, using a mandoline or similar slicing device. Remove any seeds. Very lightly oil both sides of the apple slices with a drop or two of light vegetable oil. Place the apple rounds on a baking sheet in a single layer between sheets of parchment or waxed paper. Place in the oven for 15 to 20 minutes, or until the apples are softened. Remove the top sheet of paper and return the baking sheet to the oven to allow the apples to dry completely, approximately 1 hour longer. Store in an airtight container.

CHICKEN, TURKEY, GAME HENS, QUAIL, AND SQUAB

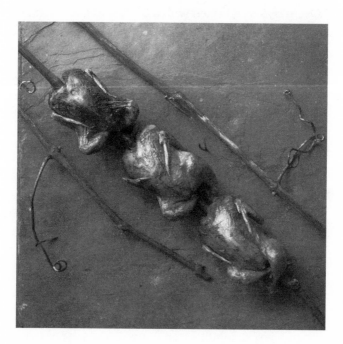

Poultry and Wine

Although squab may be more robust than the white meat of chicken, all poultry has a relatively neutral flavor, which is why it's so versatile in the kitchen. This means that the choice of wine to serve with a poultry dish depends mostly on the ingredients and cooking technique you use. As you'll see by the wine recommendations accompanying the recipes in this chapter, the wines that work with chicken and other birds are as varied as the ways of preparing them. Conversely, if you have a particular bottle of wine that you're in the mood for, you can pretty much create or choose a poultry dish to suit it.

Interesting recipes to me are those that "tickle" as many of the senses of taste as possible. In the West (the Western world, that is), we're taught that there are four senses of taste—sweet, salty, sour, and bitter—perceived by taste buds on different parts of the tongue. According to the Asian system, there is a fifth taste—pungent, or pepper—with which I certainly concur. We quickly tire with a single taste sense. What keeps the palate alive and interested is food that excites two or more of the taste senses (in some kind of harmony, of course). For example, the Chicken Breast Marinated in Yogurt and Grilled with Tropical Fruit Vinaigrette excites the sour (with the yogurt and vinegar), the sweet (from the fruit), and the pungent-pepper sense.

Wine, too, has these complex taste qualities. The most interesting wines are also those that excite as many of the taste senses as possible in a harmonious way.

Chicken Breasts Marinated in Yogurt and Grilled with Tropical Fruit Vinaigrette

The yogurt marinade adds a tart, spicy flavor to the chicken and also gives it a moist, buttery texture.

Serves 6

YOGURT MARINADE:

1   teaspoon toasted and crushed
       cumin seed (page 36)
½   teaspoon red chile flakes
2   teaspoons roasted garlic (page 247)

¼   cup minced scallions, white part only
1   cup plain yogurt
1   teaspoon paprika
1   tablespoon fresh lemon juice

6   boneless, skinless chicken breast halves

TROPICAL FRUIT VINAIGRETTE:

2   tablespoons minced scallions,
       white part only
1   cup diced mango or papaya
3   tablespoons seasoned rice wine
       vinegar (or to taste)
¼   cup corn or peanut oil
2   tablespoons minced fresh mint
       Kosher salt and freshly ground
         white pepper

2   tablespoons olive oil
4   cups young savory greens, such as
         spinach, mustard, and kale
       Garnish: Slices of kiwi, cilantro
         sprigs, and grilled pineapple
         wedges, if desired

In a medium bowl, combine the marinade ingredients. Add the chicken and marinate in the refrigerator for at least 2 hours.

While the chicken is marinating, combine the vinaigrette ingredients. Allow the vinaigrette to set at room temperature for at least 30 minutes for the flavors to develop.

Preheat the broiler or a stovetop grill. Wipe any excess marinade from the chicken. Grill or broil until the chicken is just done and juicy, about 3 to 4 minutes on each side. While the chicken is cooking, heat the olive oil in a large sauté pan and quickly sauté the savory greens until just wilted. Serve the chicken on top of the greens and drizzle with the vinaigrette to taste.

 Recommended wine: Many Chardonnays are characterized by tropical fruit flavors, which makes them an ideal match for this dish.

Breast of Chicken with a "Coat of Many Colors"

When time is short or I'm at the end of a long day, I often just grill, sauté, or poach a boneless chicken breast and then top it with a tasty little "new mother sauce." Here are four of my make-ahead favorites that work equally well with other light meats such as pork or fish.

Tomato and Golden Raisin Chutney

Makes approximately 2 cups

4 tablespoons olive oil	1 cup dry white wine
1 cup minced onions	⅔ cup white wine vinegar
1 tablespoon minced garlic	3 tablespoons sugar
1½ cups peeled, seeded, and chopped tomatoes (or canned drained, diced tomatoes)	Bouquet garni: 4 parsley sprigs, 2 bay leaves, 2 thyme sprigs, and 12 peppercorns tied in a cheesecloth bundle
Kosher salt and freshly ground black pepper	2½ cups water
1¼ pounds white pearl onions	⅓ cup golden raisins

In a medium saucepan, heat 1 tablespoon of the olive oil. Add the minced onions and garlic and sauté until soft and lightly colored. Add the tomatoes. Simmer over moderate heat until most of the liquid has evaporated. Season lightly with salt and pepper. Remove from the saucepan and reserve.

Peel the pearl onions and cut a small cross in the root end. In the saucepan, combine the onions, wine, vinegar, sugar, bouquet garni, and water. Bring to a boil. Reduce the heat to a simmer and continue to cook until the onions are tender, approximately 20 minutes, depending on their size. Remove the onions and reserve.

Over high heat, continue to reduce the liquid to 1 cup. Lower the heat to a simmer. Add the reserved tomato mixture, raisins, and onions. Simmer for 10 minutes, stirring occasionally, or until the mixture is thick and the onions are glazed and tender. Remove and discard the bouquet garni. Season to taste with salt and pepper.

This can be served right away or can be stored refrigerated for up to 3 months.

Olive-Caper Relish

Makes approximately ¾ cup

¼ cup chopped green olives	2 teaspoons balsamic vinegar
1 teaspoon roasted garlic (page 247)	3 tablespoons seeded and chopped plum tomatoes
¼ cup chopped fresh parsley	2 tablespoons chopped oil-packed, sun-dried tomatoes
2 tablespoons drained and chopped cornichon pickles	2 tablespoons oil from the tomatoes
1½ tablespoons drained and chopped capers	Freshly ground black pepper
1 teaspoon Dijon-style mustard	

Combine all the relish ingredients, seasoning to taste with pepper. This can be served right away or can be stored covered in the refrigerator up to 3 weeks.

Sun-Dried Tomato Pesto

Makes approximately 1¼ cups

1½ cups fruity red wine, such as Gamay or Pinot Noir	¼ cup grated aged dry goat cheese such as Tomme (or a good Parmesan or dry Jack)
1 cup dried tomatoes (*not* packed in oil)	3 tablespoons chopped fresh basil
1 tablespoon tomato paste	½ cup or so extra-virgin olive oil (or to taste)
¼ cup lightly toasted and chopped pistachios or almonds	Salt and freshly ground black pepper
2 tablespoons roasted garlic (page 247)	

Warm the wine to a simmer, remove from the heat, and add to the tomatoes in a small bowl. Set aside and allow the tomatoes to plump and soften (approximately 1 hour). Drain and press the tomatoes lightly to extract excess liquid. (Save the wine for stock, if desired). Put the tomatoes into a food processor along with the remaining ingredients except the olive oil and salt and pepper and process in one or two short bursts. With motor running, gradually add the oil to desired consistency. Season to taste with salt and pepper. Store covered in the refrigerator for up to 2 weeks. Pesto can be thinned with reserved wine or stock if desired.

Note: A thin layer of olive oil on top of any pesto helps preserve its color and flavor.

Jicama-Carrot Salsa

Makes approximately 2 cups

½ cup finely diced jicama
⅓ cup finely diced carrot
½ cup seeded and diced ripe plum tomato
¼ cup diced red onion or scallions
1 teaspoon minced garlic
2 tablespoons fresh lime or lemon juice

½ teaspoon seeded and minced habañero chile (or to taste)
¼ cup roughly chopped fresh cilantro
2 tablespoons olive oil
   Honey, salt, and pepper

Combine all ingredients, adding honey, salt, and pepper as desired. Store covered in the refrigerator up to 3 days.

 ## Chicken Breasts Steamed in Cabbage with Cider Cream Sauce

This is an elegant preparation for chicken, elevating the humble bird to new heights. By enveloping the chicken breasts in cabbage, they remain moist and juicy.
   Serves 4

   Cider Cream Sauce (recipe follows)
4–8 large leaves of napa or other green cabbage
   3 tablespoons unsalted butter or olive oil
   2 cups peeled and sliced tart apples, cut approximately ¼ inch thick
   2 tablespoons slivered shallots

1 teaspoon high-quality curry powder
   Kosher salt and freshly ground black pepper
4 6-ounce boneless, skinless chicken breast halves
1 cup thinly sliced mushrooms
⅓ cup dry white wine
   Garnish: Roasted baby carrots and onions, fresh thyme leaves

Make the Cider Cream Sauce and set aside.

In lightly salted boiling water briefly blanch the cabbage leaves, about 30 seconds. Remove and plunge immediately into ice water to stop the cooking, then drain and set aside. In a medium sauté pan, heat 2 tablespoons of the butter or oil and sauté the apples and shallots until tender. Add the curry powder and sauté until fragrant, approximately 1 to 2 minutes. Season with salt and pepper.

Divide the sautéed apples among the four cabbage leaves. Place a chicken breast on top of the apple mixture and fold over the cabbage leaves to completely enclose. If necessary, place a second cabbage leaf around the mixture. In a large sauté pan, heat the remaining tablespoon of butter or oil. Add the sliced mushrooms and sauté 1 minute. Place the cabbage packets on top of the mushrooms, add the wine, cover, and steam over moderate heat for 7 to 10 minutes or until the breasts are just done, but moist.

To serve, remove the cabbage packets and mushrooms with a slotted spoon and place on warm plates on a pool of the Cider Cream Sauce. Garnish with the baby vegetables and a scattering of thyme leaves.

Cider Cream Sauce

5 tablespoons unsalted butter, at room temperature	⅔ cup apple cider or ⅓ cup applejack brandy
½ cup sliced mushrooms	2 cups rich chicken stock
1½ cup minced scallions, white part only	1 tablespoon fresh lemon juice
	¾ cup heavy cream
1 cup peeled, cored, and roughly chopped tart apples	1 tablespoon drained green peppercorns

In a medium saucepan, heat 1 tablespoon of the butter and sauté the mushrooms, scallions, and apples until lightly browned. Add the cider or brandy, stock, and lemon juice and reduce by half. Add the cream and reduce to a light sauce consistency. Remove from the heat, whisk in the remaining 4 tablespoons butter, and strain the sauce. Slightly crush the green peppercorns and add to the sauce, which can be kept warm in a thermos for up to 3 hours.

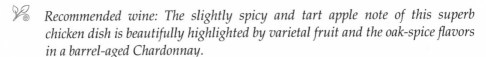

Recommended wine: The slightly spicy and tart apple note of this superb chicken dish is beautifully highlighted by varietal fruit and the oak-spice flavors in a barrel-aged Chardonnay.

Smoking Foods

Smoking adds delicious flavor to many foods and, of course, is a terrific way of linking food to the smoky, toasty flavors in barrel-aged and fermented wines.

Food can either be flavored with a bit of smoke and then cooked conventionally or cooked and smoked at the same time. The former is usually called "cold" smoking in which little or no heat is used while the latter is called "hot" smoking.

There are all kinds of smokers available on the market today including many that can be used right in the kitchen on top of the stove. These, of course, require a good ventilation system over the stove.

Any hardwood can be used for smoking, such as oak, hickory, or alder, and fruitwoods, such as apple or cherry, also give great flavor. I also like to smoke with fresh herbs. Rosemary grows like a weed in the wine country and we often throw bunches of it right on the coals to add a smoky, herbal flavor to meats, fish, or vegetables. End-of-summer herbs that are bolting, such as basil, dill, or fennel, are also great right on the coals.

A simple stovetop method to add some smoky flavor to meats or vegetables is to line a wok with heavy foil and then place hardwood shavings or sawdust in the bottom. You then place a rack with the food to be smoked on it at least 2 inches above the wood. Place the wok on the stove over moderate heat, and as soon as it begins to smoke, cover the top lightly with foil and/or a lid and allow the food to smoke for at least 3 or 4 minutes. Remove the wok from the heat, remove the lid (either with good ventilation or outside), and finish cooking the food on top of the stove or in the oven as needed.

One of my favorite quick recipes for smoked chicken or shrimp uses a marinade of the Oriental Orange Vinaigrette (page 15) with shrimp or boneless chicken breasts. These are marinated for at least 30 minutes and then wok smoked as described above. Shrimp are completely cooked in 3 to 4 minutes while boneless chicken breasts are usually done in 6 to 8 minutes.

Green Peppercorns

Green peppercorns are available either freeze-dried or in brine packed in a can. They are the immature berry of a tropical vine native to India and Indonesia. Black peppercorns are also the immature fruit, but they are dried in the sun to develop a more pungent flavor. White peppercorns fare from the mature berry, left on the vine until fairly ripe and red in color. The red skin is removed by soaking and rubbing and then the peppercorns are dried. Pink peppercorns are not a true peppercorn, but rather the dried berries of the *Baies* rose plant, grown in Madagascar.

Chile-Rubbed Roast Chicken with Tortilla-Chile Sauce

This spicy roast chicken can be done either in the "green" version, as below, or in a "red" version with the following substitutions: red onions for the yellow onions, 2½ ounces stemmed and seeded ancho or New Mexico dried chiles for the poblanos, and drops of fresh lime or lemon juice for seasoning. Both versions make a great party dish served with Green Chile and Cheese Rice (page 289).
Serves 4

Chile Rub (recipe follows)
1   3½-pound chicken, all fat removed
¾   pound tomatillos, husked
1¼ pounds yellow onions, quartered
12 garlic cloves, peeled
2   large poblano chiles, seeded
2   small serrano chiles, stemmed
    Olive oil
2   8-inch corn tortillas, lightly toasted

1¼ cups rich chicken stock
½   cup fruity white wine, such as Riesling
1   cup chopped spinach leaves
2   large bunches fresh cilantro, stemmed and chopped
    Kosher salt and freshly ground black pepper
    Garnish: Cilantro sprigs and toasted pumpkin seeds

Prepare the Chile Rub and coat the outside of the chicken. Set aside in a small roasting pan.

On a lightly oiled jelly roll pan, arrange the tomatillos, onions, garlic, poblanos, and serranos in a single layer. Place under a hot broiler until lightly browned and remove. Set the oven temperature to 450 degrees. Insert half of the roasted vegetables into the cavity of the chicken. Cut the tortillas into ½-inch wide strips and scatter them and the remaining vegetables in the bottom of the roasting pan. Truss the chicken and place on top, breast side down. Roast for 15 minutes. Turn the chicken over and lower the oven temperature to 375 degrees. Roast for another 45 to 50 minutes or until the juices run clear when the joint between the leg and thigh is pierced.

Remove the vegetables from the cavity. Set the chicken aside and keep warm. In a food processor or a blender, purée, in batches if necessary, the vegetables, tortillas, pan juices, including any browned bits, the chicken stock, white wine, spinach, and cilantro leaves. (The purée should be bright green and really smooth.) Strain the purée and season to taste with salt and pepper. Briefly warm the sauce. Carve the chicken into serving pieces and serve immediately with the sauce. Garnish with cilantro sprigs and toasted pumpkin seeds if desired.

Chile Rub

1 tablespoon California or New Mexico chile powder	2 teaspoons kosher salt
	1 teaspoon dried Mexican oregano
1 teaspoon fennel seed	½ teaspoon ground cinnamon
1 teaspoon coriander seed	2 tablespoons olive oil

Place all ingredients except the olive oil in a spice grinder. Grind finely. Alternately, grind by hand with a mortar and pestle. Remove to a bowl and stir in the olive oil to make a smooth mixture. Store covered at room temperature for up to 3 days.

 Recommended wine: A fruity Gewürztraminer or Johannisberg Riesling provides refreshing contrast to this zesty dish.

 Corned Chicken

This is an excellent technique for "corning" chicken, not unlike the technique used for corning beef. The uncooked chicken is "pickled" in a brine of salt, sugar, and sweet spices in the refrigerator for 4 days; the salt is soaked out and then the chicken is roasted. Once cooked, the chicken can be used in main courses, soups, or sandwiches, in salads, or for corned chicken hash!

Serves 4

¾ cup kosher salt	12 whole cloves
⅓ cup firmly packed light-brown sugar	1 teaspoon freshly grated nutmeg
2½ quarts water	1½ tablespoons crushed juniper berries
3 large garlic cloves, crushed	1 3½-pound chicken

In a large saucepan, combine the salt, sugar, and 2½ quarts of water. Simmer until the salt dissolves. Remove from the heat and stir in the garlic, cloves, nutmeg, and juniper berries. Allow the mixture to cool to room temperature.

Put the chicken in a nonreactive bowl or pot and cover with the salt-sugar mixture, adding additional water, if necessary, to barely cover the chicken. Cover the bowl or pot tightly and refrigerate for 4 days, turning the chicken once a day.

Drain the chicken, rinse it well, and cover with cold water. Submerge the chicken, using a weight if necessary. Return the pot, covered, to the refrigerator for 3 hours, changing the water at least 3 times.

Preheat the oven to 375 degrees. Drain the chicken and pat dry. Truss and roast it on a rack for 1 hour or until the juices run clear.

 Recommended wine: A fruity Riesling, Gewürztraminer, or Chenin Blanc with a little residual sugar will play off the sweet-salty "corned" flavor of this chicken.

As you may have surmised by looking at the above recipe, there is no corn in "corned" chicken—or in "corned" beef. The term comes from the old English tradition of salting meats to preserve them. For this purpose, the English used a special kind of salt (not unlike kosher salt) whose large, coarse crystals resembled grain—what the English called "corn"—in size and shape.

 ## Smoked Chicken Burritos

You can serve these burritos assembled or as part of a "burrito bar," letting everyone make his or her own. The idea for this dish came from Lee Stephens, who worked with me at Valley Oaks; we had to do a quick lunch one day, and this was the result. I make these at home a lot.

Serves 6

1 cup thinly sliced red bell pepper
1 cup thinly sliced yellow bell pepper
1 cup thinly sliced cucumber (peel, seed, and depulp before slicing)

½ cup julienned jicama
1 cup thinly sliced red onions
Orange-Cumin Vinaigrette (recipe follows)

6 12-inch flour tortillas, preferably
    homemade (page 362)
    Chipotle Mayonnaise (recipe
    follows)
1¼ pounds smoked chicken,
    julienned

¼ cup loosely packed cilantro leaves
    Garnish: Avocado Salsa (page 212)
    and/or Roasted White Corn
    Salsa (page 147), and cilantro
    sprigs

In a large bowl, combine the bell pepper, cucumber, jicama, and red onions with the Orange-Cumin Vinaigrette. Allow to stand at room temperature for at least 30 minutes. Drain and set aside.

Warm the tortillas briefly over a gas burner or cover with a damp towel and steam in a 350-degree oven for about 6 minutes, until soft and pliable. Spread the Chipotle Mayonnaise on the tortillas. Top with the drained bell pepper mixture, julienned smoked chicken, and cilantro leaves.

Fold the top and bottom of the tortilla partially over the filling. Roll the tortilla to completely enclose the filling. Serve with a couple of tablespoons of either or both of the salsas and cilantro sprigs.

Orange-Cumin Vinaigrette

⅓ cup fresh orange juice
2 tablespoons fresh lime or lemon
    juice
1 teaspoon toasted and ground
    cumin seed (page 36)

¼ teaspoon ground cinnamon
1 teaspoon minced fresh mint
3 tablespoons olive oil
    Kosher salt and freshly ground
    black pepper

In a small bowl, whisk together all ingredients but the salt and pepper until well combined. Season to taste. Store covered in the refrigerator up to 3 days.

Chipotle Mayonnaise

1 egg
2 teaspoons chopped garlic
2 tablespoons chopped scallions,
    white part only
1 teaspoon chopped chipotle in
    adobo

2 tablespoons fresh lime juice
½–¾ cup olive oil
    Salt and freshly ground black
    pepper

In a food processor, combine the egg, garlic, scallions, chipotle, and lime juice. Process briefly. With the motor running, slowly add enough oil to form a thick emulsion. Season to taste with salt and pepper. Store refrigerated for up to 3 days.

Recommended wine: The Chipotle Mayonnaise is pretty spicy and smoky. A slightly sweet well-chilled Chenin Blanc or Riesling would work nicely.

My Grandmother's Fried Chicken

Just to show you that wine country cooking still has room for time-honored traditions like fried chicken, here's my grandmother's version. The presteaming guarantees moist chicken, and also reduces the time the chicken spends frying, which gives it a crisp crust and makes it less greasy. It would be wonderful on a picnic with the Lemony Potato Salad with Olives, Corn, and Cashews (page 38) and a great summer cobbler, like the Cherry and Almond Cobbler (page 315).

Serves 4

1 3 ½-pound chicken	½ teaspoon freshly ground black
1 large egg	pepper
1½ cups buttermilk	1½ quarts vegetable oil
1 cup flour	(or, traditionally, lard)
1 teaspoon kosher salt	

In a soup kettle bring 2 inches of water to a boil. Place a rack over the water, setting the chicken on top. Cover the pot and steam the chicken whole until it is almost cooked, approximately 15 to 18 minutes.

Remove the chicken from the pot and cool. Cut into 8 serving pieces. In a medium bowl whisk the egg and buttermilk together. In a separate bowl, combine the flour, salt, and pepper. Marinate the chicken in the buttermilk mixture for a few minutes, then remove from the buttermilk and dredge in the seasoned flour.

In a large skillet or Dutch oven, heat the oil to 365 degrees. Fry the chicken, in batches if necessary, for approximately 7 minutes. Turn the chicken and fry until golden brown, about 7 minutes more. Remove the chicken to paper towels and drain. Serve immediately.

Recommended wine: A buttery Chardonnay emphasizes the succulent chicken perfectly.

Oven-"Fried" Chicken with a Cornmeal Crust

This technique gives a crisp, crunchy crust with a minimum of fat. You could also remove the skin before coating and baking, which also reduces fat substantially; the marinated chicken baked without the coating is also very tasty and quick to prepare. Either way, this chicken is superb hot or at room temperature.

Serves 4

¾ cup buttermilk
¼ cup fresh lemon juice
1 tablespoon grated lemon zest
¼ cup olive oil
2 tablespoons finely minced
    shallots
1 tablespoon chopped fresh thyme
    or rosemary leaves (or
    ½ teaspoon dried)
1 tablespoon kosher salt
1 tablespoon pure New Mexico or
    California chile powder

1 3-pound chicken, cut into
    8 serving pieces
½ cup yellow cornmeal
½ cup Panko or other dry
    breadcrumbs
⅔ cup freshly grated Parmesan or
    dry Jack cheese
3 tablespoons minced fresh parsley
    or basil
2 eggs beaten with 2 tablespoons
    water
2 tablespoons unsalted melted butter

In a medium bowl, whisk together the buttermilk, lemon juice, 1 teaspoon of the lemon zest, the olive oil, shallots, thyme, 2 teaspoons of the salt, and 2 teaspoons of the chile powder. Add the chicken, turning the pieces to coat them. Marinate, refrigerated, for 4 hours.

In a separate bowl combine the cornmeal, breadcrumbs, Parmesan, parsley, and the remaining lemon zest, salt, and chile powder. Remove the chicken from the marinade and drain briefly. Coat the pieces in the egg mixture and dredge in the cornmeal mixture, patting to coat. The chicken can be prepared up to this point 3 hours in advance and kept uncovered in the refrigerator.

Preheat the oven to 425 degrees. On a lightly oiled baking pan, arrange the chicken skin side up. Drizzle with the butter. Bake for 35 minutes until crisp and golden. Remove to paper towels and drain. Serve warm or at room temperature.

Recommended wine: A crisp, tart Sauvignon Blanc is my favorite wine with this dish. It reflects the tart flavors from the lemon and buttermilk.

Grilled Tamarind-Glazed Chicken with Sesame Spinach

This simple, marvelous dish owes its unusual flavor to tamarind, a tart fruit used in Latin American and Asian cooking, which can be found in markets carrying Latin American products. The chicken improves with a good, long marinating, so don't hesitate to prepare it the day before and leave it in the refrigerator overnight.

Serves 4

⅔ cup firmly packed light-brown
    sugar
⅔ cup red wine vinegar
1 cup rich chicken stock
1 cup seeded and chopped ripe
    tomatoes
1 tablespoon whole mustard seed
½ teaspoon seeded and minced
    serrano chile

3 tablespoons tamarind pulp or
    concentrate
1 3½-pound chicken
    Sesame Spinach (recipe follows)
    Garnish: Curry oil (page 68),
        toasted sesame seeds (page 36),
        and cilantro sprigs

In a saucepan, combine the sugar, vinegar, stock, tomatoes, mustard seed, chile, and tamarind. Bring to a simmer and cook over moderate heat for 10 minutes, stirring occasionally until thickened. Cool slightly, purée in a food processor, and set aside.

Split the chicken in half; remove and discard the wing tips, back, and rib bones. Coat with the tamarind purée and marinate, refrigerated, for 4 hours or overnight.

Prepare a charcoal fire or preheat the broiler. Grill or broil the chicken halves on both sides until crusty, rich brown, and cooked through, approximately 20 minutes. Cut into serving pieces and arrange on warm plates on a bed of Sesame Spinach. Drizzle with drops of curry oil and garnish with a sprinkling of sesame seeds and cilantro sprigs. Serve immediately.

Sesame Spinach

1 tablespoon olive oil
1 tablespoon dark sesame oil
2 large bunches spinach (about
    1 pound), washed and stemmed
    Kosher salt and freshly ground
    black pepper

    Fresh lemon juice
2 tablespoons toasted sesame seeds,
    both white and black seeds, if
    available (page 36)

In a large pot or wok, heat the olive and sesame oils. Add the spinach, in batches if necessary, and sauté over high heat for 1 minute or until the spinach just begins to wilt. Season with salt, pepper, and drops of lemon juice to taste and sprinkle with the sesame seeds.

 Recommended wine: A fruity Gewürztraminer or Johannesburg Riesling would play off the sweet-tart flavor of the tamarind glaze.

 # *Soy-Poached Game Hens*

This is an Oriental-style poultry dish in terms of flavoring and how it is served. Star anise is a special Asian ingredient with a pronounced licorice flavor and aroma. It's available in Asian markets and many health food stores. The hens may be halved for a main course or chopped in smaller pieces as an appetizer. Here, the hens are placed on savory baby greens, but soba noodles or even whole-wheat thin noodles like angelhair would be delicious too. The dish should be served at room temperature.

Serves 4 as a main course

4   cups water
¾   cup dark soy sauce
⅓   cup sugar
⅓   cup Chinese black or balsamic
      vinegar
4   tablespoons chopped fresh ginger
      Juice and half the peel of
      1 medium orange
4   large garlic cloves, peeled and
      bruised
¾   teaspoon fennel seed
1   large star anise pod
1   3-inch piece cinnamon stick

¼   teaspoon red chile flakes
2   large game hens, or 3-pound
      frying chicken with all fat
      removed, or 3 pounds chicken
      thighs with skin removed
3   tablespoons dark sesame oil
6   cups savory baby greens, such as
      red mustard, arugula, savoy
      cabbage, and mizuna
   Garnish: Toasted sesame seeds
      (page 36), diagonally sliced
      whole scallions, and cilantro
      sprigs

In a medium stockpot, combine the water, soy sauce, sugar, vinegar, ginger, orange juice and peel, garlic, and dry spices. Simmer, covered, for 5 minutes.

Add the whole game hens or chicken and gently simmer, covered, for 35 minutes. (If using thighs, cook only for 12 minutes.) Remove from heat and allow the poultry to stand in the poaching liquid for at least 30 minutes. (The longer the hens stand, the more color and flavor they will absorb from the poaching liquid. They'll be fine for up to 3 hours.)

To serve, remove the hens to a cutting board, pat dry, and sprinkle liberally with the dark sesame oil. Cut whole birds into serving pieces; chicken thighs may be left whole. On a platter, arrange the hens on top of the savory greens, drizzle a bit of poaching liquid over all, and garnish with sesame seeds, scallions, and cilantro.

Note: The soy poaching liquid can be reused. Strain, remove all fat, and store, covered, refrigerated up to 3 weeks or frozen indefinitely.

 Recommended wine: I enjoy a fruity Gewürztraminer or Riesling to contrast the sweet-salty flavors of this dish.

 # Herb-Roasted Game Hens

I wanted to come up with a version of the ever-popular roasted poultry that would take advantage of all the wonderful herbs grown in the Valley Oaks garden. Jim Rhodes, who has one of the best senses of taste that I know, came up with this approach, which works wonderfully for birds that are oven-roasted, grilled, or spit-roasted.
Serves 4

HERB RUB:

2 tablespoons dried oregano
2 tablespoons dried tarragon
3 tablespoons dried lemon thyme or English thyme
1 tablespoon dried rosemary
2 imported bay leaves, center ribs removed
1 teaspoon dried lavender flowers (optional)
1 tablespoon toasted fennel seed (page 36)
1 teaspoon toasted coriander seed

1 tablespoon coarsely ground black pepper
2 tablespoons minced dried orange peel
1 tablespoon minced dried lemon peel
Kosher salt
Balsamic vinegar
Extra-virgin olive oil

4 game hens, 16–18 ounces each
1 large lemon, sliced
8 garlic cloves, peeled and smashed

To prepare the herb rub: Combine the oregano, tarragon, thyme, rosemary, bay leaves, and lavender flowers, if using, in a bowl. In a dry sauté pan over medium heat, toast the herb mixture until fragrant. This will take only a few minutes. You will smell the wonderful aroma. Do not burn. Return to the bowl. Add the fennel, coriander, pepper, and orange and lemon peel and stir to combine. In a spice grinder or with a mortar and pestle, coarsely grind the mixture. To use the herb rub, combine 5 parts of the coarsely ground mixture with 1 part kosher salt, 3 parts balsamic vinegar, and 3 parts extra-virgin olive oil.

Rinse the game hens well and pat dry. Rub the herb rub liberally over the inside and outside of the hens. Allow to marinate, covered, in the refrigerator for 8 hours or overnight.

Preheat the oven to 425 degrees. Evenly divide the lemon slices and garlic, placing them in the cavity of each hen. Truss the hens. Place them on a rack in a roasting pan, breast side down. Roast for 10 minutes. Turn the hens breast side up, reduce heat to 350 degrees, and continue roasting for another 20 to 25 minutes or until cooked through and the juices run clear. Allow to rest 10 minutes before carving. Serve warm or at room temperature.

 Recommended wine: These herb-roasted birds go well with a barrel-aged Chardonnay or a lighter-style red with herbaceous notes, such as a Pinot Noir or Merlot.

DRIED CITRUS PEEL

Dried citrus peel is a flavorful addition to many dry herb mixes. For some reason the dried peel you buy in the spice section of your supermarket rarely has any flavor at all. When I get nice oranges in the winter I use my vegetable peeler to remove the orange skin, leaving the white bitter pith behind. Take these strips of orange skin and microwave them on medium or medium-low for 2 to 3 minutes until leathery. Let them sit at room temperature for a few hours until dry, then finely chop and store them in an airtight container for up to 3 months. You can do the same with lemons, limes, or grapefruit.

Asian Marinated Breast of Squab

This is a delicious recipe that works equally well with the breast of any bird: Quail, hen, chicken, or pheasant would all be wonderful. Adjust the cooking time as needed. You'll note that I recommend cooking the squab breast on the bone. This ensures that the breast will keep its shape and not shrivel up. Also, cooking on the bone keeps the meat moist and adds flavor. I'm accompanying the squab here with cooked greens, but they would be equally delicious on fresh, spicy greens. Try the Oriental Orange Vinaigrette (page 15) on the fresh greens.

Serves 4

ASIAN MARINADE:

⅛ cup finely crushed star anise pods
¼ cup roughly chopped fresh ginger
2 tablespoons soy sauce
2 tablespoons fresh lime juice
1 cup olive oil
2 teaspoons Chinese five-spice powder
1 tablespoon dark sesame oil
2 teaspoons freshly ground black pepper
¼ cup finely chopped lemon grass or 1 tablespoon grated lemon zest

4 whole squab, cleaned
5 tablespoons olive oil
2 tablespoons minced shallots
½ pound chanterelle or shiitake mushrooms
   Salt and freshly ground black pepper
6 cups savory young greens, such as spinach, chard, mustard, or a combination

In a nonreactive bowl, combine the marinade ingredients. Marinate the squabs for 4 hours or overnight in the refrigerator, turning them occasionally. Remove the whole (bone-in) breast from each squab and very quickly brown the breasts in 2 tablespoons of the oil over high heat, about 2 minutes. Set aside. Save the remainder of the carcass to make stock or remove the leg/thigh portions and brown them to use as garnish.

Preheat the oven to 425 degrees. Place the bone-in breasts (and leg portions, if using) in a single layer in a roasting pan and roast for 6 to 8 minutes or until the breasts are cooked medium rare. (If using the leg portions, cook them 3 minutes longer or until they are tender.) The flesh of the breasts should be pink and rosy. Set aside and keep warm.

In a sauté pan, heat 2 tablespoons of the olive oil and sauté the shallots and mushrooms until they just begin to soften. Season with salt and pepper, set aside, and keep warm. Add the remaining 1 tablespoon oil to the pan and sauté the greens until just tender. Season to taste with salt and pepper. To serve, arrange the greens on warm plates. Carefully cut breasts from bone and arrange on top of the greens with the mushrooms alongside. Spoon a little of the marinade around and garnish with the roasted leg portions, if using.

 Recommended wine: If using squab breast, which is a dark, rich meat, I'd serve a nontannic Merlot or Pinot Noir. If using a white-meat breast, from chicken or game hens, a rich, barrel-aged Chardonnay would accentuate the Asian flavors in the marinade without overpowering the bird.

CHINESE FIVE-SPICE POWDER

This standard of Chinese cooking is a blend of five different aromatic spices. Choice of ingredients varies depending on the maker. Sometimes licorice root is substituted for the fennel or anise. Five-spice powder can be purchased ready-mixed, but like all ground spices it quickly loses its flavor, and I think it's best to make your own from spices that are freshly ground.

CHINESE FIVE-SPICE POWDER

Makes about 3 tablespoons

1 tablespoon freshly ground Szechuan peppercorns (1 heaping tablespoon before grinding)

½ teaspoon ground cloves, preferably freshly ground (about ½ teaspoon before grinding)

1 tablespoon ground cinnamon, preferably freshly ground (about 6 inches of stick cinnamon before grinding)

1 tablespoon freshly ground fennel seed (1 heaping tablespoon before grinding)

6 whole star anise, ground

Mix the spices, then regrind them together until the mixture is very fine. Store refrigerated in a jar with a tightly fitting cover.

Squab with Fig-Port Sauce

In *American Game Cooking*, I explored the world of game birds in great detail, and I haven't stopped cooking squab or loving its flavor and juicy texture. Remember, the squab needs to be cooked "pink," or medium rare. Since the bird has little fat, cooking past this point renders it dry and tasteless. This is another super-easy dish, for entertaining or eating elegantly at home without company.

Serves 4

2   whole squab, halved, wing tips
      removed
    Kosher salt and freshly ground
      black pepper

1   tablespoon vegetable oil
    Fig-Port Sauce (recipe follows)
    Garnish: Fresh thyme sprigs

Season the squab with salt and pepper. In a medium sauté pan, heat the oil until sizzling. Sauté the squab, skin side down, for 4 to 5 minutes, or until the skin is richly browned. Turn and cook for just 2 to 3 minutes. Do not overcook—squab should be juicy and pink inside. Spoon the sauce on warm plates and place half a squab on top. Garnish with thyme sprigs.

Fig-Port Sauce

Makes about 3 cups

1   tablespoon olive oil
⅓ cup minced yellow
      onion
1   cup port
2½ cups rich chicken stock
½ cup chopped dried figs

1   4-inch cinnamon stick, broken
      into 3 or 4 pieces
2   star anise pods
2   teaspoons minced fresh thyme
    Kosher salt and freshly ground
      black pepper

In a saucepan, heat the olive oil and sauté the onion until lightly browned. Add the port, stock, figs, cinnamon, and star anise and bring to a boil. Reduce heat and simmer for 5 minutes. Strain through a fine sieve. Stir in the fresh thyme. Season to taste with salt and pepper and keep warm. A thermos is useful for this.

Recommended wine: This intense, fig-infused sauce requires a hearty Zinfandel, Petite Sirah, or Syrah to match its power.

Grilled Quail with Citrus-Muscat Sauce

Quail pick up flavors very well and benefit greatly from marinating. This citrus-based marinade and sauce complement them beautifully. The dish is easier to prepare than it looks, as long as you can buy the quail already deboned. If it's barbecue weather, this is a perfect dish for elegant but easy entertaining. I like to serve the quail with the Chile Corn Cakes on page 284.

Serves 4

MARINADE:

2 tablespoons olive oil	1 shallot, chopped
Juice of 3 tangerines	½ teaspoon kosher salt
Juice of 1 lemon	
1 tablespoon chopped fresh thyme (or ½ tablespoon dried)	8 boneless quail
	Citrus-Muscat Sauce (recipe follows)

In a small bowl, mix all the marinade ingredients together. In a baking dish large enough to hold the quail in a single layer, place the quail and pour the marinade over. Refrigerate covered for 2 to 3 hours, turning occasionally. (Make the Citrus-Muscat Sauce while the quail are marinating.) Remove the quail from the marinade. Reserve the marinade for basting.

Prepare a charcoal fire, using mesquite wood, if possible. When the coals are white, grill the quail skin side down for 3 to 4 minutes. Turn, baste with the reserved marinade, and grill for just 2 to 3 minutes. (The quail should remain juicy and pink inside.) Do not overcook. Serve topped with the Citrus-Muscat Sauce.

Citrus-Muscat Sauce

Makes about 2 cups

1 tablespoon vegetable oil	Juice of 1 lime
1 carrot, chopped	Juice of 3 tangerines
1 stalk celery, chopped	1½ cups chicken stock
1 shallot, chopped	1 tablespoon chilled unsalted butter (optional)
2 cloves garlic, chopped	
4 thyme sprigs	
2 cups Black Muscat wine or sweet sherry	

In a large saucepan over medium heat, heat the oil. Add the chopped carrot, celery, shallot, garlic, and the thyme and sauté until the vegetables are lightly browned. Add the wine and the lime and tangerines juices. Bring to a boil, scraping up any brown bits to deglaze the pan. Reduce the heat and simmer for 10 to 12 minutes or until reduced by half. Add the stock and continue cooking for 12 to 15 minutes or until the mixture reaches a light sauce consistency. Remove from the heat. Whisk in the chilled butter, if using. Keep the sauce warm.

Recommended wine: The citrusy tang to this dish suggests a fine barrel-aged Chardonnay or a cherry-tinged Pinot Noir.

Grilled Quail with Pickled Figs and Prosciutto

Grilled quail, succulent little devils that they are, are extremely versatile. This preparation features the quail with sweet-tart pickled figs and the contrasting flavor of salty prosciutto. If you make the figs ahead, refrigerate them in their poaching liquid and return them to room temperature before serving. You get a bonus with this recipe: The leftover fig-poaching syrup is delicious on grilled meats or even ice cream! The figs are served at room temperature, but the quail should be hot, right off the grill.
    Serves 4

8 boneless quail	Pickled Figs (recipe follows)
2 tablespoons vegetable oil	12 thin slices prosciutto
Kosher salt and freshly ground black pepper	

Prepare a charcoal fire (using mesquite wood, if possible) or preheat the broiler. Brush the quail with the oil and season with salt and pepper. Grill the quail, skin side down, 4 to 5 minutes. Turn and continue cooking until nicely browned, just 2 to 3 minutes. Or place the quail skin side up on a baking sheet and broil until crisp on the outside, approximately 3 to 4 minutes. Turn and continue broiling for 2 to 3 minutes, until done. The quail should be slightly pink and juicy inside. Do not overcook.
    Wrap each pickled fig with a slice of prosciutto and serve alongside the quail.

Pickled Figs

1   cup sugar
1¼   cups red wine vinegar
¼   cup balsamic vinegar
1   3-inch cinnamon stick, broken
        into 3 pieces
6   cardamom pods, crushed

3   star anise pods
6   thin coins peeled fresh ginger
4   thin slices lemon
6   whole black peppercorns
12   small fresh figs (Black Mission
        or Kadota)

In a small, nonreactive pot, place the sugar, vinegars, cinnamon, cardamom, star anise, ginger, lemon, and peppercorns. Simmer for 10 minutes. Add the figs, cover, and continue simmering for 3 minutes. Remove from the heat and let the figs cool in the syrup. (Figs can be prepared to this point and stored in their syrup in the refrigerator indefinitely. Their flavor will get stronger over time, so you probably should use them within 2 weeks.) Using a slotted spoon, carefully remove the figs, reserving the poaching syrup for another use.

 Recommended wine: The sweet-tart flavors of the pickled figs are challenging for wine. However, an off-dry Gewürztraminer, Johannisberg Riesling, or Gamay Beaujolais will provide the necessary fruitiness.

 # Barbecued Turkey with Jambalaya Stuffing

In California, we barbecue virtually year round. This turkey recipe has graced our family's Thanksgiving table for many years. It is far more Southern than it is wine country, but so much for strict regionality. For those not so fortunate to enjoy such forgiving climates, you might want to consider this recipe for outdoor summer entertaining. Once you experience turkey cooked on the grill, you are not likely to ever want to cook it in the oven again, so unbelievably succulent and delicious is the meat.
Serves 10 to 12

MARINADE:

6   tablespoons vegetable oil
1   tablespoon Worcestershire sauce
3   tablespoons paprika
1   tablespoon dry mustard
2   tablespoons dried thyme

2   tablespoons dried oregano
½   teaspoon cayenne pepper
1   tablespoon chopped garlic
1   tablespoon kosher salt

1   15-pound turkey

In a small bowl, combine all the marinade ingredients and whisk together. Rub the marinade over the outside of the turkey as well as underneath the skin by gently using your fingers to separate the skin from the breast. Refrigerate the turkey for at least 2 to 3 hours.

JAMBALAYA:

4 tablespoons olive oil
1 pound andouille sausage or other highly seasoned sausage, such as chorizo, linguiça, or Italian, diced
2 cups diced green bell peppers
2 cups diced red bell peppers
4 cups diced yellow onions
2½ cups diced celery
1 tablespoon chopped garlic
1 teaspoon seeded and minced serrano chile
4 teaspoons chopped fresh thyme
4 teaspoons chopped fresh basil
1 tablespoon crumbled dried oregano
1 teaspoon freshly ground black pepper

½ teaspoon toasted and ground cumin seed (page 36)
2 teaspoons filé powder
2 bay leaves
2½ cups converted rice
1 28-ounce can Italian tomatoes, drained and diced
1 tablespoon tomato paste
  Kosher salt
4 cups hot rich chicken stock
1 cup diagonally cut scallions, ¼-inch lengths
2 tablespoons minced fresh parsley
  Kosher salt and freshly ground black pepper

In a large saucepan, sauté the andouille sausage in 2 tablespoons of the olive oil until golden brown. Using a slotted spoon, remove the sausage and set aside, leaving the oil in the pan. Add the remaining 2 tablespoons oil, the peppers, onions, celery, garlic, and serrano and sauté until deep golden brown (this may take as long as 20 minutes). Add the thyme, basil, oregano, pepper, cumin seed, filé powder, and bay leaves and stir to thoroughly combine. Add the rice, tomatoes, and tomato paste and sauté until the rice grains are translucent, about 5 minutes. Add 1 teaspoon salt to the hot stock, then pour the stock into the rice mixture. Stir well to fully incorporate and bring to a boil. Reduce heat to a simmer, cover, and cook for 20 minutes or until the rice is just tender.

Remove the bay leaves from the rice. To the rice, add the diced andouille, sliced scallions, and minced parsley. Stir gently to combine. Season to taste with salt and pepper. Refrigerate for 2 hours or until chilled. Spoon the chilled jambalaya into the turkey cavity and truss the cavity closed.

Build a charcoal fire (mesquite preferred) around the edges of a large grill. As soon as the coals are hot, push the coals to the edge, leaving a space to place a large dripping pan in the center. Replace the grill and put the trussed turkey directly over the dripping pan so that all juices drip into the pan and not onto the coals. Cover the grill, leaving the vents partially open. Add coals as necessary to keep the heat even.

Barbecue the turkey for 1½ hours or until a meat thermometer inserted between the leg and thigh registers 160 degrees. Do not overcook. Remove the turkey from the grill. Cover with a tent of foil for 15 to 20 minutes before carving. Serve the sliced turkey with the jambalaya stuffing.

 Recommended wine: This festive dish can be served with many different wines—a chilled Gamay Beaujolais, a slightly sweet Gewürztraminer, a fruity Chardonnay, a spicy Zinfandel.

 # Turkey Saltimbocca with Egg-Lemon Sauce and Butter-Braised Spinach

I created this dish for a class called "New Wave Thanksgiving"; the idea was to use traditional ingredients in a different way. The menu included Orange, Olive, and Fennel Salad with Cranberry Vinaigrette (page 13) and Corn Pudding (page 283), plus a pumpkin crème brûlée. The Egg-Lemon Sauce here is based on the Greek avgolemono sauce.

Serves 4

2 10- to 12-ounce turkey tenderloins, tendon removed	Butter-Braised Spinach (recipe follows)
2 ounces thinly sliced prosciutto	Egg-Lemon Sauce (recipe follows)
4 ounces thinly sliced smoked mozzarella cheese	Garnish: Baked cherry tomatoes and fresh sage sprigs
16 large fresh sage leaves	

Butterfly the tenderloins by slicing them lengthwise down the middle without cutting all the way through to the opposite side (you should be able to open up the tenderloin like a book). Using a mallet or a meat pounder, gently flatten the tenderloins between sheets of lightly oiled plastic wrap to a thickness of ¼ inch. Remove the top sheet of plastic wrap. Place single layers of prosciutto and smoked mozzarella on the turkey, leaving a border approximately ½ inch around the perimeter of the tenderloin. Place the sage leaves down the center. Using the plastic wrap and starting with a long side, roll the turkey tightly to form a sausage shape covered in plastic. Twist the ends tightly and tie securely with kitchen twine. Repeat with the other tenderloin.

In a stockpot large enough to hold the turkey rolls, heat water to a simmer. Place the turkey rolls in the simmering water and poach for 20 minutes or until cooked through (160 degrees on an instant-read thermometer). Remove from the water, unwrap, and discard the plastic. Slice into medallions ¼ to ½ inch thick.

To serve, place the spinach on warm plates and arrange the medallions attractively on top. Spoon the Egg-Lemon Sauce around and garnish with the cherry tomatoes and herb sprigs.

Butter-Braised Spinach

2 tablespoons unsalted butter
1 tablespoon minced shallots or
    scallions
1 pound spinach, washed and
    stemmed

Pinch of freshly grated nutmeg
Salt and freshly ground black
    pepper

In a large sauté pan, heat the butter and sauté the shallots until soft but not brown. Increase the heat and add the spinach all at once. Stir the spinach for a minute or two until wilted. Remove from the heat and season with nutmeg, salt, and pepper.

Egg-Lemon Sauce

1½ cups rich chicken stock
⅓ cup dry white wine
2 large egg yolks
3 tablespoons fresh lemon juice

Kosher salt and freshly ground
    white pepper
1 tablespoon minced fresh chives

In a small saucepan bring the stock and wine to a boil and reduce by half. Remove from heat. In a separate bowl, whisk together the egg yolks and lemon juice. Slowly whisk the reduced stock into the egg mixture a little bit at a time, being careful not to scramble the eggs. Return the mixture to the saucepan and cook over moderate heat, stirring constantly, until the sauce thickens slightly. Do not let the sauce simmer. Immediately strain, then season to taste with salt and pepper. Stir in the chives. Keep warm in a thermos until ready to serve.

Recommended wine: A crisp, lemon-tinged Fumé/Sauvignon Blanc provides the balancing acidity required for this dish.

BEEF, PORK, AND LAMB

Meat and Wine

We tend to consider all meats as the same when it comes to matching them with wines, but while there are good reasons for following tradition and partnering red meat with red wine, sweeter, lighter meats like lamb, rabbit, or pork can also match well with full-flavored white wines like Chardonnay.

A note on the wine you cook with: It's not necessary to use the same wine in a dish that you're going to drink with it, but if you're drinking an affordable wine, then by all means use the same one to cook with. When you choose a wine to cook with, be sure that it's a good wine and one that you'd enjoy drinking, but it doesn't have to be an expensive wine. You certainly don't want to cook with a great, old, priceless Cabernet any more than you want to cook with anything from the supermarket labeled "cooking wine." Also, don't make the mistake of using leftover wine that you may have kept in your refrigerator for weeks; after a few days, wine begins to oxidize and to "vinegar" a bit, which isn't necessarily complementary to the food you're cooking.

A note on cooking with wine: Many of the recipes in this chapter call for wine as an ingredient. Two of the questions I'm often asked are: (1) What does wine contribute to a dish? and (2) Does all the alcohol burn off when I cook with wine?

Wine's contribution to a recipe is generally one of being another subtle flavor, or "spice." For me, wine is every bit as important to flavor as herbs or pepper. Wine adds subtle complexity and also acts as a bridge to unify individual flavors.

With regard to alcohol and cooking, almost all (99 percent) of the alcohol in wine evaporates after only a few minutes of cooking. Most authorities seem to agree that the tiny amount of alcohol that does remain is akin to eating some very ripe fruits.

Maguelonne Toussaint-Samat's wonderful book *History of Food* contains perhaps the best desciption I know of wine's role in cooking:

"What part does wine play in the preparation of a dish? Apart from its gastronomic qualities of flavor, wine puts all its nutritional virtues at the service of the cooking and digestion of food. Wine contains glycerine, so it helps to bind sauces, and less fat can be used. Wine is well flavored, and allows the cook to go easy on salt or omit it altogether. Wine contains tannin, particularly when it has been cooked, and stimulates digestion. Wine contains alcohol, but very little once it has evaporated in being cooked. It stimulates the tastebuds, and thus the appetite. It brings out the flavor of food and helps the system to digest fat. And it is very good for morale."

Marinated and Grilled Flank Steak with Lime-Chipotle Sauce

This is a great outdoor summer dish since it doesn't involve any stovetop or oven cooking. The pronounced smoky, spicy heat of the chipotle chiles is extremely flattering to flank steak. Chipotle in adobo can be found in small cans in the Latin foods sections of the supermarket. Any leftover meat and sauce can be used in burritos.

Serves 6

MARINADE:

2 tablespoons minced chipotle in adobo
1 tablespoon minced garlic
3 tablespoons chopped fresh cilantro

⅓ cup olive oil
¾ cup red wine
½ cup soy sauce

3 pounds flank steak, well trimmed of all fat

LIME-CHIPOTLE SAUCE:

½ cup honey
2 tablespoons minced chipotle in adobo
3 tablespoons balsamic vinegar
2 tablespoons brown or Dijon-style mustard
½ cup fresh lime juice
1½ tablespoons minced garlic

1 teaspoon ground cumin
½ teaspoon ground allspice
¼ cup chopped fresh cilantro
1 teaspoon kosher salt (or to taste)
   Freshly ground black pepper
   Garnish: Grilled red onions and red and yellow peppers

In a small bowl, combine the marinade ingredients. Place the flank steak in a large baking dish, pour in the marinade, and turn the steak to coat well. Cover and marinate, refrigerated, for 4 hours or overnight.

In a food processor, combine the sauce ingredients and process briefly to blend. Season to taste with salt and pepper and set aside.

Prepare a charcoal fire. Remove the steak from the marinade, pat dry, and grill over hot coals to desired doneness, approximately 4 to 5 minutes per side for medium rare. Let the steak rest for 5 minutes before slicing.

To serve the steak, slice it thinly across the grain on an angle. Drizzle the sauce over the slices or serve on the side and accompany with grilled sweet red onions and peppers, if desired.

Recommended wine: Frankly, I like beer with this chile-laden dish.

Jalapeño-Stuffed Steaks with Poblano Chile Sauce

The filling for these steaks can also be stuffed under the skin of a chicken or used to stuff pork chops. (The poblano sauce would work equally well with those meats, too.) The recipe for the sauce makes more than enough to go with the steaks, so cover and refrigerate any unused sauce to garnish your next tostada!

Serves 6

1   tablespoon vegetable oil
3   tablespoons seeded and finely
       sliced jalapeño chiles
1   cup finely chopped onions
2   tablespoons chopped garlic
½   teaspoon cumin seed
⅔   cup grated Jack or California feta
       cheese
2   tablespoons chopped fresh cilantro

6   beef tenderloin steaks, cut
       1½–2 inches thick
    Kosher salt and freshly ground
       black pepper
    Poblano Chile Sauce (recipe
       follows)
    Garnish: Cilantro sprigs and
       roasted garlic cloves (page 247)

In a medium sauté pan, heat the oil. Add the chiles, onions, garlic, and cumin seed and sauté until soft but not brown. Remove from the pan and cool. Stir in the cheese and cilantro.

Prepare a charcoal fire or preheat a stovetop grill. Slice pockets into the steaks and fill with the jalapeño mixture. Fasten the pockets if necessary with skewers. Season the outside of the steaks with salt and pepper. Grill over hot charcoal to desired doneness, preferably rare to medium rare. To serve, spoon warm sauce onto plates and place the steaks on top. Garnish with cilantro sprigs and roasted garlic cloves, if desired.

Poblano Chile Sauce

Makes about 4 cups

1   tablespoon olive oil
1   cup chopped onions
1½ cups husked and coarsely chopped tomatillos
1   tablespoon minced garlic
1   teaspoon seeded and minced serrano chile
1   pound poblano chiles, seeded and chopped
½   teaspoon toasted coriander seed (page 36)
½   teaspoon toasted cumin seed (page 36)

2   cups rich chicken or vegetable stock
½   cup fruity white wine, such as Riesling
2   cups loosely packed cilantro leaves
½   cup toasted and chopped almonds or whole pepitas or a combination
    Kosher salt and freshly ground black pepper
    Fresh lime or lemon juice

In a medium sauté pan, heat the oil. Add the onions, tomatillos, and garlic and sauté until lightly browned. Add the chiles, coriander seed, cumin seed, stock, and wine and bring to a boil. Lower the heat and simmer for 5 to 8 minutes, uncovered, or until somewhat thickened. Cool slightly.

Transfer the mixture to a blender or food processor along with the cilantro and almonds and purée. Season to taste with salt, pepper, and drops of lime juice. Serve warm. This may be made several hours ahead.

Recommended wine: A good, hearty Zinfandel, Petite Sirah, or Syrah with forward, berry fruit will stand up to these lively flavors.

Sticky Rice "Tamales" with Star Anise Beef

The Thai red curry paste called for in the recipe is available in Southeast Asian markets. If you can't find it, substitute ⅛ teaspoon or so of cayenne pepper. I love the star anise beef filling, and if you don't feel like making the tamales, the filling is delicious rolled up warm in crisp, cold lettuce leaves.

Makes 8 tamales, serving 4

STAR ANISE BEEF FILLING:

1 tablespoon vegetable oil	¼ teaspoon red chile flakes, crushed
1½ pounds lean pot roast, tri-tip preferred, thickly cut into 2-inch strips	1 2-inch piece cinnamon stick
	½ teaspoon dried orange peel
	2 scallions, white and green parts, sliced diagonally in 2-inch lengths
1 cup water	
½ cup dry white wine	
1 tablespoon sugar	1 2-inch piece fresh ginger, peeled and cut in coins
2 whole star anise pods	

In a heavy skillet, heat the oil and quickly brown the beef strips. Remove them and set aside; discard the oil.

In a large saucepan, combine 1 cup water and all the remaining filling ingredients. Bring to a boil and add the beef. Reduce heat to a simmer, cover, and cook until the beef is very tender, approximately 1½ hours. Remove the cinnamon stick, ginger, and star anise. Cool the beef in the liquid, then remove and shred.

TAMALES:

¼ ounce dried cloud ear or shiitake mushrooms	3 tablespoons chopped fresh basil
1½ cups California short-grain rice	8 iceberg or romaine lettuce leaves
2 cups cold water	
2 tablespoons peanut oil	Garnish: Fresh cilantro sprigs and toasted black sesame seeds (page 36)
1 teaspoon kosher salt	
2 teaspoons Thai red curry paste	

Soak the mushrooms in 2 cups of warm water for 30 minutes to rehydrate. Drain well, mince, and reserve.

In a saucepan, combine the rice, cold water, 1 tablespoon of the peanut oil, the salt, and curry paste. Bring to a simmer, whisking to dissolve the curry paste. Cover and simmer over very low heat for 15 to 20 minutes, until the liquid is absorbed. Let stand, covered, for another 10 minutes. Transfer to a bowl and fold in the remaining 1 tablespoon oil, the rehydrated mushrooms, and the basil. Spread the rice onto the lettuce leaves in a uniform layer, leaving about a ½-inch border. Spoon some of the beef filling down the center of the rice, then roll and tie with kitchen twine to enclose the filled rice completely. In a steamer over boiling water, steam the tamales for 40 minutes. Remove the twine, place on a plate, and serve hot, garnished with cilantro and sesame seeds.

Recommended wine: The spicy Asian flavors require a soft, fruity wine such as Gewürztraminer or Gamay Beaujolais for contrast.

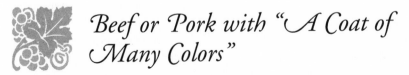

Beef or Pork with "A Coat of Many Colors"

Here are some wine country ideas for quickly saucing or topping a simple grilled or pan-sautéed piece of beef or pork.

Avocado Salsa

This is a simple salsa that is delicious with many things. (For instance, I've suggested it as a garnish for the Smoked Chicken Burritos on page 188.) When I use it with beef or pork, I rub the meat with a mixture of pure chile powder, kosher salt, and freshly ground black pepper mixed with a little olive oil before it goes on the grill.

Makes approximately 2 cups

1   large or 2 medium ripe avocados, cut into ¼-inch dice
1   medium yellow tomato, seeded and cut into ¼-inch dice
¼   cup finely chopped red onion
½   teaspoon seeded and minced serrano chile
½   teaspoon minced garlic

1   tablespoon fresh lime or lemon juice
2   tablespoons chopped fresh cilantro
   Big pinch of sugar
   Salt and freshly ground white pepper

Gently combine all the ingredients. Refrigerate if not serving immediately; however, it should be used the day it is made.

Blackberry Sage Sauce

In the summer wild blackberries are everywhere in the wine country. They are a little "seedy" to eat fresh but their flavor is fantastic. I love this sauce with grilled meats and game birds. Double the recipe and then you can store some frozen for a quick, elegant meal.

Makes approximately 1½ cups

1 tablespoon olive oil

⅓ cup chopped shallots or scallions, both white and pale-green parts

⅔ cup chopped mushrooms

2 cups hearty red wine

½ cup sweet port (or to taste)

5 cups rich chicken or beef stock

2 cups fresh blackberries

¼ cup coarsely chopped fresh sage

1 tablespoon honey (or to taste) Salt and freshly ground black pepper

In a saucepan, heat the olive oil and sauté the shallots and mushrooms until lightly browned. Add the wine, port, stock, berries, and sage and reduce the mixture to a light sauce consistency over high heat. The sauce should lightly coat the back of a spoon. Season to taste with honey, salt, and pepper. Strain through a fine-mesh strainer, pressing on the solids. The sauce may be made ahead and refrigerated up to 5 days. Warm it just before serving.

Artichoke "Pesto"

This is not a traditional pesto in that the ingredients are left chunky. The flavors are marvelous, however, and improve after sitting for a day or two. I often make a big batch of this, to use not only on grilled meats but also on pasta, rice, or a slice of good toasted peasant-style bread, such as bruschetta.

Makes approximately 2 cups

1 6½-ounce jar marinated artichoke hearts, drained and coarsely chopped (see note)

⅓ cup *each* diced green and red bell pepper

⅓ cup chopped green or black olives, or preferably a combination

⅓ cup chopped lightly toasted walnuts

¾ cup loosely packed basil leaves, chopped (⅓ cup or so)

1 tablespoon minced garlic

¾ cup extra-virgin olive oil or basil oil (see page 68)

⅓ cup freshly grated pecorino or Parmesan cheese

1 teaspoon finely grated lemon zest Drops of lemon juice Freshly ground black pepper

Combine all the ingredients, seasoning to taste with lemon juice and pepper. Store covered in the refrigerator for up to 2 weeks.

Note: Cooked fresh or frozen artichoke hearts can be substituted for the canned, marinated ones.

Peppered Brandy Cream Sauce

Every once in a while, I get a craving for a little tenderloin done with this classic "sinful" sauce. I tell myself that I have a dispensation for living an otherwise healthy life!

Makes approximately 1½ cups sauce

¼ cup minced shallots or scallions, both white and pale-green parts
2 teaspoons minced garlic
⅓ cup finely chopped mushrooms
1 cup brandy or Cognac
2 cups rich beef or chicken stock
2 teaspoons drained green peppercorns
1 teaspoon cracked black peppercorns (or to taste)

½ teaspoon fennel seed
2 tablespoons Dijon-style mustard
1¼ cups heavy cream
  Salt
2 teaspoons chopped fresh parsley
1 teaspoon chopped fresh tarragon (optional)

Sauté the shallots, garlic, and mushrooms, dry, over moderately high heat until just beginning to brown. Add the brandy, stock, green peppercorns, cracked peppercorns, fennel seed, and mustard, and over high heat reduce by half. Add the cream and reduce to desired sauce consistency. Correct the seasoning and stir in parsley and tarragon just before serving. The sauce can be made ahead and stored covered in the refrigerator for up to 3 days. Gently reheat it before serving.

Mexican Pot Roast

This is a south-of-the-border spin on a traditional pot roast, with sweet, spicy, and acidic elements that offer a lot of flavor interest.

Serves 6 to 8

3 large dried California or New Mexico chiles, ancho if available (or ¼ cup pure chile powder)
1¼ cups dry red wine

½ cup fresh orange juice
¼ cup balsamic or red wine vinegar
4 tablespoons chopped garlic
1½ tablespoons seeded and minced serrano or jalapeño chiles

2   teaspoons ground cumin
¾   teaspoon ground cinnamon
1   tablespoon fresh oregano
    (or 1½ teaspoons dried)
2   teaspoons salt
2   pounds onions, thinly sliced
⅓   cup golden raisins or
    currants

3   pounds center-cut beef brisket, fat
    removed
Garnish: Fresh tortillas, cilantro
    sprigs, lime wedges, sliced
    avocados, and queso fresco or
    fresh feta cheese

Remove the stems and seeds from the dried chiles, if using. Rinse and place in a saucepan with water to cover. Bring to a boil, then remove from the heat, cover, and let stand for 1 hour. Drain and set aside.

Preheat the oven to 350 degrees. In a blender or food processor, purée the softened chiles or chile powder with the wine, orange juice, vinegar, garlic, fresh chiles, ground spices, oregano, and salt until smooth. Scatter half of the onions and raisins in a roasting pan and place the beef on top of them. Scatter the remaining onions and raisins over the beef and then pour on the chile mixture, spreading with a spatula to evenly coat the meat.

Cover the roasting pan tightly and bake until the brisket is very tender, about 4 hours. Shred the meat with a fork and mix with the onions and juices. Serve on warmed tortillas garnished with cilantro, a squeeze of lime, sliced avocados, and crumbled cheese.

 Recommended wine: Ordinarily the chile heat would call for a fruity, lower-alcohol wine, such as a chilled Gamay. That would be nice, but I love this dish with a good Merlot.

My Grandmother's Pot Roast

My grandmother had a real touch with wholesome comfort foods, such as this savory pot roast, so I've revived it for her. The meat is cooked until it is falling off the bone, *"stracotto"* as it would be called in Italy. Styles may change; dishes like this won't.

Serves 6 to 8

3 pounds tri-tip or bottom round
    of beef
  Kosher salt and freshly ground
    black pepper
4 tablespoons olive oil
3 cups sliced onions
1 cup sliced leeks, both white and
    tender green parts
1½ cups diagonally sliced celery
1½ cups thickly sliced carrots
¼ cup slivered garlic
¼ teaspoon red chile flakes

3 cups hearty red wine
3 cups rich beef stock
2 cups seeded and diced tomatoes
2 large bay leaves
1 teaspoon fennel seed
2 teaspoons *each* minced fresh
    thyme, sage, and oregano (or
    1 teaspoon *each* dried)
2 teaspoons cornstarch (optional)
  Garnish: Roasted potatoes and
    sautéed shiitake or wild
    mushrooms

Preheat the oven to 375 degrees. Trim the beef of all visible fat and season with salt and pepper. In a large, heavy-bottomed roasting pan, heat the olive oil and quickly brown the meat on all sides. Remove the meat and add the onions, leeks, celery, carrots, and garlic and cook over moderate heat until the vegetables just begin to color and the onions are translucent.

Return the beef to the pan and add the chile flakes, red wine, stock, tomatoes, and herbs. Bring to a simmer, cover, and place in the oven for 2 to 2½ hours, or until the meat is very tender and almost falling apart.

Strain the liquid from the meat and vegetables into a bowl. Remove the meat and vegetables and set aside. Allow the liquid to sit for a few minutes so that the fat rises to the surface. Remove and discard it. Return the liquid to the empty roasting pan and over high heat simmer until the liquid is reduced by approximately a third to concentrate its flavor. (If desired, the gravy may be thickened with 2 teaspoons cornstarch dissolved in wine or water.) Season to taste with salt and pepper.

Return the meat and vegetables to the roasting pan and warm through. Slice the meat and serve in shallow bowls along with some of the vegetables. Generously ladle the reduced sauce around and garnish with roasted potatoes and mushrooms.

Recommended Wine: This is a hearty "hunter-style" dish, a great match for big, deep reds like Cabernet, Zinfandel, or Petite Sirah and other Rhône varietals.

Grilled Calves' Liver with Onions and Balsamic Vinegar Sauce

I've always liked liver *if* it's not overcooked—it should be pink and tender. It cooks very quickly, so be attentive! If you wish, you could whisk a tablespoon or two of softened butter into the stock and vinegar reduction to add body and richness to the sauce.

Serves 4

3 tablespoons olive oil	1 tablespoon *each* minced fresh parsley and chives
¼ cup chopped pancetta	
⅓ cup dry white wine	1½ pounds young calves' liver, cut into ½-inch-thick slices
½ cup rich chicken or beef stock	
5 tablespoons balsamic vinegar (or to taste)	2 large red onions, cut into thick rings
Salt and freshly ground black pepper	Garnish: Watercress sprigs and fresh blackberries, if available

In a sauté pan, heat 1 tablespoon of the olive oil and cook the pancetta until it just begins to color. Remove and set aside. Add the wine, stock, and vinegar and cook over high heat until reduced by half. Season with salt and pepper, stir in the parsley and chives, and keep warm.

Prepare a charcoal fire or preheat a stovetop grill. With the remaining 2 tablespoons olive oil, liberally coat the liver and onions and season with salt and pepper. Grill both over hot coals until the onions begin to soften and the liver is medium rare, approximately 3 to 4 minutes per side.

Serve the liver on the onions, drizzled with the warm sauce and sprinkled with the reserved pancetta. Garnish with watercress and blackberries, if desired.

 Recommended wine: A robust Zinfandel or Syrah works well with this hearty dish.

Lamb and Eggplant Rolls with Savory Tomato Sauce

This Mediterranean–East India cross is easy to make. The filled eggplant rolls can be made a day ahead and refrigerated, as can the sauce. The roasted pearl onions are best eaten the day they are cooked (see page 245 on roasting vegetables). As a final garnish you could also drizzle a little mint oil around the plate for added interest. (A discussion of infused oils is on page 67–69.)

Makes 10 to 12 rolls, serving 4 to 6

1   large globe eggplant (about 3 pounds)
    Extra-virgin olive oil
    Salt and freshly ground black pepper
½   cup finely chopped red onion
1   tablespoon finely chopped garlic
1   pound ground lamb
3   tablespoons dry couscous or fine bulgur wheat
⅓   cup plain yogurt

2   teaspoons garam masala or high-quality curry powder
3   tablespoons minced sun-dried tomatoes
½   cup steamed, chopped spinach or Swiss chard
2   teaspoons minced fresh mint
2   teaspoons grated orange zest
¼   teaspoon red chile flakes, crushed
½   cup buttermilk

COATING MIXTURE:

¾   cup finely toasted and chopped almonds
⅓   cup freshly grated dry Jack or Parmesan cheese
2   teaspoons minced fresh oregano (or 1 teaspoon dried)

½   teaspoon salt
    Savory Tomato Sauce (recipe follows)
    Garnish: Roasted pearl onions (page 245; about 3 or 4 per person) and mint sprigs

Preheat the oven to 375 degrees. Slice the eggplant into ¼-inch-thick rounds, discarding the end pieces. You should have 10 to 12 slices. On a baking sheet lined with parchment paper, lay the eggplant rounds in a single layer, brush them with olive oil, and season lightly with salt and pepper on both sides. Bake for 12 to 15 minutes or until the eggplant is lightly browned and softened. Set aside.

Combine the coating mixture ingredients and set aside.

In a small sauté pan, heat 1 tablespoon olive oil and sauté the onion and garlic over moderate heat until softened. In a medium bowl, combine the onion mixture, the lamb, couscous, yogurt, garam masala, sun-dried tomatoes, spinach, mint, orange zest, and chile flakes. Mix thoroughly. Place even amounts of filling down the center of each eggplant slice. Roll up the slices. (The eggplant may not completely envelop the filling. Use a toothpick if necessary.) Carefully dip the rolls in the buttermilk and then gently roll in the coating mixture. Place the rolls seam side down on a lightly oiled baking sheet. Bake for 20 to 25 minutes or until cooked through.

Serve the the eggplant rolls on pools of the warm tomato sauce, surrounded by roasted onions and garnished with mint sprigs.

Savory Tomato Sauce

1 tablespoon olive oil	¼ cup hearty red wine
½ cup finely chopped red onion	1 tablespoon mixed minced fresh
2 teaspoons finely minced garlic	herbs, such as rosemary, savory,
½ cup chopped carrots	and oregano
3 pounds tomatoes, peeled, seeded,	⅛ teaspoon red chile flakes
and chopped	Salt and freshly ground black
½ cup rich vegetable or chicken	pepper
stock	1 teaspoon minced fresh mint

In a medium saucepan, heat the oil. Add the onion, garlic, and carrots and sauté until soft and just beginning to color. Stir in the tomatoes and cook until they begin to release their juice. Add the stock, wine, herbs, and chile flakes, bring to a simmer, and cook uncovered for 15 minutes. Cool slightly. Transfer the mixture to a blender or food processor and purée. Return to the pan and season to taste with salt and pepper. Stir in the mint and keep warm.

   Recommended wine: I like this dish best with a fruity Cabernet that is relatively low in tannin. Cabernet often has hints of mint in it, which would reflect the flavors of the filling well. If you prefer a white, a Fumé/Sauvignon Blanc also goes nicely.

 # Lamb Osso Buco with Tomatoes, Olives, and Herbs

Braising tougher cuts of meat in liquid and seasonings adds an incredible amount of flavor and helps tenderize the meat beautifully. This dish, redolent of herbs and spices, is as satisfying as you're likely to find, perfect for a cold winter night.

Serves 8

16	center-cut, meaty lamb hind shanks, cut "osso buco" style, 2 inches thick	2½	cups dry red wine
	All-purpose flour for dredging	⅔	cup whole Niçoise, Kalamata, or other oil-cured black olives
	Kosher salt and freshly ground black pepper	2	teaspoons fennel seed
3	tablespoons olive oil	1	tablespoon minced fresh oregano (or 1 teaspoon dried)
4	cups sliced yellow onions	1½	teaspoons minced fresh thyme (or ¾ teaspoon dried)
4	tablespoons chopped garlic		
2	cups diced celery	1	teaspoon seeded and minced serrano chile (or ½ teaspoon red chile flakes)
2	cups diced carrots		
3	cups diced plum tomatoes		Garnish: Fresh herb sprigs
5	cups rich lamb or chicken stock		

LEMON ZEST MIXTURE (GREMOLATA):

| 2 | teaspoons grated lemon zest | 2 | tablespoons minced fresh parsley |
| 2 | teaspoons minced garlic | | |

Preheat the oven to 350 degrees. Dredge the lamb shanks in flour and shake off excess. Season with salt and pepper. In a deep flameproof casserole or Dutch oven, heat 2 tablespoons of the oil and brown the shanks on all sides. Remove the shanks, wipe the casserole clean, and add the remaining 1 tablespoon oil along with the onions, garlic, celery, and carrots. Sauté until lightly browned. Add the tomatoes, stock, wine, olives, and seasonings. Return the shanks to the casserole, scooping some of the vegetable mixture on top of them.

Cover the casserole and bake for 2 hours. Uncover and cook 30 minutes more or until the lamb is very tender. Remove the shanks and set aside. Strain the braising liquid and reserve the vegetables. Degrease the braising liquid and return it to the casserole. Over high heat, cook the liquid until reduced to a light sauce consistency. Return the meat and vegetables to the casserole and heat through. Adjust seasoning with salt and pepper.

In a small bowl, combine the ingredients for the gremolata.

Serve the lamb shanks in wide-rimmed soup bowls and ladle the hot braising liquid around. Sprinkle with the gremolata and garnish with herb sprigs.

Recommended wine: The robust flavors in this dish are perfect for a Zinfandel, Petite Sirah, or Rhône-style wine, such as Syrah or Mourvèdre.

Grilled Leg of Lamb with Currant–Bell Pepper Chutney

Here is another great treatment for lamb. It can be prepared under the broiler, but it really benefits from picking up smokiness from the barbecue. The wine country produces more lamb than any other red meat. Besides being a local product, lamb seems to fit with wine country cooking particularly because it has a special affinity for both savory and sweet flavors—a hallmark of wine country cuisine. The chutney, which blends sweet, tart, and spicy flavors, can be used with a wide variety of broiled or grilled meats.

Serves 4

½ leg of lamb, approximately 4 pounds, boned and butterflied, excess fat trimmed

MARINADE:

1½ cups dry red wine
1 tablespoon high-quality curry powder (page 87)
1 tablespoon crushed fresh rosemary (or ½ tablespoon dried)

1 tablespoon chopped fresh thyme (or ½ tablespoon dried)
2 garlic cloves, minced
⅛ teaspoon red chile flakes
Kosher salt and freshly ground black pepper

In a large, sealable plastic bag, marinate the lamb in a mixture of the red wine, curry powder, rosemary, thyme, garlic, and chile flakes in the refrigerator for 3 to 4 hours. Remove the lamb from the marinade and reserve marinade for use in the chutney. Pat the lamb dry and season with salt and pepper.

Currant–Bell Pepper Chutney

½ cup currants
2 tablespoons olive oil
1 cup chopped onions
1½ cups chopped red bell pepper
1 cup chicken stock
¼ cup port or cassis

1½ tablespoons sherry vinegar
Reserved marinade
1 tablespoon chopped fresh mint
Salt and freshly ground black pepper

Cover the currants in warm water for 30 minutes. Drain.

In a large sauté pan, heat the oil over medium-high heat. Add the onions and bell peppers and sauté for 3 minutes, or until the onions are just beginning to soften. Add the chicken stock, port, vinegar, and reserved marinade. Reduce over moderately high heat until most of the liquid is evaporated, about 10 to 15 minutes. Stir in the mint and season to taste with salt and pepper. Keep warm.

Grill the lamb over a mesquite or charcoal fire for approximately 8 to 10 minutes per side, or until the lamb is medium-rare and juicy inside. Carve into thin slices and top with chutney.

 Recommended wine: Bell peppers accent the herbal dimension often found in both Cabernet Sauvignon and Merlot. Cassis and currants help bring out the classic varietal fruit flavors of these wines.

 ## Leg of Lamb Stuffed with Wild Mushrooms and Figs

You can stuff a large leg of lamb with any savory stuffing. Here's one I really like. The sauce is a classic one; it is quickly made and is a good technique for any roasted meat. Make sure you have a friendly butcher who will bone the leg for you.

Serves 8 to 10

Olive oil
½ cup finely chopped shallots or scallions, both white and pale-green parts
½ cup finely chopped carrots
¼ cup finely chopped celery
2 tablespoons finely chopped garlic
1 cup coarsely chopped shiitake or cremini mushrooms
½ cup lightly toasted pine nuts
⅓ cup chopped dried figs or pitted prunes

⅓ cup bulgur wheat
¼ cup loosely packed fresh mint, chopped
1 teaspoon *each* chopped fresh thyme and rosemary
2 teaspoons grated lemon zest
1¼ pounds ground lamb
1 egg, lightly beaten
Salt and freshly ground black pepper
1 8- to 9-pound leg of lamb, boned

RED WINE DEGLAZING SAUCE:

⅔ cup diced onion
⅔ cup diced carrots
⅔ cup diced celery
3 garlic cloves, diced
1 cup hearty red wine

2½ cups rich chicken or mushroom
       stock (page 57)
2 tablespoons finely chopped fresh
       parsley

Preheat the oven to 500 degrees. In a medium sauté pan, heat 3 tablespoons olive oil. Add the shallots, carrots, celery, garlic, and mushrooms until lightly colored. Remove from the heat and transfer to a bowl. Stir in the pine nuts, figs, bulgur, mint, thyme, rosemary, and lemon zest. Allow the mixture to cool completely, then mix in the ground lamb and egg. Season with salt and pepper. (It's a good idea to sauté a tablespoonful to taste for seasoning, since this filling can't be tasted raw.)

Season the cavity of the leg of lamb with freshly ground pepper. Sew the small end of the leg with a trussing needle and twine or a skewer to close. Spoon the stuffing into the cavity and sew or skewer the opening to enclose the stuffing completely. With kitchen twine, tie the leg securely at 2-inch intervals. Rub the lamb generously with olive oil and season well with salt and pepper.

Place the lamb on a rack in a roasting pan in the middle of the oven and roast for 10 minutes. Reduce the heat to 375 degrees and roast for another 30 minutes. At this time, scatter the diced onions, carrots, celery, and the garlic cloves for the red wine deglazing sauce in the bottom of the pan. The lamb should continue to cook for about another 45 minutes until medium rare, or until an instant-read thermometer registers 125 degrees in the thickest part of the leg.

When the meat is done, transfer the lamb to a serving platter and cover very loosely with foil to keep warm.

To make the red wine deglazing sauce: Place the roasting pan over high heat and add the wine and stock. Boil for 6 to 8 minutes to reduce, scraping up any browned bits from the bottom of the pan. Carefully strain and degrease the sauce and season with salt and pepper. Stir in the chopped parsley.

Serve the lamb cut into ¼-inch slices with sauce spooned around.

 Recommended wine: This is a rich, full-flavored dish that goes with a full-flavored, hearty red, such as Cabernet or Merlot. The mint and fig flavors in the stuffing are often classic descriptors of these two wines.

Rack of Lamb with Hot-Sweet Mustard

A particularly tasty hot-sweet mustard called Mendocino Mustard, which is made in northern California, inspired this dish, but any hot-sweet mustard will do. A simple accompaniment would be some quickly sautéed savory greens.

Serves 4

2 8-bone racks of lamb (approximately 1½ pounds each)	2 tablespoons chopped shallots or scallions, white part only
Kosher salt and freshly ground black pepper	¾ cup hot-sweet mustard (see note)
2 tablespoons olive oil	4 tablespoons chopped fresh mint
2 tablespoons chopped garlic	2 tablespoons dry sherry
	½ teaspoon freshly ground white pepper

Preheat the oven to 425 degrees. Remove and discard the fat covering, known as the cap, from the racks. French-trim the bones of any additional fat, scraping them as clean as possible. Ask your butcher to do this or to show you how it is done.

Season the racks well with salt and black pepper. In a heavy-bottomed skillet, heat the oil and quickly sear the racks on all sides until nicely browned. Set aside to cool.

In a food processor or blender combine the garlic, shallots, mustard, mint, sherry, and white pepper. Process briefly to combine all ingredients—the mixture should be quite thick. Place the lamb in a shallow roasting pan with bones curved-side up. Liberally coat the top and sides of the racks with the mustard mixture.

Roast the lamb for 12 to 15 minutes for medium rare (125 degrees on an instant-read thermometer). Allow the racks to rest 5 minutes before cutting. Serve the racks cut into double chops.

Recommended wine: Mustard has a natural affinity for Pinot Noir. Classically, they both come from the same region in France and just seem to do a wonderful dance together.

Note: If you can't find a commercially prepared hot-sweet mustard in the store, take any hot mustard and add a bit of brown sugar to it. The goal is to have both the hot and the sweet come through equally. To order the "real" hot-sweet Mendocino Mustard, call 1-800-964-2270 or write to Mendocino Mustard Inc., 1260 North Main St., Fort Bragg, CA 95437.

Rack of Lamb with Sun-Dried Cherry Sauce

Sun-dried cherries are one of my favorite ingredients in meat dishes, since they mirror the flavor of many red wines, particularly Cabernet Sauvignon, which this dish showcases.

Serves 8

4   **8-bone racks of lamb, approximately 1½ pounds each**

MARINADE:

⅔ **cup olive oil**
½ **cup dry white wine**
1   **tablespoon minced garlic**
1   **tablespoon *each* chopped fresh**
       rosemary and thyme
       (or 1 teaspoon *each* dried)
1   **teaspoon salt**

2   **teaspoons freshly ground black**
       pepper

Sun-Dried Cherry Sauce
       (recipe follows)
Garnish: Fresh thyme or rosemary
       sprigs

Remove and discard the fat covering, known as the cap, from the racks. Trim the bones of any additional fat, scraping them as clean as possible. In a small bowl, whisk together the marinade ingredients. In a baking dish large enough to hold the racks in a single layer, place the racks of lamb, pour the marinade over, and marinate, refrigerated, for 6 hours or overnight, turning occasionally.

Preheat the oven to 425 degrees. Remove the racks from the marinade and place on a baking sheet. Roast the racks for 20 minutes or until rare to medium-rare (120 to 125 degrees on an instant-read thermometer). Allow the racks to rest 5 minutes before slicing.

Serve the lamb cut into double chops, with the sauce drizzled over and garnished with herb sprigs, if desired.

Sun-Dried Cherry Sauce

Makes about 2 cups

1½ tablespoons olive oil
¼ cup chopped shallots
¾ cup minced shiitake mushrooms
8 cups rich chicken or vegetable
    stock
1 teaspoon grated orange zest
1½ cups Cabernet Sauvignon

½ cup sun-dried cherries
½ cup fresh orange juice
1 tablespoon chopped fresh thyme
⅓ cup port (or to taste)
    Salt and freshly ground black
    pepper

In a saucepan, heat the olive oil and sauté the shallots and shiitakes until very lightly browned. Add the stock, orange zest, and wine and bring to a boil. Lower the heat and simmer until reduced by half. Add half the cherries, the orange juice, thyme, and port and continue simmering until reduced to a light sauce consistency. Strain the sauce and add the remaining ¼ cup cherries. Season to taste with salt and pepper. Keep warm. Can be made several hours in advance, or the morning of your dinner.

 Recommended wine: Besides the Cabernet Sauvignon the dish was designed to showcase, a fresh, young Merlot would also work beautifully.

WHY ROASTED MEAT SHOULD
REST BEFORE CARVING

Ever wonder why recipes call for allowing roasted meat to sit for a few minutes after you take it out of the oven or off the grill? The reason for this is that the meat near the surface contains less juice just off the heat than it did when you started to cook it. During cooking the juices near the surface evaporated from the heat or are driven toward the center.

If you carve immediately after cooking, while these juices are still unevenly distributed, the meat toward the edges will be dry. Also, you'll lose juices because the meat in the center can't hold all the accumulated juices that collected there during cooking.

A few minutes' rest gives the juices a chance to redistribute themselves, through osmosis, throughout the meat. So give chickens or thick steaks at least 3 to 5 minutes before cutting and large roasts such as prime rib of beef or leg of lamb at least 15 minutes.

Spicy Lamb Stew with Cracked Green Olives and Orange Rice

Every cook should have a good lamb stew as part of his or her repertoire, and here's my favorite. If you use lamb necks, the flavor will be richer, from the simmering of the bones. Like all stews, this is even better the second day.
Serves 6

3 pounds meaty lamb necks or lamb shoulder, cut into 2-inch cubes	2 teaspoons oregano leaves (or 1 teaspoon dried)
Salt and freshly ground black pepper	3 cups rich lamb or chicken stock
3 tablespoons olive oil	1¼ cups dry white wine
4 anchovy fillets, rinsed and chopped	2 cups cracked green olives, well rinsed and pitted
½ teaspoon red chile flakes	½ cup *each* coarsely chopped fresh parsley and cilantro
3 tablespoons finely slivered garlic	Red wine vinegar
2 cups chopped yellow onions	Orange Rice (recipe follows)
1 teaspoon crushed coriander seed	Garnish: Fresh parsley and cilantro sprigs, Frizzled Onions (see box, page 228)
½ teaspoon crushed cumin seed	

Lightly season the lamb with salt and pepper. In a casserole or Dutch oven, heat the olive oil and brown the lamb well on all sides. Remove the lamb with a slotted spoon and set aside. Remove all but 2 tablespoons of fat from the pan and add the anchovies, chile flakes, garlic, onions, coriander seed, and cumin seed; sauté until just beginning to color. Add the oregano, stock, and wine and return the meat to the pan. Simmer, covered, for 1½ hours or until the meat is very tender. If using necks, gently pull the meat from the bones, return the meat to the pot, and discard the bones.

Allow the stew to rest off the heat for at least 30 minutes for fat to rise to the surface. Skim fat off and discard.

At serving time, add the olives to the stew and bring to a simmer. Stir in the parsley and cilantro and season to taste with salt, pepper, and drops of vinegar. Serve with Orange Rice and garnish with fresh herb sprigs and Frizzled Onions, if desired.

Orange Rice

½ cup finely chopped onion	1 teaspoon grated orange zest
1 tablespoon unsalted butter or vegetable oil	2 teaspoons finely minced fresh ginger
1 cup basmati or other long-grain rice	1 tablespoon chopped golden raisins
1¼ cups rich chicken or vegetable stock	Salt and freshly ground black pepper
½ cup fresh orange juice	

Sauté the onion in butter or oil over moderate heat until soft but not brown. Add the rice and continue to sauté and stir for 3 minutes longer. Add the stock, orange juice, orange zest, ginger, and raisins and stir in. Lightly season with salt and pepper, reduce the heat to a simmer, and cover. Cook for 20 minutes or until all liquid is absorbed. Allow to rest off the heat for 5 minutes. Fluff with a fork and serve warm.

 Recommended wine: A hearty Zinfandel, Syrah, or Petite Sirah would be intense enough to stand up to this stew.

CRACKED GREEN OLIVES

"Cracked" refers to olives in which the meat has been split before curing to allow the curing brine to penetrate better. You can take uncracked green olives and smack them with the flat side of a chef's knife to create a similar effect.

Cracked green olives are generally available in bulk in good delicatessens. Any good black or green olive can be used, however, such as Niçoise, Kalamata, Picholine, etc.

FRIZZLED ONIONS

¾ cup unbleached all-purpose flour	Vegetable oil for frying
2 teaspoons salt	2 medium onions, sliced very thinly into rounds and separated into rings
¼ teaspoon freshly ground white pepper	
1 teaspoon pure California or New Mexico chile powder (optional)	

Combine the flour, salt, pepper, and chile powder in a bowl. In a large saucepan or a deep fryer, add oil to a depth of 2 inches and heat to 360 degrees.

Dredge the onion rings thoroughly in the seasoned flour. Shake off excess flour and deep-fry until golden brown and crisp. Drain on paper towels. The Frizzled Onions may be prepared a couple of hours in advance if necessary.

 ## *Pork and Pepper Stew with Oranges*

This stew brings together spice, fruit, and sweet flavors in a delicious way. Like all stews, it's even better the next day and it freezes well if you want to make a big batch. Almost any other meat will work here too, such as beef, veal, or chicken. Adjust the cooking time accordingly.

Serves 6 to 8

3½ pounds boneless pork shoulder or butt, cut into 2-inch cubes, excess fat trimmed away
Kosher salt and freshly ground black pepper
4 tablespoons olive oil
2 pounds onions, halved and thickly sliced
4 tablespoons thickly sliced garlic
1 cup diagonally cut celery, in ½-inch slices
3 medium poblano chiles, seeded and thickly sliced
1 teaspoon minced jalapeño chile
1 medium red bell pepper, thinly sliced
¾ teaspoon fennel seed

2 teaspoons dried oregano
2 cups canned tomatoes in juice, diced
2½ cups rich chicken or vegetable stock
½ cup dry white wine
2 tablespoons pure California or New Mexico chile powder
1 teaspoon dried shrimp powder (optional)
⅓ cup golden raisins
2 tablespoons chopped fresh cilantro
Orange-Cinnamon Rice (recipe follows)
Garnish: Orange segments and cilantro sprigs

Season the pork liberally with salt and pepper. In a heavy casserole or Dutch oven, heat 2 tablespoons of the olive oil and quickly brown the pork, in batches if necessary. Remove and set aside.

Add the remaining 2 tablespoons of the oil to the pot and sauté the onions, garlic, celery, poblanos, jalapeño, and red bell pepper over moderate heat until just beginning to color. Add the fennel seed, oregano, tomatoes, stock, white wine, chile powder, and shrimp powder and bring to a boil. Add the pork and raisins, reduce the heat, cover, and simmer gently until the pork is tender, about 35 to 40 minutes. Remove from the heat and skim any fat from the top.

Just before serving, stir in the chopped cilantro. Serve with Orange-Cinnamon Rice and garnish with orange segments and cilantro sprigs.

Orange-Cinnamon Rice

1	tablespoon olive oil or unsalted butter	2	teaspoons grated orange zest
⅓	cup finely chopped onion	1	4-inch piece cinnamon stick
1	cup basmati or other long-grain rice	1¼	cups water
		½	cup fresh orange juice
		½	teaspoon salt

In a saucepan, heat the oil or butter and sauté the onions over medium heat until soft but not brown. Add the rice and sauté 2 minutes longer, stirring occasionally. Add the remaining ingredients and bring to a boil, stirring once or twice.

Reduce the heat to a simmer, cover, and cook for 15 minutes or until all liquid is absorbed. Remove the cinnamon stick. Let the rice stand 5 minutes, partially covered, before serving.

 Recommended wine: A fruity, berry-tinged Zinfandel with its spicy and peppery complexity is just the answer for this robust stew.

Pork Chops Braised with Dried Fruits and Almonds

I entered this recipe years ago in a contest sponsored by the Pork Council. I didn't win, but I still prepare this wonderful "casserole" often in the winter, when I'm craving rich, comforting foods. These chops are delicious served with the Moroccan-Inspired Cinnamon Couscous on page 267.

Serves 6

6	center-cut pork chops, cut 1¼ inches thick and trimmed of fat	¼	cup olive oil
	Kosher salt and freshly ground black pepper	1½	cups diced red onions
		2	teaspoons minced garlic
		4	cups fresh orange juice

2 teaspoons grated orange zest
1 cup Gewürztraminer or Gamay
   Beaujolais
1 cup rich chicken stock
1 tablespoon seeded and minced
   serrano chiles
1 cup dried apple slices
1 cup dried figs or prunes, halved

3 tablespoons minced fresh ginger
1 2-inch piece cinnamon stick
1 teaspoon ground allspice
   Kosher salt and freshly ground
   black pepper
   Garnish: Toasted slivered
   almonds

Preheat the oven to 325 degrees. Season the chops with salt and pepper. In a heavy, flameproof casserole or Dutch oven, heat 2 tablespoons of the olive oil and quickly brown the pork chops on both sides. Do this in batches, to avoid crowding, if necessary. Remove and set aside. Add the remaining olive oil to the casserole and sauté the onions and garlic over moderate heat until lightly colored. Return the chops to the casserole and add all the remaining ingredients. Cover and bring to a simmer. Place in the oven and bake for 1 hour or until the chops are tender. Remove the chops and fruits to serving plates and keep warm. Discard the cinnamon stick. Reduce the juices to a light sauce consistency and season to taste with salt and pepper. Serve the pork chops with the sauce and garnish with toasted almonds.

 Recommended wine: The rich, sweet dried fruits in this dish are a great match for Gewürztraminer or a fruity Gamay Beaujolais, also recommended for the cooking wine.

I can't resist including this glaze, which is smashing on plain pork tenderloins. Make up the glaze and marinate the pork in a cup of it in the refrigerator for several hours or overnight, if you have time. Then grill or broil the pork, brushing with the remaining glaze. This recipe makes enough for 4 pounds of pork.

HONEY-MUSTARD APRICOT GLAZE

Makes about 2 cups

¼ pound dried California
   apricots
1½ cups water
2 tablespoons unsalted butter
¼ cup finely minced shallots
⅔ cup white wine vinegar

¼ cup Dijon-style mustard
½ cup honey
1 teaspoon salt
½ teaspoon freshly ground
   white pepper

In a heavy saucepan, combine the apricots and water. Bring to a boil, reduce heat, and simmer uncovered for 12 to 15 minutes or until the apricots are tender and the liquid is reduced by half. In a separate sauté pan, melt the butter and sauté the shallots until softened but not brown.

Transfer the apricot mixture and the shallots to a food processor along with the vinegar, mustard, honey, salt, and white pepper and purée until smooth. Return the mixture to the saucepan and bring to a simmer. Simmer uncovered 8 to 10 minutes or until thickened.

Cool and store covered in the refrigerator for up to 3 weeks.

Grilled Pork Tenderloin Marinated in Berry-Cherry Mostarda

This recipe gives me a chance to talk about mostarda di frutta, an old Italian concoction. It is truly an all-purpose product, which can be used as a marinade (as it is here) or reduced and used as a sauce for game, chicken, or even fresh fruits. I make it up in the summer when fresh berries and cherries are inexpensive. You can also make it from IQF (individually quick-frozen) fruits. If you marinate meats in the mostarda, you can use it again—be sure to bring to a boil and simmer for 4 to 5 minutes and then cool before reusing.

Serves 6 to 8

Berry-Cherry Mostarda (recipe follows)

**3　pounds trimmed pork tenderloin
Vegetable oil for grilling**

Make the mostarda. Place the pork tenderloin in a nonreactive bowl or pan and add enough mostarda to just cover. Marinate, covered and refrigerated, for 4 hours or overnight, turning the pork occasionally.

Prepare a charcoal fire. Remove the pork from the mostarda and gently pat off any excess marinade. Lightly brush the tenderloin with oil and grill it over medium coals until just done, about 10 minutes per side. Be careful not to overcook—the center should be pink and juicy. Serve the pork warm or at room temperature.

Berry-Cherry Mostarda

Makes about 3 cups

1 cup red wine vinegar
1 cup dry red wine, such as
 Zinfandel
1½ cups sugar
⅛ teaspoon black mustard seed

2 medium strips lemon zest
1 cinnamon stick
3 pints mixed raspberries,
 blueberries, and pitted cherries,
 well mashed

In a medium saucepan, combine the vinegar, wine, sugar, mustard seed, lemon zest, and cinnamon stick and bring to a boil. Remove from the heat and immediately stir in the fruit. Cool. The mostarda can be used at this point or it can be stored, covered and refrigerated, indefinitely.

 Recommended wine: The mostarda is a classic mirror for berry and cherry flavors in red wine, and you can adjust the recipe to suit the wine, e.g.: Add more blueberries to link it to Merlot; add more cherries to link it to Cabernet; add more raspberries to link it to Zinfandel.

BERRIES

The sheer joy of picking and eating wild berries in midsummer is one of our simplest and greatest culinary pleasures. According to American Indian legend, berries grow by the heavenly road—a wonderfully stained and thorny road it must be!

In addition to the profusion of wild berries available in many regions, many supermarkets and produce stores are beginning to carry a wider array of specialty berries during the height of the season.

The best way to store berries is unwashed, in an open or perforated basket, where they can breathe in the refrigerator to prevent molding. While the obvious use of berries is in pies, cobblers, ice creams, sherbets, and mousses, they can also be used in relishes and sauces for meat and game to add a sweet-tart tang to the dish. When used this way, berries marry beautifully to Cabernet Sauvignon, Zinfandel, and Pinot Noir.

Blackberries

There are many local varieties of blackberries in each region. Most are medium-size to large with a deep maroon or purple-black color and are usually found in large clusters on the vine. Boysenberries (a hybrid of raspberry, blackberry, and loganberry) are popular in pies and pastries.

Blueberries

Indigenous to America, this small, blue-black–skinned fruit invites instant eating, and is a favorite fruit for pies, jams, and tarts.

Currants

Red and black currants are more available than in years past. These semi-transparent berries are quite tart and are best combined with sweeter berries to offset their pungent burst of flavor. Currants are an excellent accent to game meats and can replace vinegar or lemon juice in many recipes.

Huckleberries

The small black huckleberry is virtually indistinguishable from wild blue-berries. Known for their intense tangy flavor and crunchy, edible seeds, huckle-berries must be gathered in the wild. Favored in sauces and pies, they are also irresistible by themselves and as garnishes for other foods.

Loganberries

Loganberries are considered by some to be a variety of the western dew-berry (a trailing vine blackberry), by others a hybrid dewberry-raspberry. What-ever they are, they display a purplish–dark red color; and their flavor is slightly tart and very distinctive, which makes them desirable for preserves, desserts, winemaking, cordials, and liqueurs.

Marionberries

Often difficult to find, marionberries are a real treasure. These luscious, dark, blue-black berries have a ravishing aroma, lovely texture, and superb acid balance.

Raspberries

Nearly 90 percent of the nation's supply of raspberries is raised in the Pacific Northwest and is widely available from mid-June to mid-August. Black raspber-ries are relished for their intensely concentrated sweetness, while the red and golden varieties have a mild citric, sweet character. Especially rich in pectin, all raspberries are well suited for jams, jellies, and preserves.

Spicy Braised Eggplant with Prunes and Pork

At one point in my cooking career, I did a lot of cooking with a Chinese friend, who taught me a great deal about quick cooking and Asian flavors. This recipe comes from that time, and I still cook it at home. Substitute chicken or shrimp or, for a nonmeat version, shiitake mushrooms. The hot bean paste called for in the recipe is generally available at Asian markets. If you can't find it, add a half teaspoon or so of seeded and minced serrano chile.

Serves 4 to 6

½ cup light vegetable oil	2 tablespoons dark soy sauce
1 pound diced lean pork	⅓ cup thinly sliced prunes
1 tablespoon dark sesame oil	1½ tablespoons Chinese hot bean paste
1½ pounds diced eggplant	
1 tablespoon minced garlic	1½ teaspoons cornstarch
1 tablespoon minced fresh ginger	Garnish: Lots of fresh cilantro sprigs and fine julienne of red bell pepper
½ cup thinly sliced scallions, both white and pale-green parts	
1 cup rich chicken or vegetable stock	

In a heavy-bottomed sauté pan or a wok, heat 2 tablespoons of the oil. Quickly sauté the pork until lightly browned and cooked through. Drain and set aside.

Add the remaining oil and sesame oil to the pan and quickly sauté the eggplant until lightly browned (about 4 minutes). Add the garlic, ginger, and scallions and cook 2 to 3 minutes, until the eggplant is just tender but not mushy.

Add ½ cup of the stock, the soy sauce, prunes, and bean paste and simmer for 3 minutes. In a small bowl, dissolve the cornstarch in the remaining ½ cup of stock and add to the pan. Raise the heat to high and cook 2 minutes longer or until the sauce thickens lightly. Stir in the cooked pork.

Garnish with cilantro sprigs and julienned red bell peppers.

 Recommended wine: A clean, slightly sweet Gewürztraminer or Chenin Blanc would be the best choice among wines. More often than not, I have jasmine tea with this dish.

Ribs in a Chinese Style with Spicy Cabbage Salad

These ribs carry a lot of piquant Asian flavors. Arm yourself with napkins, as they are definitely succulent finger food! The ribs can be prepared either in an oven or on the grill; I have included both methods below.

Serves 6 to 8 as an appetizer, 3 to 4 as a main course

MARINADE:

⅓ cup seasoned rice wine vinegar

½ cup light soy sauce

⅓ cup honey or pure maple syrup

⅓ cup hoisin sauce

2 teaspoons dark sesame oil

2 tablespoons minced garlic

½ teaspoon Chinese five-spice powder (page 197)

2 tablespoons minced fresh ginger

1½ teaspoons Asian chile sauce (or ½ teaspoon red chile flakes)

1 tablespoon grated orange zest

½ cup fresh orange juice

5 pounds pork spareribs, trimmed of white membrane and excess fat

Spicy Cabbage Salad (recipe follows)

In a medium bowl, combine all the marinade ingredients. In a container large enough to hold the ribs with the marinade, coat the ribs thoroughly. Cover and marinate, refrigerated, for 4 hours or overnight.

To prepare in the oven: Preheat the oven to 375 degrees. Reserving the excess marinade for basting, transfer the ribs to a rack in a roasting pan in a single layer and bake for 1 hour, basting occasionally, or until the meat is tender.

To grill: Prepare a charcoal fire around the edges of the grill, leaving room in the center to place a pan with which to catch the drippings. Replace the grill rack. Reserving the excess marinade for basting, transfer the ribs to the grill, centering them over the drip pan. Grill the ribs for 45 minutes, basting occasionally, or until the meat is tender.

Serve the ribs warm or at room temperature, accompanied by the Spicy Cabbage Salad.

Spicy Cabbage Salad

Serves 6

1½ pounds finely shredded red and/or green cabbage	2 tablespoons minced fresh ginger
1 tablespoon kosher salt	½ cup chopped fresh cilantro
¾ cup rice wine vinegar	½ teaspoon red chile flakes (or to taste)
½ cup sugar	1 cup finely shredded carrots

In a colander, toss the cabbage with the salt. Weight the cabbage down with a plate and a can or other heavy object. Let stand and drain for 1 to 2 hours at room temperature. In a large bowl combine the vinegar, sugar, ginger, cilantro, and chile flakes. Add the drained cabbage and the carrots and stir to combine. Chill for at least 2 hours, stirring occasionally. The salad can be made a day ahead and kept, covered and refrigerated.

 Recommended wine: The sweet, smoky flavors of the ribs are nicely contrasted by a fruity Gamay Beaujolais. An ice-cold Bud (or locally made Red Tail Ale if you're in northern California) isn't bad in a pinch either!

Rabbit with Ancho Chile Sauce and Black Bean Salsa

I explored the world of rabbit in great detail in *American Game Cooking,* but this new recipe begged for inclusion in this book. I continue to be dazzled by the incredible culinary versatility of rabbit, notwithstanding its great value as a lean, very low-fat meat. You'll have more than enough ancho sauce for this recipe. Save the remainder covered in the refrigerator for up to 5 days or freeze indefinitely.

Serves 4

MARINADE:

8 teaspoons ground coriander	8 loins from 4 large rabbit saddles
4 teaspoons ground cinnamon	16 thin slices high-quality bacon or pancetta
½ teaspoon salt	**Ancho Chile Sauce** (recipe follows)
1 teaspoon freshly ground black pepper	**Black Bean Salsa** (page 144)
2½ tablespoons olive oil	**Garnish:** Cilantro sprigs
4 teaspoons dried marjoram	

In a bowl, combine the marinade ingredients. Thoroughly rub the marinade on the rabbit loins and refrigerate for at least 30 minutes.

Remove the rabbit from the refrigerator. Lay 2 bacon strips side by side. Place 2 of the loins across one end of the bacon strips. Roll the bacon tightly around the pair of loins. Repeat this process with the remaining loins. You should now have 4 bacon-wrapped bundles.

Prepare a charcoal fire or preheat the broiler. Grill the rabbit over medium heat or broil until just cooked through and brown on all sides, 4 to 6 minutes. (If the charcoal is too hot, the fat from the bacon may flare up and char the bundles.)

To serve, spoon a pool of the Ancho Chile Sauce on warm plates, then spoon a tablespoon or two of the Black Bean Salsa decoratively over the sauce. Slice the grilled rabbit bundles on the diagonal and place the slices on top of the salsa. Garnish with cilantro sprigs.

Ancho Chile Sauce

4	large ancho chiles (dried poblanos)	1	cup peeled, seeded, and diced tomatoes
1	tablespoon peanut oil	½	teaspoon ground cinnamon
1½	cups finely chopped onions	½	cup heavy cream (optional)
1	tablespoon fennel seed	2	teaspoons honey (or to taste)
2	tablespoons finely chopped garlic	1	tablespoon fresh lime juice (or to taste)
1	teaspoon seeded and minced serrano chile	¼	cup minced fresh cilantro Kosher salt and freshly ground black pepper
1½	cups rich chicken stock		
½	cup dry red wine		

In a bowl, cover the chiles with hot water, place a small plate on top of them to keep them submerged, and soak for 30 minutes. Drain, remove the stems and seeds, and set aside.

In a medium saucepan, heat the oil and sauté the onions for 2 to 3 minutes until softened and translucent. Add the fennel seed, garlic, and serrano and sauté 3 minutes longer. Add the stock, wine, tomatoes, cinnamon, and the reserved anchos and simmer uncovered for 15 to 20 minutes. Add the cream, if using, and heat through. Cool slightly.

In a food processor or blender, purée the sauce until smooth. Add the honey and lime juice to taste. Strain if desired. Just before serving, stir in the minced cilantro and season to taste with salt and pepper.

Recommended wine: With their earthy, almost sweet character, ancho chiles go well with Pinot Noir. But if the final dish ends up having a lot of chile heat, then go to a slightly chilled Gamay Beaujolais.

 # Grilled Veal Chops with Cabernet– Wild Mushroom Sauce

Veal has come into some disfavor because of the way it has traditionally been raised for the commercial market. There are now a number of "ethical" veal producers who raise their animals in a kind and humane way. Be sure to ask your butcher or meat department what the source of the veal is. Veal is a sweet, delicious meat that I think is best grilled. The red wine reduction sauce used here can be made a day or two ahead of time and reheated at serving time.

Serves 6

HERB MARINADE:

½ cup chopped onions	6 veal loin chops, cut 1¼ inches
2 tablespoons minced garlic	thick
3 tablespoons minced fresh basil	Cabernet–Wild Mushroom Sauce
1½ tablespoons minced fresh mint	(recipe follows)
¼ cup dry white wine	Garnish: Grilled shiitake and/or
2 tablespoons white wine vinegar	other wild mushrooms and
1 teaspoon salt	fresh herb sprigs
1 teaspoon cracked black pepper	
⅓ cup olive oil	

In a blender or food processor, combine all the marinade ingredients except the olive oil. Process with 3 or 4 short bursts. Remove to a bowl and whisk in the olive oil separately.

In a pan large enough to accommodate the loin chops and the marinade, combine the chops and the marinade, turning to coat evenly. Cover and marinate, refrigerated, for at least 2 hours.

Prepare a charcoal fire or preheat the broiler or a stovetop grill. Remove the chops from the marinade and grill or broil until just done, approximately 5 to 6 minutes per side. The veal should remain slightly pink and juicy inside. Serve the veal chops surrounded with the sauce and garnished with grilled mushrooms and herb sprigs.

Cabernet–Wild Mushroom Sauce

2 tablespoons olive oil
½ cup sliced shallots
½ cup chopped shiitake
     mushrooms
1 tablespoon chopped garlic
½ ounce dried porcini mushrooms
1 cup seeded and chopped fresh
     tomatoes
5 cups rich beef or chicken stock

2 cups hearty red wine, preferably
     Cabernet Sauvignon
2 bay leaves
2 teaspoons fresh thyme leaves (or
     1 teaspoon dried)
1 tablespoon Dijon-style mustard
2 teaspoons minced fresh mint
     Salt and freshly ground black
     pepper

In a medium saucepan, heat the olive oil and sauté the shallots, shiitake mushrooms, and garlic until lightly browned. Add the porcini, tomatoes, stock, wine, bay leaves, thyme, and mustard and bring to a boil. Simmer over medium heat until reduced to a light sauce consistency, which could take from 40 minutes to 1 hour. Strain through a fine-mesh strainer, pressing down on the solids. Add the mint and season to taste with salt and pepper. The sauce can be kept, covered and refrigerated, for up to 2 days. Reheat before serving.

Recommended wine: With Cabernet Sauvignon being used in the sauce, it's only natural to use it on the table as well.

DEBORAH JONES

Zucchini Filled with Feta and Roasted Tomatoes, with Roasted Corn Vinaigrette

Corn Cakes shown with Sage Butter Sauce

Grilled Salmon with Roasted White Corn Salsa

Pecan–Polenta Salad with Grilled Scallions and Crème Fraîche

Chicken Breast Steamed in Cabbage with Cider Cream Sauce

"Soup of Fruits" with *Chardonnay Sabayon and Coconut Shortbreads*

ED AIONA

Fresh Peach and Almond Tart

Fresh Fruits and Berries with Hazelnut Biscotti

VEGETARIAN MAIN COURSES AND SPECIAL SIDES

Vegetables with Wine

Until recently, no one thought much about the relationship of vegetables and wine except to occasionally pronounce that they didn't go together. Not going together meant either that the vegetables would ruin the wine (asparagus and artichokes being two famous "wine ruiners") or that the wine would overpower the vegetables, which were too delicate to hold their own. But as we've expanded our ideas of what vegetables can be and how they can be prepared, we've discovered that vegetable-based dishes and even individual vegetables can go wonderfully with many wines. I am a great enthusiast of roasting and grilling vegetables. Both of these methods develop in the vegetable a complexity and depth of flavor that can match up to even a rich red wine. Try roasted young beets with a good California Pinot Noir or Merlot—delicious together!

Most of the recipes in this section are relatively rich, full-bodied dishes, designed for the center of the plate. You'll note that several contain a fair amount of cheese (in fact, some are entirely cheese based), but you can certainly use less cheese if you are concerned about fat. This is not, strictly speaking, a "vegetable" chapter, because in this book, as in wine country cuisine, the vegetables are everywhere, not segregated to the side of the plate. Look to the chapters titled *Salads, Soups,* and *Pastas, Pizzas, Risottos, and Gnocchis* for more vegetable and vegetarian ideas.

GRILLING AND ROASTING VEGETABLES

The simplest way to bring out the flavor of vegetables, other than eating them fresh and raw, is to grill or roast them. Traditionally, most of us were taught to use water to cook vegetables, through boiling, blanching, steaming. The trouble is that when you cook with water, flavor drains away from the vegetables into the water and, as a result, you have to add flavor back to the poor depleted things through the use of rich sauces or other toppings. Steaming does the least damage, but it also contributes nothing to flavor. I rarely use water or steam to cook vegetables any more.

In grilling and roasting you don't lose flavor to water. In fact, these dry-heat methods actually concentrate flavor by evaporating water in the vegetables. This also concentrates the natural sugar in the vegetables, which caramelizes and browns, yielding a golden exterior that is full of flavor. Because of the rich flavors and textures that result, grilled and roasted vegetables can certainly compete with meat for the center of the plate.

To grill vegetables:

My favorite vegetables on the grill are thick slices of red onion, eggplant, summer squash, and tomatoes. The simplest and most straightforward way to season vegetables for the grill is to toss them with a little olive oil, a drop or two of balsamic vinegar, and a sprinkling of kosher salt and freshly ground black pepper. As with other cooking techniques, if you are preparing more than one kind, make sure they are of a variety and size that will cook in the same time. (And if you're cutting them, be sure to leave them large enough so they don't fall through the grill!) I typically grill vegetables over a fairly hot bed of coals so the vegetables will cook quickly and retain their texture. A lot of fire also helps caramelize and develop flavors quickly.

For flavor variety, you can give vegetables a quick dip in any of the vinaigrettes in the book, such as the Lemon-Garlic Cream on page 20 or the Oriental Orange Vinaigrette on page 15 before grilling.

For more complex flavors, here are three marinades I especially like with vegetables. All yield about 2½ cups of marinade. These may be made a day ahead and stored in the refrigerator.

MUSTARD MARINADE

¾ cup olive oil
⅓ cup finely minced scallions,
    both white and pale-
    green parts
½ cup dry white wine

4 tablespoons roasted garlic
    (page 247)
1 cup Dijon-style mustard
1½ tablespoons sugar
    Salt and freshly ground black
    pepper

Whisk all ingredients together until combined, seasoning to taste.

BASIL-PARMESAN MARINADE

2 cups loosely packed basil
    leaves, chopped
1⅓ cups olive oil
½ cup white wine vinegar
2 tablespoons minced garlic

⅔ cup freshly grated
    Parmesan cheese
    Salt and freshly ground
    black pepper

Place all ingredients but the salt and pepper in a food processor or blender and pulse in short bursts until just combined; season to taste. The marinade should have a bit of texture. This marinade is especially good with grilled tomatoes and onions.

THAI-STYLE MARINADE

6 tablespoons Thai fish sauce
½ cup firmly packed light-
    brown sugar
¼ cup soy sauce
1 cup unsweetened coconut
    milk

¾ teaspoon red chile
    flakes (or to taste)
2 tablespoons curry powder
6 tablespoons fresh lime juice
6 tablespoons chopped fresh
    cilantro

Place all ingredients in a food processor or blender and process in short bursts until smooth. This marinade goes especially well with eggplant and sweet peppers.

To roast vegetables:

The most commonly roasted vegetables are root vegetables—carrots, onions, beets, parsnips, potatoes, and the like—but many other vegetables are also wonderful roasted, such as cauliflower, artichokes, broccoli, and garlic, which has become a staple in my kitchen.

The technique I use is very simple: Coat the vegetables with a little olive oil and season lightly with kosher salt and freshly ground black pepper. Toss. Place them whole (halved or quartered if they're really huge) in a single layer in a baking pan and cover with aluminum foil. Place in a preheated 400-degree oven and roast until the vegetables are half-cooked and just beginning to soften. Uncover the pan and finish cooking, allowing the vegetables to brown lightly and develop their sweet, wonderful flavor. Cooking times will vary depending on size and the particular vegetable used. I start them covered in order to allow the internal water to "steam" and soften the vegetables a bit; then they won't dry out too much. The goal is to have soft, luscious interiors and browned exteriors without too much shriveling.

Roasting peppers to remove the skin:

Peppers are roasted or charred to remove the skin, but in the process something wonderful happens to the flavor. Once you've tasted fresh roasted peppers with their sweet, smoky flavor you'll never again be satisfied with their poor canned cousins, like pimientos.

To roast peppers, use a long-handled fork and char them over an open flame until they are blackened all over. Or you can place them under a preheated broiler about 2 inches from the heat and turn occasionally until they are well blackened. Place the blackened peppers in a bowl and cover with plastic wrap and let them steam for a few minutes. With your fingers and/or the point of a knife, remove the blackened skin. DO NOT wash the peppers—this washes away much of that lovely flavor you've developed from the charring.

Cut off the tops and discard the stem and seeds. Roasted peppers freeze well indefinitely and are also delicious stored in olive oil in the refrigerator for up to 3 weeks.

Use rubber gloves if you're roasting and peeling chiles and you're sensitive to the capsaicin in them.

Roasting tomatoes for stocks and sauces:

Especially in the winter, store-bought tomatoes often lack flavor and appeal. For a sauce or soup, I think canned tomatoes are often a better choice, because they have a bit more flavor than fresh. One way of developing flavor in fresh tomatoes is to roast them. Remove the stems and place the tomatoes in a crowded single layer on a clean, lightly oiled baking sheet with sides (a jellyroll pan is ideal). If the tomatoes are large, cut them in half and place cut side down. There's no need to oil them. Roast in a preheated 375-degree oven until the tomatoes are well browned. The tomatoes will collapse and look a little abused, but that's okay. Depending on the tomatoes, it can take an hour or two for the tomatoes to brown. Be sure not to burn them. Transfer the tomatoes to a food processor, making sure to scrape all the browned bits and pieces out of the pan, and pulse a few times to make a chunky sauce. The browning, or caramelization, has heightened the tomato flavor, and now you have something wonderful to use in stocks, sauces, and vinaigrettes.

Roasting garlic:

Roasted garlic is a staple in my kitchen and appears in many recipes throughout the book. I consider it to be part of the basic larder of ingredients everyone should have on hand—almost up there with salt and pepper. I keep several heads of roasted garlic on hand at all times to add to soups, sauces, marinades, dressings, to toss with hot pasta. When garlic is roasted, it changes from the bold, sharp pungent flavor we associate with raw garlic to something subtle, sweet, and buttery soft. And since it's roasted whole in the husk, you can easily squeeze out just what you need.

To roast garlic: Cut off the top quarter inch or so of the garlic head to reveal the cloves. Drizzle a little olive oil over and season lightly with kosher salt and pepper. Wrap each individual head completely in aluminum foil and place in a preheated 350-degree oven for 25 to 30 minutes or until the garlic is very soft when squeezed. You can also open up the foil for the last 10 minutes or so to allow the garlic to caramelize a bit, which adds another interesting flavor note. Cool and store roasted garlic in the refrigerator in a sealed container for up to 3 weeks or freeze if you have a bumper crop from your garden.

Creamy Garlic Polenta with Wild Mushrooms and Tomato-Fennel Broth

Creamy polenta is a wonderful dish for a chilly fall or winter evening. (The recipe calls for ½ cup of heavy cream, but if you're indulging, a full cup gives a wonderful texture.) I've surrounded this polenta with Tomato-Fennel Broth, but you could use any of the vegetable stocks in the soup chapter or simply warm the fresh tomato and fennel juices together and season lightly with salt and pepper. At Valley Oaks, when we're awash in fragrant ripe tomatoes, we simply juice and can them, unseasoned, to use in recipes like this.

Serves 6 to 8

½   ounce dried porcini mushrooms
¼   cup olive oil
1   cup finely chopped yellow onions
½   cup coarsely chopped fresh
    mushrooms
1   tablespoon minced garlic
1   tablespoon minced fresh basil
½   teaspoon minced fresh oregano
    (or ¼ teaspoon dried)
4   cups vegetable or chicken stock
1   cup dry polenta

    Kosher salt and freshly ground
      white pepper
½   cup heavy cream
⅓   cup freshly grated Asiago or
    fontina cheese
    Tomato-Fennel Broth (recipe
    follows)
    Garnish: Sautéed fresh porcini or
    chanterelle mushrooms, if
    desired, and fresh basil sprigs

Rinse the dried porcini. Place in a small bowl and cover with warm water. Weight the mushrooms down with a small plate to submerge them completely. Let stand 1 hour. Drain and reserve.

In a large saucepan, heat the olive oil and sauté the onions, fresh mushrooms, garlic, and rehydrated porcini until very lightly colored. Add the basil, oregano, and stock and bring to a boil.

Slowly add the polenta by handfuls, stirring constantly with a wooden spoon to prevent lumps. Reduce the heat and simmer slowly for 30 minutes, stirring regularly. The polenta will be thick and creamy. Add more stock if necessary. Season with salt and pepper.

To serve, add the cream and cheese, stirring vigorously. Spoon onto warm plates, and ladle a ring of warm Tomato-Fennel Broth around the polenta. Garnish with sautéed wild mushrooms, if using, and basil sprigs. Save any remaining broth for another use.

Tomato-Fennel Broth

Makes approximately 3 cups

1   tablespoon olive oil
2   cups chopped onions
½   cup chopped fresh mushrooms
1   teaspoon chopped garlic
1   cup chopped fresh fennel
    bulb
1   teaspoon fennel seed
½   cup dry white wine

1   cup corn or mushroom stock
    (pages 56 and 57)
3   tablespoons chopped sun-dried
    tomatoes
¾   cup fresh fennel juice (page 59)
¾   cup fresh tomato juice
    Kosher salt and freshly ground
    black pepper

In a large saucepan, heat the olive oil and sauté the onions, mushrooms, garlic, fennel, and fennel seed until they just begin to color. Add the wine, stock, and sun-dried tomatoes. Simmer slowly for 10 minutes. Remove from the heat and strain. Return the liquid to the pan and add the fresh fennel and tomato juices. Season to taste with salt and pepper. The Tomato-Fennel Broth can be made ahead and stored, covered and refrigerated, for 3 days. Reheat gently before serving.

 Recommended wine: A Chianti Classico reflects the flavors and feeling of this rustic dish. A mature California Pinot Noir would also be a great match, echoing the earthiness of the mushrooms; the tomato broth would help accent the bright fruit and slightly herbal tastes of the wine.

Eggplant Sandwiches on Baby Greens with Tomato-Balsamic Vinaigrette

This is a great dish for a summer luncheon or al fresco dinner. Its background is clearly Italian. I love the anchovy in this recipe, but if you prefer a vegetarian version, substitute slivered Niçoise or oil-cured black olives to get the same salty, briny effect.
Serves 6

2 medium eggplant, cut into 12 1-inch-thick slices	½ cup finely chopped walnuts
¼ cup olive oil	1 cup all-purpose flour
Kosher salt and freshly ground black pepper	3 large eggs, lightly beaten
	Vegetable oil for frying
¾ pound fresh mozzarella cheese, cut into 6 slices	3 cups savory baby greens, such as arugula, frisée, red mustard, flowering kale, and spinach
½ cup loosely packed basil leaves	Tomato-Balsamic Vinaigrette (recipe follows)
12 rinsed and dried anchovy fillets	Garnish: Deep-fried capers (page 21) and fresh rosemary leaves
1½ cups Panko or other dry breadcrumbs	

Preheat the oven to 400 degrees. Lightly brush both sides of the eggplant slices with the oil and season with salt and pepper. Place in a single layer on a baking sheet and roast until lightly brown and tender, about 20 minutes.

Arrange the mozzarella slices on 6 of the eggplant slices. On a cutting board, coarsely chop the basil and anchovy together and sprinkle over the cheese. Top with a second eggplant slice to form a sandwich.

In a small bowl, combine the breadcrumbs and walnuts. Dredge the sandwiches in flour, patting off the excess. Dip them in the beaten egg and then in the breadcrumb mixture. The sandwiches may be prepared up to this point and kept loosely covered in the refrigerator for up to 8 hours.

Add vegetable oil to a sauté pan to a depth of ½ inch. Heat oil to to 350 degrees. In batches, sauté the sandwiches in a single layer, turning once to brown both sides. This will take only a few minutes per side. As they are done, remove to paper towels to drain. Keep warm. These sandwiches may be cooked up to 4 hours in advance and reheated in the oven at serving time.

To serve, toss the greens with a little of the vinaigrette and serve the hot eggplant sandwiches on a bed of the lightly dressed greens. Scatter with deep-fried capers and rosemary leaves, if desired. Serve immediately.

Tomato-Balsamic Vinaigrette

2 teaspoons minced garlic	1 teaspoon chopped fresh mint
⅓ cup balsamic vinegar	2 tablespoons minced oil-packed
⅔ cup tomato juice	sun-dried tomatoes
¼ cup extra-virgin olive oil	Kosher salt and freshly ground
1 tablespoon fresh lemon juice	black pepper
2 tablespoons chopped fresh basil	

In a small bowl, whisk together all ingredients, seasoning to taste. Allow to stand at least 1 hour before using. Store any unused vinaigrette, covered and refrigerated, up to 10 days.

 Recommended wine: A grassy, herbal Sauvignon Blanc as well as a soft, fruity Cabernet or Cabernet Franc would be wonderful with this dish. I've also liked a good Chianti as a match.

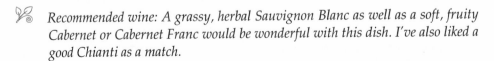

REDUCED BALSAMIC VINEGAR

Reduced balsamic vinegar as a garnish used to "paint" the plate adds interesting acid-sweet flavors.

To reduce balsamic vinegar, put it in a saucepan and let it simmer until reduced by half. Allow it to cool. You can keep it indefinitely in the refrigerator. I keep reduced balsamic vinegar in a squeeze bottle with a narrow tip—it's handy for squeezing out small amounts for flavoring and great for decorating.

Parmesan Soufflé Rolled with Greens and Leeks with a Red Bell Pepper Sauce

This beautiful dish is full of color and flavor and is marvelous for entertaining. The greens and leek filling and the Red Bell Pepper Sauce can be prepared a day ahead. The soufflé layer can be prepared several hours ahead. You'll need no more than 15 or 20 minutes before serving time to assemble the elements and heat them up.

Serves 8

Garnish: Curry-saffron oil (page 68) and rosemary sprigs with flowers, if available

GREENS AND LEEK FILLING:

3 tablespoons olive oil	1 pound washed, stemmed, and chopped baby greens, such as spinach leaves, chard, or kale
2 cups chopped red onions	
2 teaspoons minced garlic	
1 cup thinly sliced leeks, both white and tender green parts	2½ cups coarsely grated Gruyère cheese
¾ cup dry white wine	1¾ cups coarsely grated dry Jack or Asiago cheese
2 tablespoons *each* minced fresh tarragon and basil (or 1 tablespoon *each* dried)	Kosher salt and freshly ground black pepper

In a large sauté pan, heat the olive oil and sauté the onions until lightly brown and caramelized. Add the garlic and leeks and sauté for 3 minutes longer or until soft. Add the wine and herbs. Cook until most of the liquid has evaporated. Add the greens and cook until just tender, approximately 1 minute for spinach and longer for heartier greens. Remove to a colander, drain, and cool. Gently squeeze the greens to remove any excess moisture. Place the greens in a bowl and lightly toss with the cheeses. Season with salt and pepper. The filling can be stored, covered and refrigerated, for 1 day.

RED BELL PEPPER SAUCE:

2	tablespoons unsalted butter	1	cup rich vegetable stock
1	cup chopped yellow onions	1	teaspoon pure chile powder
4	cups chopped red bell peppers		(optional)
	(about 5 large peppers)		Kosher salt and freshly ground
1	cup dry white wine		white pepper
2	tablespoons tomato paste		

In a saucepan, melt the butter and sauté the onions and peppers until soft but not brown. Add the wine, tomato paste, stock, and chile powder. Bring to a simmer and reduce over moderate heat by half. Transfer to a blender and purée. Strain the sauce. Season to taste with salt and pepper. If necessary, thin the sauce with additional stock. The sauce can be stored, covered and refrigerated, for 1 day. Reheat gently before serving. For a richer tasting sauce, try roasting the peppers first and substituting a half teaspoon or so of chipotle chile in place of the chile powder.

SOUFFLÉ LAYER:

5	large eggs, separated	1½	teaspoons kosher salt, plus a
1½	cups half-and-half		pinch for the egg whites
4	tablespoons unsalted butter, plus	½	teaspoon freshly ground white
	additional for the baking sheet		pepper
5	tablespoons all-purpose flour,	¼	teaspoon freshly grated nutmeg
	plus additional for the baking	½	cup freshly grated Parmesan
	sheet		cheese

Preheat the oven to 400 degrees. In a medium bowl, lightly beat the egg yolks and set aside.

In a small saucepan, heat the half-and-half to scalding. In a separate small saucepan, melt the butter and add the flour, stirring to make a roux. Cook for 3 minutes without browning. Whisk the scalded half-and-half into the roux, and cook, stirring constantly, for another 3 minutes until thickened. Remove from the heat. Stir in the salt, pepper, and nutmeg. Gradually whisk the warm mixture into the egg yolks and set aside.

In a medium bowl, beat the egg whites, with a pinch of salt, until they hold stiff peaks. Stir a quarter of the beaten egg whites and half of the Parmesan into the egg-yolk mixture to lighten it. Gently fold in the rest of the whites.

Butter a 10- by 15-inch jellyroll pan and line with waxed paper. Lightly butter the paper and dust with flour. Pour the soufflé mixture onto the prepared baking sheet, spreading evenly to the corners. Sprinkle with the remaining ¼ cup Parmesan. Bake for 15 minutes, until the top is browned and puffed. Remove from the oven and cool. Invert and remove the waxed paper. Invert again so the top faces up. The soufflé may be made in advance to this point, wrapped in plastic wrap and refrigerated.

To assemble the soufflé roll: Preheat the oven to 350 degrees. Evenly spread the greens and leeks filling on top of the soufflé layer. Starting with a long edge, carefully roll the soufflé, jellyroll-style.

Place the rolled soufflé on a baking sheet and bake for 8 to 10 minutes or until heated through and the cheese is melted. Remove from the oven.

To serve, spoon the warm red bell pepper sauce in the center of warm plates. Slice the rolled soufflé and arrange in the center of the plates. Garnish with a drizzled ring of the curry-saffron oil and rosemary sprigs, if desired.

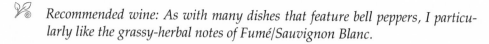

Recommended wine: As with many dishes that feature bell peppers, I particularly like the grassy-herbal notes of Fumé/Sauvignon Blanc.

GREENS

Greens are a fixture of wine country cooking, but the use of greens is so interwoven in the rich heritage of Southern cooking that it falls into the realm of folklore as much as it does cuisine. Often referred to in the South as "a mess of greens," the earthy, soul-satisfying, slightly bitter taste of mustard and turnip greens, collards, kale, and Swiss chard appears on Southern tables with great regularity. Served on New Year's Day with black-eyed peas and ham, they symbolize good luck and monetary gain. More contemporary uses call for them in pastas, in pizzas with herbs and sausage, or with black-eyed peas and tomatoes in comforting winter soups. Nutritionally, greens are very high in vitamin A, calcium, and potassium, and they are very low in calories.

Greens should be used as soon after purchasing them as possible, and they should always be thoroughly washed. Most dishes made with greens match nicely with a crisp, herbal-tinged Fumé Blanc.

Mustard greens:

The slightly frilly, bright-green oval leaves have a sharp, mustardy tang with a hint of hot radish. They make a wonderful addition to salads and stir-fries.

Turnip greens:

The leafy green tops to the turnip plant are said to do everything from curing hangovers to awakening "slumbering sexual desires." Turnip greens find their contemporary place in soups and stir-fries, where their slightly bitter, chewy edge can be toned down with other flavors.

Kale:

The ruffly, green-purple leaves of kale are quite dramatic and are often used ornamentally, as well as in soups, stews, and sautés. The Dutch, British, Germans, and Scots all prize this humble member of the cabbage family and value its mystical properties.

Collards:

Legendary in the South, hearty collards, a relative to cabbage, originated in Africa. Collard leaves should be separated from the tougher stems and ribs, and simmered in seasoned broth for a few hours, or for a quarter to half hour if a crunchier texture is desired. They also blend beautifully with pork and ham hocks and other smoky, salty, and spicy flavors.

Swiss chard:

This member of the beet family is a mainstay of southern French cooking and is infinitely versatile. Green and red (or rhubarb) chard are the most common varieties. Chard is used as an excellent flavor and textural addition to pastas, salads, sausage, and soups, particularly when combined with olive oil, pine nuts, mushrooms, garlic, and currants or raisins.

Dandelion greens:

Long a staple in the South, where they are traditionally braised or sautéed with pork, the notched leaves of this bitter delicacy are now more commonly found in contemporary salads. Dandelion greens adapt well to hot dressings with oil, balsamic vinegar, bacon bits, hot pepper sauce, and perhaps cheese or croutons. Dandelion greens need to be cooked for only a short time.

FRESH TOMATO PASTE

During the summer, when tomatoes are at their peak, I like to make my own fresh tomato paste. It doesn't have the strongly cooked flavor of canned paste, and I much prefer it. Here's what I do:

Peel and seed dead-ripe tomatoes and purée them with a food mill or in a food processor. Pour the purée into a cotton jelly bag (generally available wherever canning supplies are sold) and hang it up over a bowl; let the clear liquid drip off for several hours or overnight. Save the drippings for stock and freeze the paste in ice cube trays. When frozen, pop out the tomato cubes and store in airtight bags in the freezer. You'll have approximately 2 tablespoons of paste per ordinary-sized cube.

 Eggplant Torta with Smoked Tomato Sauce

You'll need a 9-inch springform cake pan for this recipe. You can add any other vegetable to the filling that you like, such as sautéed mushrooms or sautéed zucchini. You'll have more than enough Smoked Tomato Sauce for this recipe. Save the remainder to toss with pasta for a quick meal.

Serves 8 to 10

6   medium eggplants, sliced lengthwise into ⅓-inch-thick slices
    Extra-virgin olive oil
    Kosher salt and freshly ground black pepper
3   tablespoons minced garlic
2½ pounds fresh ripe tomatoes, peeled, seeded, and chopped
1   cup loosely packed basil leaves, roughly chopped
1   teaspoon crushed fennel seed

½   cup dry white wine
¾   cup freshly grated Parmesan cheese, plus additional for top
½   pound grated mozzarella cheese or Monterey Jack
3   large eggs, beaten until light with 2 tablespoons water
    Smoked Tomato Sauce (recipe follows)
    Garnish: Arugula leaves and roasted baby vegetables, if desired

Preheat the oven to 400 degrees. Lightly brush the eggplant slices with some of the olive oil and season with salt and pepper. Place on a baking sheet in a single layer and bake for 20 minutes or until lightly brown and soft. Remove and cool. Lower the oven temperature to 350 degrees.

Meanwhile, in a saucepan, heat 2 tablespoons olive oil and sauté the garlic for 2 minutes. Add the tomatoes, basil, fennel seed, and wine. Simmer until thick, about 20 minutes. Season with salt and pepper.

Lightly oil the bottom and sides of a 9- by 2-inch springform pan. Line the bottom and sides of the pan with a layer of the eggplant slices; the eggplant should extend (hang) over the rim by at least 3 inches. Spoon in one third of the tomato mixture. Top with one third of the Parmesan and mozzarella. Add another layer of eggplant, trimming to fit snugly. Add the second third of the sauce, followed by a second third of the cheeses. Add a third layer of the eggplant, followed by the remaining sauce and cheeses. Top with the remaining eggplant. Using a sharp knife or metal skewer, poke holes down through the layers. Pour the egg mixture over the top so that it soaks in evenly. Fold the overlapping edges of eggplant over the top and sprinkle with a little Parmesan.

Bake the eggplant torta on a baking sheet at 350 degrees for 35 to 40 minutes. Remove and let stand at least 10 minutes before serving. Run a knife around the edge of the pan before releasing the spring.

Serve the torta sliced into wedges and surrounded by the Smoked Tomato Sauce. Garnish with arugula and roasted baby vegetables, if desired. The torta may be served warm or at room temperature.

Smoked Tomato Sauce

Makes about 2 cups

1½ pounds plum tomatoes,
      seeded and halved
2   tablespoons olive oil
1   cup diced red onions
½   cup diced red bell
      pepper
2   teaspoons roasted garlic
      (see page 247)

1   tablespoon chopped fresh
      oregano (or 1 teaspoon
      dried)
⅓   cup dry white wine
     Kosher salt and freshly ground
      black pepper
     Balsamic vinegar

Place the tomatoes in a single layer in a roasting pan. In a smoker or grill that can be enclosed, place on the hot coals green fruitwood or wood chips that have been soaked in water for 3 to 4 hours. Replace the grill rack. Set the roasting pan of tomatoes on the grill. Cover the grill, leaving a small vent to keep the coals burning. Smoke the tomatoes at least 45 minutes to develop flavor.

In a sauté pan, heat the olive oil and sauté the onions, pepper, roasted garlic, and oregano until the onions are soft but not brown. Add the wine. Increase the heat and reduce the liquid by half. Add the smoked tomatoes. Simmer, uncovered, for an additional 10 minutes to thicken the mixture. Transfer the mixture to a blender or food processor and purée. Return the sauce to the pan. Season to taste with salt and pepper and drops of balsamic vinegar.

 Recommended wine: This is a robust dish, and the smokiness goes well with a Fumé/Sauvignon Blanc or a barrel-aged red without too many tannins, like Merlot or Pinot Noir.

 # Mediterranean Polenta Tamales with Ratatouille Filling and Pepper-Corn Cream Sauce

This is another of the "Here today, gone tamale" explorations from the global tamale book I never wrote. (I did teach a class on tamales once: The final course was a dessert tamale, chocolate-mocha with a raspberry sauce, which is *not* included in this book!) You can explore tamales on your own. Although this recipe looks complicated, it's really a skeleton with total flexibility. In place of the ratatouille filling, try any cooked vegetable mixture: leftover Roasted Eggplant Caponata (see page 280) would be a great substitution. And there are numerous sauces throughout the book that you could use in place of the Pepper-Corn Cream: Ancho Chile Sauce (page 238) or Smoked Tomato Sauce (page 256). Have fun!

Makes 8 to 10 tamales, serving 4 to 5

8 **large dry corn husks, soaked for 2 hours in warm water**

Garnish: Red bell pepper strips, if desired

RATATOUILLE FILLING:

½ cup diced eggplant
½ cup diced yellow squash
½ cup diced zucchini
½ cup quartered red or yellow pear
     tomatoes
¼ cup diced wild mushrooms, such
     as porcini (if dried, soak 30
     minutes, then rinse and dice)
1 cup diced red onions
1 tablespoon minced fresh basil
1 teaspoon minced fresh parsley
     (½ tablespoon dried)

1 teaspoon minced shallots or
     scallions
½ teaspoon minced fresh oregano
     (¼ teaspoon dried)
¼ teaspoon kosher salt
⅛ teaspoon freshly ground black
     pepper
   Pinch of red chile flakes
1 tablespoon dry white wine
2 tablespoons olive oil

In a medium bowl, combine all the ingredients. Toss to coat thoroughly. Cover and let stand at room temperature for 1 hour. Transfer the vegetables to a roasting or sauté pan and roast in a preheated 375-degree oven or sauté until crisp-tender. Roughly chop and reserve.

PEPPER-CORN CREAM SAUCE:

1 tablespoon olive oil
¼ cup minced shallots
1 teaspoon seeded and minced
     serrano chile (or to taste)
1 cup dry white wine
2½ cups rich vegetable stock
1 cup heavy cream
2 tablespoons minced red bell
     pepper

2 tablespoons minced yellow bell
     pepper
2 tablespoons minced green bell
     pepper
   Kosher salt and freshly ground
     white pepper
   Drops of fresh lemon or lime
     juice
1 cup young fresh raw corn kernels

In a medium saucepan, heat the olive oil. Add the shallots and serrano and sauté until soft but not brown. Add the wine and stock. Bring to a boil and reduce the liquid by half. Add the cream and continue to boil until reduced to a light sauce consistency. Stir in the bell peppers. Season with salt, pepper, and drops of lemon juice. Stir in the corn kernels. Keep warm.

POLENTA DOUGH:

2 cups water
½ cup yellow cornmeal
½ cup dry polenta
¼ cup freshly grated Parmesan cheese
2 tablespoons minced green bell pepper

2 tablespoons minced red bell
   pepper
¼ cup unsalted butter
   Kosher salt and freshly ground
   black pepper

In a medium saucepan, bring 2 cups water to a boil. Slowly pour in the cornmeal and polenta, stirring constantly. Lower the heat and continue stirring until very thick, about 5 minutes. Fold in the Parmesan, minced peppers, and butter. Stir and cook until the butter melts. Season with salt and pepper. Let the dough cool a little.

To assemble the tamales: Remove the husks from the water, drain, and pat dry. Spread out the corn husks on a dry work surface. Pinch off an egg-sized piece of the polenta dough mixture. Pat it onto the corn husk, flattening the dough to approximately 4 inches square and ¼ inch thick, leaving a border of husk at least ½ inch wide around the perimeter of the dough. Spread a tablespoon of the Ratatouille Filling lengthwise in the center of the dough. Fold the husk together until the edges overlap and the polenta and its filling are completely enclosed by the husk.

Gently flatten the top and bottom of the husk and fold the ends up to enclose. Place the tamales folded side down in a steamer over boiling water and steam for 20 minutes. Remove and allow to cool 10 minutes. To serve, open the husks to reveal the tamales. Drizzle with some of the Pepper-Corn Cream Sauce and garnish with strips of red bell pepper if desired.

Recommended wine: A number of wines can work here. A clean, crisp Chardonnay goes wonderfully with the sweet corn and bell pepper flavors in the sauce. A slightly grassy-herbal Sauvignon Blanc would highlight those flavors of the filling.

Herbed Crêpes with Roasted Vegetables and Goat Cheese Sauce

This combination of vegetables provides a wonderful variety of flavors and textures, but I encourage you to experiment with other combinations. The crêpes themselves can be made in advance and refrigerated or frozen; the Goat Cheese Sauce is easy and irresistible.

Serves 8

1   small eggplant, sliced ½ inch
        thick
     Olive oil
     Kosher salt and freshly ground
        black pepper
½   pound turnips or parsnips,
        scrubbed and quartered
½   pound red bell peppers, quartered
½   pound fennel bulb, sliced ½ inch
        thick
2   medium red onions, sliced ¼ inch
        thick

½   pound ripe plum tomatoes,
        stemmed and seeded
2   tablespoons red wine vinegar
⅓   cup chopped fresh basil
1   teaspoon minced garlic
     Herbed Crêpes (recipe follows)
     Goat Cheese Sauce (recipe
        follows)
     Garnish: Fresh thyme sprigs and
        baby greens, such as mizuna,
        mustard, tatsoi, spinach, and/or
        lettuces, are optional

Preheat the oven to 375 degrees. Lightly brush the eggplant slices with olive oil, season with salt and pepper, and arrange in a single layer on a baking sheet. On another baking sheet or in a roasting pan, lightly toss the remaining vegetables with a little olive oil and season with salt and pepper. Roast all the vegetables for 20 to 25 minutes or until lightly browned. Set aside. (The fennel, onions, eggplant, and tomatoes can be charcoal-grilled over moderate coals. The peppers and turnips are best roasted in the oven.)

Roughly chop all the cooked vegetables into ½-inch pieces. In a large bowl, combine the vinegar, basil, and garlic. Add the vegetables, toss, and add enough olive oil just to coat. Season with salt and pepper. Divide the filling among the crêpes. Roll into neat cones. Place on a baking sheet lined with waxed paper.

To serve, briefly warm the crêpes in a preheated 350-degree oven until heated through. Serve 2 crêpes apiece on warm plates with the Goat Cheese Sauce spooned around. Garnish with fresh herb sprigs and baby greens, if desired.

Herbed Crêpes

Makes 16 8-inch crêpes

1   cup all-purpose flour
1   cup plus 2 tablespoons whole milk
3   large eggs
2   tablespoons unsalted butter,
        browned and cooled

1   teaspoon salt
2   tablespoons *each* minced fresh
        parsley, chives, and tarragon
     Vegetable oil

In a blender or food processor, combine the flour, milk, eggs, butter, and salt and process for 15 seconds. Turn off the motor. Using a rubber spatula, scrape down the sides of the container. Blend the batter for 20 seconds more, then transfer it to a bowl. Stir in the herbs and let the batter stand at room temperature, covered, for 1 hour. The batter may be made 1 day in advance and kept covered and refrigerated.

Lightly oil an 8-inch crêpe or sauté pan and heat over moderate heat. (Oil the pan each time.) Add 2 tablespoons of the batter and swirl the pan to coat the bottom with the batter. Cook until lightly brown, about 1 minute. Turn the crêpe over and cook 30 seconds more. Remove from the pan and place on a square of waxed paper. Top with another square of waxed paper. Repeat until all the batter is used, layering sheets of waxed paper between each crêpe to prevent sticking. The crêpes can be wrapped well in plastic wrap and refrigerated for 2 days or frozen for up to 1 month.

Goat Cheese Sauce

⅔ **cup fresh, soft cream cheese- or log-style goat cheese**
¾ **cup rich vegetable stock, heated**
1 **tablespoon minced fresh chives**
1 **tablespoon minced fresh basil**

2 **teaspoons fresh lemon juice**
1 **teaspoon minced garlic**
   Kosher salt and freshly ground white pepper

In a medium bowl, whisk together all the ingredients but salt and pepper until smooth. The sauce should be pourable and not too thick: add more stock as necessary. Season to taste with salt and pepper. Warm the sauce slightly before serving.

 Recommended wine: As with many vegetable dishes, a good chilled Fumé/ Sauvignon Blanc seems to lift out the flavors beautifully. The acidity of the goat cheese is also mirrored nicely in this wine.

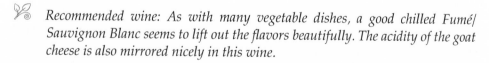

Beggar's Purses with Savory Greens and Warm Lemon Sauce

This is a very pretty dish that requires a bit of work, but it's worth it. The filling can be made a day ahead and refrigerated. The crêpes can be made a couple of weeks ahead and frozen. (Be sure to put a sheet of waxed paper between each crêpe before freezing to ensure that you'll be able to get them apart after thawing.) The sauce should be made no more than a few hours before serving; keep it warm in a thermos. I love this sauce as an accompaniment to almost every green vegetable. First-of-the-season crisp-cooked asparagus in a pool of the lemon sauce is sublime!

Serves 8

4   tablespoons olive oil
2   cups chopped red onions
2½ cups diced fresh shiitake or
     cremini mushrooms
1½ pounds spinach leaves, washed
     and trimmed
¼   teaspoon freshly grated
     nutmeg
4   tablespoons minced fresh
     basil
⅔   cup grated dry Jack or Gruyère
     cheese

Kosher salt and freshly ground
   black pepper
Whole chives or strips of leek for
   tying purses
Basil Crêpes (recipe follows)
Warm Lemon Sauce (recipe
   follows)
Garnish: Diced red and yellow
   peppers and fresh thyme,
   marjoram, or tarragon sprigs,
   if desired

In a large sauté pan, heat 2 tablespoons of the olive oil. Add the onions and sauté for 2 minutes. Add the mushrooms and continue cooking until the onions are soft and translucent. Remove from the heat, transfer to a medium bowl, and set aside.

Add the remaining 2 tablespoons olive oil to the pan and increase the heat to high. Add the spinach leaves and stir to wilt. Remove from the pan, cool, and blot dry with paper towels. Roughly chop the spinach and combine with the onion-mushroom mixture. Stir in the nutmeg, basil, and cheese. Season to taste with salt and pepper.

To serve, place a dollop of the filling in the center of each of the 16 crepes. Gather the crêpe together just above the filling and tie very gently with a chive or leek green. Spoon the Warm Lemon Sauce into the center of each plate. Place two purses on top of the sauce. Garnish with diced peppers and herb sprigs, if desired. The beggar's purses may be served warm or at room temperature, although the sauce should be warm.

Basil Crêpes

Makes 16 8-inch crêpes

1   cup water
1   cup whole milk
1½ cups all-purpose flour
4   large eggs

6   tablespoons olive or vegetable oil
¾   teaspoon salt
5   tablespoons minced fresh basil

In a blender or food processor, combine the water, milk, flour, eggs, 3 tablespoons of the oil, and salt. Blend until smooth, about 15 seconds. Add the basil and pulse once to just mix in. Cover and chill for at least 1 hour or overnight.

Using the remaining 3 tablespoons oil for *all* the crêpes, lightly oil a 10-inch crêpe pan or sauté pan and place over moderate heat. When the pan is hot, pour in ¼ cup of the batter and tilt the pan in all directions to cover the bottom of the pan. Pour out any excess to the batter bowl. Cook until the center of the crêpe is dry and the bottom lightly browned, approximately 1 minute. Turn and cook the other side for 30 seconds. Remove and cool on a rack. The crêpes may be made ahead of time: Cool, separate the crêpes with sheets of waxed paper, then wrap in plastic. Store, refrigerated, for 2 days or frozen for up to 2 months.

Warm Lemon Sauce

Makes approximately 1½ cups

1½ **cups rich vegetable or chicken stock**
½ **cup dry white wine**
3 **large egg yolks**

5 **tablespoons fresh lemon juice**
   Kosher salt and freshly ground white pepper
2 **tablespoons minced fresh chives**

In a small saucepan, bring the stock and wine to a boil. Reduce by half. In a bowl, whisk together the egg yolks and lemon juice. Slowly whisk the reduced stock into the egg mixture, a bit at a time, being careful not to scramble the eggs. Return the mixture to the saucepan and place over moderate heat. Cook, stirring constantly, until the sauce thickens slightly. Strain immediately and season with salt and pepper. Stir in the chives. Keep warm until ready to serve.

 Recommended wine: A crisp, lemon-tinged Fumé/Sauvignon Blanc or Sémillon captures the tart freshness of this dish.

BASIL

One of the most popular of all herbs, basil is a member of the mint family. "Basil" comes from the Greek word for "king," which gives you some idea of how important it has been to the kitchen throughout the centuries. The varieties of basil are endless, ranging from the tiny piccolo fino verde (considered the connoisseur's basil) to the pungent cinnamon, lemon, and licorice basils that can be grown easily in a small herb garden.

Basil appears in almost as many cuisines as cilantro does, with a special prominence in the Mediterranean and Southeast Asia. In the Valley Oaks garden, each year we've grown at least 20 different basils, and next to the 105 varieties of tomatoes I think it's the part of the garden that cooks love the most.

Ricotta Cheese–Lemon Thyme Tart with Sweet Cornmeal Crust

For me, this recipe has symbolic meaning: It is the one that indirectly brought me to Fetzer. Sid and I developed the recipe for a wine country promotion, during which I had a chance to visit. Once set loose in the expansive Valley Oaks garden to harvest the herbs, I couldn't turn back. The crust, a real favorite of mine, is particularly good for showcasing savory fillings. For an added flavor dimension, try adding a thin layer of slow-roasted tomatoes (see page 246) to the prepared tart shell before you pour in the filling mixture.

Serves 8 to 12

CORNMEAL CRUST:

½ cup unsalted butter, softened
2 tablespoons sugar
1 cup yellow cornmeal

2 eggs, at room temperature
1 teaspoon salt
1½ cups all-purpose flour

In the bowl of an electric mixer, combine the butter and sugar. Beat until smooth. Add the cornmeal, eggs, and salt. Beat until well combined. Add the flour and mix until the dough forms a ball. The mixture should be soft and moist. Wrap in plastic wrap and chill for 1 hour.

Preheat the oven to 350 degrees. Butter a 9-inch tart pan with a removable bottom. On a floured work surface, roll out the dough to fit the pan. Roll the dough up onto the rolling pin to transfer to the tart pan. Press the dough into the pan, trimming any excess. Prick the dough with the tines of a fork. Bake for 8 to 10 minutes or until just lightly browned. Any leftover dough may be wrapped and frozen; it makes great biscuits.

RICOTTA CHEESE–LEMON THYME FILLING:

1   tablespoon unsalted butter
4   tablespoons minced shallots or
    scallions, both white and pale-
    green parts
⅔   cup heavy cream
½   cup dry white wine
½   teaspoon kosher salt
¼   teaspoon freshly black ground
    pepper

¾   pound fresh ricotta cheese
3   eggs
1½ tablespoons chopped fresh
    herbs, such as lemon thyme,
    chives, parsley, or basil, or a
    combination

In a medium sauté pan, melt the butter and sauté the shallots until soft but not brown. Add the cream, wine, salt, and pepper. Bring to a simmer and reduce by half. Remove to a bowl and cool. Add the ricotta, eggs, and thyme. Beat until smooth. Pour into the prepared tart shell.

Bake at 350 degrees for 35 to 40 minutes, or until the filling is just set and lightly browned. Serve warm or at room temperature. Garnish with a sprinkling of thyme or whatever other herb you used in the filling.

 Recommended wine: The crisp, distinctively herbaceous flavors of a Fumé/ Sauvignon Blanc are perfect counterpoints to the tart.

Surprisingly, this cornmeal crust comes from an old French recipe. Cornmeal is not usually thought of as being part of the French pantry, but I encountered it at a tiny little roadside cafe in the French countryside. Rather than using it as a tart crust, the proprietors had made it into little cookies to serve alongside the local red wine, similar to what the Italians do with biscotti.

Zucchini Filled with Feta and Roasted Tomatoes, with Roasted Corn Vinaigrette

This recipe brings together the best of summer flavors and is a good use for zucchini that have gotten too large! The filling is also terrific tossed with your favorite pasta.

Serves 4

2 large zucchini
1 small eggplant, sliced into
     ½-inch-thick rounds
7 tablespoons olive oil
4 halved and seeded plum
     tomatoes
   Kosher salt and freshly ground
     black pepper
1 cup minced onions
2 teaspoons minced garlic
¼ cup chopped red bell pepper
½ teaspoon seeded and minced
     serrano chile (or big pinch red
     chile flakes)

¼ cup chopped fresh parsley
2 tablespoons chopped fresh mint
1 cup diced or crumbled feta or
     aged California goat cheese
¼ cup toasted pine nuts
2 cups mixed baby savory greens,
     such as arugula, frisée, and
     watercress
   Roasted Corn Vinaigrette (recipe
     follows)

Preheat the oven to 400 degrees. Halve the zucchini lengthwise and carefully scoop out the flesh, leaving a ¼-inch-thick shell. Chop and reserve the flesh. Set the zucchini shells aside.

Lightly brush both sides of the eggplant rounds with 3 tablespoons of the olive oil. In a bowl, lightly toss the tomatoes with 1 tablespoon of the olive oil. Place the tomatoes and eggplant slices in a single layer on a baking sheet, season with salt and pepper, and roast for 10 minutes or until the eggplant is lightly browned and softened. Roughly chop both tomatoes and eggplant and set aside.

In a sauté pan, heat the remaining 3 tablespoons of olive oil. Add the onions, garlic, and bell pepper and sauté until soft but not brown. Add the reserved zucchini flesh and cook 1 minute, stirring. Combine with the eggplant mixture. Stir in the serrano, parsley, mint, feta, and pine nuts. Season to taste with salt and pepper. Divide the filling among the zucchini shells, mounding it slightly. Place in an oiled ovenproof baking dish. Broil the filled zucchini until the filling is bubbling and lightly browned, approximately 5 minutes.

To serve, arrange the greens on plates. Spoon the Roasted Corn Vinaigrette over the greens and around the plate and place a filled zucchini on top. The zucchini can be served warm or at room temperature.

Roasted Corn Vinaigrette

1 cup fresh raw corn kernels (about 2 large ears), cobs reserved
2 tablespoons olive oil
   Kosher salt and freshly ground black pepper
¾ cup rich chicken or vegetable stock

¼ cup dry white wine
1½ tablespoons minced shallots
2 tablespoons sherry vinegar
1 teaspoon seeded and minced serrano chile (or to taste)

Preheat the oven to 375 degrees. In a medium bowl, toss the corn kernels with 1 tablespoon of the olive oil. Season lightly with salt and pepper. Spread in a single layer on a baking sheet and roast in the oven until lightly browned around the edges, approximately 12 to 15 minutes. Remove and cool.

Meanwhile, in a small saucepan, combine the stock and the wine. Break up the cobs and add to the liquid. Bring the liquid to a boil, lower the heat to a simmer, and reduce by half. Strain the liquid and discard the cobs. Let the liquid cool.

In a large bowl, whisk the reduced stock, shallots, sherry vinegar, serrano, and remaining 1 tablespoon olive oil to combine. Stir in the roasted corn. Season to taste with salt and pepper.

Recommended wine: A crisp non-oaked Chardonnay is lovely with this, as is a slightly chilled Gamay.

Moroccan-Inspired Cinnamon Couscous with Sweet Spice Vegetables

This rich, satisfying main course helps make the point that vegetables can provide a meal as hearty as any that is based on meat. The spices are reminiscent of those used in Moroccan cooking. The "chutney" is a kind of takeoff on the hot Moroccan condiment called harissa; you can certainly make the recipe without it, but I think even a teaspoonful enlivens the dish.

Serves 6 to 8

¼ cup olive oil
2 cups red onion cut in ½-inch
   wedges
1 cup leeks cut in ¼-inch rounds,
   both white and pale-green parts
1 cup diagonally cut carrots, in
   thick slices
1 cup thickly sliced parsnips
2 cups peeled and cubed sweet
   potatoes
1½ pounds plum tomatoes, peeled,
   seeded, and coarsely chopped
1 tablespoon minced fresh ginger
2 teaspoons ground cinnamon
½ teaspoon ground allspice
¼ teaspoon cayenne pepper (or to
   taste)

2 cups rich vegetable or chicken
   stock
1 cup cooked garbanzo beans, or
   canned beans, drained and
   rinsed
½ cup golden raisins
1 teaspoon honey (or to taste)
   Kosher salt and freshly ground
   black pepper
   Cinnamon Couscous (recipe
   follows)
   Red Pepper Chutney (recipe
   follows)
   Garnish: Toasted slivered
   almonds and mint sprigs

In a large skillet over moderate heat, heat the olive oil and sauté the onions and leeks until they just begin to soften. Add the carrots, parsnips, and sweet potatoes and sauté for 3 minutes. Add the tomatoes, spices, stock, garbanzos, raisins, honey, and salt and pepper to taste. Simmer briefly for 5 minutes to combine the flavors. Do not overcook; the vegetables should remain firm.

To serve, spoon the Cinnamon Couscous into warm bowls. Add the vegetables and top with a teaspoonful of Red Pepper Chutney. Garnish with toasted slivered almonds and mint sprigs.

Cinnamon Couscous

1¼ cups rich vegetable or chicken
   stock
¼ teaspoon saffron threads
2 tablespoons olive oil
2 teaspoons roasted garlic (see
   page 247)
¼ teaspoon ground cumin
¼ teaspoon ground coriander

½ teaspoon ground cinnamon
¼ teaspoon freshly grated nutmeg
   Kosher salt and freshly ground
   black pepper
1 cup quick-cooking couscous
½ cup minced scallions, both white
   and pale-green parts
⅓ cup toasted pine nuts

In a medium saucepan, heat the stock and saffron. Bring to a simmer, remove from the heat, and let stand for 15 minutes. Return the pan to the heat and add the oil, garlic, cumin, coriander, cinnamon, and nutmeg. Bring to a boil. Season to taste with salt and pepper. Place the couscous in a bowl. Pour the hot stock mixture over the couscous, stirring briefly with a fork. Cover and let the couscous stand for 5 minutes to absorb the stock. Add the scallions and pine nuts and fluff gently with a fork.

Red Pepper Chutney

Makes 1 cup

½ cup roasted and finely minced red
    bell pepper (page 246)
2 teaspoons minced garlic
1 teaspoon toasted and crushed
    cumin seed (page 36)
¼ cup finely chopped fresh cilantro
¼ cup finely chopped fresh mint
¼ cup finely chopped Kalamata olives

2 tablespoons drained and finely
    chopped capers (optional)
1 teaspoon seeded and minced
    serrano chile or ¼ teaspoon
    cayenne pepper (or to taste)
  Kosher salt and freshly ground
    black pepper

Combine all the ingredients in a bowl. Store, covered, in the refrigerator for up to 2 weeks.

Recommended wine: There are a lot of strong flavors happening in this dish, but the sweet spices are a great link to Gewürztraminer or Viognier, both of which have spicy, floral qualities.

Serrano and Garlic Jack Cheese Soufflé

This soufflé and a fresh green salad would make a perfect light supper. Garlic Jack cheese, made in the wine country, has bits of fresh garlic and parsley incorporated into it. If you can't find garlic Jack, substitute cheddar or a soft goat cheese with a little age on it. One other note: Serranos can vary in their heat. The only way I know to determine the heat of an individual serrano is to taste a little tiny piece. You may want to adjust the amount of chiles you use accordingly.

Serves 4

3 tablespoons unsalted butter, plus
   more for buttering the soufflé
   dish
3 tablespoons all-purpose flour
3 tablespoons minced shallots
3 tablespoons seeded and minced
   serrano chiles (or to taste)
1 cup half-and-half
4 large eggs, separated

2 cups freshly grated garlic Jack
   cheese
⅓ cup freshly grated Parmesan cheese
4 tablespoons minced fresh cilantro
4 tablespoons finely diced red bell
   pepper
   Kosher salt and freshly ground
      black pepper
   Garnish: Salsa Cruda (page 167)

Preheat the oven to 350 degrees. Butter a 1½-quart soufflé dish. In a medium saucepan, melt the butter. Add the flour, shallots, and serranos. Cook over moderate heat, stirring constantly, to make a roux, approximately 3 minutes—do not brown. Add the half-and-half in a slow stream, whisking constantly. Bring just to the boil. Lower the heat and simmer for 2 minutes to cook the flour and make a thick sauce, whisking continually. Remove from the heat and whisk in the egg yolks, one at a time. Stir in the cheeses, cilantro, and red pepper. Season with salt and pepper.

In a separate bowl, beat the egg whites until stiff but not dry. Stir one quarter of the egg whites into the cheese mixture to lighten it. Carefully but thoroughly, fold in the remaining whites. Gently pour the mixture into the prepared dish. Bake for 25 to 30 minutes or until the soufflé is puffed and golden.

Serve with Salsa Cruda.

 Recommended wine: Chile heat goes well with a fruity, lower-alcohol wine such as Riesling or Gewürztraminer.

 Summer Vegetable Tarts

This sounds like a complicated recipe but it's actually very simple. It is a cake(s) made up of five layers of vegetables topped with a little tabbouleh garnish. I've given you my five favorite vegetable layers, but feel free to make up your own. If you want to go all out with garnish, you could drizzle a little tomato oil and reduced balsamic vinegar around the plate. It's a strikingly beautiful dish. The "tart" molds may be purchased in a cookware store or you can use, as I do, 6½-ounce tuna cans with both ends removed. You could also use an 8-inch springform pan. The presentation's less elegant, but the assembly's a lot easier.

Serves 8

Eggplant layer (recipe follows)	Tomato layer (recipe follows)
1 cup rinsed and chopped Kalamata or Niçoise olives	Zucchini layer (recipe follows)
	Tabbouleh Salad (page 273)
Potato layer (recipe follows)	Garnish: Tomato oil (page 68),
½ cup toasted pine nuts	reduced basalmic vinegar
Olive oil	(page 250), if desired
Spinach layer (recipe follows)	

Using a round, lightly oiled mold 3 inches in diameter and 2 inches high as a guide, cut the center out of a prepared eggplant round.

To assemble each tart: Put an eggplant circle in the bottom of the mold and spread 2 tablespoons of the chopped olives over the eggplant. Add ¼ cup of the potato mixture, pressing to fill. Sprinkle 1 tablespoon pine nuts over the potato layer. Follow with a layer of the spinach mixture and then a layer of the tomato mixture. Place the zucchini rounds in a spiral fashion on top of the tomato layer and press down gently. Place the tarts on an oiled baking sheet and warm them in a preheated 350-degree oven for 10 to 15 minutes.

To serve, place the tarts on warm plates. Gently unmold the tarts and mound a tablespoon of the tabbouleh on top. Decoratively drizzle tomato oil and balsamic vinegar, if desired, around the plate and serve immediately.

Eggplant Layer

1 1½-pound globe eggplant, at least 3 inches wide	½ teaspoon freshly ground black pepper
½ cup grated Parmesan cheese	3 eggs, lightly beaten
	½ cup dry breadcrumbs
1 teaspoon kosher salt	4 tablespoons olive oil

Cut the eggplant into 8 rounds approximately ¾ inch thick. Combine the breadcrumbs, Parmesan, salt, and pepper. Dip the eggplant rounds into the beaten egg, allowing excess egg to drip off. Then dredge them in the breadcrumb mixture, patting to evenly coat. In a medium sauté pan, heat the olive oil over moderately high heat. Add the coated eggplant and sauté, turning once to brown both sides, about 3 minutes.

Remove to paper towels to drain. Cool.

Potato Layer

1 pound baking potatoes, peeled and quartered	1 tablespoon roasted garlic (page 247)
¼ cup half-and-half	Kosher salt and freshly ground black pepper
1 tablespoon unsalted butter	

In a saucepan of lightly salted cold water, place the potato quarters and bring to a boil. Lower the heat and simmer until tender, about 15 to 20 minutes. Drain and transfer to a bowl.

In a separate saucepan, combine the half-and-half, butter, garlic, salt, and pepper. Heat until the butter melts. Add the mixture to the potatoes and mash until relatively smooth, with some small chunks remaining.

Spinach Layer

2   tablespoons unsalted butter
1   pound fresh spinach, washed and stemmed

Kosher salt and freshly ground black pepper

In a large sauté pan, melt the butter. Add the spinach and sauté over moderately high heat until the spinach is wilted but still bright green. Season, then transfer the spinach to a strainer to cool and drain. Squeeze out excess liquid and roughly chop.

Tomato Layer

1   tablespoon olive oil
½   cup minced red onion
1   teaspoon minced fresh oregano
2   teaspoons minced fresh basil

1½ cups seeded and diced tomatoes
1   tablespoon minced fresh chives
1   tablespoon drained capers

In a small sauté pan, heat the olive oil. Add the onion, oregano, and basil and sauté until the onion just begins to soften. Add the tomatoes and sauté briefly. Remove from the heat, cool, then stir in the chives and capers.

Zucchini Layer

3   small zucchini

Slice the zucchini in rounds as thin as possible. In a saucepan of lightly salted boiling water, blanch the zucchini for 5 to 10 seconds. Drain and immediately plunge into ice water to set the color. Drain and pat dry with paper towels.

 Recommended wine: Since there is such a complexity of flavor in this dish, either a crisp white wine—which would go with the eggplant and spinach layers—or a lighter-body red wine like Pinot Noir—which would go with the tomato and zucchini—would be fine. My suggestion is have a glass of both.

TABBOULEH SALAD

There is great debate among cooks from the Middle East about the ratio of bulgur to parsley in a tabbouleh. I've been told that it should be at least 8 parts parsley to 1 part bulgur wheat. In this version I've added a bit more wheat. To serve this salad on its own, try adding a wine country twist: Slow-roast some plum tomatoes on a parchment-lined baking sheet at 275 degrees for 5 hours, until they're very lightly browned. Something magical happens when you cook them for a long time at a low temperature—the flavors become very concentrated and sweet. They are a perfect foil for the lemony–herb tabbouleh.

⅓ cup fine bulgur wheat
⅓ cup rich vegetable stock,
    heated to boiling
2 tablespoons olive oil
2 cups minced fresh parsley
3 tablespoons minced fresh mint

1 tablespoon minced scallion
2 teaspoons minced garlic
2 tablespoons fresh lemon juice
1 teaspoon grated lemon zest
  Salt and freshly ground
    black pepper

In a bowl, combine the bulgur, the boiling stock, and the olive oil and cover. Allow to stand for at least 30 minutes, then uncover and fluff with a fork. Stir in the parsley, mint, scallion, garlic, lemon juice, and lemon zest. Correct the seasoning with salt and pepper.

Vegetarian Red Chile with Pepitas

I like to use a variety of exotic beans in this chile just for the pleasure of the different shapes, colors, and patterns, but it could certainly be prepared with any single kind of bean. The chile stock is delicious, great in any recipe that calls for a richly flavored stock.

Serves 8 to 10

2   cups assorted dried beans, such
      as annelino, painted desert,
      scarlet runner, calico lima, and
      Appaloosa (keep each variety
      separated)
    Red Chile Stock (recipe follows)
2   tablespoons olive oil
1½ cups diced yellow onions
¾   cup diced carrots
2   tablespoons thinly sliced garlic
½   cup diagonally cut celery
1½ teaspoons toasted cumin seed
      (see page 36)
1½ teaspoons toasted coriander seed
½   teaspoon toasted caraway seed
1   teaspoon oregano leaves
1   cup hearty red wine

½   cup diced fennel bulb
½   cup diced red bell pepper
½   cup diced yellow bell pepper
½   cup diced green bell pepper
1½ cups seeded and diced ripe plum
      tomatoes
1   cup diced zucchini
    Kosher salt and freshly ground
      black pepper
    Fresh lime or lemon juice
⅓   cup chopped fresh cilantro
½   cup diced shiitake mushrooms,
      quickly sautéed in a few drops
      of olive oil (optional)
    Garnish: Toasted pepitas
      (pumpkin seeds) and queso
      fresco (Mexican fresh cheese)

Keeping each variety separate, soak the beans at least 5 hours with water to cover by 2 inches or more. If possible, change the water once or twice. Drain the beans. Alternately use the quick soak method on page 276. In individual saucepans, cover the beans with chile stock. Bring to a boil. Reduce the heat and simmer until just cooked. Each variety will take a slightly different amount of time, but it will be approximately 1 hour. Add additional stock as necessary to keep the beans covered.

Meanwhile, in a large stockpot, heat the olive oil. Add the onions, carrots, garlic, and celery and sauté until the vegetables just begin to color. Add the cumin, coriander, and caraway seed, and the oregano leaves. Sauté for 5 minutes. Add the red wine and all of the beans, along with their cooking liquid. Add additional stock as needed to cover. Bring to a boil, reduce the heat, and simmer for 5 to 10 minutes. Add the fennel, peppers, tomatoes, and zucchini. Return to a simmer and cook an additional 5 to 10 minutes, stirring occasionally and adding stock as needed.

The vegetables should still have some texture. Season to taste with salt, pepper, and drops of fresh lime or lemon juice.

To serve, stir in the chopped cilantro and sautéed shiitake mushrooms, if using. Ladle into warm bowls and garnish with toasted pepitas and queso fresco.

Red Chile Stock

Makes 4 quarts

6 ounces ancho chiles
3 tablespoons olive oil
2 cups coarsely chopped onions
2 cups coarsely chopped leeks
2 cups coarsely chopped carrots
2 cups coarsely chopped celery,
     leaves included
1 cup peeled and chopped parsnips
2 cups chopped waxy potatoes
2 cups chopped mushrooms
1 tablespoon fennel seed
1 tablespoon coriander seed
2 teaspoons cumin seed

¾ cup coarsely chopped fresh parsley
3 large bay leaves
3 tablespoons chopped fresh sage
     (or 2 teaspoons dried)
1 teaspoon dried oregano
2 teaspoons dried thyme
6 cups coarsely chopped fresh or
     canned tomatoes, with their
     juice
2 cups dry red wine
4 quarts water
   Salt and freshly ground black
     pepper

Cover the ancho chiles with warm water. Weight down with a plate to submerge. Let stand 1 hour to soften.

In a large stockpot, heat the olive oil. Add the onions, leeks, carrots, celery, parsnips, potatoes, and mushrooms. Sauté until they just begin to color. Drain the anchos and remove the seeds and stems; then add them to the stockpot along with the spice seeds, herbs, tomatoes, red wine, and water. Bring to a boil. Reduce the heat and simmer, partially covered, for 1 hour. Season with salt and pepper. Strain carefully, to remove all the solids. Cool. The stock can be covered and stored in the refrigerator for up to 3 days, or frozen indefinitely.

Note: If more "heat" is desired, leave half the seeds in the ancho chiles. The seeds of chiles contains more of the heat than the flesh.

COOKING DRIED BEANS

There are hundreds of varieties of dried beans, and if you add the rest of the legume family, including lentils and peas, there are well over two thousand varieties that we know of. There has been an amazing resurgence of interest in beans in recent years. We've come to understand not only how good they are for us (being the most inexpensive and healthiest source for protein, since they contain no associated fat) but also how they have a myriad other positive health benefits. With their abundance of dietary fiber they seem to help prevent a number of cancers as well as alleviate blood glucose problems.

Beyond health, however, beans are beautiful and delicious! They are poetic, with names like painted pony, Jacob's cattle, European soldier, yin-yang, scarlet runner, and rattlesnake. They come in every shape, size, and color imaginable. Flavor and texture also vary dramatically. The exotic varieties beyond the usual navy, pinto, lima, and black are also becoming much more available. Three good sources for unusual bean varieties are:

- The Bean Bag, in Oakland, California (800) 845-2326
- Phipps Ranch, in Pescadro, California (415) 879-0787
- Galina Canyon Ranch, in Santa Fe, New Mexico (505) 982-4149

The last two grow a wide variety of beans and all three can send you a catalog on request.

To cook beans:

Most recipes call for soaking dried beans overnight, which is fine if you've thought ahead. An alternative "quick soak" method also works very well. Simply wash the beans well and place them in a pot covered by at least 2 inches of cold water. Put the pot over high heat and bring to a rolling boil. As soon as the beans boil take the pot off the heat and allow to sit for 1 hour. This duplicates the overnight soak. One added advantage of the method is that if you pour off this water, up to 85 percent of the oligosaccharides (the compounds that cause beans to give us gas) go down the drain, making beans much more friendly! The small drawback when you pour off the "quick soak" water is that you pour off some of the color from the beans along with a small bit of the vitamins and minerals (but not enough to worry about).

Whether you soak beans conventionally or via the "quick-soak" method, to finish cooking make sure the beans are covered by at least 2 inches of fresh water, *not* the soaking water. Most cooks advise against adding salt to beans until they are tender. You can, however, add ½ teaspoon salt per cup of dry beans and any herbs or other seasonings you like. *DO NOT* add tomatoes or other acidic ingredients until the beans are almost done, otherwise the beans will be tough. My grandmother used to add a pinch of baking soda for each cup of dry beans, which apparently raises the PH of the water, making it less acid, which in turn makes the beans more soluble and quicker cooking. This does, however, destroy some nutrients so even though my grandmother did it—don't!

Bring the beans to a simmer, cover, and simmer gently until done. Covering helps insure that the beans will cook evenly. Check the liquid from time to time to make sure the beans are covered. That's all there is to it!

One cup of dried beans will yield approximately 2 to 3 cups of cooked beans. Cooked beans freeze wonderfully in their liquid, so be sure to cook up an extra batch for freezing and quick use later on. Also save any bean-cooking liquid. It makes a tasty alternative vegetable stock to substitute for or use with meat stock.

Veggie Burger

Colleen Stewart of the Valley Oaks staff cooks delicious vegetarian dishes. This recipe of hers is one I really love (besides, how could you have a cookbook from California without including at least one squeakie-clean veggie burger kind of recipe!). I like to top the burgers with a Salsa Cruda (page 167) and serve with a little salad of savory greens dressed with a lemony vinaigrette. Add or substitute any vegetables or even nuts if you like. A slice of a special cheese—such as Cindy Callahan's Bell Weather Farms fresh pecorino or a nutty Gruyère—melted over the burger is fantastic.

Makes enough for 6 burgers

4 tablespoons olive oil
1 cup finely chopped onions
1 tablespoon minced garlic
1 cup finely diced carrots
½ teaspoon seeded and minced serrano chile (or to taste)
½ teaspoon ground ginger
1 teaspoon ground cumin
1 cup chopped roasted eggplant, including skin
1 cup chopped firm-cooked red potatoes, unpeeled

1 cup coarsely grated zucchini, squeezed dry in a clean tea towel
3 tablespoons chopped fresh cilantro
2 tablespoons whole-wheat flour
1 egg, lightly beaten
1 cup soft whole-wheat breadcrumbs
Salt and freshly ground black pepper

In a large sauté pan, heat 2 tablespoons of the olive oil and sauté the onions and garlic over medium heat until they just begin to color. Add the carrots, chile, ginger, and cumin and continue to cook until the carrots just begin to soften. Stir in the eggplant, potatoes, zucchini, and cilantro and cook for 2 to 3 minutes, stirring occasionally. Remove from the heat.

When cool enough to handle, gently mix in the flour, egg, and breadcrumbs.

Season to taste with salt and pepper and shape into patties. Sauté the patties in the remaining 2 tablespoons olive oil until golden brown on both sides.

  Recommended wine: A number of wines could work depending on what you serve with the burger. If I were serving a lemony salad, mentioned above, I'd go toward a Fumé/Sauvignon Blanc. With the addition of a full-flavored cheese, try a barrel-aged Chardonnay or even a soft Pinot Noir.

Baked Olives and Vegetable Crudités with Warm Garlic Dipping Sauce

This is really two appetizers in one: the olives and the raw vegetables with the dipping sauce. The latter is reminiscent of the classic Italian dish bagna caôda. It makes a great starter for a big family meal or as an hors d'oeuvre for entertaining. Baking the olives subdues their briny flavors.

Serves 8

BAKED OLIVES:

2   cups mixed oil-cured olives, such as Kalamata and Sicilian green, rinsed and drained

⅔   cup dry white wine

¼   cup extra-virgin olive oil

1   tablespoon slivered garlic

3   tablespoons minced fresh parsley

2   tablespoons minced mixed fresh herbs, such as basil, oregano, thyme, chervil (or 2 teaspoons dried)

¼   teaspoon red chile flakes, crushed
    Freshly ground black pepper

Preheat the oven to 375 degrees. In a baking dish, arrange the olives in a single layer. Add the wine and 2 tablespoons of the oil. Cover tightly with foil. Bake until the olives are fragrant, approximately 45 minutes. Most, but not all, of the liquid should be absorbed; the olives should be tender and somewhat plump.

Meanwhile, using a mortar and pestle, combine the garlic, parsley, mixed herbs, chile flakes, and the remaining olive oil. Mash to form a paste. (This may also be done in a food processor, although the texture will not be the same.) When the olives are out of the oven and still hot, combine with the garlic paste, tossing thoroughly to mix. Add black pepper to taste. Let the olives marinate for several hours or overnight before serving. The olives may be stored, refrigerated, for several weeks. Bring the olives to room temperature before serving.

CRUDITÉS:

6   cups mixed crisp peeled vegetables, such as carrots, celery, scallions,
     parsnips, jicama, and red bell pepper, cut into thick strips

WARM GARLIC DIPPING SAUCE:

4   tablespoons unsalted butter
10 garlic cloves, finely slivered
10 anchovy fillets, well rinsed and
     chopped

1   cup olive oil
2   tablespoons sherry vinegar
3   tablespoons chopped fresh
     parsley

In a saucepan, melt the butter. Add the garlic and sauté until soft but not brown. Stir in the anchovies, olive oil, vinegar, and parsley and heat through. Keep warm.

Serve the olives and crudités arranged on a platter or on individual plates around a ramekin filled with the warm dipping sauce. Serve immediately with lots of crusty French bread.

 Recommended wine: These recipes are very reminiscent of food you might find in a simple restaurant in Italy. The wine choice, then, would be something similar to the country wines of Italy—I'd go for a lighter-style Pinot Noir, Merlot, or Zinfandel.

PEELING GARLIC

Most cooks have heard about smashing a clove of garlic with the side of a chef's knife to loosen the surrounding papery husk. The problem, however, is that unless you hit it just right, some of the husk gets driven into the meat of the clove. Then you get garlic-smelling fingers as well as cutting board. Also the smashing and breaking of the clove means that the fresh garlic flavor and aroma will start to oxidize and change.

I've found two easy alternative ways to peel garlic and keep the clove whole:

1. Soak the whole head overnight in cold water. In the morning you can easily remove the husk.

2. Dry-roast whole cloves in a sauté pan over moderate heat for 3 or 4 minutes, which also adds an interesting "charred" flavor to the garlic. Again, the husk will slip off very easily.

Once peeled, store garlic cloves in a sealed container in your refrigerator for up to 10 days. I prefer storing them in olive oil.

Roasted Eggplant Caponata

This is a dish that is better made ahead to allow the flavors to marry. It's perfect for a picnic or as part of a summer buffet and can be the basis for a tasty eggplant and pasta salad. As with many wine country dishes (even those appropriated from other cultures!), there is a mix of sweet and savory flavors happening here. The caponata is a good accompaniment for grilled meats, poultry, and seafood; it's also terrific spread on grilled bread.

Serves 6 to 8

2 pounds eggplant, any variety, sliced lengthwise into ¼-inch slices	2 tablespoons drained capers
	3 tablespoons toasted pine nuts
	2 tablespoons golden raisins or currants
3 tablespoons olive oil	
¾ cup chopped yellow onions	16 chopped Kalamata olives
5 garlic cloves, roasted (page 247)	2 tablespoons light-brown sugar
1 cup diced celery	⅓ cup red wine vinegar
1½ cups seeded and chopped tomatoes, fresh or canned	Kosher salt and red chile flakes

Preheat the oven to 400 degrees. Lay the eggplant slices on a baking sheet in a single layer. Roast for 20 to 25 minutes or until tender and lightly browned. Remove. Dice and reserve.

In a large sauté pan over medium heat, heat the oil and sauté the onions, garlic, and celery until the onions are translucent, stirring occasionally. Add the tomatoes and cook for 2 to 3 minutes. Add the eggplant, capers, pine nuts, raisins, olives, brown sugar, and vinegar. Over moderate heat, cook for 6 to 8 minutes, stirring frequently. Season with salt and chile flakes. Refrigerate, covered, for 4 hours or overnight. Bring to room temperature before serving. May be kept, refrigerated, for up to 5 days.

Recommended wine: A crisp, well-chilled Fumé/Sauvignon Blanc or chilled Gamay or Grenache Rosé will contrast the sweet-tart flavors in this summery dish.

THE WORLD OF EGGPLANT

If you need another reason to be glad you live in the twentieth century, consider what people used to think about eggplant. "Doubtless these apples have a mischievous quality," wrote Englishman John Gerard in his 1597 *Herball*. "Eat at your own risk," he warned.

And he wasn't alone. The French suspected the curvaceous eggplant of causing epilepsy and fevers and disdained it until the nineteenth century. And although the ever-curious Thomas Jefferson grew eggplant at Monticello, Americans didn't really embrace it until the modern wave of immigrants—southern Italians, Chinese, Middle Easterners, and Indians—showed us irresistible ways to prepare it.

Thank goodness for progress. Today's cookbooks overflow with ideas for this versatile vegetable, and farmers offer every size, shape, and color imaginable. From the small egg-shaped white varieties that gave the eggplant its name to the shiny purple globe eggplants best known to American shoppers, all are eminently worth eating.

In farmers' markets and Asian markets, look for the cherry-size eggplants that Southeast Asians prize for pickling. Italian, Chinese, and Japanese cooks prefer the long, slender varieties that are now commonplace in many markets; ranging from lavender to deep purple, they usually have a more tender skin, milder flavor, and firmer flesh than their large counterparts do. Halve and grill them, brushed with oil. Cut them in chunks and braise them with tomatoes, bell peppers, and zucchini to make a French ratatouille. Or steam them, shred them, and season with soy sauce and a little sesame oil.

The familiar plump globe eggplants are perfect for making large round slices for eggplant parmigiana, or for stuffing and rolling. Be wary of overripe ones; they can be seedy and bitter. Unsure? Try the touch test: If the flesh stays indented after you press it gently, the eggplant is overripe.

For adventuresome cooks, eggplant is the chameleon of the kitchen: It adopts the flavor and style of whatever you put with it. Give it a Mediterranean influence with capers, olives, and tomatoes; or veer toward Turkey with garlic, mint, and yogurt; or dress it Indian-style with fresh coriander, spicy chiles, and tomato. As vegetarians around the world know, eggplant is a satisfying and low-calorie meat substitute.

Radicchio Baked with Cream and Dry Jack Cheese

In this recipe, the bitterness of radicchio contrasts with the sweet cream and slightly salty cheese. This is rich food, but perfect as a side dish for simple roasted poultry or meats or as an intriguing first course when there isn't much other cream/butter/cheese on the menu.

Serves 4

4   medium heads radicchio
3   tablespoons unsalted butter, plus additional for the baking dish
    Kosher salt and freshly ground black pepper

¾   cup heavy cream
4   tablespoons freshly grated dry Jack or Parmesan cheese
4   tablespoons paper-thin shavings of dry Jack or Parmesan cheese

Preheat the oven to 425 degrees. Cut the radicchio heads in half lengthwise through the core. In a saucepan of lightly salted boiling water, in batches if necessary, blanch the radicchio halves for 1 minute. Drain and gently squeeze to remove any excess water. Place the radicchio on several layers of paper towels to drain further.

In a large sauté pan, melt the butter over low heat. Add the radicchio in one layer. Season with salt and pepper. Sauté for 4 to 5 minutes, turning frequently and gently.

Lightly butter a baking dish large enough to hold the radicchio in one layer. Arrange the radicchio halves cut side down. Pour the cream over. Sprinkle with the grated cheese and top with the shavings.

Bake for 20 minutes or until the cream thickens and begins to bubble.

  Recommended wine: I like the buttery, creamy texture of Chardonnay as a contrast to the slight bitterness of radicchio. The rich, nutty flavors of the cheese act as a bridge between the wine and the food.

RADICCHIO

A few years ago, this member of the chicory family was all the rage in upscale restaurants. Most radicchio was imported from Italy, where varieties were named after towns or regions where it was grown—e.g., radicchio di Verona or radicchio di Treviso. Many varieties of radicchio are now grown in California and, although we always tend to think of it as a red, compact-headed plant, there are also green and golden varieties that look much like romaine lettuce. Radicchio has a distinctive flavor that is mellowed when it is cooked as in this recipe. My other favorite preparation for radicchio is to halve it, lightly oil it, season with salt and pepper, and grill it. Served warm with a few drops of a good balsamic vinegar and a shaving or two of Parmesan or dry Jack cheese, it makes a perfect course on its own.

Corn Pudding

This is a terrific side dish that could be baked right along with a roast chicken. I've also served this as a main dish, accompanied by the Smoked Tomato Sauce on page 256.

Serves 6 to 8 as a side dish

2 tablespoons unsalted butter, plus additional to coat the baking dish	½ teaspoon dry mustard
	¼ teaspoon freshly grated nutmeg
1 cup minced yellow onions	1¼ cups half-and-half
⅓ cup minced green bell pepper	3 eggs, separated
⅓ cup minced yellow bell pepper	2½ cups fresh raw corn kernels (about 4 large ears)
1 tablespoon cornstarch, dissolved in 2 tablespoons dry white wine	Kosher salt and freshly ground black pepper

Preheat the oven to 350 degrees. In a medium sauté pan, melt the butter and sauté the onions and peppers until soft but not brown. Remove to a large bowl to cool. When cool, add the cornstarch mixture, mustard, and nutmeg and stir to combine. In a separate bowl, beat the half-and-half and egg yolks. Stir into the onion mixture. Add the corn. Season with salt and pepper.

In a separate bowl, beat the 3 egg whites until they hold stiff peaks. Fold carefully into the corn mixture. Pour into a buttered 1½-quart baking dish. Bake for 30 to 40 minutes or until lightly browned and puffed. Serve immediately.

Note: The pudding may also be baked in individual ramekins; reduce the cooking time accordingly.

 Recommended wine: Chardonnay that has been barrel-aged and sweet, summer corn are one of the great wine-food combinations.

Chile Corn Cakes

These slightly spicy corn cakes, or fritters, are an excellent accompaniment to poultry and meat dishes.

Serves 4

4   tablespoons olive oil
½   cup chopped red bell pepper
¼   cup chopped yellow bell pepper
2   cups fresh raw corn kernels
        (about 4 large ears)
⅔   cup chopped yellow onions
1   tablespoon pure California or
        New Mexico chile powder
1   teaspoon ground cumin
¼   cup rich chicken stock
¾   cup all-purpose flour
1   teaspoon baking powder

½   cup yellow cornmeal
1   egg, lightly beaten
½   cup milk
1   tablespoon melted unsalted butter
2   tablespoons chopped fresh
        cilantro
    Kosher salt and freshly ground
        black pepper
    Vegetable oil for sautéing
    Garnish: Sour cream mixed with
        chopped jalapeños and cilantro

In a large saucepan over medium-high heat, heat 2 tablespoons of the olive oil and sauté the peppers, corn, and onions for 2 to 3 minutes or until the onions begin to soften. Add the chile powder and cumin and cook for 2 minutes, stirring constantly. Add the chicken stock and stir, scraping up any browned bits from the bottom of the pan. Continue cooking until most of the liquid has evaporated. Remove from the heat and set aside.

Into a small bowl, sift together the flour and baking powder. Add the cornmeal, egg, milk, and butter. Stir until very smooth. Add the corn mixture and cilantro. Season to taste with salt and pepper.

In a large sauté pan over medium high heat, heat some vegetable oil. In large dollops add the corn batter and sauté until golden brown, 3 to 4 minutes on each side. Remove to paper towels to drain. Cook in batches, adding additional oil as necessary. Serve warm with the sour cream garnish if desired.

 Recommended wine: The sweet corn and spicy chile powder suggest a fruity Gewürztraminer or Chenin Blanc with a bit of residual sugar.

SAGE CREAM SAUCE

This sauce would make an elegant accompaniment for the Chile Corn Cakes, whether you are serving them alone, alongside meat, poultry, or fish, or alongside other vegetables for a vegetarian main course.

1 tablespoon unsalted butter	⅓ cup chopped fresh sage
3 tablespoons chopped shallots	½ cup heavy cream
½ cup sliced mushrooms	Salt and freshly ground white
1 cup chicken stock or rich mushroom stock (page 57)	pepper
	Fresh lemon juice
1 cup dry white wine	

In a medium saucepan, heat the butter and sauté the shallots and mushrooms until they just begin to color. Add the stock, wine, and all but 2 tablespoons of the sage. Bring to a boil and reduce by half. Lower the heat to a simmer, add the cream, and simmer until reduced to a light sauce consistency. Season to taste with salt, pepper, and drops of lemon juice. Strain. Stir in the reserved chopped sage. Keep warm.

Deep-Dish Potato and Olive Cake

This crisp potato cake is excellent with roasted meats or topped with a fresh salsa or herbed mayonnaise and served as a first course. The secret to achieving crispness is using a glass pie plate.

Serves 4 to 6

2 pounds scrubbed baking potatoes, such as russets	2 tablespoons minced mixed fresh herbs, such as parsley, chives, tarragon, mint, and chervil
4 tablespoons extra-virgin olive oil	
1 cup minced red onions	4 tablespoons minced Niçoise or Kalamata olives
Kosher salt and freshly ground black pepper	

Preheat the oven to 375 degrees. Slice the potatoes very thinly lengthwise. Do not peel. Rinse in cold running water until the water runs clear, about 3 minutes. Pat dry with paper towels.

In a sauté pan, heat 2 tablespoons of the olive oil and sauté the onions until soft but not brown. Remove from the heat and set aside.

Lightly oil a 9-inch deep-dish glass pie plate. Using one third of the potatoes, arrange an overlapping layer of potatoes on the bottom of the plate and lightly season with salt and pepper. Layer with half of the onion mixture, half of the herbs, and half of the olives. Top with an overlapping layer of the second one third of the potatoes. Repeat the process, first seasoning the potatoes, then layering with the remaining onions, herbs, and olives. Finish with the remaining potatoes. Drizzle with the remaining 2 tablespoons olive oil and season again with salt and pepper. Firmly press on the potatoes to form a compact cake.

Bake the "cake" in the oven for 40 minutes, pressing occasionally with a spatula to make it compact. Raise the oven temperature to 450 degrees and bake for another 15 to 18 minutes or until the potatoes are tender and the top is golden brown and crisp.

To serve, slice into wedges and serve warm or at room temperature.

 Recommended wine: A crisp dry white wine such as Fumé/Sauvignon Blanc would seem to be the choice here, but I also love this dish with a rich, mellow Merlot, which often has olive-herbal flavors. Merlot would be an especially good choice if you served this cake with roasted red meat.

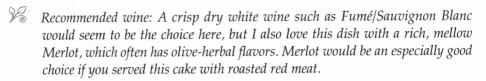

HOW TO STORE POTATOES

Ideally, potatoes should be stored in a dry root cellar at about 50 degrees. Since almost no one has root cellars any more, we need to find another cool, dry place in our kitchen. Do not store potatoes in the refrigerator. Anything below 45 degrees causes the starch to turn to sugar, giving the potato an undesirable sweet flavor. Also, don't store onions and potatoes together. Onions give off gases that cause potatoes to decay faster.

Fried Green Tomatoes with Caper-Herb Aïoli

In spite of the recent "discovery" of fried green tomatoes, brought on by the movie of the same name, this dish has long been a great way to utilize underripe tomatoes with delicious results. These are a good accompaniment to poultry and seafood dishes. Aïoli (a kind of garlic mayonnaise not traditionally accompanied by fried green tomatoes!) is made in a mortar and pestle, with the eggs and garlic being mashed together and the oil slowly added. The texture is indescribable and worth trying when you have the time. For convenience, I'm using the food processor. Any unused aïoli may be kept covered and refrigerated for up to 5 days. It's good on everything, except ice cream!

Serves 4 to 6 as a sidedish

1 cup all-purpose flour
2 large eggs, lightly beaten with 1 tablespoon water
1 cup Panko or other dry breadcrumbs
⅔ cup freshly grated Asiago or Parmesan cheese
2 teaspoons minced fresh chives
2 teaspoons minced fresh basil
½ teaspoon red chile flakes, crushed

1½ pounds large, firm, green tomatoes, cored and sliced ⅓ inch thick
⅓ cup olive oil
Kosher salt and freshly ground black pepper
Caper-Herb Aïoli (recipe follows)

Have the flour and the beaten eggs in separate bowls. In a third bowl, combine the breadcrumbs, cheese, chives, basil, and red chile flakes.

Dredge the tomato slices in the flour. Dip into the eggs. Toss gently in and pat with the breadcrumb mixture.

In a heavy-bottomed sauté pan, heat the olive oil. Sauté the tomato slices, in batches as necessary, turning once until golden brown. Remove to paper towels to drain. Serve warm, seasoned with salt, pepper, and a dollop of Caper-Herb Aïoli.

Caper-Herb Aïoli

Makes about 1 cup

2 tablespoons roasted garlic
      (page 247)
1 teaspoon chopped garlic
2 egg yolks
2 teaspoons fresh lemon
      juice
¾ cup extra-virgin olive oil

3 tablespoons mixed, finely chopped
      fresh herbs, such as chives, basil,
      parsley, and tarragon
1 tablespoon rinsed and chopped
      capers
   Kosher salt and freshly ground
      black pepper

In a food processor, combine the two kinds of garlic, the egg yolks, and the lemon juice. Process for 30 seconds. With the motor running, slowly add the oil to form a thick emulsion. Add the herbs and capers and pulse to combine. Season to taste with salt and pepper. Cover and refrigerate at least 1 hour before using to allow flavors to blend.

Recommended wine: The creamy aïoli and tart green tomatoes are ideal flavor foils for a crisp Fumé/Sauvignon Blanc.

The Best "Stewed" Tomatoes

When good tomatoes are abundant, this simple dish is hard to beat. It's a great addition to a picnic buffet. Chop it coarsely to make a wonderful sauce for pasta or as a topping on grilled meats and fishes. For those uses, don't peel the tomatoes. For a completely vegetarian dish, substitute chopped capers or olives for the anchovies.

Serves 4 to 6

¾ cup chopped fresh parsley
¾ cup chopped fresh basil
2 teaspoons minced fresh
      rosemary
2 tablespoons minced garlic
½ cup Panko or other dry
      breadcrumbs

¾ cup freshly grated Parmesan or
      dry Jack cheese
2 tablespoons rinsed and dried
      chopped anchovies
   Extra-virgin olive oil
¼ cup dry white wine, heated with
      2 tablespoons unsalted butter

| 3 | pounds ripe tomatoes, peeled and cored (see note) | Kosher salt and freshly ground black pepper |

Preheat the oven to 425 degrees. In a bowl, combine the herbs, garlic, bread-crumbs, cheese, and anchovies. Toss with a little olive oil until lightly coated but not soggy. Lightly butter a baking dish just large enough to hold the tomatoes in a crowded single layer and arrange the tomatoes in the dish. Drizzle the warm wine-butter mixture over them. Season with salt and pepper and top with the herb mixture. Bake for 15 minutes. Lower the heat to 350 degrees and bake for 15 to 20 minutes longer or until the topping is browned and the tomatoes are very soft. Remove from the oven.

Serve warm or at room temperature.

 Recommended wine: Tomatoes and red wines that are fruity and fresh without too much tannin are terrific together. I'd go for a Gamay or young red Zinfandel.

Note: To peel tomatoes, plunge them into boiling water and submerge for 15 to 20 seconds. Remove and plunge immediately into ice water. The skin should loosen and easily peel off. If not, repeat the process.

Green Chile and Cheese Rice

This rice makes a delicious accompaniment to almost anything. I love the idea of burying little "presents" in the rice to discover as you serve. For a simple meatless meal, serve the rice with some grilled or roasted tomatoes and a salad of savory greens.

Serves 4

½	pound Jack cheese, cut into ½-inch cubes	½	cup minced onion
	Fresh cilantro leaves	1	tablespoon minced garlic
2	large roasted and seeded poblano chiles (page 246), cut in ½-inch strips, lengthwise	1	cup basmati or other long-grain rice
1	tablespoon unsalted butter or vegetable oil	1	teaspoon dried oregano
		½	teaspoon fennel seed
		1¾	cups rich chicken or chile or corn stock (pages 275, 56)

Make the little "presents" by wrapping each cube of cheese with a cilantro leaf in a strip of roasted poblano. Set aside.

In a medium saucepan over moderate heat, melt the butter and sauté the onion and garlic until soft but not brown. Add the rice, oregano, and fennel seed. Continue to sauté for 2 minutes more, stirring occasionally.

Add the stock and bring to a boil. Lower the heat to a simmer, cover, and cook for 10 minutes; the stock will be mostly absorbed but still visible. Gently poke the chile-wrapped cheese into the rice in various spots. Replace the cover and continue to cook for 5 minutes or until all the stock is absorbed. Remove from the heat and let stand, uncovered, for 3 to 5 minutes before serving.

 Recommended wine: If the rice is being served alone, I would choose a simple, crisp non-oaked Chardonnay. If the rice is being offered as part of a larger meal with a lot of additional chile heat, then I'd recommend a fresh, off-dry wine, such as Riesling or Gewürztraminer.

 # Roasted Garlic–Tarragon Custards

These savory custards can be featured either as a first course on a bed of baby greens or as a side dish with grilled meats and poultry.
Serves 6

3 tablespoons tarragon leaves	¾ cup half-and-half or whole milk
3 large eggs	
4 tablespoons roasted garlic (page 247)	¾ cup rich vegetable or chicken stock
1 teaspoon kosher salt	Garnish: 12 tarragon leaves
½ teaspoon freshly ground black pepper	

Preheat the oven to 350 degrees. In a small saucepan in lightly salted boiling water, blanch the 3 tablespoons tarragon for 5 seconds. Drain and immediately plunge into ice water to set the color. Drain again, pat dry, and set aside.

In a blender or food processor, combine the tarragon, eggs, garlic, and salt and pepper. Pulse until smooth. Blend in the half-and-half and stock.

Lightly butter or oil 6 4-ounce ovenproof ramekins. Evenly divide the egg mixture among them. Place 2 tarragon leaves on top of each. Place the ramekins in a baking pan just large enough to hold them. Pour in boiling water three quarters of the way up the sides of the ramekins.

Bake for 30 to 35 minutes or until the center of the custards is just set and lightly browned. Remove the ramekins from the pan and let them stand for 5 minutes.

Run a sharp knife around the sides of the ramekins to release and unmold. Invert the custards so the browned top is up. Serve warm.

Note: The custards can also be made in 12 2-ounce ramekins, a better size if they are to accompany meat or poultry. Reduce the cooking time to 15 to 20 minutes.

 Recommended wine: Tarragon goes well with very crisp white wines that have a bit of a "green" note to them. Either a Chardonnay or Sauvignon Blanc made in this style would work.

Rosemary-Parmesan Polenta Cakes

This is a tasty dish to go with grilled or roasted meats such as lamb or chicken. You can make the polenta a day or two ahead of time. Store it covered in the refrigerator and allow it to return to room temperature before heating it with the Parmesan.

Serves 6 to 8 as a side dish

3½ cups rich vegetable or corn stock (page 56)
½ cup dry white wine
1 cup dry polenta
1½ teaspoons minced fresh rosemary
1 teaspoon minced fresh sage
1 teaspoon minced fresh thyme
2 tablespoons chopped scallions, white part only

3 tablespoons minced red bell pepper
2 tablespoons unsalted butter
Kosher salt and freshly ground black pepper
½ cup freshly grated Parmesan cheese

In a large saucepan, combine the stock and wine. Bring to a boil. Slowly pour in the polenta, stirring constantly. Reduce the heat to a simmer and continue cooking for 15 minutes, stirring frequently. Add the herbs, scallions, red pepper, and butter. Cook for 10 minutes longer, stirring frequently. Correct the seasoning with salt and pepper.

Lightly oil an 8- by 8-inch baking dish. Pour in the polenta, spreading it evenly. Refrigerate for at least 3 hours. Slice into diamonds or desired shapes. Bring to room temperature before serving.

To serve, top with the cheese. Broil until the cheese is melted and the polenta is warmed through. Serve immediately.

Recommended wine: The rosemary in this dish is a great link to the herbal flavors in hearty red wines like Zinfandel or Cabernet.

 # Fried Stuffed Squash Blossoms

Many people have never experimented with stuffing the beautiful blossoms of baby squash. If this technique seems a little daunting, try the recipe with the vegetable itself: Scoop out the insides of baby summer squash or zucchini, stuff with the filling, and bake for 6 to 8 minutes in a preheated 375-degree oven. They are delicious plain, but if you wanted to put a little sauce on top, choose something simple and light, such as a fresh tomato sauce. And now for the blossoms . . .

Makes 16 stuffed squash blossoms, serving 8

FILLING:

¼ cup white wine
3 tablespoons golden raisins
1 cup whole-milk ricotta cheese
3 tablespoons chopped oil-packed sun-dried tomatoes
3 tablespoons chopped fresh basil
¼ cup chopped shiitake mushrooms, lightly sautéed in olive oil and cooled
2 tablespoons grated Parmesan cheese

¾ teaspoon minced lemon zest
2 tablespoons toasted pine nuts
1 teaspoon minced garlic
2 teaspoons chopped fresh parsley

16 squash blossoms, with baby squash attached
Vegetable oil for frying
Beer Batter (recipe follows)

In a small saucepan, heat the wine. Remove from the heat and add the raisins. Let stand 30 minutes to plump. Drain, discarding the wine. Chop the raisins.

In a medium bowl, combine all the filling ingredients, including the plumped raisins. Gently open the squash blossoms. Place a heaping tablespoon of filling inside. Gently twist the end of each blossom together to completely enclose the filling.

In a large saucepan, pour the vegetable oil to a depth of 2 inches. Heat to 360 degrees. Dip each stuffed blossom into the Beer Batter, allowing excess batter to drip off. Place in the hot oil and fry 3 to 4 minutes or until golden brown. Remove to paper towels to drain thoroughly. Keep warm while frying the remaining blossoms.

Beer Batter

1 cup beer
1 cup all-purpose flour
1 teaspoon kosher salt

1½ teaspoons sweet paprika
     Pinch of cayenne pepper

In a medium bowl, whisk together all ingredients.

 Recommended wine: An herbal-tinged Fumé/Sauvignon Blanc plays nicely off the savory stuffing.

Male versus Female Squash Blossoms

Either blossoms will, of course, work, but if you are picking blossoms off the plant, you'll note that some have long, narrow stems (male) while others have swollen stems or even a little zucchini in place of the stem (female). If I have a choice, I use the male blossoms, leaving the female to continue to produce.

DESSERTS

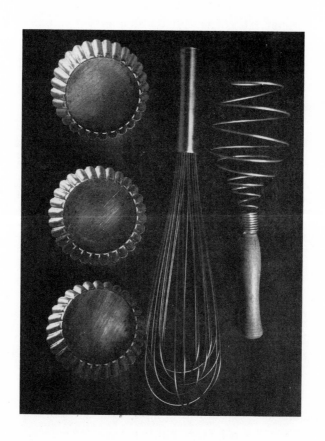

Apple-Jack Tart with Ginger Custard Sauce   *297*

Baked Apples with Sherry Custard Sauce and Amaretti Snow   *301*

Banana-Mango Fritters   *302*   Blueberries and Cream   *304*

Compote of Fresh and Dried Fruits   *305*

Coffee-Poached Pears with Cinnamon Twists   *307*

Bread Pudding with Apples, Prunes, and Walnuts   *309*

California Almond Cake with Balsamic Strawberries and Orange Mascarpone   *310*

California Four-Nut Torte   *311*

Caramel, Chocolate, and Macadamia Nut Tart   *312*

Fresh Cherry Flan   *314*   Cherry and Almond Cobbler   *315*

Chocolate Soufflé   *316*   Espresso Brownie Tart   *317*

Flourless Walnut Cake   *318*   Grapefruit-Banana Brûlée Tart   *318*

Honey Rice Pudding   *320*   Jack Daniel's Sun-Dried Cherry Tart   *321*

Lemon-Glazed Persimmon Bars   *322*

Lemon Polenta Cake with Warm Spiced Apricot Sauce and Fresh Mascarpone   *324*

Lemon Tartlets with Fresh Berries and Fresh Plum Sauce   *325*

Mango Crème Brûlée   *327*

Nectarine Upside-Down Cake in a Skillet   *328*

Old-Fashioned Fresh Fruit Crisp   *329*   Peaches and Dumplings   *330*

Fresh Peach and Almond Tart   *331*   Ricotta, Honey, and Fig Tart   *332*

"Soup of Fruits" with Chardonnay Sabayon and Coconut Shortbreads   *334*

Walnut Orange Tart   *335*

Frozen Desserts

Wine and Fresh Fruit Ice   *336*   Roasted Banana Ice   *337*

Meyer Lemon Sorbet   *338*   Watermelon Granità   *338*

Peach-Mint Granità   *339*

Fresh Blackberry Ice Cream and Walnut Shortbreads   *339*

Fresh Corn Ice Cream with Almond Lace Cookie Fans   *341*

Fresh Peach Ice Cream with Blueberry and Thyme Sauce   *342*

Lemon Verbena Ice Cream   *343*

Vanilla Bean Ice Cream with Burnt Almond Caramel Sauce   *344*

Frozen Orange Soufflés   *345*   Ginger, Fig, and Cranberry Semifreddo   *346*

Wine and Desserts

Because desserts typically contain a lot of sugar, matching wine to a sweet dessert can be a real challenge. Champagne or a California sparkling wine (true Champagne only comes from the Champagne region of France) is often considered the proper dessert accompaniment, but I find most rich desserts overwhelm the lovely delicacy of a good sparkler. Sweet wines such as Late Harvest Rieslings, ports, Late Harvest Zinfandels, and Sauternes can work with desserts, but these wines are so wonderful by themselves that they *are* dessert! When I'm lucky enough to get one of these great sweet wines I typically either enjoy it on its own or contrast it with a savory cheese. Here some of the traditional matches are wonderful: port with English Stilton, Late Harvest Rieslings or Sauterne with creamy blues such as Roquefort or American blues such as Maytag or Dietrich's. But other than these traditional matches, dessert is often better enjoyed on its own.

 ## Apple-Jack Tart with Ginger Custard Sauce

Nothing beats a good apple tart. The cheese in the topping is a takeoff on that great Midwestern tradition of serving warm apple pie with a slice of cheddar cheese. If you don't have time to make the crust, the dessert works equally well without the crust as a crisp, baked in an 8-inch square baking dish. Make the Ginger Custard Sauce ahead; it's lovely to serve it cold with the warm tart. If you're looking for applejack spirits here, there aren't any. I'm referring to the combination of apples and California dry Jack cheese—a Monterey Jack that has been aged for two or more years. In my opinion dry Jack is America's answer to great Italian Parmesan.

Makes 1 9-inch tart

CRUST:

6 tablespoons (¾ stick) chilled
   unsalted butter
1 cup all-purpose flour
1 tablespoon sugar

Big pinch of salt
½ teaspoon grated lemon zest
1 egg yolk, beaten

Cut the butter into ¼-inch bits; in a bowl, cut in the flour, sugar, salt, and zest with the butter until it resembles coarse cornmeal. Add the beaten egg yolk and mix quickly until just combined: This can all be done quickly in a food processor by pulsing all the ingredients together 6 to 8 times. Add drops of water if needed. Gather the dough and gently press together into a flattened cake. Wrap in plastic wrap and chill until firm, 2 hours or overnight. Lightly butter and flour a 9-inch tart pan. On a lightly floured work surface, roll out the dough into a circle at least 10 inches in diameter. Roll the dough up onto the rolling pin and transfer to the tart pan, evenly pressing the dough into the sides. Trim the excess dough and prick the crust well.

APPLE FILLING:

4 cups peeled and sliced tart green apples, such as Newtown Pippin or Granny Smith
1 tablespoon fresh lemon juice
¼ teaspoon freshly ground white pepper

1 tablespoon sugar
1 tablespoon all-purpose flour
1 teaspoon ground cinnamon
¼ teaspoon freshly grated nutmeg
2 tablespoons light-brown sugar
¼ cup golden raisins (optional)

TOPPING:

¼ cup sugar
¼ cup all-purpose flour
6 tablespoons (¾ stick) chilled unsalted butter, cut into small bits
⅔ cup coarsely grated dry Jack, aged Asiago, or Parmesan cheese

2 tablespoons finely chopped toasted almonds (optional)
Ginger Custard Sauce (recipe follows)

Preheat the oven to 350 degrees. In a mixing bowl, toss all the apple filling ingredients to combine. Evenly fill the prepared tart shell with the mixture.

To make the topping, combine the sugar, flour, and butter in a food processor. Pulse until the mixture resembles very coarse cornmeal. Add the cheese and almonds and continue to pulse to combine.

Scatter the topping evenly over the apples. Bake for 45 minutes or until the top is golden and the apples are tender.

Serve the tart warm, spooning the Ginger Custard Sauce over and around the individual slices.

Ginger Custard Sauce

Makes approximately 3 cups

¼ cup roughly chopped fresh ginger	2 cups half-and-half
½ cup sugar	1 teaspoon pure vanilla extract
¼ cup water	6 egg yolks

In a small saucepan, place the ginger, ¼ cup of the sugar, and the water. Simmer over very low heat for approximately 10 minutes; the syrup should be thick but not brown. Remove from the heat and let stand for 30 minutes. Return to the heat, add the half-and-half and vanilla, and bring just to the simmer over medium heat.

Meanwhile, in a separate bowl, beat the egg yolks with the remaining ¼ cup sugar until light and lemon colored. Slowly pour in the hot cream, whisking to combine. Return the mixture to the saucepan and heat over medium-low heat, stirring constantly, until the sauce begins to thicken and coats the back of a wooden spoon (it will register about 180 degrees). Immediately strain and chill, covered. To prevent a skin from forming, one trick is to cover with plastic wrap right down on the surface of the custard.

APPLES

Ever since Eve took her fateful bite of apple, the glorious fruit has been immortalized, and has been utilized as a symbol of temptation and seduction. The apple tree is native to Europe and western Asia and started rapidly gaining popularity in North America in the seventeenth century. Dwarf apple trees are the best choice for the home gardener since they can be more easily maintained than standard apple trees and will bear fruit within two to three years, as opposed to five or six.

At the Valley Oaks garden, we organically grow over 85 different apple varieties to explore their different color, shape, texture, and taste. There are over 7,000 varieties known but only about 100 are grown commercially.

Apples have the ability to act as a ripening agent for many other plants by emitting ethylene gas. To speed the ripening of tomatoes, place them in a paper bag with an apple or two and they'll ripen quickly. This can also have a downside. Storing a number of apples in the refrigerator can cause lettuce to brown, carrots to become bitter, and cucumbers to turn yellow.

Of those varieties commercially available, here are my favorites:

Golden Delicious: Originated in West Virginia in the early 1900s. Green-yellow to bright yellow skin, firm flesh, juicy, crisp, and sweet. Mid-season ripener. A good keeper and an excellent all-around apple for eating out of hand or cooking.

Gravenstein: Originated in the early 1800s in Germany and Sweden. Favored now in northern California. Greenish yellow to orange-yellow with light red stripes. Aromatic, crisp, juicy flesh. An early ripener. They are good out of hand when just picked but don't hold up to storage. Gravensteins make wonderful applesauce and cider and they're a favorite in the wine country.

Northern Spy: Originated in New York supposedly from an errant seed sprouted near Canandaigua around 1800. Skin is red and yellow. Firm, tender, crisp, and juicy. It stores well and is one of the best apples for pie.

Empire: Developed in the 1960s in New York. A Red Delicious–McIntosh cross with lovely aromatic qualities. Dark red/yellow skin. An excellent eating apple for kids. Crisp, juicy flesh. Also known as the Royal Empire, it stores well and makes a great cider.

Granny Smith: Originated in Australia, supposedly sprouting from a pile of apples tossed out by a southeastern Australian named Mrs. Smith in 1868. Grass-green skinned. Crisp and tart. Requires a long season to ripen. A good keeper with tart, simple flavor. Not nearly as interesting as Newtown Pippin.

Newtown Pippin: Originated in Long Island in the early 1700s. It is the oldest commercially grown variety in America. The first American apple to gain popularity in Europe. Green or yellow skin with pinkish blush at the base. Juicy with fine-grained flesh. Late season ripener and a good keeper, it is a great cooking apple.

McIntosh: A Canadian variety from the 1800s. Green-red skin. Tender and aromatic. Excellent for eating, sauce, and especially cider. Mid-season ripener, this variety turns mealy if stored too long.

Jonagold: This cross between Jonathan and Golden Delicious was first released in 1968. It has become the leading variety grown in the Pacific Northwest. It is an excellent sweet-tart dessert apple that makes a great pie.

Fuji: This variety was developed from American parents: Ralls Janet and Red Delicious. It is now the most popular apple in China and Japan. It is the best keeper of all the sweet apples and will last up to a year if kept refrigerated.

Gala: This is a strikingly beautiful red-yellow apple that was originally developed in New Zealand by crossing Golden Delicious and Kidd's Orange Red. Great out of hand, it also makes great sauce and cider.

Winesap: This apple has a pungent sweet-sour flavor with fine aroma. It's an important late season apple that does equally well in sauces, pies, and cider.

Baked Apples with Sherry Custard Sauce and Amaretti Snow

This is an upscale version of that old standard, baked apples. The custard sauce and amaretti cookies should be made in advance. For peeling the apples, I like to use the old-fashioned peeler-slicer, which is available in most cookware stores.

Serves 8

⅓ cup golden raisins
⅓ cup fruity, slightly sweet wine, such as Riesling or Gewürztraminer
8   medium-tart baking apples, such as Newtown Pippin, peeled and cored
½ cup toasted pine nuts
⅓ cup melted unsalted butter

½ cup light-brown sugar
½ cup dry white wine
1   teaspoon grated lemon zest
    Sherry Custard Sauce (recipe follows)
    Amaretti Cookies, crushed (recipe follows)
    Garnish: 8 large mint sprigs, if desired

Preheat the oven to 375 degrees. In a small saucepan, combine the raisins and wine and bring to a simmer. Remove from the heat and let stand 15 minutes to allow the raisins to plump. Strain the raisins and drain well, reserving any liquid.

Place the apples in a baking dish just large enough to hold them. Combine the raisins with the pine nuts and fill the cavities of the apples. Put the butter, brown sugar, white wine, lemon zest, and the reserved raisin liquid in the saucepan and simmer to melt the sugar, approximately 2 minutes. Drizzle over the apples. Bake for 25 to 30 minutes or until the apples are tender when pierced with a toothpick, basting occasionally with the juices.

Serve the warm apples in shallow wide-rimmed bowls. Spoon the Sherry Custard Sauce around and sprinkle with crushed Amaretti Cookies. Garnish with the mint sprigs, if desired.

Sherry Custard Sauce

3   egg yolks
¼ cup sugar
1¼ cups half-and-half

2   tablespoons dry sherry (or to taste)
    Drops of lemon juice

In a bowl, whisk the egg yolks and sugar together until pale yellow. In a small saucepan, heat the half-and-half to steaming but do not boil. Slowly pour the hot cream into the yolk mixture, whisking constantly to prevent the yolks from scrambling. Pour the mixture back into the saucepan and cook over low heat, stirring constantly until the sauce thickens slightly. Remove from the heat and strain immediately into a metal bowl. Add the sherry. Place the bowl into a larger bowl filled with ice water, or refrigerate. Stir occasionally to speed the cooling.

Store, covered, in the refrigerator up to 3 days.

Amaretti Cookies

Makes about 24 cookies

1¼ cups blanched and lightly toasted almonds	2 large egg whites
¾ cup powdered sugar	⅓ cup granulated sugar
2 teaspoons all-purpose flour	1 teaspoon grated lemon zest
	1 teaspoon almond extract

In a food processor, grind the almonds to a powder by pulsing off and on to keep the powder loose. Mix the almonds with the powdered sugar and flour.

In a separate bowl, beat the egg whites to soft peaks. Gradually beat in the granulated sugar until stiff. Fold in the lemon zest and almond extract.

Pipe the mixture with a pastry bag using a round ¼-inch tip into 1½-inch rounds onto baking sheets lined with lightly buttered waxed paper or parchment. Bake in a preheated 275-degree oven for 1 hour, checking to make sure the amaretti don't brown. Turn off the oven and let the amaretti dry out for an additional hour—they should be very crisp. Store them in an airtight container in the refrigerator or freezer.

 # Banana-Mango Fritters

This was a recipe created out of panic one day when we didn't have a dessert to serve for unexpected guests. (We had wonton skins left over from one of our guest chefs who had made scallop ravioli, so this seemed a perfect idea.) I've served it several times, varying the dipping sauces. It's best to make for a small group, so you can serve the fritters just as hot and crisp as possible.

Serves 4

32 wonton skins
 2 large bananas, diced
 2 large mangoes, seeded and diced
    Vegetable oil for frying

Powdered sugar
Orange Caramel Dipping Sauce
    (recipe follows) or Berry-Cherry
    Mostarda (page 233)

Lay 16 wonton skins on a work surface and place a small amount of the diced banana and mango on each, being sure to leave a border all around. Lightly paint the border with a little water and place the remaining 16 skins on top of the fruit. Gently but firmly, seal the edges of the wontons with the tines of a fork. Place the fritters on a baking sheet lined with waxed paper. (They can be stored, uncovered, in the refrigerator until ready to fry.)

Just before serving time, pour vegetable oil to a depth of 2 inches in a large pan and heat to 360 degrees. Carefully drop the fritters into the hot oil and fry until golden brown on both sides, 30 to 40 seconds per side. Dust with powdered sugar and serve immediately with Orange Caramel Dipping Sauce or Berry-Cherry Mostarda.

Orange Caramel Dipping Sauce

Makes 1½ cups

½ cup heavy cream
¾ cup fresh orange juice
1¼ cups sugar
¾ cup water
 5 tablespoons chilled unsalted
    butter, cut into small bits

1 teaspoon pure vanilla extract
⅛ teaspoon kosher salt
2 tablespoons brandy or bourbon
1 teaspoon grated orange zest

In a saucepan, combine the cream and orange juice and heat until just beginning to simmer. Remove from the heat and keep warm.

In a separate, deep saucepan, combine the sugar and water. Bring to a boil, then reduce the heat to a simmer, washing down any sugar crystals clinging to the side of the pan with a pastry brush dipped in water. Swirl the pan occasionally until the syrup turns golden brown.

Remove from the heat and carefully whisk the cream mixture into the caramelized sugar. The caramel sauce will bubble dramatically, so be careful. Whisk in the butter in small increments until completely combined. Stir in the vanilla, salt, brandy, and orange zest.

Store indefinitely, covered, in the refrigerator. Serve warm or at room temperature.

Blueberries and Cream

The cream part of this recipe is my grandmother's. I've seen variations of it referred to as Russian or French cream—to me, it's Grandma's cream. I love to serve this with the Almond-Orange Biscotti on page 365.

Serves 4 to 6

2 **pints fresh blueberries**	¼ **cup dry red wine**
¼ **cup sugar**	1 **teaspoon minced fresh mint**
1 **teaspoon grated lemon zest**	**Garnish: Fresh mint sprigs**

In a small saucepan over moderate heat, combine 1 pint of the blueberries, the sugar, lemon zest, and red wine. Simmer, uncovered, for 5 minutes or until the mixture is syrupy. Remove from the heat and cool. Stir in the remaining blueberries and mint. Store, covered, in the refrigerator for up to 2 weeks.

Cream

2 **teaspoons unflavored gelatin**	1 **cup sour cream**
1 **cup heavy cream**	1 **teaspoon pure vanilla extract**
½ **cup sugar**	1 **teaspoon lemon zest**

In a saucepan over moderate heat, combine the gelatin, cream, and sugar. Using a wooden spoon, stir until the sugar is dissolved. Put into a bowl the sour cream, vanilla, and lemon zest. Gradually add the hot cream mixture, stirring until the mixture is smooth.

Rinse a 2½-cup metal mold with cold water (or use individual ramekins). Shake out the excess water but do not dry. Pour the cream mixture into the wet mold. Refrigerate for 4 hours or overnight, until the mixture is set and firm.

To serve, unmold the cream by placing the mold in a warm water bath for a few seconds to loosen the cream. Invert the mold onto a cutting board. Slice the cream into serving pieces and with a spatula lift them onto chilled plates. Spoon the prepared blueberries around. Garnish with mint sprigs.

Compote of Fresh and Dried Fruits

For this simple dessert you can use whatever dried or fresh fruits you have on hand; just try to make it a colorful assortment. I've suggested serving the compote with a dollop of yogurt or yogurt cheese, but ice cream, sour cream, mascarpone, or nothing at all are equally satisfying. When they are available in the fall, I love garnishing this compote with a sprinkling of fresh pomegranate seeds.

Makes approximately 2 quarts

2 **750 ml bottles dry white wine**	1 **tablespoon chopped crystallized**
¼ **cup fresh lemon juice**	**ginger**
1 **cup sugar**	1 **pound fresh, firm ripe pears**
2 **4-inch cinnamon sticks**	**and/or apples, peeled, cored,**
2 **large bay leaves**	**and cut into thick wedges**
1 **tablespoon coriander seed,**	1½ **cups fresh or individually**
slightly crushed	**quick-frozen (IQF)**
2 **teaspoons whole black**	**blueberries, raspberries,**
peppercorns	**cherries, or a combination**
1 **pound mixed dried fruits, such as**	**Garnish: Yogurt or yogurt cheese**
figs, pears, and peaches	**(page 306)**
¼ **cup dry sherry**	

In a nonreactive saucepan, combine the wine, lemon juice, sugar, cinnamon, bay leaves, coriander seed, and peppercorns. Cover, bring to a simmer, and simmer for 15 minutes. Remove from the heat, cool slightly, and strain.

Transfer the liquid to a stockpot or large saucepan and add the dried fruits, sherry, and ginger; simmer, covered, for 10 minutes. Add the fresh fruit and simmer until just tender, about 3 to 5 minutes. Remove from the heat and cool to room temperature. Add the berries. The compote can be served at room temperature or chilled. Store well covered in the refrigerator for up to 10 days.

YOGURT CHEESE

This is a simple, relatively low-fat cheese (depending on the type of yogurt used) that is easily made. I recommend using a plain whole-milk yogurt that is not too tart. Start with twice as much yogurt as you'd like to end up with. (In other words, use 4 cups yogurt to make 2 cups yogurt cheese.)

To make the cheese: Line a strainer with a double thickness of cheesecloth that has been well rinsed. Set in a bowl so that the strainer is suspended. Scoop the yogurt into the strainer, cover lightly, and refrigerate overnight or for up to 2 days, depending on how thick you'd like the yogurt cheese to be. When the cheese stops dripping, transfer it to a suitable container and store refrigerated.

The cheese can be used as is or it can be flavored. To make a dessert cheese, add a little sugar and vanilla or finely grated citrus zest. For a savory cheese, mix in some chopped fresh herbs, salt, and pepper.

DRYING FOODS

The most ancient technique for preserving food is by drying it. Over the centuries, different cultures devised all kinds of clever ways to dry foods. In the Middle East, fruits were wrapped in dried palm leaves and then buried in hot sand to dry out. In the Mediterranean, tomatoes and other fruits and vegetables were sliced, liberally salted to discourage spoilage and bugs, and then dried in the hot summer sun.

All kinds of machines are available now for drying foods at home. Additionally, your home oven (especially if it's a convection oven) can be used to dry almost anything. The only appliance I cannot make work successfully for drying is the microwave oven. Despite the claims of manufacturers, food dried in the microwave always seems to turn out overcooked for me. A good book on drying foods at home is Mary Bell's *Complete Dehydrator Cookbook*, published by Morrow (1994).

Coffee-Poached Pears with Cinnamon Twists

The idea for this recipe came from my grandmother, who, being a frugal Scotch-German woman, never wasted anything. With my eye on the leftover coffee I always seem to have around, I developed this poaching liquid for pears. Classically, red wine is used to poach fruits and, as I thought about it, coffee has many of the same qualities as wine: acidity, tannin, and rich flavor. The Cinnamon Twists, which I find irresistible, came later.

Serves 8

6 cups strong coffee	8 small firm, ripe pears, peeled and cored
2½ cups dark-brown sugar	
Zest and juice of 2 large oranges.	¾ teaspoon cornstarch or arrowroot
	¼ cup fresh orange juice
3 tablespoons chopped fresh ginger	Garnish: Fresh orange segments and mint sprigs
1 3-inch cinnamon stick	Cinnamon Twists (recipe follows)

In a large, wide nonreactive saucepan, combine the coffee, brown sugar, zest and juice of the oranges, ginger, and cinnamon stick and bring to a boil. Lower the heat and simmer for 4 minutes. Add the pears and return to the simmer. Gently simmer until the pears are cooked through and tender, testing the pears with a toothpick. The cooking time will vary greatly depending on the type and size of pear used. When tender, remove from the heat. Scoop 1 cup of the poaching liquid into a small saucepan. Leave the pears in their liquid while making the sauce.

Dissolve the cornstarch in the orange juice and add to the small saucepan containing the cup of poaching liquid. Bring to a simmer and cook for 3 minutes until lightly thickened. Remove from the heat and set aside to cool.

Serve the pears sliced and fanned in shallow bowls or on plates. Spoon some of the sauce over and around the slices; garnish with 2 or 3 orange segments and mint sprigs. Serve the Cinnamon Twists on the side.

Cinnamon Twists

Makes approximately 30 twists

1½ cups all-purpose flour	½ cup finely chopped almonds
1 cup (2 sticks) unsalted butter, cut into bits	½ cup sugar
½ cup sour cream	1½ tablespoons ground cinnamon

In a food processor, combine the flour and butter. Pulse 2 or 3 times until the mixture resembles very coarse cornmeal. Add the sour cream and pulse briefly until the dough just begins to come together. Do not overmix. Form into a disk, wrap in plastic, and refrigerate for 4 hours or overnight.

Preheat the oven to 400 degrees. Line a baking sheet with aluminum foil or parchment. In a medium bowl, combine the almonds, sugar, and cinnamon. Sprinkle the almond-sugar mixture over a work surface, place the disk of dough on top, and roll out into a 9-by-12-inch rectangle approximately ⅛ inch thick, encrusting the underside of the dough with the almond-sugar mixture. Trim the edges and cut into even strips, 9 inches long by ½ inch wide.

Gently pick up the ends of the strips and twist 2 or 3 times to form a corkscrew shape and place on the baking sheet. Bake the twists for approximately 15 minutes or until they're brown and crisp. Remove to a rack and allow to cool. The twists should be stored in an airtight container even for a few hours and are best eaten the same day they are baked.

SWEET ROSEMARY SYRUP

This herb-infused syrup for serving with fresh fruits is a magic elixir. Try other herbs, such as lemon thyme, lavender, or sage, in place of the rosemary. I love a combination of fresh figs, pears, and raspberries served with a slice of fresh young goat cheese and drizzled with a few tablespoons of the syrup. Hazelnut Biscotti (page 364) are a perfect complement.

ROSEMARY SYRUP

½ cup sugar	1 large bay leaf
½ cup dry white wine	1 1-inch strip lemon zest
¼ cup water	½ teaspoon peppercorns
4 tablespoons whole rosemary leaves	2 tablespoons balsamic vinegar

In a saucepan, combine all the ingredients. Bring to a boil and reduce the heat. Cover and simmer for 6 minutes. Cool, strain, and store refrigerated, indefinitely.

Bread Pudding with Apples, Prunes, and Walnuts

This is a hearty winter dessert. I think everyone should have a good bread pudding as part of their repertoire.

Serves 8

6 tablespoons (¾ stick) unsalted butter, softened	½ teaspoon salt
½ pound sliced egg bread such as challah or Brioche (page 355)	3 cups half-and-half
	2 teaspoons pure vanilla extract
2 cups peeled and sliced tart green apples, such as Newtown Pippin or Granny Smith	1 teaspoon ground ginger
	½ cup chopped lightly toasted walnuts
6 large eggs	1 cup chopped prunes
⅔ cup sugar	Garnish: Orange Caramel Dipping Sauce (page 303)

Use 4 tablespoons butter to coat one side of the slices of bread. Set aside. In a sauté pan, melt the remaining 2 tablespoons butter. Add the apple slices and sauté quickly to lightly brown them. Set aside.

In a large bowl, beat the eggs, sugar, and salt. In a saucepan over moderate heat, heat the half-and-half until scalded (a skin will begin to form on top). Slowly whisk the hot cream into the egg mixture, taking care that the eggs don't "scramble." Stir in the vanilla and ginger.

Preheat the oven to 350 degrees. In an 8-cup soufflé dish, arrange the bread, walnuts, prunes, and sautéed apples in alternate layers, making sure that you end with a layer of bread. Pour the egg mixture over and allow to stand for 30 minutes. Place the soufflé dish in a larger baking pan and pour enough hot water into the pan to come halfway up the sides of the dish. Bake for 45 minutes or until the center of the custard is just set. Remove and allow to stand for 15 minutes before serving.

Serve warm or at room temperature with Orange Caramel Dipping Sauce.

California Almond Cake with Balsamic Strawberries and Orange Mascarpone

This almond cake is very moist and can certainly be made in advance. It is a great cake to freeze and have on hand for unexpected company. Serving strawberries dressed with balsamic vinegar and pepper is an old Italian tradition.

Serves 8 to 10

Butter and flour for the cake pan

8   ounces almond paste

½   cup (1 stick) unsalted butter, softened

¾   cup sugar

3   large eggs

2   teaspoons grated lemon zest

2   tablespoons Grand Marnier or other orange brandy

¼   cup all-purpose flour

½   teaspoon baking powder

Garnish: Powdered sugar

Balsamic Strawberries (recipe follows)

Orange Mascarpone (recipe follows)

Preheat the oven to 350 degrees. Lightly butter and flour an 8-inch round cake pan. In the bowl of an electric mixer, combine the almond paste, butter, and sugar. One at a time, beat in the eggs, followed by the lemon zest and brandy. Sift the flour and baking powder together over waxed paper. Beat the flour into the almond-egg mixture until just combined. Pour the batter in the prepared pan and bake for 35 to 40 minutes. A toothpick inserted in the center should come out clean. Cool on a rack before removing the cake from the pan.

Serve a wedge of the cake with a scoop of the Balsamic Strawberries. Dust with a sprinkling of powdered sugar and pipe a small rosette of the Orange Mascarpone from a pastry bag or simply place a dollop on the cake.

Balsamic Strawberries

2   pints ripe strawberries, stemmed and halved

⅓   cup balsamic vinegar

2   tablespoons honey

½   teaspoon freshly ground black pepper

1   tablespoon drained and rinsed green peppercorns, slightly crushed

In a bowl, gently combine all ingredients. Allow to stand, refrigerated, for at least 1 hour before serving.

Orange Mascarpone

3   ounces fresh mascarpone cheese
1   teaspoons grated orange zest

1   teaspoon Grand Marnier or other
     orange brandy

In a bowl, combine all the ingredients and beat well. Let stand, refrigerated, at least 1 hour before serving.

 California Four-Nut Torte

This cake is very rich and delicious. I usually serve it with some ripe, unsweetened fruit, such as peaches or strawberries, and a dusting of powdered sugar. It really doesn't need anything more. The shredded coconut called for in the filling can be either sweetened or unsweetened depending on your preference—I usually use sweetened.

Makes 1 8-inch cake

NUT CRUST:

½   cup coarsely ground almonds
½   cup coarsely ground hazelnuts or
     filberts
3   tablespoons all-purpose flour

2   tablespoons sugar
⅓   cup (5⅓ tablespoons) chilled
     unsalted butter, cut into small
     bits

Lightly butter an 8-inch round cake pan. In the bowl of an electric mixer fitted with the paddle attachment, combine all the ingredients for the crust and mix until well combined and no lumps of butter are visible; the mixture should be somewhat crumbly. Work quickly so that the butter does not melt. This may also be done in a food processor with the steel blade. Evenly press the mixture onto the bottom and sides of the pan; the mixture will reach approximately two thirds of the way up the sides.

NUT FILLING:

1   cup light-brown sugar
3   eggs
1   teaspoon baking powder
½   cup chopped pine nuts
1   cup chopped walnuts

1   cup shredded coconut
½   cup all-purpose flour

Garnish: Powdered sugar

Preheat the oven to 350 degrees. In a mixing bowl, combine the brown sugar, eggs, and baking powder and beat until well mixed. Beat in the pine nuts, walnuts, coconut, and the flour.

Pour the filling into the prepared crust. Bake for approximately 25 minutes. Do not overbake—the cake should be soft and caramelly in the center. Cool on a rack for 10 minutes before removing the cake from the pan. This cake may be made up to 5 days in advance and stored, wrapped in plastic, in the refrigerator; return to room temperature before serving.

To serve, use a serrated knife to cut the torte into small wedges, since it is very rich. Accompany with a fresh fruit of your choice, and a dusting of powdered sugar.

Caramel, Chocolate, and Macadamia Nut Tart

This dessert, created by Dawn Bailey at my restaurant, John Ash & Company, became a signature dish. Every time we tried to take it off the menu, we'd be bombarded with groans and moans. So it stayed. If you are unable to track down unsalted macadamia nuts, you can use the salted ones, simply rinse them, pat dry with paper towels, and proceed to toast as called for in the recipe. This tart keeps very well in the refrigerator, but allow it to come to room temperature before serving, otherwise the caramel is too hard.

Makes 1 9-inch tart

CRUST:

1½ cups all-purpose flour	½ teaspoon kosher salt
⅓ cup (5⅓ tablespoons) chilled unsalted butter, cut into small bits	1 large egg yolk, lightly beaten
	2–4 tablespoons ice water

In the bowl of an electric mixer fitted with the paddle attachment, quickly combine the flour, butter, and salt until just blended; or, by hand, cut in the flour, butter, and salt very quickly to resemble coarse cornmeal. Add the egg yolk and 2 tablespoons of the water and mix until the dough just comes together. If too dry, add a little more cold water. This may also be made in a food processor using the plastic or metal blade. Wrap the dough in plastic and chill for at least 2 hours or overnight. This dough freezes well.

Preheat the oven to 375 degrees. Lightly butter the bottom and sides of a 9-inch tart pan with a removable bottom. On a lightly floured work surface, roll out the dough to a diameter of at least 10 inches. Roll the dough onto the rolling pin and transfer to the tart pan. Gently press the dough into the bottom and sides of the pan. Trim off any excess and prick the dough with a fork. Line the dough with heavy foil and fill with dried beans to weight the dough. Bake for 5 to 7 minutes or until the dough is partially cooked but not brown. Carefully remove the foil and the beans; continue to bake 3 to 4 minutes longer until lightly brown. Remove and set aside to cool.

CARAMEL FILLING:

½ cup sugar
1¼ cups heavy cream
½ cup dark corn syrup

¼ cup (½ stick) butter
1½ cups unsalted macadamia nuts,
     lightly toasted

In a heavy saucepan over medium high heat, combine the sugar, ½ cup of the cream, the corn syrup, and the butter. Bring the mixture to a boil, stirring occasionally, and cook until it reaches 240 degrees on a candy thermometer, the soft-ball stage. Slowly, as it will bubble up, add the remaining ¾ cup cream. Return the mixture to the boil and cook until it reaches 220 degrees. Remove from the heat and cool slightly. Arrange the nuts evenly in the baked tart shell and pour the warm caramel over. Cool and refrigerate until firm.

CHOCOLATE GLAZE:

3 ounces bittersweet chocolate
⅓ cup heavy cream

3 tablespoons sugar

Place all the glaze ingredients in a double boiler and cook over medium-low heat just until the chocolate melts. Remove from the heat and whisk until smooth.

Quickly pour the chocolate glaze over the top of the chilled tart. Rotate and tilt the tart to spread evenly. Chill again to firm the chocolate. Return the tart to room temperature before serving.

Fresh Cherry Flan

This version of a classic French clafouti works equally well with any other fresh, ripe fruit, such as blackberries, apricots, peaches—but I love cherries.
Serves 6 to 8

Butter for the baking dish	1 **cup all-purpose flour**
3½ **cups sweet, ripe cherries, any**	3 **tablespoons dark rum**
variety	1 **teaspoon grated lemon zest**
½ **cup sugar**	1 **cup milk**
2 **egg yolks**	**Garnish: Powdered sugar and**
1 **egg**	**crème fraîche (see below)**
⅓ **cup (5 tablespoons) unsalted**	
butter, melted	

Carefully pit the cherries, leaving them whole.

Preheat the oven to 400 degrees. Butter a 9-inch baking dish. In a large bowl, combine the sugar, egg yolks, and egg and mix until smooth. Beat in the melted butter, followed by the flour, rum, lemon zest, and milk. The batter should be very smooth. Alternatively, the batter may be quickly made in a blender or food processor.

Arrange the cherries in the bottom of the prepared dish and pour the batter on top. Bake for 35 to 40 minutes or until golden brown and lightly puffed and set.

Serve warm with a dusting of powdered sugar and a dollop or two of crème fraîche.

MAKING CRÈME FRAÎCHE

There are a few commercial brands of crème fraîche available, and you may find it in a gourmet store if not in the supermarket, but you can easily make your own.

In a saucepan, combine 2 cups heavy cream and 1 cup cultured sour cream or 3 tablespoons cultured buttermilk. Warm gently to about 90 degrees (barely warm to the touch). Remove from the heat and pour into a clean jar. Cover the opening with a clean tea towel or cheesecloth and allow the mixture to sit at room temperature (75 to 80 degrees) for 6 to 8 hours or overnight, until the cream is very thick. Stir it gently, cover, and refrigerate for up to 2 weeks. The crème fraîche will become more tart as it ages.

Cherry and Almond Cobbler

In California the cherry season is very short, just a few weeks during midsummer. This cobbler and the flan are two ways to take advantage of cherry's short stay. IQF (individually quick-frozen without sugar) cherries are occasionally available in the market and can be substituted, but of course they are not as good as fresh ones. In place of whipped cream, I like to serve this cobbler with a scoop of Vanilla Bean Ice Cream.

Serves 6 to 8

Butter for the baking dish
5 **cups fresh, pitted Bing or Royal Ann cherries**
¾ cup sugar
2½ tablespoons fresh lemon juice
3 tablespoons arrowroot or cornstarch
¼ teaspoon almond extract
1 teaspoon grated lemon zest
½ teaspoon ground cinnamon
1 cup all-purpose flour
1½ teaspoons baking powder

½ teaspoon salt
¼ cup (½ stick) chilled unsalted butter, cut in small bits
½ cup half-and-half or milk
1 large egg
½ teaspoon pure vanilla extract
⅓ cup blanched and coarsely chopped almonds
Garnish: Lightly sweetened whipped cream or Vanilla Bean Ice Cream (page 344)

Preheat the oven to 400 degrees. Lightly butter a 2-quart baking dish. In a saucepan, combine the cherries, ½ cup of the sugar, the lemon juice, arrowroot, almond extract, grated lemon zest, and cinnamon. Cook over low heat, stirring occasionally, and bring to a simmer, approximately 4 to 5 minutes. Pour into the prepared baking dish.

In a food processor, combine the flour, the remaining ¼ cup sugar, baking powder, and salt and pulse 2 or 3 times to mix. Add the butter and pulse until the mixture is just combined but still crumbly. Add the half-and-half, egg, and vanilla and pulse again to form a smooth batter.

Drop the batter by heaping teaspoons on top of the cherry mixture, leaving some space in between them. Scatter the almonds over. Bake for 20 minutes or until the top is lightly browned and the cherry mixture is bubbling.

Serve warm or at room temperature with lightly sweetened whipped cream, if desired, or Vanilla Bean Ice Cream.

 Chocolate Soufflé

This soufflé is a little denser than traditional versions. Its great attribute, however, is that it can be made ahead and held in the refrigerator for up to a day before baking. Allow a little longer baking time if you are taking it straight from the refrigerator. The idea for this recipe came from Alice Medrich, author of *Cocolat*, who is the master of all things chocolate.

Makes 1 1½-quart soufflé or 8 ½-cup soufflés

Butter and sugar for the soufflé dish(es)	4 eggs, separated
8 ounces bittersweet chocolate, coarsely chopped	2 teaspoons grated orange zest
	¼ teaspoon cream of tartar
	Pinch of kosher salt
1 tablespoon unsalted butter	¼ cup sugar
1 tablespoon all-purpose flour	Garnish: Powdered sugar and
⅓ cup milk	strained fresh raspberry purée,
1 teaspoon pure vanilla extract	if desired.

Preheat the oven to 375 degrees. Lightly butter the soufflé dish or dishes and sprinkle with granulated sugar.

Place the chocolate in the top of a double boiler over simmering water and melt, stirring occasionally. When melted, set aside. Meanwhile, in a separate saucepan, melt the butter, add the flour, and cook, stirring, over low heat for 3 minutes. Add the milk and whisk until the mixture is smooth and lightly thickened. Cook for 5 minutes or until the mixture thickens. Remove from the heat, whisk in the melted chocolate, vanilla, egg yolks, and zest. Transfer to a large bowl and set aside.

In a separate bowl, beat the egg whites with the cream of tartar and salt until they hold soft peaks. Sprinkle in the sugar gradually, continuing to beat until the whites are stiff but not dry. Stir one quarter of the whites into the chocolate mixture to lighten it. Carefully fold in the remaining whites.

Pour the mixture into the prepared soufflé dish or dishes and set on a baking sheet. (The soufflé can be prepared to this point and held in the refrigerator overnight.) Bake for 35 to 40 minutes (15 to 17 minutes for the individual soufflés) or until a toothpick inserted in the center comes out moist but not wet.

Remove from the oven, dust with powdered sugar, and serve immediately with the raspberry purée, if desired.

 ## Espresso Brownie Tart

You could bake this in a conventional 8- by 8-inch pan and cut it in squares like brownies, but this is so wonderfully chocolate that I like to present it as a tart. It stores very well for up to a week, well wrapped, or in the freezer for a month or two.

Makes 1 8-inch tart

Butter and cocoa powder for
    dusting the tart pan
¼ cup (½ stick) unsalted butter
8 ounces semisweet chocolate,
    coarsely chopped
½ cup cocoa powder
¼ cup instant espresso powder
3 large eggs

1½ cups sugar
½ cup all-purpose flour
1 teaspoon baking soda
¼ teaspoon salt
1 cup chopped walnuts
    Garnish: Powdered sugar,
      unsweetened whipped cream,
      and chocolate shavings

Preheat the oven to 350 degrees. Butter and lightly dust with cocoa powder an 8-inch tart pan; save any excess for the ½ cup needed. Melt the butter and chocolate in the top of a double boiler and stir in the cocoa powder and espresso powder until smooth. Pour into the bowl of an electric mixer fitted with the paddle attachment, or a regular electric mixer; at low speed, mix in the eggs one at a time, alternating with the sugar. Continue mixing at medium speed for 6 to 8 minutes.

In a separate bowl, sift together the flour, baking soda, and salt. Fold the dry ingredients into the chocolate mixture along with the nuts. Pour into the prepared tart pan and bake for 25 minutes. The tart will be very soft when it comes out of the oven.

Refrigerate at least 2 hours before serving. Even chilled it will still have a chewy center.

Serve the tart cut into wedges and topped with a sprinkling of powdered sugar, unsweetened whipped cream, and chocolate shavings.

Flourless Walnut Cake

This is a very simple recipe that depends entirely on the quality of the walnuts. If you suspect your walnuts have been in storage for a while, place them on a baking sheet in a preheated 375-degree oven and lightly toast for 3 to 4 minutes to refresh their flavor. This is a great cake to serve with Late Harvest Riesling or sweet Orange Muscat wines.

Makes 1 8-inch cake

Butter and flour for the cake pan	¾ **pound walnuts, finely ground**
4 **large eggs, separated**	**(do this in a food processor)**
1 **cup plus 1 tablespoon sugar**	**Garnish: Powdered sugar, cocoa,**
2 **teaspoons grated lemon zest**	**and fresh berries**

Preheat the oven to 375 degrees. Lightly butter and flour an 8-inch round cake pan. Using an electric mixer, beat the egg yolks and sugar together until light and fluffy, approximately 4 minutes. Stir in the lemon zest.

In a separate bowl, beat the egg whites until they hold stiff peaks. Fold one quarter of the whites into the egg-yolk mixture to lighten it. Add the ground walnuts, stirring until thoroughly blended. Carefully fold in the remaining egg whites to maintain a light texture.

Pour the batter into the prepared pan and bake for 55 to 60 minutes or until firm and golden brown. Cool on a rack before removing the cake from the pan.

To serve, slice into wedges. Dust alternately with powdered sugar and cocoa and arrange with fresh berries.

Grapefruit-Banana Brûlée Tart

"Brûlée" is the technique of caramelizing sugar until it is brown and crisp, to give added flavor and texture. At home, this is usually done under a broiler, but the easiest way to caramelize the sugar is with a propane torch—which you can buy at a hardware store. It works quickly and you don't run quite the risk of melting your tart if the broiler is not hot enough. The combination of the tart grapefruit and the sweet banana in this recipe is very intriguing. I'm a great fan of grapefruit and think we don't use them nearly enough. This tart needs to be started well ahead of serving—the dough needs to be chilled before rolling, then frozen before filling, and the filling should chill several hours before going under the broiler or torch. The final step (caramelizing the sugar) takes just a few seconds.

Makes 1 9-inch tart

CRUST:

1 **cup all-purpose flour**	½ **cup (1 stick) chilled unsalted**
Pinch of kosher salt	**butter, cut into small bits**
1 **tablespoon sugar**	½ **teaspoon pure vanilla extract**
¼ **cup toasted, skinned, and**	2–4 **tablespoons ice water**
chopped hazelnuts	**Butter for the tart pan**

In a food processor, combine the flour, salt, sugar, and hazelnuts. Pulse 2 or 3 times to combine. Add the butter and pulse until the dough resembles very coarse cornmeal. Add the vanilla and water and pulse until the dough just begins to come together. Remove the dough and flatten it into a disk. Wrap in plastic wrap and refrigerate for at least 2 hours.

Lightly butter a 9-inch tart pan with a removable bottom. Roll out the dough to a circle at least 10 inches in diameter. Roll the dough onto the rolling pin and transfer to the prepared tart pan, pressing the dough into the bottom and sides. Trim off any excess and prick the bottom with a fork. Freeze the shell for at least 1 hour before baking.

Preheat the oven to 375 degrees. Line the shell with heavy-duty aluminum foil and fill with dry beans to weight down. Bake for 6 to 8 minutes. Carefully remove the foil and the beans and bake 4 minutes longer or until the dough is very lightly browned. Cool in the pan and set aside.

GRAPEFRUIT-BANANA FILLING:

2 **small, firm ripe bananas**	3 **egg yolks**
½ **cup fresh grapefruit juice**	**Pinch of kosher salt**
2 **teaspoons grated lemon zest**	⅓ **cup (5⅓ tablespoons) unsalted**
¾ **cup sugar plus ⅓ cup for the top**	**butter, melted**
½ **teaspoon cornstarch**	**Garnish: Fresh raspberry purée**
2 **eggs**	**and mint sprigs, if desired**

Slice the bananas and arrange evenly over the bottom of the prepared tart shell. In a stainless-steel bowl, whisk together the grapefruit juice, lemon zest, sugar, cornstarch, eggs, yolks, salt, and melted butter. Transfer to the top of a double boiler over simmering water and whisk until thick. Pour over the bananas in the tart shell. Refrigerate at least 3 hours or until firm.

Just before serving, lightly but evenly coat the top of the tart with the remaining ⅓ cup sugar. Place under a hot broiler and broil until the sugar caramelizes to a dark brown. Or hold a propane torch 3 inches from the tart and flame the sugar. It takes about a minute.

If desired, serve the tart surrounded by a spoonful of the raspberry purée and garnished with the mint sprigs.

For a really simple grapefruit dessert, try putting a good layer of either light- or dark-brown sugar on a cold grapefruit half and then caramelizing it quickly under the broiler or with a torch. The tart-sweet-crunchy taste sensation rush is wonderful.

 Honey Rice Pudding

As a kid I loved rice and tapioca puddings. In this version I've prepared the pudding in a cake pan so that it can be presented a little more elegantly. Nevertheless, it's still just homey old rice pudding.

Serves 8

1 teaspoon unsalted butter or vegetable oil for the cake pan	½ cup honey
	1 teaspoon pure vanilla extract
1¼ cups water	2 teaspoons grated lemon zest
¾ cup long-grain white rice	¼ teaspoon kosher salt
2½ cups milk	¼ teaspoon freshly grated nutmeg
3 large eggs	¼ cup golden raisins, plumped in
3 egg yolks	warm water or rum for 30 minutes

Preheat the oven to 300 degrees. Butter an 8-inch (1-quart capacity) cake pan or baking dish. In a small saucepan bring the water to a boil, add the rice, and reduce to a simmer. Cover and cook for approximately 10 minutes or until the water is absorbed. Transfer the rice to a bowl and cool.

In a small saucepan, heat the milk to scalding. Meanwhile, in a separate bowl, combine the eggs, egg yolks, honey, vanilla, lemon zest, salt, and nutmeg, beating until smooth. Add the hot milk in a slow stream, stirring continuously to prevent scrambling the eggs. Drain the raisins and add to the mixture along with the cooled rice.

Pour the rice mixture into the prepared dish and place the dish in a larger pan. Add enough hot water to the pan to come two thirds of the way up the side of the dish. Bake for 1 hour and 10 minutes or until custard is just set. Transfer to a rack and let cool. Cover and refrigerate for at least 4 hours. Cut the pudding into wedges and serve on chilled plates.

Note: For an interesting "brûlée" presentation, remove the pudding from the refrigerator and sprinkle ¼ cup superfine sugar over the top. With a propane torch (page 318), glaze the sugar until it caramelizes and is golden brown. You could also bake the pudding in buttered individual ramekins. The baking time will be approximately 45 minutes for 4-ounce ramekins.

 Jack Daniel's Sun-Dried Cherry Tart

I believe I developed this recipe for a contest sponsored by (you guessed it) Jack Daniel's. I didn't win, but I still like the tart. The approach is similar to the traditional linzertorte: a fruit filling cooked until almost jammy, baked in a textured, nutty dough. Use any fruit you'd like, including dried apricots or pears, or golden raisins.
Makes 1 10-inch tart

FILLING:

2 **cups roughly chopped dried cherries**	¾ **cup Jack Daniel's whisky**

In a small saucepan, simmer the cherries and the Jack Daniel's until the whisky is absorbed and the cherries are soft. Remove from the heat and cool.

GLAZE:

½ **cup Jack Daniel's whisky**	1 **3-inch strip of orange zest**
3 **tablespoons sugar**	

Combine all the ingredients in a small saucepan. Bring to a boil and reduce by half. Remove the orange zest.

CRUST:

¾ cup all-purpose flour

2 tablespoons cocoa powder

½ teaspoon ground cinnamon

¼ teaspoon baking powder

5 ounces (1¼ sticks) unsalted butter, softened

½ cup plus 2 tablespoons sugar

1 large egg yolk

½ teaspoon almond extract

2 cups finely ground almonds (do this in a food processor with the metal blade)

In a bowl, sift together the flour, cocoa, cinnamon, and baking powder. In another bowl, cream the butter and sugar together, then add the egg yolk and almond extract and mix well. Mix in the flour mixture and then the almonds.

Preheat the oven to 350 degrees. Divide the dough in half. Press half of the dough on the bottom and one third the way up the sides of a 10-inch springform pan. Divide the remaining dough into 8 pieces and roll into 10 inch-long "ropes" for use on top of the tart. Fill the tart shell with the filling and arrange the "ropes" of dough in a lattice design on top of the tart.

Place the tart on a baking sheet and bake for 30 minutes or until the edges start to brown and the dough is set. Cool the tart on a wire rack for 5 to 10 minutes. Paint the entire top of the tart evenly with the glaze. Gently run a knife around the edges to loosen and remove the sides of the springform pan. Serve warm or at room temperature.

 Lemon-Glazed Persimmon Bars

In the fall, when persimmons are ripe, this is one of my favorite desserts. I often serve the bars warm with a scoop of homemade ice cream.

Vegetable oil and flour for the jellyroll pan

1 cup Hachiya persimmon pulp

1 teaspoon soda water (club soda or seltzer)

1 egg

1 cup sugar

½ cup vegetable oil

1¾ cups sifted all-purpose flour

1 teaspoon kosher salt

½ teaspoon ground cloves or ginger (or mixed)

1 teaspoon ground cinnamon

½ teaspoon freshly grated nutmeg

¾ cup chopped walnuts, almonds, or other nuts

¾ cup coarsely chopped dates or raisins

Lemon Glaze (recipe follows)

Preheat the oven to 350 degrees. Lightly oil and flour a jellyroll pan. Mix the persimmon pulp with a beater or whisk until smooth, stir in the soda, and set aside. In a separate bowl, beat the egg lightly. Add the sugar and oil and mix well. Add this mixture to the persimmon mixture. In a separate bowl, combine the flour, salt, and spices; then stir in the persimmon mixture, the nuts, and the dates. Spread the mixture in the pan. Bake for 25 minutes or until golden brown. Glaze while hot with the Lemon Glaze. Cut into bars.

Lemon Glaze

1   cup sifted powdered sugar   **3   tablespoons fresh lemon juice**

Combine the sugar and lemon juice in a saucepan. Bring to a simmer and stir until the sugar is melted. Remove from the heat and set aside.

PERSIMMONS

Native to China and Japan, persimmons are grown widely in California as well as around the Mediterranean. There are hundreds of varieties of persimmons, but the most widely known and grown is the variety called Hachiya. When firm it can be quite tart and astringent, but as it softens and ripens, it becomes very sweet and honeylike. Its pulp is delicious in breads, puddings, sauces, and similar recipes. Since persimmons on the tree tend to ripen simultaneously, there often is a glut of fruit all at once in the fall. A trick that local growers use is to cut off the very tip of the persimmon to allow for expansion and then wrap and freeze the fruit. Then they partially defrost it and eat it like a frozen mousse or ice. You can use the pulp from a frozen persimmon exactly as you would use the pulp from a fresh one.

In recent years, another variety of persimmon called Fuyu has started to show up in the market. This persimmon is different from Hachiya in that it is best eaten firm, almost like an apple. It is sweet when firm with no astringency and perfect in salads or desserts in its raw form.

Lemon Polenta Cake with Warm Spiced Apricot Sauce and Fresh Mascarpone

This is a rustic, peasant-style cake. Polenta, a coarsely ground cornmeal, is a staple in the northern Italian kitchen. The polenta found in American markets is of a coarser texture than the true Italian polenta, so in this recipe I've used stone-ground cornmeal. The crunch of the polenta adds an interesting texture that I like. The warm spiced apricot sauce seems to make this a perfect dessert for late fall and winter. Mascarpone is the fresh Italian thickened cream "cheese" that is made simply from sweet cream; the addition of citric and tartaric acids gives it its unique tart, rich flavor. You can purchase it ready-made or substitute a good sour cream.
Serves 8

1 cup stone-ground cornmeal (or ¾ cup cornmeal plus ¼ cup polenta)	2 tablespoons softened unsalted butter
½ cup unbleached all-purpose flour	½ cup plain yogurt
1½ teaspoons baking powder	1½ tablespoons grated lemon zest
¼ teaspoon kosher salt	2 tablespoons lemon juice
1 cup sugar	Warm, Spiced Apricot Sauce (recipe follows)
2 large eggs plus 2 egg whites	½ cup fresh mascarpone, lightly whipped
¼ cup vegetable oil plus additional for the pan	

In a bowl, sift together the cornmeal, flour, baking powder, and salt. Set aside.

In a separate bowl, beat the sugar, eggs, and egg whites until creamy. Add the oil, butter, yogurt, lemon zest, and lemon juice and beat until smooth. Fold in the dry ingredients until combined. Do not overmix.

Line the bottom of an 8-inch cake pan with lightly oiled waxed paper. Pour the batter into the prepared pan and smooth the top with a spatula. Place in a pre-heated 350-degree oven and bake for 40 minutes, or until a toothpick inserted in the center of the cake comes out clean.

Cool for 15 minutes on a rack. Invert and peel off the paper. Cool completely before serving.

To serve, slice the cake and place on plates. Spoon the Warm Spiced Apricot Sauce over the cake and put a dollop of fresh mascarpone on top.

Warm Spiced Apricot Sauce

3-inch cinnamon stick, broken into 3 or 4 pieces	3 tablespoons honey (or to taste)
8 whole cloves	2 tablespoons brandy
1½ cups dry white wine	¼ cup dried currants
3 ounces diced dried apricots	1 teaspoon grated lemon zest

Place the cinnamon sticks and cloves on a square of cheesecloth and tie loosely to form a bag. In a small saucepan, combine the spice bag, wine, apricots, and honey. Bring to a boil, reduce heat, and simmer uncovered for 10 to 15 minutes or until slightly thickened, stirring often.

Remove the spice bag and discard. Add the brandy, currants, and zest and simmer for 2 minutes. Allow to cool. Store covered in the refrigerator for up to 2 months.

 ## Lemon Tartlets with Fresh Berries and Fresh Plum Sauce

I fell in love with lemon curd years ago while staying at bed and breakfast inns in England. It seemed there was always a jar of curd at the breakfast table to spread on warm scones. In this dessert, I've taken lemon curd and put it in a flavorful shortbread shell and served it along with a scattering of fresh berries. Yum! I've given directions for a very elegant presentation, but the components are very simple to make and all can be prepared ahead.

Makes 10 tartlets

LEMON CURD:

1 cup fresh lemon juice	2 tablespoons grated lemon zest
1¼ cups sugar	
1 teaspoon cornstarch	Garnish: Fresh raspberries and blackberries, Orange-Ginger Star Cookies (see below), and mint sprigs
4 eggs	
6 egg yolks	
½ teaspoon kosher salt	
¾ cup (1½ sticks) unsalted butter, melted	

In a double boiler over simmering water, combine all the lemon curd ingredients, whisking until thick. Remove from the heat and cool. Chill the curd, covered, for 4 hours or overnight until set. Store any curd, tightly covered, in the refrigerator for up to 1 month.

FRESH PLUM SAUCE:

1½ pounds halved and pitted fresh
        Santa Rosa or other plums
  3 tablespoons sugar
  2 teaspoons grated lemon zest

¼ cup slightly sweet white wine,
      such as Riesling or
      Gewürztraminer

In a saucepan, combine all the ingredients and simmer, uncovered, until thick. Transfer to a food processor and purée. Strain through a medium sieve. Store, covered, in the refrigerator.

ORANGE-GINGER SHORTBREAD DOUGH (FOR TARTLETS AND STAR COOKIES)

½ cup plus 1 tablespoon sugar
2 tablespoons minced crystallized
      ginger
¾ cup (1½ sticks) unsalted butter,
      softened

1 teaspoon pure vanilla extract
½ teaspoon kosher salt
2 teaspoons grated orange zest
1½ cups all-purpose flour

In a food processor, combine the sugar and ginger and process until the ginger is pulverized. In the bowl of an electric mixer, cream the sugar mixture and the butter until light and fluffy. Beat in the vanilla, salt, and orange zest. Add the flour and mix until well blended.

Divide the dough in half. Take one portion and divide it into 10 walnut-sized balls. Make tartlet shells by pressing each ball into a cup in a tartlet tin; chill for at least 30 minutes. Roll out the remaining dough and, using a small, star-shaped cutter, cut out stars and place them on a lightly buttered baking sheet. Chill 30 minutes.

Preheat the oven to 350 degrees. Bake the star cookies for 8 to 10 minutes and the tartlets 12 to 15 minutes or until lightly browned. Remove and cool. Store in an airtight container.

To serve, use a pastry bag to pipe the curd into the prepared shells or simply spoon it in. Place 1 or 2 tartlets on a plate. Drizzle the Plum Sauce around and garnish with a scattering of berries, an Orange-Ginger Star Cookie, and a mint sprig.

Mango Crème Brûlée

Mangoes are not a native California fruit, but we do see a great number of them, beginning in January, imported from Mexico and Central America. As a result, I always think of mangoes as one of the wintertime fruits—perfect for this brûlée. (The recipe would be just as delicious with papaya.)

Serves 8

4 cups heavy cream
1 4-inch vanilla bean
   Pinch of salt
8 egg yolks
¾ cup sugar
⅔ cup diced fresh mango

4 tablespoons light-brown sugar for caramelizing
4 tablespoons granulated sugar for caramelizing
   Garnish: Mint sprigs and fresh berries, if desired

Preheat the oven to 300 degrees. In a saucepan, heat the cream, vanilla bean, and salt to scalding. Remove the vanilla bean from the hot cream. Slit it open with a knife and scrape the tiny seeds back into the cream. In a bowl, beat the egg yolks and the sugar until well mixed and light in color. Slowly add the hot cream, stirring constantly to melt the sugar and not let the eggs scramble. Strain. Skim off any bubbles. Gently stir in the mango.

Divide the mixture among 8 ramekins. Place the ramekins in a roasting pan. Fill the pan with boiling water to reach halfway up the sides of the ramekins. Cover loosely with foil and bake for 55 to 65 minutes or until the center is just beginning to set and no longer liquid.

Remove the ramekins from the oven and cool. Refrigerate, covered, for at least 3 hours or overnight. Close to serving time, combine the sugars in a small bowl. Preheat a broiler and sprinkle 1 tablespoon of the mixed sugars evenly over the surface of each custard. Broil (as quickly as possible) until the sugar is caramelized. Alternately, you can caramelize the sugar with a propane torch (page 318). Serve within 1 hour to maintain the crispness of the sugar topping.

Serve garnished with mint sprigs and fresh berries, if desired.

Nectarine Upside-Down Cake in a Skillet

This cake is best eaten the day it is made, but that shouldn't be a problem because it's so good. Make sure your cast-iron skillet is well seasoned. If not, scrub it well with a nonmetallic scrubber, dry it, and lightly coat the interior with vegetable oil. Place the skillet in a 350-degree oven for 3 to 4 hours. Remove and cool. Wipe the skillet clean and you should end up with a smooth, shiny surface that's essentially nonstick. Wash with water only (no soap!) and coat with oil after every use; you'll have a pan that you'll use often because cast iron is such a wonderful heat conductor.

Serves 6

¾ cup sugar	2 eggs, separated
2 pounds large, firm ripe nectarines, cut into eighths	1 teaspoon ground ginger
	2 teaspoons baking powder
⅓ cup (5⅓ tablespoons) unsalted butter, softened	1 cup all-purpose flour
	1 teaspoon ground cinnamon
¼ cup sugar	1 teaspoon grated lemon zest
¼ cup pure maple syrup	Garnish: Lightly whipped cream

Preheat the oven to 350 degrees. In a 9-inch cast-iron skillet, melt the sugar with 2 tablespoons water. Gently rotating the pan to evenly coat the bottom, cook until the sugar caramelizes to a medium gold. Remove from the heat and *carefully* place the nectarine slices in a circular pattern on top of the caramel, without touching the hot sugar with your fingers. Set aside.

In the bowl of an electric mixer, beat the butter until soft. Add the sugar and maple syrup and mix until smooth. One at a time, add the egg yolks, beating thoroughly after each addition. Remove the bowl from the mixer.

In a separate bowl, sift together the ginger, baking powder, flour, and cinnamon. Fold the dry ingredients into the egg batter along with the lemon zest until well combined. Beat the egg whites until stiff but not dry. Mix one quarter of the beaten egg whites into the batter to lighten it and then carefully fold in the remaining whites. Spread the batter over the top of the nectarines in the skillet. Bake for 20 to 25 minutes or until the cake is golden brown and it springs back when touched.

Remove the skillet from the oven and allow the cake to cool for 10 minutes. Run a knife around the edge of the skillet to loosen the cake. Place a serving platter over the top of the skillet and invert the cake quickly onto the platter.

Serve warm or at room temperature with lightly whipped cream.

Old-Fashioned Fresh Fruit Crisp

I really love fruit crisps. They're a wonderful way to highlight any fruit that's in season; they're easy to make; and they fall into that "comfort food" zone that we all need to visit. For a real warm-weather treat, serve this with Vanilla Bean Ice Cream. You may have noticed that I use grated Asiago cheese in the topping—not, strictly speaking, a traditional fruit crisp ingredient, but it's so good that I'm sure you'll excuse me.

Serves 8 to 10

6   cups fresh seasonal fruits, such as peaches, blackberries, figs, strawberries, plums, apples, pears, or a combination, sliced if necessary

1½ cups dark-brown sugar

1½ cups old-fashioned rolled oats (not instant)

1   cup all-purpose flour

½   cup freshly grated Asiago or Parmesan cheese

1   teaspoon kosher salt

¾   cup (1½ sticks) chilled unsalted butter, cut into bits

Garnish: Lightly whipped cream, sweetened with powdered sugar or Vanilla Bean Ice Cream (page 344), if desired

Preheat the oven to 375 degrees. Lightly butter a 9- by 12-inch glass or enamel baking dish.

Place the fruit in the baking dish. In a bowl, combine the sugar, oats, flour, cheese, and salt and mix. With a hand mixer or using your fingertips, quickly mix the bits of butter into the sugar mixture to form a coarse meal. The mixture should be loose and crumbly. Work quickly to avoid melting the butter.

Gently sprinkle the topping mixture over the fruit. Bake for 35 minutes or until the top is lightly browned and the fruits are bubbling.

Serve warm with whipped cream or a scoop of Vanilla Bean Ice Cream.

Peaches and Dumplings

If it seems as though many of my fruit desserts are old-fashioned preparations, you're right! I think they excel in showing off seasonal fruits. This dish is best served when the dumplings are still hot. You may, however, hold the dessert for up to an hour before serving it.

Serves 4 to 6

1	cup all-purpose flour	¼	teaspoon ground cinnamon
1	cup plus 2 teaspoons sugar	½	teaspoon ground ginger
1½	teaspoons baking powder	4	cups sliced ripe peaches
½	teaspoon baking soda	1	cup fresh blackberries or
¼	teaspoon kosher salt		blueberries
1	large egg, separated		Garnish: Crème fraîche (page 314)
½	cup plus 2 tablespoons buttermilk		and mint sprigs
1	tablespoon unsalted butter, melted and cooled		

In a large bowl, sift together the flour, 2 teaspoons of the sugar, the baking powder, baking soda, and salt. In a separate bowl, combine the egg yolk, buttermilk, and melted butter. Quickly add the buttermilk mixture to the flour mixture, stirring just to combine. In a separate bowl, beat the egg white until soft peaks are formed. Fold into the batter and set aside.

In a 4-quart Dutch oven or other nonreactive pan with a lid, combine 2 cups water, the remaining 1 cup sugar, the cinnamon, and the ginger and bring to a boil. Add the fruit, reduce to a simmer, and cook for 3 minutes. Do not overcook the fruit.

Drop the dumpling batter by spoonfuls onto the simmering fruit. Cover and cook for 8 to 10 minutes, without uncovering, until the dumplings are firm.

Serve in warm bowls with a dollop of crème fraîche and a sprig of mint.

Fresh Peach and Almond Tart

This is one of my favorite summer desserts, and it works equally well with nectarines or apricots. The tart is best eaten the day it's made, so plan ahead, because the dough needs to chill for 2 hours before being rolled out and then for another hour before being filled. You can prepare the peaches while the dough is chilling, but make the filling just before baking. The dough makes a really wonderful crust and it keeps well in the freezer, so you might want to make a double batch and roll it out and freeze it, unbaked, for another use. Another bonus of this recipe is the peach-poaching liquid, which should be saved. It's delicious drizzled on fruits or pancakes and can be used again to poach more fruits.

Makes 1 9-inch tart

CRUST:

1½ cups all-purpose flour
1   tablespoon sugar
⅓   cup (5⅓ tablespoons) chilled
    unsalted butter, cut into small
    bits

2   tablespoons chilled vegetable
    shortening
    Pinch of kosher salt
⅓   cup ice water
    Butter for the tart pan

In a food processor, combine the flour, sugar, butter, shortening, and salt and pulse just to blend. Add the ice water and pulse briefly; the dough should just pull together.

Transfer the dough to a lightly floured work surface. Gather the dough into a ball (it will seem slightly dry) and knead it briefly with the heel of your hand. If the dough seems too dry, add a few more drops of ice water. Form the dough into a disk, wrap with plastic wrap, and refrigerate for at least 2 hours before using.

Lightly butter a 9-inch tart pan. Roll out the dough into a circle 10 inches in diameter. Then roll it up onto the rolling pin and transfer to the prepared tart pan. Gently press the dough into the bottom and sides of the pan, trimming off the excess. Prick the dough with a fork and return to the refrigerator for at least 1 hour.

Preheat the oven to 350 degrees. Line the tart shell with heavy-duty aluminum foil and fill with dry beans to weight down the dough. Bake for 5 minutes. Carefully remove the foil and beans and bake the tart shell for 3 minutes longer or until the dough is set and lightly browned.

PEACHES:

4	large (or 6 small) firm ripe peaches	2	3-inch strips of lemon zest
3½	cups dry white wine	1	3-inch vanilla bean
1½	cups sugar	3	whole cloves
1	cup water	1	teaspoon whole black peppercorns

Cut the peaches in half and remove their pits. In a medium saucepan, combine the wine, water, the sugar, lemon zest, vanilla bean, cloves, and peppercorns. Bring to a boil and reduce the heat. Add the peaches and simmer for 4 to 5 minutes or until just barely tender. Remove the peaches with a slotted spoon. Peel and set aside.

FILLING:

½	cup (1 stick) unsalted butter	2	teaspoons grated lemon zest
½	cup powdered sugar	¼	cup ground almonds (do this in a food processor)
⅓	cup all-purpose flour		
½	cup almond paste	2	egg whites, beaten until foamy

Preheat the oven to 375 degrees. In a medium bowl, combine the butter, sugar, flour, almond paste, lemon zest, and almonds and beat until smooth. Quickly stir in the foamy egg whites and spread evenly in the bottom of the prepared tart shell.

Arrange the poached peach halves in a circle, cut side down, on top of the filling. Bake the tart for 25 to 30 minutes or until the filling is set and lightly colored. Remove and allow to cool.

Ricotta, Honey, and Fig Tart

This is a very simple dessert that requires exceptionally good ricotta and honey. You can make your own ricotta (page 333) or get some from a good delicatessen or cheese shop. Regular supermarket ricotta just doesn't have enough flavor. My favorite ricotta is a sheep's milk version made by Cynthia Callahan at Bellweather Farms (page 401). Good honey is also essential. I prefer honey made from flower pollens such as orange, star thistle, or heather.

Makes 1 8-inch tart

1½   cups hazelnut biscotti crumbs
        (page 363) or other cookie
        crumbs
¼   cup (½ stick) unsalted butter,
        melted
2   cups whole-milk ricotta cheese
⅓   cup honey

        Pinch of kosher salt
1   tablespoon grated lemon zest
½   cup heavy cream
2   teaspoons unflavored gelatin
2   pounds ripe figs
        Garnish: Bittersweet chocolate
          shavings

Preheat the oven to 375 degrees. In a medium bowl, mix the biscotti crumbs with the butter. Press into an 8-inch tart pan with a removable bottom. Place the tart pan on a baking sheet and bake for 8 to 10 minutes or until the crust is set and lightly browned. Remove and allow to cool. Set aside.

In a food processor, combine the ricotta, honey, salt, and lemon zest. Process until the mixture is smooth, approximately 60 seconds. Scoop the mixture into a bowl.

Place the cream in a small saucepan and sprinkle the gelatin on top. Allow the gelatin to soften for 3 minutes. Over low heat, stir until the gelatin is dissolved. Then whisk the cream-gelatin mixture into the ricotta mixture and pour into the prepared shell. Chill for at least 2 hours or until firm.

To serve, remove the tart from the pan and place on a serving plate. Slice the figs, two or three lengthwise slices each, and arrange on the tart. Garnish with chocolate shavings.

MAKING RICOTTA CHEESE

There are many different recipes for making your own ricotta cheese. One of the simplest and best that I know is the version from Deborah Madison's book *The Savory Way*. It's a magical process to participate in and the result is wonderful. A thermometer is helpful here. My bet is that once you make your own ricotta you'll never again buy the little white tubs in the supermarket.

Makes 3 to 4 cups

1   gallon whole milk
6   tablespoons lemon juice

        Sea salt to taste

Combine the milk and lemon juice in a nonreactive pan over very low heat. Gradually bring the milk up to 180 degrees; it should take 25 to 30 minutes. A fine skin will form and there will be tiny bubbles all around the edge of the milk. When the milk reaches 180 degrees, remove the pan from the heat, cover, and leave it in a warm spot (an oven with the pilot light on is perfect) for 6 hours. The curds will have formed and separated from the whey.

Line a sieve or colander with a well-rinsed double layer of cheesecloth and set it over a larger bowl. Ladle the curds into the sieve and season lightly with salt. Refrigerate overnight until the cheese is well drained. For a thicker, firmer cheese you can tie the filled cheesecloth into a pouch and hang it from a refrigerator shelf with a bowl underneath for up to 1 day. Remove the cheese from the cloth, place it in a covered container, and store for up to 1 week. The whey that has been drained off can be used in baking (my grandmother used to add it to her pancakes).

"Soup of Fruits" with Chardonnay Sabayon and Coconut Shortbreads

Not a cooked fruit soup at all, this interesting dessert depends on finding the best fresh fruits available. I like to use a combination of fresh kiwi and berries along with tropical fruits such as mango, miniature bananas, passion fruit, papaya, and star fruit.
Serves 6 to 8

CHARDONNAY SABAYON:

7 large egg yolks	2 pounds assorted berries, tropical
½ cup sugar	fruits, and stoned fruits, peeled
Pinch of kosher salt	if necessary and cut into bite-
1 cup Chardonnay	sized pieces
3 tablespoons kirsch or brandy	Coconut Shortbreads (recipe
¾ cup heavy cream, whipped to soft	follows)
peaks	

In a medium bowl, beat the egg yolks, sugar, and salt until light. Place the mixture in the top of a double boiler over simmering water and whisk in the Chardonnay and kirsch. Continue whisking, over low heat, until the mixture mounds and quadruples in volume. Remove from the heat, pour into a bowl, and allow to cool. Carefully fold the whipped cream into the cooled mixture. Refrigerate and use within 4 hours.

The sabayon can also be served warm: Omit the cream and serve warm as soon as the mixture quadruples in volume.

To serve, ladle the Chardonnay sabayon into shallow soup bowls. Attractively arrange the cut fruits on top along with a wedge or two of the Coconut Shortbreads.

Coconut Shortbreads

Makes 32 cookies from 2 9-inch tart pans with removable bottoms

2 cups all-purpose flour	1 cup (2 sticks) chilled unsalted
⅔ cup sugar	butter, cut into bits
½ teaspoon kosher salt	1½ teaspoons pure vanilla extract
4 cups shredded unsweetened coconut	

Preheat the oven to 350 degrees. Lightly butter 2 9-inch tart pans with removable bottoms. In the bowl of an electric mixer fitted with the paddle attachment, combine all the ingredients and mix until the dough just comes together. This may be done in a food processor with the plastic or metal blade. Divide the dough in half and press evenly into the prepared tart pans. Chill for 30 minutes. Bake for 25 to 30 minutes or until the dough is golden brown.

Cool the shortbreads in the pans for 2 minutes. Remove the metal rings, leaving the shortbreads on the metal bottoms. Cut into wedges while still warm and on the metal bottom. (If the shortbreads seem too moist or soft, return to the oven and bake an additional 3 to 5 minutes or until crisp.) Allow to cool. Then refrigerate.

Refrigerating the cookies on the metal pan bottom before removing them makes them easier to handle. Store the wedges in an airtight container in the refrigerator or freezer.

 Walnut Orange Tart

This is a simple tart to make and it keeps very well. You can use any kind of nut you want—a combination of walnuts, pecans, and hazelnuts is great!
One 9-inch tart

CRUST:

1 cup all-purpose flour	1 teaspoon pure vanilla extract
½ cup (1 stick) chilled unsalted butter, cut into bits	1–2 tablespoons ice water (if needed) Butter for the tart pan

In a food processor, combine the flour, butter, and vanilla. Pulse until the dough resembles coarse oatmeal. If the dough is too dry, add a little ice water. Gather the dough into a ball and wrap well with plastic wrap. Chill for at least 30 minutes.

Preheat the oven to 350 degrees. Lightly butter a 9-inch tart pan with a removable bottom. On a lightly floured work surface, roll out the dough to approximately 10 inches in diameter. Then roll the dough up onto the rolling pin and transfer it to the prepared tart pan, trimming any excess. Gently press it into the bottom and sides of the pan. Prick the dough with a fork. Bake for 6 to 7 minutes or until the crust is just set and very lightly browned. Press the dough down gently with an oven mitt (hot pad) should it puff up while baking. Remove and allow to cool.

WALNUT-ORANGE FILLING:

¾   cup heavy cream
¾   cup sugar
    Grated zest from 1 orange
½   teaspoon pure vanilla extract
    Big pinch of kosher salt

2   tablespoons Grand Marnier or other orange brandy
1½   cups walnut halves
    Garnish: Fresh berries and sliced mango or papaya

In a saucepan, combine the cream and sugar. Heat, stirring, until it just simmers and the sugar dissolves. Stir in the orange zest, vanilla, salt, and Grand Marnier. Remove from the heat.

Place the walnut halves in an even layer on the bottom of the prepared crust. Pour the cream mixture over the nuts. Place the tart on a baking sheet and bake at 350 degrees for 30 to 35 minutes. The tart should be lightly browned on top; it will bubble as it bakes. Remove and cool briefly. Do not refrigerate.

Serve the tart warm or at room temperature. Garnish with berries and sliced mango or papaya.

Frozen Desserts

 # *Wine and Fresh Fruit Ice*

This is a basic recipe to make any kind of fresh fruit ice. You can also make the finished product more sorbetlike by folding a lightly whipped (until frothy) egg white into the other ingredients when they go into the ice cream freezer. The wine choice is up to you, but I'd use a white wine for light-colored fruits, such as peaches, melons, and apples, and a red wine for dark fruits, such as blueberries, blackberries, and the like. Do experiment! A pinch of ground cinnamon or cloves is also a nice addition with most fruits.

Makes approximately 1 quart

1¼ cups red or white wine
¾ cup sugar (or to taste)
2 cups puréed unsweetened fresh
   fruit (strained if desired)

1 tablespoon fresh lemon juice
  Dark rum to taste (optional)

In a small saucepan, heat the wine and sugar and cook over moderate heat, stirring, until the sugar is dissolved. Stir the hot syrup into the fruit purée and add lemon juice and rum, if using. Chill the mixture in the refrigerator or over a bowl of ice until very cold. Freeze in an ice cream maker according to the manufacturer's directions.

Roasted Banana Ice

Originally I made this with regular fresh bananas, but my colleague Mark Gordon suggested roasting them first. We both loved the result. This creamy ice is a wonderfully refreshing finish to a spicy meal. You can try substituting coconut milk for part of the water and adding a pinch of nutmeg or cinnamon to the mix.

Makes approximately 2 quarts

2 pounds ripe bananas
1½ cups sugar
3 cups water
⅓ cup fresh orange juice

2 tablespoons fresh lime or
  lemon juice
2 tablespoons dark rum

Preheat the oven to 375 degrees. Set the whole, unpeeled bananas on a baking sheet and roast them for 15 minutes or until their skin is black and just beginning to split. Remove from the oven and, when cool enough to handle, discard the skin. You should have 2 cups of banana pulp.

While the bananas are roasting, in a medium saucepan over moderate heat, stir the sugar with the water and simmer, stirring, until the sugar is completely dissolved. Remove from the heat and cool.

In a bowl, combine the banana pulp, cooled sugar syrup, the citrus juices, and rum. Refrigerate the mixture for 2 hours or until very cold. Freeze in an ice cream maker according to the manufacturer's directions. Transfer to a storage container and place in the freezer for a few hours to allow the flavors to mellow. This ice is best served within 2 days.

Meyer Lemon Sorbet

Meyer lemons are a special fruit in the wine country. Thought to be a cross between an orange and a lemon, they have a yellow-orange flesh that is very aromatic and not as tart as that of ordinary lemons. They prefer the colder climate of the wine country to those hot subtropical areas where lemons are ordinarily grown. Most of the crop comes from backyard gardeners, although some Meyers are now being grown commercially, so they are increasingly available in markets around the country. You can use regular lemons to make this sorbet but it won't be quite the same. I'd suggest substituting one-third fresh orange juice for the regular lemon juice to better approximate the distinctive Meyer lemon taste.

Makes 1½ quarts

1 cup fresh Meyer lemon juice	1¼ cups sugar
2 tablespoons grated Meyer lemon zest	⅛ teaspoon salt
	4 cups half-and-half

In a bowl, mix all the ingredients together and pour into an ice cream maker; the cream will look curdled but will smooth out when frozen. Freeze according to the manufacturer's directions.

Allow the sorbet to soften slightly before serving.

Watermelon Granità

Traditionally, granitàs are frozen in a tray and then scraped into a glass to eat. I never found this scraping process particularly successful and have preferred using a food processor to make the final product. Be careful not to overprocess. Granitàs should have fine, delicate icy particles; they shouldn't be smooth like sorbets. They're magnificent on a hot summer day!

Serves 6

5 cups seeded and diced watermelon pulp (about a 6-pound whole melon)	¼ cup fresh lime juice
	2 teaspoons grated lime zest
⅓ cup sugar	¼ cup sweet white wine, such as Riesling

In a food processor, purée the watermelon until smooth and set aside.

In a small saucepan combine the sugar, lime juice, zest, and wine. Simmer, stirring, until the sugar dissolves. Remove from the heat, cool, and add to the puréed watermelon. Pour the mixture into ice cube trays and freeze until solid.

To serve: Place the frozen cubes in a single layer in the bowl of a food processor and pulse 9 or 10 times until very finely chopped but still frozen. Serve immediately in frozen stemmed glasses.

Peach-Mint Granità

This is a cool, sophisticated summertime dessert, even lovelier when served with some lightly sweetened sliced strawberries.
Serves 4

1 **pound ripe peaches, peeled and sliced**	⅓ **cup sugar (or to taste, depending on the sweetness of the peaches)**
2 **teaspoons chopped fresh mint**	
¾ **cup fruity white wine, such as Riesling or Gewürztraminer**	1 **tablespoon fresh lemon juice**

Place all the ingredients in a blender or food processor and process until smooth and the sugar is completely dissolved. Strain through a fine-mesh sieve and discard the pulp. Pour the mixture into ice cube trays and freeze until solid.

To serve: Place the cubes in a single layer in a food processor and pulse several times to create uniform ice particles. Repeat as necessary with the remaining cubes and serve immediately in frozen stemmed glasses.

Fresh Blackberry Ice Cream and Walnut Shortbreads

Wild blackberries grow all over the wine country, and their flavor, when ripe, is like nothing else in the world. The Walnut Shortbreads that accompany this recipe are equally good made with pecans or almonds.
Makes 1½ quarts

2   cups half-and-half
2   cups heavy cream
6   egg yolks
1¼ cups sugar
1   tablespoon grated lemon zest
4   cups ripe wild blackberries,
      puréed and strained of seeds

Walnut Shortbreads (recipe follows)
Garnish: Sliced nectarines, and tiny
   blue or purple flower petals, such
   as Johnny jump-up or bachelor's-
   button, if available (page 397)

In a saucepan, combine the half-and-half and heavy cream. Heat just to a simmer. Remove from the heat and set aside.

In a bowl, beat the egg yolks, sugar, and lemon zest together until lightly colored. Slowly beat in the hot cream mixture, being careful not to scramble the eggs. Return the mixture to the saucepan and cook over moderately low heat, stirring constantly, until the mixture thickens (180 degrees). Remove from the heat and stir in the blackberry purée. Place in an ice cream maker and freeze according to the manufacturer's instructions. Transfer to a storage container and freeze until firm.

Serve a scoop of the Blackberry Ice Cream on top of some sliced nectarines and accompany with one or two Walnut Shortbreads. Scatter the flower petals, if using.

Walnut Shortbreads

Makes 16 shortbreads

1   cup all-purpose flour
½   cup granulated sugar
½   cup (1 stick) unsalted butter, cut
      into 8 slices
1¼ cups lightly toasted walnuts or
      pecans

2   teaspoons grated orange zest
1   tablespoon coarse (pearl or
      decorator's) sugar

Preheat the oven to 350 degrees. In a food processor, combine the flour, granulated sugar, and butter. Pulse 8 to 10 times or until the mixture resembles coarse cornmeal. Be careful not to overmix. Add the nuts and orange zest and continue to pulse until the nuts are coarsely chopped.

Evenly press the mixture into the bottom of a 9-inch tart pan with a removable bottom and sprinkle with the coarse sugar. Bake for 25 to 30 minutes or until golden brown. Immediately remove the sides of the pan and cut the shortbread into 16 wedges.

Fresh Corn Ice Cream with Almond Lace Cookie Fans

This may sound a little strange but it's quite delicious. The recipe requires fresh sweet corn; frozen or canned just doesn't make it. To extract even more flavor, run the point of the knife down the center of each row of kernels before scraping them off the cob to release the milk and then scrape the cobs well to extract every bit of the sweet corn milk. I've included an optional addition of fresh chile for the adventurous. Also try the ice cream with a little toasted curry powder or ground ginger in place of the chile.

Makes 2 quarts

3 cups fresh sweet, raw corn kernels (about 2 to 3 ears), cobs reserved and broken into 3-inch lengths	½ cup light honey
4 cups half-and-half	1 teaspoon grated lemon zest
1 3-inch vanilla bean	1 teaspoon seeded and minced serrano chile (optional)
8 egg yolks	Almond Lace Cookie fans (recipe follows)
½ cup sugar	Garnish: Mint sprigs

In a blender or food processor, combine the corn and 1 cup of the half-and-half and process in short bursts to combine and purée the corn. Transfer the mixture to a large saucepan and add the remaining 3 cups half-and-half, the corn cobs, and the vanilla bean. Bring to a simmer over moderate heat for 1 to 2 minutes or until the corn is tender. Remove from the heat.

In a medium bowl, combine the egg yolks, sugar, honey, lemon zest, and chile, if using and mix well. Remove and discard the cobs from the corn-cream mixture; remove the vanilla bean, split it, and scrape the seeds into the mixture. In a slow, steady stream, whisk the hot corn-cream mixture into the egg yolk mixture.

Return the mixture to the saucepan and cook over low heat, stirring constantly, until it just begins to thicken (approximately 180 degrees). Be careful not to boil it or the mixture will curdle. Strain through a fine-meshed sieve and cool. Place in an ice cream maker and freeze according to the manufacturer's directions. If not using immediately, transfer to a storage container and place in the freezer.

Serve in chilled bowls with Almond Lace Cookie fans and mint sprigs, if desired.

Almond Lace Cookies

Makes 16 to 20 cookies

Butter and flour for the baking sheets	**½ cup (1 stick) unsalted butter or margarine, softened**
¾ cup ground almonds (do this in a food processor)	**1 tablespoon all-purpose flour**
	2 tablespoons milk
½ cup sugar	**1 teaspoon grated orange zest**

Preheat the oven to 350 degrees. Lightly butter and flour at least 2 baking sheets. In a large sauté pan, combine the remaining ingredients. Stir over low heat with a wooden spoon until the butter melts and the ingredients are well mixed. Remove from the heat.

Place heaping teaspoons of the batter about 5 inches apart. (The batter will spread during baking.) Bake for 8 to 10 minutes or until evenly browned. Remove from the oven. Using a wide spatula, remove the cookies from the baking sheet and immediately shape as desired, into tightly rolled cigarettes, or fans, or allow to cool and serve flat.

Store in airtight containers for 2 days or in the freezer for up to a month.

 Fresh Peach Ice Cream with Blueberry and Thyme Sauce

The combination of thyme and blueberries in the sauce and fresh, ripe peaches in the ice cream makes this a wonderfully aromatic dessert.

Makes 2 quarts

2 cups half-and-half	**1½ cups sugar**
2 cups heavy cream	**Blueberry-Thyme Sauce (recipe follows)**
9 egg yolks	**Garnish: Fresh thyme sprigs**
2½ cups peeled and finely chopped ripe peaches tossed with 2 tablespoons fresh lemon juice	

In a saucepan, combine the half-and-half and heavy cream. Heat just to a simmer. Remove from the heat and set aside.

In a bowl, beat the egg yolks and sugar together until light and thickened. Slowly beat in the hot cream. Return the mixture to the saucepan and cook over moderately low heat, stirring constantly, until the mixture thickens (180 degrees). Remove from the heat and stir in the chopped peaches. Place in an ice cream maker and freeze according to the manufacturer's directions. Transfer to a container and store in the freezer.

To serve, allow the ice cream to soften at room temperature for 10 to 15 minutes before scooping. Scoop into chilled bowls and spoon the Blueberry-Thyme Sauce around. Garnish with thyme sprigs.

Blueberry-Thyme Sauce

Makes 3 cups

3 cups fresh blueberries	1 2-inch piece vanilla bean
⅓ cup dry red wine	2 tablespoons honey
1 tablespoon thyme leaves (lemon thyme preferred)	1 teaspoon grated lemon zest

In a saucepan, combine all the ingredients and simmer for 4 to 5 minutes. Remove from the heat and allow to cool to room temperature. Remove the vanilla bean.

The sauce may be used as is or strained through a coarse sieve for a smoother consistency. Store, covered, in the refrigerator for up to 2 weeks. Serve warm or at room temperature.

Lemon Verbena Ice Cream

The distinct lemon taste and aroma of lemon verbena is really intriguing. Try this same ice cream substituting other lemon-scented herbs, such as lemon thyme, lemon basil, or lemon-scented geraniums (not the common garden geranium, which is inedible).

Makes 1½ quarts

1½ cups milk	6 large egg yolks
1½ cups heavy cream	⅔ cup honey
½ cup coarsely chopped fresh lemon verbena	Garnish: Finely chopped fresh lemon verbena

In a saucepan combine the milk, cream, and lemon verbena and bring to a simmer. Remove from the heat and cool.

In a bowl, beat the egg yolks and honey together until light. Whisk in the hot milk mixture and return to the saucepan. Cook over moderately low heat, stirring constantly, until the mixture begins to thicken (180 degrees). Remove from the heat and immediately strain and cool. Pour the mixture into an ice cream maker and freeze according to the manufacturer's directions. Transfer to a container and freeze until firm. Allow the ice cream to soften for a few minutes before serving. Garnish with finely chopped fresh lemon verbena.

LEMON VERBENA

A shrub native to Chile and Argentina, lemon verbena was brought to Europe by the Spanish explorers. It has a very distinctive and pungent lemon flavor and aroma. Lemon verbena is used in a variety of ways, most often as a tea, which is said to aid digestion. It's a good substitute for lemon grass in Southeast Asian dishes. It's very easy to grow and quite attractive. Lemon verbena is very sensitive to frost, so most gardeners grow it indoors in containers.

 ## *Vanilla Bean Ice Cream with Burnt Almond Caramel Sauce*

This is my favorite recipe for vanilla ice cream. Other flavorings, such as coffee or chocolate, can be added. The Burnt Almond Caramel Sauce can also be canned: Pour the hot sauce into sterilized jars and process for 15 minutes in a water bath. It makes a great gift.

Makes 2 quarts

4 cups milk	1¼ cups sugar
2 3-inch pieces of vanilla bean, split	2 cups heavy cream, whipped to
10 egg yolks	soft peaks

In a saucepan, combine the milk and vanilla beans over moderate heat until the milk just begins to simmer. In a separate bowl, beat the egg yolks with the sugar until light and thick. Slowly, in a thin stream, whisk the hot milk into the egg mixture. Return to the saucepan and heat gently over moderate heat until the mixture just begins to thicken (180 degrees).

Remove the mixture at once from the heat and strain into a bowl. Remove the vanilla beans. Cool the mixture, then pour it into an ice cream maker. Freeze according to the manufacturer's directions. When the ice cream is partially frozen, add the whipped cream and continue freezing until the ice cream is firm. Transfer the ice cream to a storage container and keep in the freezer.

Allow the ice cream to soften slightly before serving it. Scoop out into chilled bowls and pour warm Burnt Almond Caramel Sauce on top.

Burnt Almond Caramel Sauce

1 cup blanched slivered almonds	Kosher salt
5 tablespoons unsalted butter	½ cup Gewürztraminer
¾ cup dark-brown sugar	1 cup heavy cream
3 tablespoons hot water	1 tablespoon instant espresso powder
Pinch of cream of tartar	1 teaspoon pure vanilla extract

Preheat the oven to 350 degrees. Spread the almonds on a baking sheet and toast for 10 minutes or until golden; then remove them and turn off the oven. Dot the almonds with 2 tablespoons of the butter and return to the oven for another 10 minutes (the oven should remain off).

In a saucepan, combine the sugar, the remaining 3 tablespoons butter, hot water, cream of tartar, and a pinch of salt. Cook the mixture over moderate heat until a candy thermometer reads 230 degrees. Add the wine, cream, espresso powder, vanilla, and almonds very carefully, since the caramel sauce will boil up. Stir over low heat until combined and smooth. Increase the heat and simmer for 5 minutes. Remove from the heat and allow to cool. Store covered in the refrigerator. Serve warm or at room temperature.

 Frozen Orange Soufflés

This simple dessert always seems to capture people's attention. It can be made a day ahead of time, if desired.
Serves 8

8 medium oranges	2¼ cups heavy cream, whipped to
⅔ cup sugar	firm peaks
2 teaspoons grated lemon zest	6 tablespoons Grand Marnier or
6 large egg yolks	other orange-flavored liqueur
2 teaspoons minced fresh mint	Garnish: Cocoa powder

Cut one third of the top off each orange and scoop out all flesh, reserving it and any juice. Strain the flesh, firmly pressing down to extract as much juice as possible. In a saucepan, combine the juice, sugar, and lemon zest and reduce by half over high heat, stirring to help the sugar melt. Set aside and cool.

In a mixing bowl, beat the egg yolks and juice mixture together until light and thick. Carefully fold in the mint, whipped cream, and Grand Marnier.

Using a pastry bag or a spoon, pipe the mixture into the orange shells. Freeze for at least 3 hours or until the mixture is firm. Serve garnished with a dusting of cocoa powder on top.

Ginger, Fig, and Cranberry Semifreddo

Semifreddos, which translates to "half frozen" in Italian, are very easy to make and keep. This is one I like to do in the winter. You could substitute whatever dried fruits you like in the semifreddo. For the purée, use IQF (individually quick frozen) blackberries—simply thaw and purée them, strain, and flavor to taste with drops of lemon juice and honey.

Makes 1 2-quart terrine

2¾   cups heavy cream
8   egg yolks
⅔   cup sugar
¼   cup minced crystallized ginger
⅓   cup coarsely chopped dried figs
⅓   cup coarsely chopped dried
       cranberries (or cherries)

2   tablespoons grated orange
       zest
       Garnish: Fresh blackberry purée,
       mint springs, and biscotti
       (pages 363–66)

Beat the cream until stiff and set aside. In a separate bowl, beat the egg yolks until light. Gradually beat the sugar into the yolks and continue beating for several minutes until light and fluffy. Gently fold the egg and cream mixtures together. Fold in the ginger, figs, cranberries, and zest.

Line a 2-quart terrine with plastic wrap and fill with the mixture. Cover the top with plastic and freeze for at least 6 hours or overnight.

To serve, unmold the semifreddo, cut it into slices, and surround each serving with fresh blackberry purée, mint sprigs, and a few biscotti.

BREADS, SPREADS, AND OTHER BAKED GOODS

In many of the bread recipes following, I call for the use of a mixer. I find that a good, heavy-duty mixer, such as that made by Hobart, to be one of the "indispensable" pieces of equipment in my kitchen (*no*, I don't own any Hobart stock!). Though expensive, they last a lifetime and are ideal for mixing and kneading yeast doughs. If you don't have a mixer, you can also make any of the breads entirely by hand. The mixing and kneading will take longer to get to the satiny-feeling and -looking dough described in the recipes.

Focaccia

There is really no difference between focaccia and pizza. Carol Field, in her wonderful book *The Italian Baker*, points out that "both are flat round breads seasoned with oil and cooked in the oven or over embers and are called *pizza* in the south and *focaccia* in the north."

Here are two of my favorite focaccia recipes; here I've made them rectangles.

Basic Focaccia

Makes 1 12- by 17-inch focaccia

1	**tablespoon plus ½ teaspoon active dry yeast**
1½	**cups warm water (100 degrees)**
½	**cup fruity olive oil**
3¾	**cups unbleached all-purpose flour**
2½	**teaspoons salt**

1–2 **tablespoons fresh herbs (optional)**
Optional toppings: Thinly sliced red onions, seeded slivered tomatoes, grated cheese

In a large bowl, stir the yeast into the warm water and let stand approximately 10 minutes. Stir in ¼ cup oil, then the flour, salt, and herbs, if desired. Turn the dough out onto a lightly floured surface and knead until smooth and elastic, 8 to 10 minutes.

Lightly oil a large clean bowl and add the dough, turning to coat it. Cover the bowl tightly with plastic wrap and let the dough rise until doubled, 1 to 1½ hours.

Lightly oil a 12- by 17-inch jellyroll pan. Flatten and stretch the dough to cover as much of the pan as possible, then dimple the top quite vigorously with your fingertips to stretch it some more. Cover with a towel and let it relax 10 minutes.

Dimple and stretch the dough again to completely cover the pan. Cover with a towel and let it rest another 30 minutes. Preheat the oven to 425 degrees.

Brush the dough with the remaining ¼ cup olive oil and bake on the upper rack until it just starts to turn golden, 12 to 15 minutes. Scatter whatever toppings you desire over the top and continue to bake until golden brown, approximately 10 to 15 minutes longer. If desired, remove the focaccia from the pan at this point and finish cooking it directly on the oven shelf for a crisp bottom crust.

Onion, Sun-Dried Tomato, and Oregano Focaccia

This is a delicious bread in which you can substitute or add to any of the flavorings, such as rosemary for the oregano. The dough can even be made a day ahead and kept covered with plastic in the refrigerator until you're ready to bake it—just be sure to let the dough come to room temperature before baking.

Makes 1 12- by 17-inch focaccia

1   package (2½ teaspoons) active dry yeast
2   teaspoons honey
1½ cups warm water (100 degrees)
4–5 cups unbleached all-purpose flour
1½ teaspoons sea salt
5   tablespoons extra-virgin olive oil

¼   cup drained, minced sun-dried tomatoes packed in oil
2   tablespoons chopped fresh oregano (or 2 teaspoons dried)
½   cup very thinly sliced red onion
1   tablespoon kosher salt
    Optional topping: ¾ cup finely slivered olives, such as Niçoise or Sicilian green

In the bowl of a electric mixer fitted with a dough hook, or by hand as on page 350, stir together the yeast, honey, and water and allow the mixture to sit for 10 minutes or until foamy. Stir in 4 cups of the flour, the sea salt, and 2 tablespoons of the olive oil and knead until the dough is well combined. Scrape down the sides of the bowl and hook occasionally to make sure the dough is smooth. You may need to add up to an additional cup of flour in order to form a soft, slightly sticky dough.

Lightly oil a large clean bowl with 1 tablespoon of the olive oil and add the dough, turning to coat it. Cover loosely and let it rise undisturbed in a warm place for 1 to 2 hours or until doubled in bulk. Punch down and knead in the sun-dried tomato and oregano.

Oil a 12- by 17-inch jellyroll pan well and lightly oil your hands. Press the dough into the pan. Cover loosely and allow to rise in a warm place for 40 minutes.

Preheat the oven to 425 degrees. Dimple the dough all over with the tips of your fingers and gently brush the remaining 2 tablespoons olive oil over it. Top with onion, kosher salt, and olives if using and bake on the upper rack of the oven for 25 to 30 minutes or until the focaccia is golden brown and cooked through. Remove and cool on a rack for a few minutes. Cut the focaccia into squares and serve warm or at room temperature.

Grilled Flat Bread

This is fun to do right after you've grilled vegetables or meats. You could also add tomatoes, cheese, and herbs after the first turn and have a savory, smoky pizza that is as good as or better than anything done in an oven. Grilled flat breads are also an ideal base for smoked or cured salmon (page 151) with a sprinkling of sweet red onions and a dollop of sour cream or crème fraîche.

Makes 6 8- to 10-inch rounds

2½	cups warm water (100 degrees)	3½–4½	cups all-purpose flour
1	package (2½ teaspoons) active dry yeast	1½	cups mixed chopped fresh herbs, such as basil, parsley, chives, and savory, or a mixture of your choice
1	teaspoon honey		
1½	cups whole-wheat flour		Kosher salt
2	teaspoons salt		
1	cup or so extra-virgin olive oil		

Make a "sponge" by mixing the warm water, yeast, and honey together in a bowl and letting it stand until the mixture is foamy, about 10 minutes. Stir in the whole-wheat flour, cover with plastic wrap, and let the sponge stand at room temperature for 4 hours or overnight.

Put the sponge in the bowl of an electric mixer fitted with a dough hook and add the salt, 2 tablespoons of the olive oil, and 3½ cups of the all-purpose flour and beat for 3 to 5 minutes or until the dough is smooth. The dough should be soft but not sticky. Beat in additional flour ¼ cup at a time until the dough feels right. You may also do this by hand using a wooden spoon or spatula.

Oil a clean bowl and add the dough, turning to coat it. Cover the bowl loosely and allow the dough to rise in a warm place until doubled, 1 to 2 hours. (It can be chilled overnight at this point.) Punch the dough down and divide into 6 equal balls.

Working with one piece of dough at a time, keeping the other pieces covered, roll it out on a lightly floured board into a round 8 to 10 inches in diameter. Brush with approximately 2 tablespoons olive oil, sprinkle with 2 tablespoons chopped herbs, and gently press them in. Turn the bread over and similarly coat with olive oil and herbs. Sprinkle kosher salt over both sides to taste. Set aside and shape and season the remaining balls.

Allow the dough to rest for 15 to 20 minutes before grilling. Lightly oil the grill with additional olive oil. Grill the breads on both sides over medium coals until cooked through and a light speckled brown on top. Cooking time will be approximately 6 to 8 minutes total.

Serve the breads warm or at room temperature.

 # Garden Herb and Cheese Bread

This is a bread for taking advantage of the herbs in the summer garden. It's delicious as a sandwich bread and is also nice grilled for bruschetta. (The dough is also wonderful made into individual rolls.) You can certainly follow this recipe to the letter, but if you have an interest in exploring the subtleties of bread baking, you can try a slow-rise method by placing the dough in the refrigerator overnight before forming it into loaves. The slow rise intensifies the flavor of the herbs and, I think, gives the bread a better texture.

Makes 3 loaves

3 tablespoons active dry yeast	1½ tablespoons salt
3 cups warm water (110 degrees)	2 teaspoons freshly ground black pepper
9 cups unbleached all-purpose flour	3 tablespoons coarse cornmeal
4 tablespoons olive oil	1 large egg, beaten with 1 tablespoon water
½ cup mixed fresh herbs, such as chives, tarragon, and basil	
1⅓ cups coarsely grated cheese, such as Asiago, fontina, or Gruyère	

Place the yeast and water in the bowl of an electric mixer fitted with the paddle and stir. Mix in 2 cups of the flour and let sit undisturbed until bubbly, approximately 15 minutes. This may be done in a large mixing bowl as well.

Add 3 tablespoons of the olive oil, the herbs, cheese, salt, and pepper, and the remaining flour 1 cup at a time with the machine running. Continue adding flour until the dough pulls away from the sides of the bowl. Depending on the flour and humidity, more or less flour may be needed.

Using a dough hook or by hand, knead the bread for 4 to 5 minutes until the dough is satiny and smooth. Coat a clean bowl with the remaining 1 tablespoon olive oil and add the dough, turning to coat. Cover with a damp towel or plastic wrap and let the dough rise in a warm spot until doubled, 1 to 1½ hours. Punch down, knead briefly, and form into 3 individual loaves.

Preheat the oven to 375 degrees. Place the loaves on a baking sheet that has been lightly coated with cornmeal. Cover lightly and let the loaves rise until doubled, about 30 minutes. Carefully paint the top of the loaves with the egg wash and bake in the lower third of the oven for 30 to 35 minutes or until the loaves are golden brown and the bottoms sound hollow when thumped. Place the loaves on racks and allow to cool before slicing.

 # Winter Squash Bread

If you're going to make the Garden Herb and Cheese Bread in the summer, here's a bread to make in the winter. It really is worth the little bit of extra effort to use freshly baked squash or pumpkin instead of canned. A general bread note: I know it's hard not to cut into freshly baked bread right out of the oven, but you should always allow bread to cool thoroughly; it's still cooking internally from its own heat and needs to finish. It will taste better and last longer if you can resist.

Makes 2 10-inch round (country) loaves or 20 to 22 small rolls

1	package (2½ teaspoons) active dry yeast	1	cup winter squash or pumpkin purée, canned or homemade (see note)
¼	cup light-brown sugar	1	tablespoon salt
1½	cups warm water (100 degrees)	½	cup yellow cornmeal
2	eggs	5½–6	cups unbleached all-purpose flour

Sprinkle the yeast and a pinch of brown sugar over the water in a large bowl. Stir to combine and let stand until foamy, approximately 10 minutes.

With a whisk, beat the eggs and squash purée into the yeast mixture. Add the remaining brown sugar, salt, cornmeal, and 2 cups of the flour. Beat hard with a whisk until smooth, approximately 3 minutes. Add the flour ½ cup at a time and beat with a wooden spoon until a soft dough is formed.

Turn the dough out onto a lightly floured surface and knead vigorously for about 5 minutes to create a soft, smooth, and elastic dough. Add enough flour for the dough to hold its own shape. Grease a clean bowl and add the dough, turning to coat. Cover with plastic wrap and let the dough rise at room temperature until doubled, 1 to 1½ hours.

Preheat the oven to 450 degrees. Lightly grease a baking sheet or line with parchment. Sprinkle the baking sheet or parchment with cornmeal. Gently deflate the dough and turn out onto a lightly floured surface. Form the dough into 2 large country loaves and place these on the prepared baking sheet. Cover the loaves loosely with plastic wrap and let them rise for 30 minutes, or until doubled. If available, heat a baking stone in the oven while the loaves are rising. Dust the tops of the loaves with flour.

Slash the loaves decoratively with a serrated knife, then slide them onto the stone, if using. Place the loaves on the middle rack in the 450-degree oven, then immediately reduce the temperature to 375 degrees and bake 45 to 50 minutes or until the loaves are lightly browned. Remove and cool on a rack before serving.

Note: *To make squash purée:* Pumpkin or any kind of squash, such as delicata, acorn, butternut, or Hubbard, can be used. Wash the squash, cut in half, and scoop out and discard the seeds. Place the squash in a baking dish, flesh down, with a little water. Bake at 350 degrees for 1 to 1½ hours, or until tender. Drain, cool, and scoop out the flesh. Purée the flesh until smooth in a blender or food processor.

 Brioche

Buttery brioche is one of life's great pleasures. It can be shaped into familiar rolls with a topknot or baked in a loaf pan. It's delicious toasted and is the basis for the very best bread puddings. For a savory treat, try baking brioche rolls with a little square of creamy goat cheese or Camembert placed in the center of the dough. Brioche also makes the most wonderful toast to eat as is or to use as the base of a simple winter dish of creamed mushrooms and leeks. My grandmother used to do a variation of this by adding sliced hard-boiled eggs and a little sherry to the cream sauce.

Makes 2 medium loaves or approximately 20 rolls

¾ **cup milk**	2 **teaspoons salt (omit if using**
¼ **cup sugar**	**salted butter)**
3 **packages (2½ teaspoons** *each*)	4–5 **cups unbleached all-purpose**
active dry yeast	**flour**
6 **whole eggs plus 3 egg yolks at**	½ **pound unsalted butter, very soft**
room temperature, lightly	1 **egg beaten with 1 tablespoon**
beaten	**milk**

In a saucepan, heat the milk and sugar, stirring, so that it is just warm to the touch (120 degrees). Pour the liquid into a mixing bowl and sprinkle the yeast on top. Stir briefly to dissolve and let the mixture sit for 5 to 10 minutes until it begins to foam. Add the beaten eggs, salt if using, and 3 cups of the flour to the bowl and beat until the mixture is smooth. This is most easily done with the paddle blade in an electric mixer, but may be done by hand with a wooden spatula or spoon. Add the butter a tablespoon or two at a time and beat into the dough. Add the remaining flour ½ cup at a time, beating continuously until the dough is shiny and no longer sticky, about 5 minutes. Transfer the dough to a large, lightly oiled bowl, and turn to coat it. Cover the bowl with a towel and let the dough rise until doubled, about 1 hour. Punch down and knead briefly. Divide the dough among buttered loaf pans or other molds. Let it rise until doubled, approximately 1 hour.

Preheat the oven to 400 degrees. Brush the tops of the brioche with the beaten egg-milk glaze. Bake on the center rack for approximately 25 minutes for loaves and 12 to 14 minutes for rolls. Check periodically—the brioche should be a rich golden brown and firm to the touch. Remove from the oven and cool slightly before turning out from the pan.

Biscuits

While bread baking has become a high art, we forget how easy and tasty good biscuits can be. Here are four of my favorite biscuits to enjoy with any meal.

The secret of producing light, delicate biscuits is to work or knead the dough as little as possible. Mix just enough to combine the ingredients. They can and should look a little "lumpy" before baking. The one exception is when you use whole-wheat flour, as in the Parmesan-Tomato Biscuits. Here you need to knead a little more, just enough to make a smooth dough.

 Potato Biscuits

Makes approximately 20 biscuits

½ pound (¾ cup) peeled, cooked, and mashed waxy or boiling potatoes	1 teaspoon salt (omit if using salted butter)
¼ cup (½ stick) unsalted butter, melted	1 teaspoon sugar
1⅓ cups flour	2 tablespoons chopped fresh chives
1 tablespoon baking powder	⅓ cup buttermilk
1 teaspoon baking soda	1 egg white beaten with 1 tablespoon water

Preheat the oven to 425 degrees. In a large bowl, mix the potato and butter together until combined. Sift the flour, baking powder, baking soda, salt, and sugar into the bowl along with the chives and scoop and lift until well combined. The objective is to keep the mixture light and crumbly and not turn it into a paste.

Add the buttermilk and stir until the dough just comes together. Roll out on a lightly floured surface to form a cake about ½ inch thick. With a 2-inch cutter, cut out rounds of dough and transfer to an ungreased baking sheet. Gather up scraps and reroll the dough, then cut out more rounds, utilizing all the dough.

Brush the tops lightly with egg white wash and bake in the middle of the oven for 15 minutes or until the biscuits are puffed and golden. Serve warm or at room temperature.

 Herb Drop Biscuits

Makes approximately 16 biscuits

1½ cups unbleached all-purpose flour	2 eggs, lightly beaten
4 teaspoons baking powder	1 tablespoon *each* chopped fresh chives, basil, and savory or any
1 teaspoon sugar	combination equaling
½ teaspoon salt	3 tablespoons
1 cup heavy cream, whipped to hold soft peaks	

Preheat the oven to 425 degrees. Sift the flour, baking powder, sugar, and salt together in a bowl. Fold the cream, eggs, and herbs carefully into the flour mixture until just combined.

Drop by heaping tablespoons onto an ungreased baking sheet, 3 to 4 inches apart. Bake in the middle of the oven for 12 to 15 minutes or until lightly browned. Serve warm.

Poppy Seed–Buttermilk Biscuits

Makes approximately 20 biscuits

2 cups unbleached all-purpose flour	⅓ cup (5⅓ tablespoons) chilled butter, cut into tiny bits
2½ teaspoons baking powder	⅔ cup buttermilk
1½ teaspoons sugar	2 tablespoons melted butter
1 teaspoon salt (omit if using salted butter)	¼ cup poppy seed
	1 tablespoon kosher salt (optional)

Preheat the oven to 450 degrees. Sift the flour, baking powder, sugar, and regular salt together in a bowl. Add the butter and blend quickly with a fork (or in a food processor) until it resembles coarse cornmeal. Add the buttermilk and mix and knead until the dough just comes together, 20 to 30 seconds.

On a lightly floured surface, roll out the dough ½ inch thick and cut out rounds with a 2-inch cutter. Reroll the scraps and cut the remaining dough, utilizing all the dough. Place the biscuits on an ungreased baking sheet and brush the tops with the melted butter. Generously top with poppy seed and kosher salt if using. Bake the biscuits in the middle of the oven for 12 to 15 minutes or until puffed and golden. Serve warm.

Parmesan-Tomato Biscuits

Makes 12 to 14 biscuits

1 cup unbleached all-purpose flour	⅔ cup tomato juice (preferably fresh)
1 cup whole-wheat flour	2 tablespoons finely minced sun-dried tomato (optional)
1 tablespoon baking powder	½ cup (1 stick) unsalted butter, melted
1 teaspoon salt	
¼ cup freshly grated Parmesan cheese	
1 teaspoon *each* minced fresh oregano and basil	

Preheat the oven to 450 degrees. Sift the flours, baking powder, and salt together in a bowl. Stir in the Parmesan, herbs, tomato juice, sun-dried tomato, and all but 2 tablespoons of the melted butter; mix until the dough comes together.

On a lightly floured board, knead the dough briefly to make a fairly smooth dough. Roll out the dough ½ inch thick and cut out rounds with a 2-inch cutter. Gather scraps and reroll, utilizing all the dough.

Place the dough rounds on an ungreased baking sheet and brush the tops with the remaining 2 tablespoons melted butter. Bake in the upper third of the oven for 10 to 12 minutes or until the biscuits are puffed and lightly browned. Serve warm.

BAKING POWDER AND SODA

There are two ways of leavening, or causing doughs or batters to rise during baking. We can use natural dry yeast, but it will work only in doughs in which the gluten has been kneaded and developed and made elastic enough to capture the bubbles of carbon dioxide the yeast slowly releases, akin to a balloon bumping up to the ceiling.

The other way is to use chemical leaveners, such as baking powder or soda, which release carbon dioxide much more quickly. Both work as a result of the action between two opposing forces—acid and alkaline. The alkaline component is almost always baking soda, or sodium bicarbonate. (Potassium bicarbonate is available for those on severely sodium-restricted diets, but it tends to absorb moisture readily, it reacts prematurely, and it sometimes has a bitter taste.)

You can use baking soda alone if the dough or batter has enough acid in it from other ingredients, such as yogurt or sour milk, which contains lactic acid. (Sweet milk can be soured by adding 2 teaspoons of lemon juice or vinegar to each cup of milk.)

Commercial baking powders contain both the alkaline soda and an acid, usually sodium aluminum sulfate or phosphate, and often some inert starch to absorb moisture from the air and prevent premature reaction. This produces "double-acting" powder, which means that some carbon dioxide is produced when the powder is mixed with a liquid in a batter and then a second charge of gas occurs in response to the heat of the oven.

Aluminum-based ingredients are of concern to some people; in response, commercial baking powders have become available that use monosodium phosphates instead of aluminum. Rumford is the best-known brand in the United States.

You can make a perfectly acceptable nonaluminum "simple-acting" baking powder at home by mixing ¼ teaspoon baking soda with ½ teaspoon cream of tartar. This is equivalent to 1 teaspoon baking powder in a recipe. My grand-mother always made her own because she felt commercial baking powders had a "chemical" taste.

Favorite Corn Muffins

I love corn muffins of all kinds and here are two of my favorites, which are a little different from the standard.

 ## *Sage-Corn Muffins*

This recipe works best with fresh sage and corn, but it's also good with dried sage and frozen corn. Try other fresh herbs, such as savory, oregano, and rosemary, in place of the sage—and add more chiles if you like!

Makes 12 muffins

1½ cups unbleached all-purpose flour	2 eggs, beaten
⅔ cup yellow cornmeal	1 cup buttermilk
1½ tablespoons sugar	1 tablespoon minced fresh sage
1 tablespoon baking powder	(1 teaspoon dried)
½ teaspoon baking soda	1 cup fresh, sweet raw corn kernels
1 teaspoon salt	1 teaspoon seeded and minced
¼ cup (½ stick) unsalted butter	serrano chile (optional)
¼ cup minced scallions, both white and pale-green parts	

Preheat the oven to 375 degrees. Lightly grease a muffin pan. Sift the flour, cornmeal, sugar, baking powder, baking soda, and salt together in a bowl. In a small sauté pan, melt the butter and sauté the scallions slowly until softened but not browned and add to the flour mixture. Add the eggs, buttermilk, sage, corn, and optional chile and stir just to combine.

Divide the batter among 12 muffin cups (fill two thirds full) and bake on the middle rack for 25 to 30 minutes or until the muffins are puffed and golden. Serve warm.

Crab-Corn Muffins

We tend to get carried away in California about Dungeness crab. It's sweet and meaty, and I think it's the best-tasting crab there is (although I get lots of arguments from crab lovers in other parts of the country). Use whatever crab is available to you.

A salad of savory greens and these hearty muffins make a perfect summer meal for me. You could also make mini Crab-Corn Muffins, split them, and layer them with some thinly sliced cucumbers, sweet red onion, and smoked salmon for a dynamite hors d'oeuvre or first course.

Makes 10 muffins

1 cup unbleached all-purpose flour	1 large egg, beaten
1 cup yellow cornmeal	1 cup buttermilk
1 teaspoon sugar	¼ cup chopped chives or scallions, both white and pale-green parts
2 teaspoons baking powder	
1 teaspoon baking soda	
½ teaspoon salt	2 tablespoons chopped fresh parsley
¼ cup (½ stick) unsalted butter	
½ cup finely diced yellow onion	1 cup Dungeness crabmeat, shredded and picked over to remove any shell
¼ cup finely diced red bell pepper	
2 tablespoons finely diced Anaheim chile peppers (optional)	

Preheat the oven to 375 degrees. Butter a muffin pan well. Sift the flour, cornmeal, sugar, baking powder, baking soda, and salt together in a bowl and set aside.

In a small sauté pan, melt the butter and sauté the onion and the pepper until soft but not brown. Cool and add to the flour mixture. Add the egg, buttermilk, chives, parsley, and crab and stir just to combine.

Divide the batter among 10 muffin cups (fill two thirds full) and bake on the middle rack for 25 to 30 minutes or until the muffins are puffed and browned. Serve warm or at room temperature.

Flour Tortillas

While flour tortillas are generally available in supermarkets, fresh homemade tortillas are demonstrably better and worth making. Traditionally, the fat used in tortilla making is lard and although we've called for vegetable shortening here, you might try substituting part lard for some of the shortening to get a sense of the authentic flavor. A detailed discussion of tortilla making can be found in Rick Bayless's wonderful book *Authentic Mexican*.

Makes 16 8-inch tortillas

3 cups unbleached all-purpose flour	⅓ cup solid vegetable shortening, chilled
2 teaspoons salt	1 cup or so warm water (120 degrees)
2 teaspoons baking powder	

In a food processor, combine the flour, salt, and baking powder. Add the shortening and process in short bursts until the mixture resembles coarse cornmeal. Add the water in a steady stream and process until the dough just comes together. Turn out onto a lightly floured surface and knead for 4 to 5 minutes or until the dough is smooth and silky.

Divide the dough in 4 equal pieces and then divide each of those into 4, forming them into balls. Shape each ball into a flat, round circle, pulling the dough from the center to form a somewhat thick mushroom cap shape about 3 inches in diameter. Cover both balls and rounds with a damp towel to keep them from drying out. After all the balls are shaped into rounds, let them rest covered for 15 minutes.

On a lightly floured surface, roll out each round about ¹⁄₁₆ inch thick and 8 inches in diameter. Repeat with the remaining dough, keeping the tortillas covered with the damp towel.

To cook: Heat an ungreased griddle or cast-iron skillet over moderately high heat until a drop of water "sizzles" on contact. Cook a tortilla until one side is a lightly speckled brown and small bubbles appear on top, about 30 seconds. Turn and cook the other side until speckled. Place on a plate to cool and cook the remaining tortillas. Wrap in a dry towel and serve.

To heat: Wrap the tortillas in aluminum foil and place in a 325-degree oven for 4 minutes. Tortillas can be frozen but are best eaten soon after being made.

Cream Cheese Straws

I love these very simple little straws as an appetizer all by themselves or served alongside a savory salad or antipasto plate of cold meats. The addition of fresh chopped herbs, such as chives and/or tarragon, to the dough is a tasty variation.
Makes about 4 dozen straws

1 cup (2 sticks) unsalted butter, softened	⅓ cup heavy cream
1 cup cream cheese (natural, without emulsifiers and thickeners, preferred), softened	2½ cups unbleached all-purpose flour
⅓ cup grated Parmesan cheese	1½ teaspoons salt (or to taste)
	⅛ teaspoon cayenne pepper (or to taste)

In a mixer bowl combine the butter and cheeses and cream until smooth. Beat in the cream and then gradually beat in the flour, salt, and pepper. Gather up the dough, dust it lightly with flour, and wrap in plastic, then refrigerate for at least 2 hours.

Preheat the oven to 350 degrees. Roll out the dough to ⅓-inch thickness and cut it into pencil-thin strips approximately 4 inches long. Place them on ungreased baking sheets and bake in the middle of the oven for 10 to 12 minutes or until very lightly browned. Cool and store airtight for up to 5 days.

Poppy Seed Straws

Beat ¾ cup poppy seed into the dough along with the flour and proceed as above.

Salt Straws

Roll and cut the dough as directed above. Beat 1 large egg yolk with 2 teaspoons milk and brush the straws with the mixture. Carefully roll the straws in an equal mixture of kosher salt and caraway seed and bake as above.

Biscotti

Biscotti are a rather ancient cookie, or cracker. In Italy, where they originated, they were a staple of sailors or travelers who went to sea for months at a time. As their name indicates, they are twice baked, *"bis cotto,"* to make them very dry, so they'll last a long time and not mold or otherwise deteriorate.

Because they are crisp and crunchy, they are ideal with fresh fruits and ice creams. I also love (as the Italians do) dunking them in good coffee or a tumbler of young, robust red wine.

 ## Hazelnut Biscotti

Makes about 24 biscotti

1 cup hazelnuts, lightly toasted and skinned	3 large eggs
1 cup sugar	3 cups unbleached all-purpose flour
½ cup (1 stick) unsalted butter, melted	2 teaspoons baking powder
4 tablespoons hazelnut liqueur or brandy	¼ teaspoon salt

Preheat the oven to 350 degrees. Coarsely chop the hazelnuts. In a bowl, combine the nuts, sugar, butter, liqueur, and eggs and mix well.

Stir in the flour, baking powder, and salt. Turn the dough out onto a floured surface and knead briefly; then form into a long loaf about 2 inches wide. Place the loaf on a parchment-lined or lightly oiled cookie sheet and bake in the middle of the oven for 25 minutes or until firm. The loaf will have a cakelike texture. Remove from the oven and cool.

Cut the loaf diagonally into ½-inch slices and lay these out on a cookie sheet. Bake for 20 minutes more, turning them once until both sides are lightly browned and toasted. Cool and store in an airtight container.

Almond-Orange Biscotti

Makes about 36 biscotti

3 large eggs, separated	2 tablespoons Grand Marnier or other orange-flavored liqueur
1½ cups sugar	
⅓ cup (5⅓ tablespoons) butter, melted and cooled	2 tablespoons chopped candied orange peel or 3 tablespoons finely grated orange zest
1 cup lightly toasted and coarsely chopped almonds	3½ cups unbleached all-purpose flour
	1½ teaspoons baking powder

Preheat the oven to 325 degrees. Butter a baking sheet or line it with parchment. In a large bowl, beat the egg yolks with ¾ cup of the sugar until light and the sugar is dissolved. Stir in the melted butter, almonds, Grand Marnier, and orange peel. In a separate bowl, beat the egg whites until they just begin to form peaks and gradually beat in the remaining ¾ cup sugar until the whites form stiff peaks.

Sift the flour and baking powder together. Fold one third of the flour into the yolks; then fold one third of the egg whites in. Repeat, alternating, until well combined. The dough will be firm and slightly sticky. If the dough is too soft, add more flour. With floured hands, divide the dough into two logs approximately 1½ inches wide. Arrange the logs on the prepared baking sheet and bake for 20 to 25 minutes or until they are lightly brown and firm to the touch. Remove from the oven and set the baking sheet on a rack for 10 minutes. On a cutting board, cut the logs on the diagonal into slices ½ inch wide. Return the slices to the baking sheet and bake for 5 to 7 minutes on each side or until the biscotti are very lightly browned and crisp. Cool on racks and store airtight.

Chocolate-Mint Biscotti

- Omit almonds, Grand Marnier, and orange peel.
- Add 6 ounces bittersweet chocolate melted with 1 tablespoon cocoa.
- Add 4 tablespoons finely chopped fresh mint.

Rosemary-Walnut Biscotti

- Substitute lightly toasted and coarsely chopped walnuts for the almonds.
- Omit the Grand Marnier and orange peel.

- Add 1 teaspoon vanilla extract.
- Add 2 tablespoons finely chopped fresh rosemary.

Almond-Raisin Biscotti

- Add ½ cup golden raisins that have been plumped in ⅔ cup fruity white wine, such as Riesling or Gewürztraminer. Drain them first.
- Omit the Grand Marnier.

Whole-Wheat and Pear Biscotti

This recipe is one of Carol Field's that I've come to like a lot. She is an extraordinary baker and I can't recommend her books highly enough.

Makes about 32 biscotti

1 cup whole-wheat flour	3 large eggs
1½ cups unbleached all-purpose flour	2 tablespoons dry red wine
1 cup sugar	1 cup coarsely chopped store-bought dried pears
1 teaspoon baking soda	1 cup lightly toasted and coarsely chopped walnuts
¼ teaspoon salt	
½ teaspoon cinnamon	

Preheat the oven to 325 degrees. Lightly oil a baking sheet or line it with parchment. In the bowl of an electric mixer fitted with the paddle or in a large mixing bowl with a wooden spoon, beat the flours, sugar, soda, salt, cinnamon, eggs, and wine together until a smooth dough is formed. Stir in the pears and walnuts. Turn the dough out onto a lightly floured board and knead it briefly.

With floured hands, divide the dough in half and form into logs approximately 2 inches in diameter. Place these on the prepared baking sheet and bake for 25 to 30 minutes or until the logs are lightly browned and firm to the touch. Cool on the pan on a rack for 10 minutes and then cut the logs crosswise on the diagonal into ¾-inch slices.

Lay the biscotti on the baking sheet and bake them for 5 minutes on each side or until they are very lightly browned. Cool the biscotti on racks and store airtight.

Spreads for Breads

 Herb Butter

This is really more a method than a hard-and-fast recipe. We use it often at Valley Oaks, and I think we get more recipe requests for this than for anything else! Petra Arguelles, one of the cooks at Valley Oaks, has a great gift for putting together delicious combinations.

For each pound of good butter (we generally use Plugra brand) mix in:

- 1 cup or so minced shallots or scallions (both white and pale-green parts) that have been slowly sautéed in butter and a splash of white wine until very soft but not brown;
- 3 tablespoons or so small edible flower petals, such as Bachelor's-button, calendula, and/or herb flowers;
- ⅓ cup or so chopped tender, young herbs, such as chives, tarragon, dill, parsley, or a combination;
- salt and freshly ground white pepper.

We make up a lot of this butter in the spring, when the herbs are tender and fresh, and then roll it into logs, wrap them in aluminum foil, and freeze for later use.

To serve: Cut the butter into thick rounds and place on a butter plate on top of a nasturtium leaf or grape leaf if you'd like.

Black Bean Spread

Makes about 2½ cups

1 cup dried black beans	1 tablespoon olive oil
1 pound red onions, chopped	2 tablespoons tomato paste
2 tablespoons minced garlic	1 teaspoon adobo sauce from
1½ teaspoons seeded and minced	chipotle in adobo
serrano chiles	1 tablespoon sherry vinegar
½ teaspoon fennel seed, crushed	1½ tablespoons minced fresh
½ teaspoon ground cumin	cilantro
½ teaspoon ground cinnamon	Kosher salt and drops of Tabasco

Sort the beans, rinse them well, and soak overnight in lots of cold water. Change the water several times if possible. Cover with fresh water and cook over moderate heat until very tender, about 1 hour. While the beans are cooking, slowly sauté the onions, garlic, serranos, fennel seed, cumin, and cinnamon in the olive oil in a covered pot until very tender, about 10 minutes. Purée the onion mixture.

Drain and mash the beans or purée them in a food processor until very smooth, adding a tablespoon or two of cooking liquid if necessary. (For a very smooth spread, press the mixture through a strainer to remove bean skins.) Combine the beans and the onion purée. Stir in the tomato paste, adobo sauce, sherry vinegar, and cilantro. Season to taste with salt and drops of Tabasco. Store covered in the refrigerator up to 10 days.

Curried Red Lentil Spread

This simple spread was concocted by Jim Rhodes. Add more or less chile as your taste dictates.

Makes about 2 cups

1 tablespoon minced shallots	1 teaspoon black mustard seeds
2 teaspoons minced garlic	½ teaspoon seeded and minced
1 teaspoon curry powder	serrano chile

4 tablespoons extra-virgin olive oil
2 cups cooked red lentils, liquid
     reserved

¼ cup chopped fresh cilantro
     Kosher salt and freshly ground
       black pepper

Sauté the shallots, garlic, curry powder, mustard seeds, and serrano in 2 table-spoons of the olive oil over moderate heat until fragrant and the shallots are softened, about 3 minutes. Scrape into a food processor along with the lentils, cilantro, the remaining olive oil, and enough cooking liquid to make a spreadable mixture. Season to taste with salt and pepper. Store covered in the refrigerator for up to 3 days.

White Bean and Olive Spread

Makes about 2½ cups

1 cup dried Great Northern or
     navy beans
1 pound yellow onions, chopped
2 teaspoons roasted garlic
     (page 247)
1 tablespoon olive oil
1½ tablespoons minced Kalamata or
     other dry-cured olives
1½ tablespoons minced, drained
     sun-dried tomatoes in oil

2 teaspoons minced fresh tarragon
1 tablespoon minced fresh chives
1 teaspoon white-wine
     Worcestershire
1 teaspoon grated lemon zest
1 teaspoon drained and minced
     capers
     Drops of lemon juice
     Salt and freshly ground white
       pepper

Sort the beans, rinse them well, and soak overnight in lots of cold water, chang-ing it several times if possible. Cover with fresh water and cook over moderate heat until very tender. While the beans are cooking, slowly sauté the onions and garlic in the olive oil in a covered pot until very tender. Do not let the onions brown. Purée the onion mixture. Drain and mash the beans or purée them in a food proces-sor until very smooth, adding a tablespoon or two of cooking liquid if necessary. (For a very smooth spread, press through a strainer to remove the bean skins.)

Combine the mashed beans and the onion purée. Stir in the olives, sun-dried tomatoes, tarragon, chives, Worcestershire, lemon zest, and capers. Season to taste with lemon juice, salt, and pepper. Store covered in the refrigerator up to 5 days. Best served warm or at room temperature.

Eggplant–Roasted Garlic Spread

Makes 2 cups

1 large eggplant, approximately
   3 pounds
2 tablespoons olive oil
   Kosher salt and freshly ground
   black pepper

2 tablespoons roasted garlic
   (page 247)
2 tablespoons sherry vinegar
1½ cups loosely packed basil leaves,
   chopped

Preheat the oven to 400 degrees. Cut the eggplant into 1-inch slices. Brush lightly with olive oil and sprinkle with salt and pepper. Roast until brown and soft, approximately 20 minutes.

When cool, chop the eggplant coarsely. In a food processor, combine the eggplant with the remaining ingredients and process until smooth. Season to taste with salt and pepper.

This spread can be stored refrigerated for up to 1 week.

DRINKS

Apple–Rose Hip Iced Tea

Rose hips are available at health food stores and are very rich in vitamin C. They also add a rosy hue to the drink.

Makes 2 drinks

½ cup apple juice or white grape juice
2 teaspoons dried rose hips (or 4 rose hip or hibiscus tea bags)
Finely crushed ice

¼ cup ginger ale
1 teaspoon fresh lemon juice
Garnish: Mint sprig and slice of your favorite apple

Heat the apple juice and rose hips and simmer for 3 minutes. Remove from the heat and allow to cool. Strain and chill.

Fill a tall glass half full of crushed ice and pour in the juice mixture, ginger ale, and lemon juice. Garnish with an apple slice and mint.

Fire and Ice

This is an amusing takeoff from the Fire and Ice Melon with Figs salad on page 9. I often garnish this drink with a spear or two of fresh melon.

Serves 6 to 8

⅔ cup sugar
½ cup water
2 teaspoons seeded and finely
     minced serrano or jalapeño
     chiles
2 tablespoons minced red bell
     pepper

2 tablespoons minced fresh mint
½ cup fresh lime or lemon juice
2 cups sparkling mineral water
4 cups apple juice or
     Gewürztraminer or another
     fruity white wine

Bring the sugar and water to a boil in a small saucepan and cook, stirring, until the sugar is dissolved, approximately 2 minutes. Remove from the heat, stir in the chiles, and cool.

Combine the syrup with the remaining ingredients and pour over ice in wine glasses.

 # Ginger-Mint Tea

This can be made with or without the wine, as you choose. Both ginger and mint have extraordinary abilities to soothe the stomach and aid digestion. Ginger is also touted as a natural alternative to medicines for motion sickness. I just know that this tea makes me feel very good.

Serves 4

3 ounces fresh ginger, sliced into
     thin coins
   3-inch strip orange zest
   3-inch strip lemon zest
   3-inch piece of cinnamon stick,
     broken into 3 pieces

2 tablespoons honey (or to taste)
1 cup fruity white wine, such as
     Riesling or Gewürztraminer
     (optional)
4 cups water
⅓ cup loosely packed mint leaves

Place the ginger, zests, cinnamon pieces, honey, wine, and water in a saucepan and bring to a simmer. Let the mixture steep over very low heat for 10 minutes. Add the mint leaves and steep for 10 minutes more. Strain carefully and serve hot or iced.

Ginger is also legendary for its power as an aphrodisiac, which, of course, ensured its success in the kitchen! From the medieval Salerno School of Hygiene and Diet, ginger is described as follows:

> Within the stomach, loins and in the lung
> praise of hot ginger rightly may be sung.
> It quenches thirst, revives, excites the brain
> and in old age awakens young love again!

Honeydew Lemonade

This is a simple drink to make, and any sweet, ripe melon can be used. The idea for drinks of this kind comes from the "agua frescas" found in Mexico.
Makes 8 cups

Zest of 2 lemons cut in strips
1   cup fresh lemon juice
¾   cup sugar
1   honeydew melon (about 3 pounds),
      seeds and rind removed and cut
      into 1-inch cubes

2   cups sparkling or still water
      Garnish: Thin lemon slices and
      mint sprigs

In a small saucepan, combine the lemon zest, lemon juice, and sugar and bring to a boil. Simmer, stirring occasionally, for 5 minutes or until the sugar dissolves. Strain the syrup and cool it.

In a food processor, purée the honeydew, then force the purée through a fine sieve, if desired. In a pitcher, combine the purée and cooled syrup and mix well. Chill. Just before serving, add 2 cups plain or sparkling water and serve over ice. Garnish with lemon slices and mint.

Hot "Beau"

Hot "beau" is short for Beaujolais, that amiable, fruity red wine. This is a spin on hot, mulled wine that's perfect for the holidays, or with a "hot beau" if you so choose. The drink was developed by one of our talented culinary students at Valley Oaks, Jim Mitchell (who also does a mean Elvis impression).

Makes 8 6-ounce drinks

1	orange	¼	cup sugar
12	whole cloves	12	cinnamon sticks
1	750 ml bottle Gamay Beaujolais	¼	teaspoon freshly grated nutmeg
1	cup fresh orange juice	½	teaspoon ground allspice

Heat the oven to 325 degrees. Stud the orange with the cloves. Place the orange in a baking dish and roast it until it becomes soft (about 30 to 45 minutes). Combine the roasted orange, Gamay Beaujolais, orange juice, sugar, 4 of the cinnamon sticks, nutmeg, and allspice in a nonreactive saucepan over medium-high heat. Heat the mixture, stirring frequently, until the sugar dissolves and the liquid almost comes to a boil. Divide the drink among 8 cups or coffee glasses. Garnish each with a cinnamon stick.

Orange-Gewürztraminer Lift

I enjoy inventing new drinks that use wine in them. This is a refreshing warm or cold drink featuring spicy, fruity, floral Gewürztraminer.

Serves 4 to 6

1	750 ml bottle Gewürztraminer	½	teaspoon finely minced lemon zest
½	cup fresh orange juice	½	teaspoon finely minced orange zest
6	cinnamon sticks		
2	whole cloves		Garnish: Long mint sprigs and orange slices
½	teaspoon finely minced lime zest		

In a saucepan, combine the wine, orange juice, cinnamon sticks, and cloves. Bring to a boil and simmer for 2 minutes. Remove the cinnamon sticks and cloves. Add the citrus zests. Serve hot, or chilled over ice. Garnish with fresh mint sprigs and an orange slice on the rim of the glass.

Peach–Opal Basil Lemonade

Opal, or purple, basil is one of the dozens of basil varieties. It gives this drink a beautiful pink cast. You can use regular basil if opal is not available.
Serves 4

2 cups fruity white wine, such as Riesling	⅔ cup fragrant honey, such as orange blossom
2 cups water	¾ cup fresh lemon juice
1 cup loosely packed opal basil leaves	Garnish: Opal basil sprigs and ripe peach slices
1½ cups peeled and chopped ripe peaches	

In a saucepan, combine the wine, water, basil, chopped peaches, and honey and bring to a boil. Lower the heat, cover, and simmer for 5 minutes or until the peaches are very soft. Remove from the heat and let the mixture cool. Strain through a very fine mesh strainer, pressing down on the solids. Stir in the lemon juice, adjusting the sweetness level with more honey if desired, and chill. To serve, pour over ice cubes and garnish with basil sprigs and slices of fresh peach.

Strawberry Sunset

When strawberries are at their peak in summer, this is a tasty drink with which to watch the sun go down. The recipe will serve eight if you fill the glasses only halfway and top off with a chilled crisp California sparkling wine (in which case omit the yogurt).
Serves 4

2   cups sliced ripe strawberries
2   cups fresh orange juice
2   tablespoons honey (or to taste)
3   tablespoons balsamic vinegar

⅓   cup yogurt
¾   cup crushed ice
     Garnish: Fresh mint sprigs

In a blender, purée the strawberries, orange juice, honey, and vinegar. Add the yogurt and crushed ice and blend briefly to combine. Pour into tall glasses and garnish with mint sprigs.

 # Tamarind Tea with Scented Geraniums

One of the most flavorful herbal teas I know is one made from scented geraniums (not common garden geraniums). Scented geraniums are easy to grow and come in a wide variety of scents, including nutmeg, cinnamon, rose, etc. My favorite for tea is an old heirloom variety of lemon geranium called Mabel Grey. To make scented geranium tea, simply steep the leaves of scented geraniums in hot water until the flavor develops. Strain and serve hot or cold. In this recipe I've added tamarind pulp, which gives an added flavor dimension. Tamarind pulp is available both in Hispanic and Southeast Asian markets; it is used extensively in those cuisines.
Serves 4

2½   tablespoons tamarind pulp or
      concentrate
2   tablespoons honey (or to
      taste)

2½   cups dry white wine, water, or
      apple juice
3–4   large lemon geranium leaves *or*
      the zest from 1 small lemon

Place all the ingredients in a saucepan and bring to a simmer. Partially cover and simmer slowly for 3 minutes. Remove from the heat and allow the mixture to steep and cool. Strain and serve hot or cold over ice cubes.

SCENTED GERANIUMS

Scented geraniums are simple to grow, especially in pots. Two good mail order sources are Mountain Valley Growers (for seedlings) and Shepherds (for seeds)—see pages 409–10. Besides tea, scented geraniums make an interesting base for sorbet, and they can be substituted for mint in any recipe that calls for it. They can also be used to flavor oils and vinegars.

Zinfandel Sangría

This is a (grown-up) summer fruit salad in a glass! Be sure to give the fruit time to macerate and flavor the drink.
Serves 6

1 750 ml bottle Zinfandel	1 small orange, thinly sliced
Juice of 4 large oranges, strained (about 1¼ cups)	1 small red apple, cut into wedges
Juice of 4 large limes, strained (about ⅓ cup)	½ cup raspberries and/or blackberries
⅓ cup sugar, preferably superfine (or to taste)	

In a large pitcher, combine the wine, citrus juices, and sugar and stir vigorously to dissolve the sugar.

Add the orange slices, apple wedges, and berries and refrigerate the sangría for 6 hours or overnight to let the flavors develop. Serve in tall glasses over ice cubes with some of the macerated fruit for garnish.

MATCHING WINE WITH FOOD

"Cuisine is when things taste like themselves," wrote Curnonsky many years ago. In California's wine country, this observation defines the essence of our cuisine. Clean, vivid flavors are artfully created by integrating superb fresh ingredients with classic yet simple cooking techniques. Not surprisingly, it is *wine itself* that seems to most enhance the food of the wine country.

Over the years, considerable discussion has taken place about the "marriage" of food and wine. Almost scientifically, we in the wine industry have scrutinized the intricacies of which wine should go with which dish, partly because wine is not as deeply imbedded in America's culture and table as it is in Europe. In treating wine intellectually, we've created unnecessary impediments for people to make wine more a part of their daily lives. This complication translates, unfortunately, into intimidation about wine for some people who might otherwise enjoy it more often.

Whether it's the confusion of making the proper varietal or brand selection, the ritualistic act of opening the bottle using a corkscrew, or the proper pouring of the wine with the requisite smelling and sniffing ritual, there is a certain mystique about wine for many Americans. But, it's really very simple! And this chapter will, I hope, explain the basics.

I'm also reminded that no matter how much we might talk about the principles of matching food and wine, that when the two are enjoyed within the company of good friends and loved ones, a far deeper, more spiritual connection takes place that makes most any food and wine combination work wonders.

Tasting and Appreciating Wine in Five Easy Steps

Wine appreciation is developed almost completely from experience and memory. More often than not, this "skill" is nurtured by tasting alongside more experienced wine tasters who can articulate their impressions and help develop a point of reference for less experienced tasters. Therefore, it is highly recommended that anyone interested in learning more seek out information through local tasting groups. A good wine store might be a source for information about such groups, and often such stores have these kinds of tastings themselves.

To help further understanding about wine tasting, I'm going to try to demystify some of the older rituals about wine and hopefully lead you to more enjoyment and appreciation of one of the world's most pleasurable beverages. Here are some simple steps to help you develop your wine-tasting ability:

1) OBSERVE COLOR AND APPEARANCE

- You can tell a lot about a wine from its color. The easiest way to evaluate color in wine is against a white backdrop, ideally a tablecloth. Tilt the glass slightly away from you to get a better angle.
- In white wines, a clear, pale, or straw color should indicate a lighter style wine in the mouth; a more golden color suggests either an older or more full-bodied wine.
- With red wines, lighter shades, such as ruby and crimson, indicate lighter to medium body; scarlet, dark red, and purple usually indicate either a youthful or more full-bodied wine. As red wines age, they turn slightly brickish-orange around the rim of the glass.
- By swirling the liquid slightly in the glass and observing the "legs" (called rivulets) of the wine as they run down the side of the glass, it's possible to assess the wine's body as well. An oily coating that runs slowly down the glass usually indicates a full-bodied wine that is often slightly higher in alcohol than less full-bodied wines.

2) SWIRL TO OPEN UP AROMATIC ELEMENTS

- Place the glass on the table with just an ounce or two of wine in it. Take the bottom of the stem of the glass between your thumb and first two fingers. Using a steady, consistent motion, move the glass in small circles. This allows the wine to swirl around the glass in a similar manner. (You might want to practice on something other than Grandma Minnette's white embroidered tablecloth!) The complex aromatic components of the wine are exposed to air, making the wine much easier to smell. In wine terms, it "opens up."

3) SMELL FOR SUBTLETY—"THE NOSE"

- Bring the wine to your nose immediately after swirling and take a long, slow inhalation.

- Let the wine make its aromatic impression on you. The bouquet of the wine is called "the nose," and it is an important part of the wine's subtlety, personality, and taste.
- As a point of differentiation, "aroma" usually refers to the smell of the varietal grape itself, whereas "bouquet" refers to the subtleties that emerge from the winemaking process, such as exposure of the wine to small oak barrels for aging.
- Use free association to describe the wine: Is it like a freshly cut green apple? A cigar box? Grandmother's sachet drawer? A bowl of cherries? A slice of pineapple? A basket of peaches? Childhood references often work; so do food associations.
- Write down your impressions; this helps to establish "taste memory" and develop better recall.

Since the sense of smell, called the olfactory sense, is directly connected to the sense of taste, these first impressions you get from the nose will greatly magnify the "taste" of the wine.

4) Taste the Wine

- Immediately after smelling the wine, take a small taste. Gurgle the wine softly on your tongue. This allows the wine to interact with air and cover the entire mouth. Swallow and evaluate.
- Notice how the wine strikes you. Is it light or heavy? Dry or sweet? Tart or smooth? Does it have layers of flavors or just one dimension? Does it seem balanced or unbalanced? Try to describe the flavors you're experiencing just as you did with the wine's aroma and bouquet. Let the wine speak to you.

All wine is a combination of five basic components of taste, each experienced in a different place on the tongue. The ideal wine is a perfect *balance* of these components:

Sweet: Tip of the tongue (shows residual sugar)
Sour: Side of the tongue (indicates acidity and tartness)
Salty: Center of the tongue (rarely experienced in wine)
Bitter: Back of the tongue (results from tannin, which is derived both from the skins of grapes as well as the exposure of wine to oak barrels)
Peppery or Pungent: Front part of the tongue (often associated with earthy red wines)

5) EVALUATE THE FINISH

- Swallow the wine and keep your concentration on it. Do the flavors persist and stay on your tongue a long time, or do they dissipate quickly? Do you notice other elements in the wine that you didn't when you first tasted it? Are these pleasant or unpleasant? The persistence, or length of the finish, is another good indicator of the wine's quality.

- What is your overall impression? After you've analyzed the finite points, let your own taste determine: Quite simply, did you like the wine or not? What foods does it suggest? How does it compare to other similar wines that you've tried? What do you think of its quality and price compared to other wines you have tasted?

TEN QUICK TIPS FOR PERFECT FOOD AND WINE PAIRING

There is only one reason for knowing the "right" wines to pair with the "right" food: Wine and food that complement each other enhance the flavor of both; wine and food that don't complement each other detract from both. That's it. That's the only reason.

The tips below work because they explain the experience of consuming particular foods and wines together. In other words, you can taste for yourself when a wine that you love, eaten with a certain dish, suddenly tastes sour, or when a wine, drunk alongside a familiar food, suddenly makes that food sing; these tips explain why this happens.

1. Foods that are high in natural acids (tomatoes, citrus fruits, goat cheese) are best suited to wines with higher acids: Sauvignon Blanc and certain styles of Chardonnay, Riesling, Gewürztraminer, Zinfandel, Pinot Noir.

2. Richer and fattier foods (duck, lamb, beef, cheese) go well with either slightly oaky white wines, such as Chardonnay, or with young red wines, such as Cabernet Sauvignon or Zinfandel.

3. Spicy, salty/smoky, and more heavily seasoned dishes are best paired with light, fruity wines, whether red or white, such as Gewürztraminer, Johannisberg Riesling, Gamay Beaujolais, Pinot Noir, and certain Zinfandels.

4. Foods with some sweetness (meat and poultry dishes with fruit sauces) are best paired with wines that offer some sweetness (Gewürztraminer,

Johannisberg Riesling, White Zinfandel) or sufficient ripeness (Cabernet Sauvignon or Zinfandel). If the food is sweeter than the wine, it will often make the wine taste dry, oaky, and/or tannic.

5. Generally, wines (like courses) should follow a natural progression from dry to sweet. However, if a dish with some sweetness comes early in the meal, it's best to serve a slightly sweet wine with it.

6. The texture of a wine, its body and weight in the mouth, is as important as its flavor to matching it successfully with food. (A heavy, full-bodied wine is going to overpower a simple salad.)

7. Obvious opportunities for pairing food and wine occur when a particular wine is used in the cooking process, such as in a marinade or a sauce. The table wine should mirror the dish.

8. Great food and wine combinations come not only from matching flavors, textures, and taste components, but also from contrasting them.

9. Successful food and wine pairing is highly subjective and individual—an experimental, dynamic art form more than a science. Don't be afraid to follow your own instincts.

10. Most important, the food should not overwhelm the wine any more than the wine should overpower the food. Ideally, the result is synergistic: Food and wine together are far more enjoyable than either food or wine by itself.

Cooking with Herbs and Wine

At the heart of wine country cuisine is the use of fragrant, fresh herbs. Whether in sprightly salads with flavored vinaigrettes, in aromatic marinades for grilled vegetables, seafood, poultry or meats, or in naturally reduced sauces, the creative use of herbs and wine plays a pivotal role in enhancing both the aroma and flavor of many wine country dishes.

Herbs often provide the magical connection to tying wine to a dish since many herbal qualities are found in fine varietal wines. These tips will help make that connection and show you that by cooking with herbs and wine even the simplest dishes can be enlivened as never before.

BASIL (Sweet Basil; *Ocimum basilicum*)

Large, fragrant, green leaves; rich spicy, mildly peppery flavor with a trace of mint and clove. White edible flowers. Aromatic garnish.

Pesto, salad dressing, tomato-based pasta sauces, butters, eggplant, zucchini, stews, ragoûts, tomatoes, vinegars.

White Zinfandel, Gamay Beaujolais, Zinfandel, Cabernet Sauvignon, Sauvignon Blanc.

OPAL BASIL (*O.b. purpurascens*)

Shiny, dark-purple leaves with red veins. Similar smell but spicier than sweet basil, with edible lavender flowers. Flavor lost with prolonged heat. Colorful garnish.

Use as you would sweet basil. Turns brown in pesto, but is excellent in vinegar.

White Zinfandel, Gamay Beaujolais, Zinfandel, Cabernet Sauvignon, Sauvignon Blanc.

CINNAMON BASIL (*O.b. cinnamon*)

Bright-green leaves; spicy flavor and pungent cinnamon-clove scent. Flavor intensifies with cooking. Edible white flowers. Store in oil or vinegar.

Use as you would sweet basil. Infuse in crème anglaise sauces for desserts, or add to biscotti.

White Zinfandel, Gamay Beaujolais, Zinfandel, Cabernet Sauvignon, Sauvignon Blanc.

BAY (Sweet Laurel; *Laurus nobilis*)

Glossy, tough, dark-green leaves; warm, slightly spicy, somewhat sweetish flavor. Rub to release flavors. Cook slowly to free powerful, earthy aroma. Use fresh or dried, then remove.

Spanish, Creole, and French soups, sauces, stews, marinades, game, shellfish, tomato sauces, grains, beans, fruit punches.

Cabernet Sauvignon, Zinfandel, Sauvignon Blanc.

CHERVIL (*Anthriscus cerefolium*)

Green, dainty, fernlike leaves; elegant, warm anise-parsley flavors are lost in long cooking. Pretty garnish—unusual white flowers.

Delicate French sauces, soups, green salads, fish and chicken dishes, carrots, egg dishes.

Sauvignon Blanc, Chardonnay, Johannisberg Riesling, Gewürztraminer, White Zinfandel.

CHIVES (*Allium schoenoprasum*)

Long, thin, dark-green leaves; mildest of the onion family. Tangy, sometimes hot taste. Cannot stand heat, best used raw; add last in cooking or as garnish. Round, pale-purple edible flowers.

Potato salads, green salads, butters for fish or chicken, vegetable casseroles, omelets, cheese bread.

Sauvignon Blanc, Zinfandel, White Zinfandel.

CORIANDER (Cilantro; *Coriandrum sativum*)

Green, multileafed stems; intense and very aromatic parsleylike aroma with bold sage flavor and tangy citrus taste. Use fresh leaves or dried seed. Roots have added nutty flavor.

Mexican salsa, chutneys, chicken marinades, salad dressing, Oriental stir-fry, spicy dishes.

Gewürztraminer, Sauvignon Blanc, Zinfandel.

DILL *(Anethum graveolens)*

Pale, blue-green feathery leaves; long, hollow stalks. Intense herbal aroma, spicy with mild aniseed flavor. Use fresh or stronger dried form. Snip with scissors.

Fish, especially salmon, light sauces, butters, carrot soup, breads, deviled eggs, pickles, cucumbers.

Sauvignon Blanc, Chardonnay, Johannisberg Riesling.

FENNEL (Sweet Fennel; *Foeniculum vulgare*)

Deep-green feathery leaves; a softer, nuttier version of anise with sweet aroma. Use fresh tender stems as you would celery; grind seeds. Mince stalks/bulbs for salads/soups. Fragrant garnish, with yellow edible flowers.

Salads, soups, vegetable casseroles with Parmesan cheese, seafood, breads.

Chardonnay, Zinfandel, Sauvignon Blanc.

HYSSOP *(Hyssopus officinalis)*

Rich-green, spiky leaves. A member of the mint family, slightly bitter with strong camphorlike aroma. Best fresh. Edible blue-violet flowers. Especially fragrant garnish.

Roast chicken, lamb stew, vegetable soups, fruit salads, teas.

Chardonnay, Gewürztraminer, Johannisberg Riesling, Cabernet Sauvignon.

LAVENDER *(Lavandula officinalis)*

Small, perfumy, edible lavender flowers with fresh, astringent flavor and aroma. Use sparingly, even as garnish. Excellent combined with pepper.

Dry marinades ("rubs") for poultry and game birds, jams, stews, soufflés, ice cream, sorbets. Infuse sugars, vinegars, gelatins, honeys.

Zinfandel, Pinot Noir, Petite Sirah, Cabernet Sauvignon, Chardonnay.

MINT (Garden Mint; *Mentha spicata*)

Long, green, narrow, spear-shaped leaves; sharp, cleansing taste and distinctive aroma. Fresh leaves/sprigs for garnish.

Lamb, sautéed vegetables, fruit-based soups, Mideastern salads and rice dishes, desserts, fruit beverages, chocolate, teas, coffees.

White Zinfandel, Cabernet Sauvignon, Zinfandel, Gewürztraminer.

OREGANO *(Origanum vulgare)*

Small, round, green leaves; hot, peppery flavor, warm savory taste, and pungent aroma. Good dried. Garnish with whole stems.

Vegetable soups, zucchini and eggplant dishes, marinade for beef/lamb, pizza and pastas with tomato-garlic sauce, cheese and egg dishes, breads.

Sauvignon Blanc, Zinfandel, Cabernet Sauvignon.

PARSLEY *(Petroselinum crispum)*

Green, flat or curly leaves; fresh aroma, mild, herbal flavor. Flat-leaved preferred. Add last to avoid bruising, use entire stem in stocks/soups, then remove. Garnish with whole/minced.

Grilled/sautéed meats, tomato-based pasta, butters for seafood, omelets, sauces for fish, relishes.

Johannisberg Riesling, Sauvignon Blanc, Gamay Beaujolais, Cabernet Sauvignon.

ROSEMARY *(Rosmarinas officinalis)*

Dark, green-gray, needlelike leaves; pungent, piny, mintlike, with a slight ginger finale. Crush/mince leaves or use whole, then remove. Freeze whole. Use pale-blue flowers/sprigs as garnish.

Marinade for beef, pork, lamb, hearty soups, tomato-garlic sauces, roast chicken, breads.

Cabernet Sauvignon, Zinfandel, Petite Sirah.

SAGE (Garden Sage; *Salvia officinalis*)

Silver-green velvet leaves; lemony, pleasantly bitter and aromatic, with balsamic flavor. Dried has a stronger, musty taste.

Poultry stuffings and game dishes, liver, sausages, cheese soufflés, vegetables, breads, teas.

Chardonnay, Sauvignon Blanc, Cabernet Sauvignon, Zinfandel.

SORREL (French Sorrel/Dock; *Rumex scutatus*)

Narrow, long, bright-green leaves with slightly lemony taste and sharp, acidic bite. Powerful flavor is best mixed with other herbs. Use whole leaves as garnish.

Soups, salads, cream sauces, egg dishes, salmon, as a puréed side dish, with spinach.

Sauvignon Blanc, Zinfandel.

TARRAGON (French Tarragon; *Artemisia dracunculus*)

Small, greenish-white leaves; savory anise flavor with hidden tang; overpowers other flavors; bitter if cooked long. Best fresh, frozen, or stored in white vinegar.

Cream soups, béarnaise and hollandaise sauces, mayonnaise, salad dressings, roasts, ragoûts, butters, shellfish, olives.

Chardonnay, Cabernet Sauvignon, Sauvignon Blanc.

THYME (*Thymus vulgaris*)

Tiny, gray-green leaves with pale underside; distinctive sweet aroma, pungent flavor with faint clove aftertaste. Use white-lilac flowers/sprigs as garnish.

Soups, stocks, marinades for meats, vegetable dishes, shellfish, beans, lentils.

Sauvignon Blanc, Zinfandel, Cabernet Sauvignon, Chardonnay.

LEMON THYME (*T. citriodorus*)

Dark-green, glossy leaves, broader than thyme; pronounced lemon aroma. Use sprigs with pink flowers as garnish.

Use as you would thyme. Seafood and poultry dishes, eggplants, bell peppers, lamb stew, sweet foods, teas.

Sauvignon Blanc, Zinfandel, Cabernet Sauvignon, Chardonnay.

SILVER THYME (*T. vulgaris argenteus*)

Like thyme, but plant is completely silver-tinged. Classic sweet thyme fragrance with soft, lingering clove flavor. Use whole stems as garnish.

Use as you would thyme. French, Creole, and Cajun dishes, seafood chowders.

Sauvignon Blanc, Zinfandel, Cabernet Sauvignon, Chardonnay.

WINTER SAVORY (*Satureja montana*)

Deep-green, glossy, lance-shaped leaves; strong, peppery, piny aroma with spicy, slightly bitter flavor. Use with other strong flavors.

Mediterranean stews, grilled or roasted poultry and game, eggplants, peas, beans, sauces, vinegars.

Zinfandel, Cabernet Sauvignon, Sauvignon Blanc.

CHOICE OF A WINE GLASS

Most people know that it is traditional to serve different wines in different glasses—at least to the extent of having different styles of glasses for red wine, white wine, and champagne. But did you know that there are particular styles of glasses for Chardonnay or Cabernet?

Here are my suggestions. It's not really so terribly important which glass you use unless you're a serious traditionalist. The single exception is the glass you choose for sparkling wine or champagne. For these you want a tall, straight-sided, flute-shaped glass, which encourages and shows off the bubbles. Never, never use the flat, round, saucer-shaped glass (even if it is supposedly a re-creation of Marie Antoinette's breast). For still wines choose a glass that allows you to perform the three S's easily: that is, Swirl, Sniff, and Sip. You want a good-sized bowl on the glass so that when you swirl you won't spill wine all over you, and swirling helps develop the aroma. Finally, the bowl needs to be big enough for even the largest nose to fit in, to enjoy the liberated aromas while you sip.

Remember also to choose glasses that are perfectly clear, so you can enjoy the color of the wine.

FOOD AND WINE PAIRING CHART

	Style	Aromas/Flavors	Classic Foods
Chardonnay	Light yellow, light body, emphasis on fresh fruit, crisp	Green apple, lemon, orange, grapefruit	Appetizers, soups, shrimp salad, glazed roast chicken
	Medium yellow, medium–full body, oak influence	Apple-spice, pineapple–tropical fruit, citrus, buttery, toasty	Roast turkey, roast chicken with Dijon mustard, seafood with sauces
	Medium–dark yellow, full-bodied, rich with oak emphasis	Pineapple–tropical fruit, vanilla, nutty, toasty, buttery, spicy	Crab cakes, lobster, fettuccine Alfredo, seafood with cream sauce, soft cheeses

	Style	Aromas/Flavors	Classic Foods
Gewürztraminer	Dry-sweet, Light–medium yellow, medium body, often a hint of sweetness	Apricot, peach, Oriental spice, tropical fruit, honey	Spicy appetizers, baked ham, roast turkey, prosciutto and melon, Oriental foods, picnic foods
Johannisberg Riesling	Dry-sweet, Light–medium yellow, medium body, often a hint of sweetness	Apricot, peach, pear, honey, floral, metallic	Appetizers, baked ham, lighter poultry, smoked salmon, fresh fruits, picnic foods
Sauvignon Blanc or Fumé Blanc	Medium yellow, medium body, oak influence	Fig, melon, orange, lemon, vanilla, herbal, grassy, dill	Lighter seafood, chicken with olives, steamed clams, pasta with pesto, vegetarian dishes
Cabernet Sauvignon	Crimson–medium red, medium body, smooth, fruity, soft	Cherry, berry, spice	Roast or grilled meats, beef or lamb stew, veal roast, game with fruit sauces
	Medium–dark red, medium–full body, oak influence, more complex	Cherry, currant, chocolate, cedar, mint, vanilla	Grilled meats, roast rack of lamb, roast pork or veal, hearty game
	Dark red–purple, full-bodied, strong oak influence	Currant, chocolate, cedar, tobacco, mint, vanilla, pepper	Grilled meats with peppercorn crust, hearty game, aged cheeses
Gamay Beaujolais	Ruby red, light–medium body, lively, very fruity	Raspberry, strawberry, floral	Appetizers, baked ham, roast turkey, pizza
Merlot	Medium–dark red, medium body, soft, round mouthfeel	Berry, cherry, orange zest, tea, vanilla, cedar	Roast poultry, meat-based pastas, hearty cheeses
Petite Sirah	Dark red–purple, full body, tannic	Blueberry, raspberry, jammy, spice, pepper	Pepper steak, stews, grilled meats, venison chili, hearty cheeses

	Style	Aromas/Flavors	Classic Foods
Pinot Noir	Ruby–medium red, light–medium body, soft, fruity	Cherry, spice, cedar, coffee, earthy, mushrooms	Roast chicken, grilled salmon or tuna, mushroom tart, vegetarian pastas, soft cheeses
Zinfandel	Medium–dark red, medium–full body, lively	Blackberry, raspberry, jammy, spice, pepper	Pasta with garlic-tomato sauce, grilled meats and ribs, hearty cheeses
White Zinfandel	Pink-coral, light body, hint of sweetness, lively	Strawberry, orange zest	Appetizers, barbecued chicken, pasta salad, Oriental dishes

New Varietals

California's history of varietal wine grapes has focused on the more popular varietals—Chardonnay, Sauvignon or Fumé Blanc, Gewürztraminer, Johannisberg Riesling, and Chenin Blanc in the whites; Cabernet Sauvignon, Zinfandel, Pinot Noir, Petite Sirah, and Merlot in the reds. Both retail wine stores and restaurant wine lists have featured these varietals for the past few decades to the increasing curiosity of consumers.

Recently, new varietals with origins in Europe have burst on the California wine scene and offer opportunities for wine lovers to experience a wider range of flavors. These new varietals are well suited to the assertive style of many wine country dishes. Many of these wines offer forward fruit and lower tannin, oak, and alcohol than some of the traditional wines of California.

GRENACHE

Grenache is native to Spain, but is best known in southern France, where it flourishes in the Rhône region, particularly in Bandol and Châteauneuf-du-Pape. In California, Grenache is often used in innocuous rosés that exemplify little character, but it is now being combined with Syrah and Mourvèdre to create distinctive New World blends. Grenache is most known for its ability to provide a lush, fruity quality to these blends.

MARSANNE

Marsanne is a dry southern French white wine varietal that is often blended with another varietal, Roussanne, to make stunning wines with a slight earthy-mineral character. Only a few producers from California are currently experimenting with Marsanne.

NEBBIOLO

Nebbiolo is the noble red grape of the Piedmont region of northwest Italy, known for making intense, full-bodied, long-aged red wines. Used predominantly in the Barolo and Barbaresco areas, Nebbiolo has been slow to catch on in California. When grown in the right locale, it offers a distinctive earthy, mushroomlike aroma that is very well suited to hearty braised dishes.

PINOT BLANC

Best known in the Chablis region of France, where it is often planted with Chardonnay, and in the Alsace region, where it is widely acknowledged for producing wines of delicacy and finesse, Pinot Blanc is a fine dry white wine with a long heritage in California. Despite its pleasing qualities, Pinot Blanc has not generated much enthusiasm in California, and is unfortunately viewed as a stepchild of Chardonnay.

SANGIOVESE

A great varietal from the Tuscany region in Italy, which produces Chianti, Sangiovese is a world-class grape with a great future in California as well. In Italy, Sangiovese has been blended for many years by law with other red and even white wine grapes. More recently, top producers in both Italy and California are experimenting with nontraditional blends of Sangiovese and Cabernet Sauvignon and with Sangiovese on its own, and they are achieving considerable success. Sangiovese complements a wide range of rustic Italian dishes as well as other full-flavored foods.

SYRAH

Syrah is one of the noble red grapes of the Rhône region in southern France. While often confused with Petite Sirah, it is not related. Syrah has been grown successfully in California for a number of decades and has many fans due to its peppery, spicy quality and intense, full-flavored fruit. Syrah is often blended with

Mourvèdre, another Rhône variety, and Grenache to make New World red blends that resemble Châteauneuf-du-Pape. It is often made without blending as well.

Syrah is well suited to red meat dishes, particularly grilled and braised preparations with full, robust flavors.

VIOGNIER

Viognier is a gloriously decadent white wine grape that is grown primarily in the Condrieu region of southern France. It is quite rare and, thus, commands steep prices, which has prevented it from becoming better known in California.

Over thirty producers are now making Viognier in California, and there is considerable optimism for high-quality wines at lower prices than their French counterparts.

Viognier offers a gorgeous, seductive aroma, often reminiscent of apricots, peaches, and honeysuckle. It has a lush mouthfeel and captivating flavors, making it an enjoyable diversion from Chardonnay. It is sometimes aged in oak, which adds a buttery quality to the already creamy texture of the varietal.

Enjoy Viognier with full-flavored seafood and poultry dishes and on its own as a sipping wine. The search for this rare varietal will be well worth it, as it offers pure hedonistic pleasure. This is definitely a varietal for the future.

SULFITES IN WINE

In the mid 1980s, in response to concern about how sulfites can affect asthmatics, the U.S. government began requiring a sulfite warning statement on wine labels.

It is unclear how long sulfur has been used in winemaking, but it has certainly been around for several hundred years. A small amount of sulfites occurs in all young wines, since they are a natural byproduct of fermentation. Something in the neighborhood of ten parts per million are usually present.

Winemakers historically added sulfur or sulfites to wine to help stabilize it and improve its longevity. Sulfites have both fungicidal and antioxidant properties. Back in the days before clean, modern equipment and fermentation practices, more sulfur was added than is typically used today. U.S. law allows up to 350 ppm, but most wines today are being produced at levels of less than 100 ppm.

Wine isn't the only "food" from which we get sulfites. Most dried fruits contain much more sulfur than wine. Wine writer Dan Berger has noted that ". . . you can get as much sulfite from one dried apple as from four full bottles of wine." Sulfite solutions are also often used at restaurant salad bars to keep greens bright and fresh looking.

In my view, unless you are one of the estimated 1 percent of the population sensitive to sulfites, the more important issue is other agricultural chemicals used to grow grapes, such as herbicides, pesticides, and fungicides. Labeling laws at present don't require any warning labels about residues of these substances.

Finally, there is the issue of red wine, headaches, and sulfites. Scientists say that there doesn't appear to be any connection between sulfites and headaches. Why headaches are more associated with red wine rather than white is still being explored.

Appendices

Edible Flowers

Edible flowers have had a continuing role in wine country cuisine for many years. Although it may seem like a new trend, edible flowers have had a long history in many cuisines:

- Roses and orange flowers in Middle Eastern and Persian foods
- Lilies in China
- Cherry blossoms and chrysanthemums in Japan
- Lavender in France and England
- Saffron in Spain and the rest of the Mediterranean

Flower petals can add wonderful color and sparkle to a plate, and many, such as day lilies and nasturtiums, have bold, interesting flowers.

Not all flowers, however, are edible. Cathy Barash in her book *Edible Flowers from Garden to Palate* offers these "Ten Commandments":

THE TEN COMMANDMENTS OF EDIBLE FLOWERS

1. Not all flowers are edible—some are poisonous.
2. Eat only those flowers that you can positively identify as safe and edible.
3. Eat only edible flowers that have been grown organically.

4. When eating out, do not eat flowers on your plate unless you are sure they are edible and safe to eat. (See Commandments 2 and 3.)

5. Do not eat flowers from florists, nurseries, or garden centers. (See Commandment 3.)

6. Remove pistils and stamens from most flowers before eating. Eat only the petals of most flowers.

7. If you have hay fever, asthma, or allergies, do not eat flowers.

8. Do not eat flowers picked from the side of the road. (See Commandment 3.)

9. You don't have to like all edible flowers. Flowers may vary in taste when grown in different locations. Different varieties of the same flower may vary in taste.

10. Introduce flowers into your diet the way you would new foods to a baby—one at a time and in small quantities.

Here is a list of edible flowers I have used over the years, with my "tasting notes":

FLOWERS FOR THE EATING

Name	Tasting Notes
Anise hyssop	Licorice
Apple blossom	Slight floral
Arugula	Spicy, pepper
Bachelor's button	Mild
Basils (various kinds)	Strong, spicy, herbal
Beans, snap or pole	Beany, floral
Bee balm (Monarda didyma), purple and red	Strong, hot, minty
Begonia (tuberous)	Crisp, lemony
Borage	Mild, light cucumber
Calendula (pot marigold)	Mild vegetal
Carnation	Clovelike, floral
Chamomile, German	Slightly bitter, for teas
Cherry	Sweet, floral
Chervil	Warm anise-parsley flavors
Chicory	Slightly bitter
Chives	Tangy, oniony
Chrysanthemum	Mild to strong, bitter
Cilantro, coriander	Bold sage flavor and tangy citrus taste
Citrus (lemon, orange, lime)	Tangy, rindlike
Clover, red	Herbaceous, slightly bitter
Collard greens flower	Sweet, mild
Cress	Peppery

Name	Tasting Notes
Dandelion	Mild to strong
Day lily (true lilies only, **not** calla, Aztec, or other so-called lilies, which are poisonous)	Mild, sweet, crunchy
Dianthus, pinks	Mild vegetal to sweet spice
Dill	Herbal aroma, spicy, with mild aniseed flavor
English daisy (*Bellis perennis*)	Mild vegetal
Fennel	Mild anise
Forget-me-not, cynoglossom*	Mild
Fuchsia	Acidic
Garlic, chives	Pungent, garlic flavor
Geraniums (scented, including apple, lime, lemon, rose, etc.)	Floral
Hibiscus	Tart, citrus, cranberry, tropical
Hollyhock	Vegetal, okralike, bland
Honeysuckle	Sweet nectar, mildly bitter floral
Hyssop	Slightly bitter, strong camphorlike aroma
Impatiens*	Citrusy
Jamaica flower	Cranberry
Jasmine	Slightly sweet
Johnny-jump-up	Mild, cinnamon or root beer
Judas tree (redbud)	Mild, slightly bitter
Lavender	Herbal, strongly perfumed
Lilac	Floral, strong tarragon
Mints (chocolate, apple, spearmint, peppermint)	Slightly sweet, herbal, refreshing
Mullein	Mild, vegetal
Mustard	Pleasantly hot
Nasturtium	Peppery, hot spicy flavor
Oregano	Herbal, warm savory taste
Pansy	Mild, sweet flavor, wintergreenish
Passionflower	Mild, sweet
Pea (*not* sweet pea)	Sweet, faintly floral
Petunia*	Mild vegetal, sometimes bitter aftertaste
Pineapple guava	Sweet spongy-marshmallow flavor, floral
Plum blossom	Sweet floral, faint cherry flavor, slightly bitter
Poppy—Shirley poppy only (*use only petals: avoid opium poppies*)	Mildly bitter, floral
Portulaca	Mild vegetal

*Not all edible flower references agree

Name	Tasting Notes
Primrose	Mild floral
Prune	Mild, fruity
Rocket	Sharp, strong, peppery
Rose	Mild floral; perfume varies
Rosemary	Herbal
Safflower	Slightly bitter, earthy
Sage (winter & summer)	Herbal, spicy, slightly bitter
Scarlet runner	Mild bean, slightly crunchy, sweet
Shasta daisy	Mild vegetal
Snapdragon*	Mild vegetal
Sorrel	Citrus, herbal
Squashes	Mild vegetal
Stock, mathiola*	Floral, sweet, perfumed
Strawberry	Mild
Sunflower	Mild vegetal
Tarragon	Herbal, savory anise flavor
Thyme, various	Herbal, taste varies with variety
Tulbaghia (tricolor)	Garlic
Tulip (Do *not* eat bulb)	Mild, floral, crisp
Vegetable blossoms (All *EXCEPT* tomato, potato, eggplant, peppers, and asparagus)	Mild vegetal
Viola	Mild perfume
Violet	Sweet, very floral
Woodruff, sweet	Distinctive herbal-floral flavor
Yucca	Sweet, herbal

*Not all edible flower references agree.

Farmstead Cheese Producers of America

The word "American," when applied to cheese, generally has negative connotations. It brings to mind the typically artificially colored, tasteless, processed, and uninteresting version we see in the supermarkets and fast food industry. In reality, American farmstead cheeses are quite the opposite of those orange horrors. Their superb quality matches that of European rivals. Being produced on farms throughout the country, our American cheeses are made with fresh high-protein milk from cows, goats, and sheep. They are handled with great care and reflect the regions in which they are produced.

As with the fine wines of America, American farmstead cheeses have finally come of age.

WEST

**Bandon Foods, Inc. 503/347-2456 or
800/548-8961**
Box 1668
Bandon, OR 97411
Hand-cheddared, full-cream white cheddar

Beatrice Cheese Co., 206/863-3857
1515 Puyallup St.
Summer, WA 98390 or
240 North Ave.
Gustine, CA 95322
Mozzarella, provolone, feta

**Bellweather Farms, Cynthia Callahan,
707/763-0993**
9999 Valley Ford Road
Petaluma, CA 94952
Fresh sheep cheese (ricotta, pecorino)

Besnier America, 209/667-4505
1400 West Main Street
Turlock, CA 95380
*Brie, Camembert, très blue, Belmont d'Or,
Gouda, fontina, feta, goat*

**Blue Heron French Cheese Co.,
503/842-8281**
2001 Blue Heron
Tillamook, OR 97141
Brie

**Bodega Goat Cheese, Javier Salmon,
707/876-3453**
P.O. Box 223
Bodega, CA 94922
Queso fresco, queso blanco, queso ranchero

**Bulk Farms, Walter and Lenneke Bulk,
209/838-2491**
171487 E. Lone Tree Road
Escalon, CA 95320
Gouda and Edam

**Chateau Dumas Gourmet Cheese
Makers, 206/788-7309**
Duval, WA 98019
French-style goat cheese

Cougar Gold, 509/335-4014
Washington State University
WSU Creamery
Pullman, WA 99164-4410
Cheddar, Viking (Availability seasonal)

**Cypress Grove Chevre, Mary Keehn,
707/839-3168**
4600 Dows Prairie Rd.
McKinleyville, CA 95521
*Chèvre, fromage blanc, chèvre logs,
Chevet, cheddar, feta, Parmesan,
special French-style goat cheese,
fromage à trois*

**Darigold Cheese Plant, 206/748-8826 or
206/284-7226**
67 S.W. Chehalis Ave.
Chehalis, WA 98532
Cheddar, colby, Jack

Ferrante Cheese Co., 415/372-9413
3840 Alhambra Ave.
Martinez, CA 94553
Mozzarella, bocconcini, ricotta

**Goats Leap, Rex & Barbara Backus,
707/963-2337**
3321 St. Helena Hwy North
St. Helena, CA 94574
*Estate-produced fresh chèvre and aged goat
cheese, feta, Carmela*

**Green Gold Valley Goat Dairy, Gloria
Willis, 408/663-3076**
19449 Pesante Road
Salinas, CA 93907
Teleme, cheddar, Monterey Jack

Italcheese, Inc., 310/515-1481
16919 South Broadway
Gardena, CA 90248
*Ricotta, mozzarella, bocconcini, smoked
    mozzarella, mascarpone*

Juniper Grove, Pierre Kolish, 503/923-8353
Redmond, OR
French-style goat cheese

**Laura Chenel's Chevre, Laura Chenel,
    707/996-4477**
4310 Fremont Drive
Sonoma, CA 95476
*Fromage blanc, Chabis, Pyramide, Cabecou,
    Taupinière, Calistogan, Tomme, Crottin,
    Capriccio*

Loleta Cheese Factory, 707/733-5470
P.O. Box 607
252 Loleta Drive
Loleta, CA 95551
Cheddar, Jack, Havarti, fontina

Matos, Joe, 707/584-5283
Sebastopol, CA 95472
St. George cheese (Portuguese)

**Mount Capra Cheese, 206/748-4224 or
    800/574-1961**
279 S.W. 9th St.
Chehalis, WA 98532
*Feta-style Olympic, cheddar-type Alpine,
    Renaissance Herb, Onion and Chive
    cheddar, Caraway Jack, Jalapeño Chili
    Pepper, Mineral Supplement (from
    dehydrated whey)*

Mozzarella Fresca, 707/746-6818
538 Stone Road, Unit A
Benicia, CA 94510
Mozzarella, bocconcini, ricotta

Nancy's of Oregon, 503/689-2911
Springfield Creamery, Inc.
29440 Airport Road
Eugene, OR 97402
Cream cheese, cottage cheese, yogurt

Olympia Cheese Co., 206/491-5330
3145 Hogan Bay RD N.E.
Olympia, WA 98506
*Cheddar, Jack, colby, string cheese,
    provolone, Havarti*

Peluso Cheese, Inc., 209/826-3744
429 "H" Street
Los Banos, CA 93635
*Monterey Jack, dry Monterey Jack, raw milk
    cheddar, Teleme*

Pleasant Valley Dairy, 206/366-5398
6804 Kickerville Rd.
Ferndale, WA 98248
*Raw milk classic Gouda, farmstead,
    Mutschli*

**Queso Michoacan Cheese Co.,
    707/485-0579**
9701 West Rd.
Redwood Valley, CA 95470
Queso Mexicano

**Rachel's Goat Cheese, Rachel Helm,
    707/823-1322**
Me Gusta Farm
Sebastopol, CA 95472
*French-style goat cheeses—chèvre, Chabis,
    sun-dried tomato fromage blanc*

Redwood Hill Farms, 707/823-8250
10855 Occidental Road
Sebastopol, CA 95472
Goat-milk cheeses and yogurt

**Rollingstone Chevre, Charles or Karen
    Evans, 208/722-6460**
27349 Shelton Rd.
Parma, ID 83660
Fromage blanc, aged chèvre, various tortas

Rouge et Noir, 707/762-6001
P.O. Box 99
Petaluma, CA 94953
Breakfast cheese, Camembert, Brie, Schloss

Rumiano Cheese Company, 707/465-1535
P.O. Box 305
Crescent City, CA 95531
Parmesan, dry Monterey Jack, cheddar

Salmon Valley Cheese, 208/756-3213
102 Main Street
Salmon, ID 83467
Swiss, dairy-lite Havarti, cheddar, Jack,
  mozzarella

Sea Stars Goat Cheese, Nancy Gaffney,
  408/423-7200
5407 Old Coast Rd.
Santa Cruz, CA 95060
Chèvre

Sky Hill Farms, 707/224-5002
2431 Partrick Road
Napa, CA 94558
Chèvre

Sonoma Cheese Factory, 707/996-1000
Two Spain Street
Sonoma, CA 95476
Sonoma Jack traditional, garlic, hot pepper,
  onion, and caraway, salt-free Teleme, cheddar

Tall Talk Dairy, 503/266-1644
11961 S. Emerson Rd.
Canby, OR 97013
Goat, feta, Jack

Tillamook County Creamery
  Association, 503/842-4481
P.O. Box 313
Tillamook, OR 97141
Cheddar, Monterey Jack, colby

Vella Cheese Company of California,
  Inc., 707/938-3232
315 Second Street East
P.O. Box 191
Sonoma, CA 95476
A variety of flavored Monterey Jack cheeses,
  dry Monterey, raw-milk cheddar

Yerba Santa Goat Dairy, Chris and Jan
  Twohy, 707/263-8131
Alpine Chevre
6850 Scotts Valley Road
Lakeport, CA 95453
Fresh goat cheeses: plain, dill-onion, parsley-
  garlic, black pepper; aged goat cheeses:
  shepherd's cheese, chivitos

East

American Farm Cheese Co., Robert
  LeCompte, 201/236-2369
P.O. Box 384
Lebanon, NJ 08833
Chèvre, goat cheddar, Tomme

Bel Paese Co., Bob Castellano,
  201/363-3800
1935 Swarthmore Ave.
Lakewood, NJ 08701
Bel Paese

Bongrain Cheese, Michel Duleu-Burre,
  717/355-8500
400 S. Custer Ave.
New Holland, PA 17557
All kinds of cream cheese

Blythedale Farm, Thomas Gilbert &
  Karen Galayda, 802/885-9854
669 Greeley Road
Springfield, VT 05156
Vermont Brie

Cabot Farmers' Cooperative
Box 128
Cabot, VT 05647
Vermont cheddar, Monterey Jack

Coach Dairy Farm, 518/398-5325
RD 1, Box 445
Pine Plains, NY 12567
Goat cheeses

Craigston Cheese Company, Susan Hollander
45 Dodge's Road
Wenham, MA 01984
Camembert

Crowley Cheese, Inc., 802/259-2340
Healdville, VT 05758
Colby

Empire Cheese Inc., 716/968-3699
Cuba Cheese Division
53 Genesse Street
Cuba, NY 14727
Cheddar, cheddar spread (Old York), mozzarella

F. Alleva Latticini, 212/226-7990
188 Grand Avenue
New York, NY 10013
Mozzarella, ricotta, bocconcini, Mantecche

Goat Folks, Howard Blume, 607/532-4343
8528 Tunison Rd.
Interlaken, NY 14847
Chèvre

Grafton Village Cheese Co., 802/843-2221
P.O. Box 87
Grafton, VT 05146
Premium 1-year-old cheddar

Guilford Cheese Company, 802/254-9182
RD #2, Box 182
Lee Road
Guilford, VT 05301
Verde-Monte Plain, Verde-Monte Herb, crème fraîche, Mont-Bert, Mont-Petit, Mont-Brie, Montarella

Hawthorne Valley Farm, 518/672-7500
RD 2, Box 225A
Ghent, NY 12075
Raw milk cheeses: Emmental, Gruyère, raclette, Taghkanic (a unique soft-ripened cheese)

Hollow Road Farm, Joan Snyder, 518/758-7214
Rt 1, Box 93
Stuyvesant, NY 12173
Sheep and goat cheeses

Little Rainbow Chevre, Tom and Barbara Reed, 518/325-3351
Box 379, Rodman Road
Hillsdale, NY 12529
Chèvre logs

Lively Run Creek Farm, 607/532-4222
Box 379
2027 Slaterville Road
Interlaken, NY 14847
Goat feta and blue cheese

Manny's Dairy, Maria Moreira, 508/534-5411
267 Brockelman Rd.
Lancaster, MA 01523
Fresh European-style cheese (An old Portuguese recipe handed down for generations)

Northland Sheep Dairy, Jane North, 607/849-3328
RD 1, Box 107B
Marathon, NY 13803
Sheep's-milk cheese

Orb Weaver Farm, Marjorie Susman & Marian Pollack, 802/877-3755
Box 75, RD 1, Lime Kiln Road
New Haven, VT 05472
Aged colby

Patch Road Cheese Co., Cynthia Major, 802/387-4473
RD 3, Box 276
Putney, VT 05346
Sheep's milk cheese

Plymouth Cheese Factory, 802/672-3650
Box 1
Plymouth, VT 05056
Cheddar

**Rawson Brook Farm, Wayne Dunlop &
    Sue Sellew, 413/528-2138**
Box 345, New Marlboro Road
Monterey, MA 01245
Fresh chèvres

**Sheepscot Valley Chevre, Jim & Theta
    Torbert, 207/549-3149**
RR 1, Box 1142
North Whitefield, ME 09353
Aged and fresh goat cheeses

Shelburne Farms, Inc., 802/985-8686
Harbor Road
Shelburne, VT 05482
Cheddar

**Smith's Country Cheese, Carol and
    David Smith, 509/939-5738**
20 Otter River Road
Winchendon, MA 01475
Farmstead Gouda

Sugarbush Farm, 802/457-1757
RFD 1, Box 568
Woodstock, VT 05091
Cheddar

**The Jolly Farmer, Freedom Darrow,
    603/863-2230**
Rt. 10
East Lempster, NH 03605
*Goat feta (plain and lemon pepper), chèvre,
    cheddar*

**The Squire Tarbox Inn, Karen and Bill
    Mitman, 207/882-7693**
RR 2, Box 620
Wiscasset, ME 04578
*Soft herbed fresh chèvre, hard pressed aged
    dill, feta, Caerphilly, mozzarella*

Tholstrup Cheese USA Inc., 201/756-6320
One Mountain Boulevard
P.O. Box 4194
Warren, NJ 07060-6320
*Saga blue (triple-cream, soft-ripened blue-
    veined)*

**Vermont Cheese & Butter, Alison
    Hooper, 802/479-9371**
Pitman Rd, #95
Websterville, VT 05678
*Fresh goat (plain, herb, and pepper), crème
    fraîche, fromage blanc, mascarpone, Italian
    tortas*

**Westfield Farm, Bob and Letty
    Kilmoyer, 617/928-5110**
28 Worcester Road
Hubbardston, MA 01452
Capri, Camembert, Hubbardston blue

**White Birch Farm, Beth Schmais &
    Andy Gingra, 518/325-3527**
Gingras Road
Hillsdale, NY 12529
Fresh goat cheese, chèvre logs

**Wieninger's Cheese, Sarah & John
    Wieninger, 518/263-4772**
Star Route, Box 106
Hunter, NY 12442
Raw-milk aged goat cheese

**Windy Hamlet Farm, Dorothy Benedict,
    617/867-6111**
Route 1, P.O. Box 300, Hunt Road
West Brookfield, MA 01585
Capriole (fresh chèvre log), aged Crottin

**York Hill Farm, Penny and John
    Duncan**
York Hill Road
New Sharon, ME 04955
*Hard aged cheeses: York cheddar, Capriano;
    soft fresh cheeses: chèvre, garlic and herb,
    pepper and tarragon discs, chèvre roll with
    pepper*

MIDWEST

Auricchio Cheese, Inc., 414/863-2123
Route 3
Denmark, WI 54208
Provolone, Parmesan, fontina, Toscanello

Bass Lake Cheese, Scott Erickson, 715/549-6617
598 Valley View Trail
Somerset, WI 54025
Goat cheese

Bresse Bleu Inc., Bruno Bardet, 414/261-3036
N2002 Hwy 26
Watertown, WI 53094
Classic Montrachet, Montrachet in olive oil

Capriole, Judy Schad, 812/923-9408
Fromage A Trois
10329 Newcut Rd.
Greenville, IN 47124
Goat tortas

Dancing Winds Farm, Mary Doerr, 507/789-6606
RR3, Box 161
Kenyon, MN 55946
Minnesota chèvre: plain, Mexicali, garlic, basil

Deppeler Cheese Factory, 608/325-6311
W6805 Deppeler Road
Monroe, WI 53566
Baby Swiss

Dietrich's Dairy, 217/434-8460
R. #1, Box 83
Fowler, IL 62338
Dietrich's Pure Chèvre Blue (blue-veined 100-percent goat milk)

Drangle Foods, Inc., 715/447-8241
300 South Riverside Drive
P.O. Box 187
Gilman, WI 54433
Natural cheddar

Eau Galle Cheese Factory, Inc., Leo Buhlman, 715/283-4276
Star Route Box 33B
Durand, WI 54736
Parmesan

Ed F. Steiner, Inc., 216/897-5505
Baltic, OH 43804
Swiss

Eichten's Hidden Acres, Joe & Mary Eichten, 612/257-4752
16705–310th Street
Center City, MN 55012
Gouda, baby Swiss, colby, Tilsit, Havarti

Fantome Farms, Ann Topham, 608/924-1266
Route 1
Ridgeway, WI 53582
Goat cheese

Gibbsville Cheese Company, 414/564-3242
Box 152, Route 3
Sheboygan Falls, WI 54208
Aged cheddar, colby, Monterey Jack, two-tone colby

Greater Michigan Goat Milk Inc., Marian Harris, 616/477-5613
5291 Farnsworth
Brethren, MI 49619
Chèvre

Guggissberg Cheese Inc. of Doughty Valley, 216/893-2500
Route 4
Millersburg, OH 44654
Baby Swiss, Emmental, Guggissberg

Kidron Swiss Cheese Factory, 216/857-2841
Kidron, OH 44636
Swiss

Kolb Lena Cheese Company, 815/369-4577
3990 North Sunnyside Road
Lena, IL 61048
Baby Swiss, feta, Havarti, Brie, Camembert,
Old Heidelberg, Rexoli, Lite N Lacy

La Paysanne, 612/384-6612
Route 3, P.O. Box 10
Hinckley, MN 55037
Sheep's milk cheese

Loomis Cheese Company, Bill Loomis,
313/769-4110
220 Fetch
Ann Arbor, MI 48103
Great Lakes Cheshire (a relative to cheddar)

Maytag Cheese Company, 800/247-2458
Route 1
Newton, IA
Blue cheese

Michigan Farm Cheese Dairy, Inc.,
616/462-3301
4295 Millerton Road
Fountain, MI 49410
Farmer's cheese, queso blanco, feta

Miniver Cheese Factory, Phil Mueller,
216/868-4196
Box 60
Miniver, OH 44657
Cheddar, colby, Monterey Jack, goat cheese

Morningland Dairy, Jim and Margie
Reiner, 417/469-3817
Route 1, P.O. Box 188
Mountain View, MO 65548
Monterey Jack, cheddar, Colby

Mueller's Cheese House, 216/852-2311
Sugarcreek Dairy
116 Factory Street
Sugarcreek, OH 44681
Swiss

Nauvoo Blue Cheese Co., Bill and
Marie Scully, 800/358-9143
1095 Young Street
Nauvoo, IL 62354
Cow's-milk blue cheese

Organic Valley, Harriet Behar,
608/625-2602
Box 159
La Farge, WI 54639
Organic raw-milk cheddar, colby, Jack, light
cheddar, pasteurized cheddar Jack, pepper
Jack, muenster, mozzarella, provolone,
string

Shullsburg Creamery, Inc.,
608/965-4485
208 West Water Street
Shullsburg, WI 93586
Colby, farmer's cheese, cheddar, baby Swiss

Simon's Specialty Cheese, Gary
Romanesco, 414/788-6311
P.O. Box 223
Little Chute, WI 54140-0223
Cheddar

Steve's Cheese, 414/863-2397
Route 2
Denmark, WI 54208
Blue, aged cheddar, colby, Edam, brick,
farmer's cheese, Swiss

Tupper Cheese Company, 414/893-2271
1411 Eastern
P.O. Box 24
Plymouth, WI 53073
Koch Kaese

Valley View Cheese Co-op,
608/439-5569
Route 1
6519 Larson Road
South Wayne, WI 53587
Caraway brick, raw-milk Muenster

Wen Don Alpine Dairy, Don and Wendy Reinsmith
584 West Shelby Road
Shelby, MI 49455
Mild hard pressed goat cheese

Wisconsin Hill and Valley Cheese, 608/654-5411
RD #3, Box 84A
Cashton, WI 54619
Gouda

SOUTH AND SOUTHWEST

Ashbury Fromagerie Belle Chevre, Lee Ashbury, 205/830-1400
P.O. Box 277
Ardmore, AL 35739
Goat cheese

Brier Run Farm, Greg and Verena Sava, 304/649-2975
Route 1, P.O. Box 73
Birch River, WV
Fromage blanc, Chabis, Banon, Pyramide, Crottin, Bouche

Celebrity Goat Dairy, J. Britton Pfann, 919/549-1257
Route 3, P.O. Box 390
Siler City, NC 27344
Goat cheese

Coonridge Goat Cheese, Andy & Nancy Coonridge, 505/982-2624
Star Route
Pie Town, NM 87827
Fromage blanc, goat cheese preserved in wine and Cognac, goat cheese preserved in olive oil

Glen Crannoc Farm, Richard & Jean Thornton, 707/645-7328
123 Blackberry Inn Road
Weaversville, NC 28787
Fresh, ripened, and aged goat cheeses

Landsdale Farm, 804/823-2348
Route 2, Box 288A
Crozet, VA 22932
Farmstead raw-milk Gouda

Larsen Farms Inc., Diane Larsen, 512/858-7680
H.C.01, #98B
Dripping Springs, TX 78620
Chèvre with herbs, pepper

Mozzarella Company, Paula Lambert, 214/741-4072
2944 Elm Street
Dallas, TX 75226
Mozzarella, ricotta, mascarpone, Crescenza, cream cheese, fromage blanc, crème fraîche, Smoked Scarmorza, Caciotta, Taleggio, Texas goat cheese, Montasio

Scuppernong Farm, Bonnie and George Zink, 404/466-4723
Route 1, Highway 81 North
Loganville, GA 30249
Chèvres or French goat cheeses: Montrachet, Pyramid Valencay, fromage blanc, herb-marinated chèvre, chèvre smoked salmon pâté, and Liptauer chèvre

Sharkawi Farm, Sabry Alsharkawi, 703/347-5902
Rt.1, RR 694, Box 42
Broad Run, VA 22014
Goat feta

Sierra Farms, Inc., Carmen Sanchez, 505/281-5061
P.O. Box 606
Tijeras, NM 87059
Natural goat cheese: farm cheese, ricotta, Priola, queso fuego

**Split Creek Farm, Evin Evans, 803/
287-3921**
3806 Centerville Rd.
Anderson, SC 29625
Goat cheese (French chèvre and Greek feta)

**Sweet Home Farm, Alyce Birchenough,
205/986-5663**
27107 Schoen Rd.
Elberta, AL 36530
Cow and goat cheese

**Turtle Creek Dairy, James Berke,
407/798-4628**
P.O. Box 326
Loxahatchee, FL 33470
French chèvre

Woodside, Peter and Claudia Kafer
Subtle, KY 42129
*Soft fresh goat cheeses, blue soft-ripened
cheese*

Garden Seed Sources

**Bountiful Gardens
Ecology Action**
5798 Ridgewood Road
Willits, CA 95490

Cooks Garden
P.O. Box 535
Londonderry, VT 05148

Fetzer Valley Oaks Garden
P.O. Box 611
Hopland, CA 95449

Johnny's
Foss Hill Rd.
Albion, ME 04910

Native Seed Search
2509 N. Campbell Ave. (#325)
Tucson, AZ 85719

Nichols Garden Nursery
1190 North Pacific Hwy.
Albany, OR 97321-4598

Ornamental Edibles
3622 Weedin Ct.
San José, CA 95132

Parks
Cokesbury Rd.
Greenwood, SC 29647-0001

Rogers Northrup King
P.O. Box 4188
Boise, ID 83711-4188

Ronnigers Seed Potatoes
Star Route
Moyie Springs, ID 83845

Seeds Blum
Idaho City Stage
Boise, ID 83706

Seeds of Change
1364 Rufina Circle (#5)
Santa Fe, NM 87501
505/438-8080
505/438-7052 (fax)

Seed Savers Exchange
3076 N. Winn Rd.
Decorah, IA 52101

Shepherds
30 Irene St.
Torrington, CT 06790

Stokes Seeds
183 E. Main St.
Fredonia, NY 14063-1409

Territorial Seed Co.
P.O. Box 157
Cottage Grove, OR 97424

Herb and Seedling Sources

Caprilands Herb Farm
534 Silver St.
Coventry, CT 06238
(send SASE for free catalog)

Casa Yerba Gardens
3459 Days Creek Rd.
Days Creek, OR 97429
(send SASE for price list)

Companion Plants
7247 N. Coolville Ridge Rd.
Athens, OH 45701

Country Garden
P.O. Box 3539
Oakland, CA 94609-0539

Flowery Branch Seed Co.
P.O. Box 1330
Flowery Branch, GA 30542

Fox Hill Farm
Box 9
440 W. Michigan Ave.
Parma, MI 49269

Fragrant Path
P.O. Box 328
Fort Calhoun, NE 68023

Mountain Valley Growers
38325 Pepperweed Rd.
Squaw Valley, CA 93675

Peace Seeds
P.O. Box 190
Gila, NM 88038

Richters
Goodwood, Ontario
Canada LOC1A0

Thompson & Morgan, Inc.
P.O. Box 1308
Jackson, NJ 08527

Vermont Bean Seed Co.
Garden Lane
Box 250
Fair Haven, VT 05743

Bibliography

Ash, John, and Sid Goldstein. *American Game Cooking.* Reading, MA: Addison Wesley/ Aris Books, 1991.

Ausubel, Kenny. *Seeds of Change: The Living Treasure.* San Francisco: Harper San Francisco, 1994.

Barash, Cathy Wilkinson. *Edible Flowers from Garden to Palate.* Golden, CO: Fulerum Publishing, 1993.

Bayless, Rick, and Deann Bayless. *Authentic Mexican.* New York: Morrow, 1987.

Bissell, Frances. *The Book of Food.* New York: Henry Holt, 1994.

Cader, Michael, and Debby Roth. *Eat These Words.* New York: HarperCollins, 1991.

Castle, Coralie, and Robert Kourik. *Cooking from the Gourmet's Garden.* Santa Rosa, CA: Cole Group, 1994.

Creasy, Rosalind. *Cooking from the Garden.* San Francisco: Sierra Club Books, 1988.

Devi, Yamuna. *The Art of Indian Vegetarian Cooking.* New York: Dutton, 1987.

Dille, Carolyn, and Susan Belsinger. *Herbs in the Kitchen.* Loveland, CO: Interweave Press, 1992.

Dumas, Alexandre. *Dictionary of Cuisine,* ed. and trans. by Louis Colman. New York: Simon & Schuster, 1958.

Ferrary, Jeanette, and Louise Fizer. *Season to Taste.* New York: Simon & Schuster, 1988.

Field, Carol. *The Italian Baker.* New York: Harper & Row, 1985.

Fisher, M. F. K. *An Alphabet for Gourmets.* San Francisco: Northpoint Press, 1989.

Gibbons, Euell. *Stalking the Wild Asparagus.* New York: McKay, 1978.

Goldstein, Joyce. *Back to Square One.* New York: Morrow, 1992.

Hazan, Marcella. *Marcella's Italian Kitchen.* New York: Alfred A. Knopf, 1987.

Hensperger, Beth. *Baking Bread.* San Francisco: Chronicle Books, 1992.

The Herb Companion, published bimonthly by Interweave Press, Loveland, CO.

Hillman, Howard. *Kitchen Science.* Boston: Houghton Mifflin, 1981.

Kilham, Christopher S. *The Bread and Circus Whole Food Bible.* Reading, MA: Addison Wesley, 1991.

Madison, Deborah. *The Savory Way.* New York: Bantam Books, 1990.

McGee, Harold. *On Food and Cooking: The Science and Lore of the Kitchen.* New York: Collier-Macmillan, 1984.

Medrich, Alice. *Chocolate and the Art of Low Fat Desserts.* New York: Warner Books, 1994.

Rodale's Illustrated Encyclopedia of Herbs, ed. by Claire Kowalchek and William H. Hylton. Emmaus, PA: Rodale Press, 1987.

Root, Waverly. *Food.* New York: Fireside Books, 1980.

Rosengarten, David, and Joshua Wesson. *Red Wine with Fish.* New York: Simon & Schuster, 1989.

Schneider, Elizabeth. *Uncommon Fruits and Vegetables: A Common Sense Guide.* New York: Harper & Row, 1986.

Shepard, Renee, and Fran Raboff. *Recipes from a Kitchen Garden.* Felton, CA: Shepard's Garden Publishing, 1991.

Simmons, Marie. *Rice the Amazing Grain.* New York: Henry Holt, 1991.

Tatum, Billy Joe. *Billy Joe Tatum's Wild Foods Cookbook and Field Guide.* New York: Workman Publishing, 1976.

Toussaint-Samat, Maguelonne. *History of Food,* trans. by Anthea Bell. Oxford: Blackwell Publishers, 1992.

Visser, Margaret. *Much Depends on Dinner.* New York: Collier Books, 1988.

Vongerichten, Jean-Georges. *Simple Cuisine.* New York: Prentice Hall, 1990.

Index

A NOTE ON THE TYPE

The typeface used in this book is a version of Palatino, originally designed in 1950 by Hermann Zapf (b. 1918), one of the most prolific contemporary type designers, who has also created Melior and Optima. Palatino was first used to set the introduction of a book of Zapf's hand lettering, in an edition of eighty copies on Japan paper handbound by his wife, Gudrun von Hesse; the book sold out quickly and Zapf's name was made. (Remarkably, the lettering had actually been done when the self-taught calligrapher was only twenty-one.) Intended mainly for "display" (title pages, headings), Palatino owes its appearance both to calligraphy and the requirements of the cheap German paper at the time—perhaps why it is also one of the best-looking fonts on low-end computer printers. It was soon used to set text, however, causing Zapf to redraw its more elaborate letters.